Signs, Symbols, and Architecture

Signs, Symbols, and Architecture

Geoffrey Broadbent

Head of School of Architecture
Portsmouth Polytechnic

Richard Bunt

University College London
and
School of Architecture
Portsmouth Polytechnic

Charles Jencks

Architectural Association
School of Architecture
and
University of California
Los Angeles

John Wiley & Sons
Chichester   New York   Brisbane   Toronto

Library of Congress Cataloging in Publication Data:

Main entry under title:

Signs, symbols and architecture.

Includes bibliographical references and index.
1. Signs and symbols in architecture — Addresses, essays,
   lectures.
2. Communication in architectural design — Addresses,
   essays, lectures.
3. Semiotics — Addresses, essays, lectures.
I. Broadbent, Geoffrey.   II. Bunt, Richard.
III. Jencks, Charles
NA2500.S48   720'.1   78-13557

ISBN 0 471 99718 8

Filmset by Reproduction Drawings Ltd.

Printed by The Pitman Press, Bath

Contents

List of Contributors

Judith BLAU is a post-doctoral fellow in the Department of Psychiatry at Albert Einstein Yeshiva University, New York, USA.

Juan BONTA is Professor of Architectural Design and History at Ball State University, Muncie, Indiana, USA.

Geoffrey BROADBENT is Head of the School of Architecture, Portsmouth Polytechnic, England.

Richard BUNT is an architect and teaches at University College, London, Central London Polytechnic, and also at the School of Architecture, Portsmouth Polytechnic.

Umberto ECO is Professor of Semiotics in the Faculty of Letters, University of Bologna, Italy.

Mario GANDELSONAS is Fellow and Co-Director of the Generative Design Programme at the Institute for Architecture and Urban Studies, New York, USA.

Emilio GARRONI is Professor at the Institute of Philosophy, University of Rome, Italy.

Charles JENCKS teaches Modern Architectural History at the Architectural Association School of Architecture, London, and at the University of California, Los Angeles, USA.

David MORTON is an associate editor of *Progressive Architecture*.

Maria Luisa SCALVINI is an architect working in Naples; she also teaches at the University of Naples, Italy.

Fernando TUDELA is an architect and teaches architectural theory at the University Iberoamericana in Mexico City.

Xavier Rubert de VENTOS is Professor of Aesthetics and Composition in the School of Architecture, Barcelona, Spain.

General Introduction

Geoffrey Broadbent

When it was first published the collection of papers entitled *Meaning in Architecture*, edited by Charles Jencks and George Baird was a revelation to those of us whose reading is mostly in English. It opened up a whole new approach to architecture, based on the theory of signs, which had previously been available to us only in half a dozen or so articles, scattered in various Journals—most of which, in any case, were collected into the book. But the field itself was a well-established one, which had been pioneered in the early 1950s by certain Italian theorists, from Pane (1948) onwards.

It seemed to Charles Jencks, Dick Bunt and me quite scandalous that this pioneering material—and various developments from it—were not available in English, and we have tried to correct this deficiency by collecting these papers together.

Since those pioneering days, of course, the field itself has proliferated in many directions. It was dominated initially by the writings of Ferdinand de Saussure, whose aim in exploring the nature of language (published in English as the *Course in General Linguistics*, in 1959) had been, as he says, to establish a *General* Theory of Signs—a sign in this sense being anything which can 'stand for' something else—which he called *Semiology*.

There was much debate in those early days as to which aspects of Saussurean semiology were essential to that theory, and also the levels at which his various concepts should be transferred from language into other systems of signs—including architecture.

Saussure himself was an inveterate dichotomizer; he saw everything in pairs, such as language (which is a shared public thing agreed by social contract) and speech (which is one's personal use of language). Saussure's scheme, in general, includes half a dozen such pairs of which two—it seems to me—form essential parts of the background to these papers. He distinguished between *diachronic* linguistics—concerned with changes of usage over time—and *synchronic* linguistics—concerned with the overall structure of a language, or some other sign system one may be considering, at a particular moment in time. Saussure's techniques for considering the synchronic structure of language of course, have been extended into almost every other field—starting with anthropologists such as Lévi Strauss,—to become that intellectual paradigm or academic fashion called Structuralism.

It is a staggering thought that only *one* of Saussure's pairings should have been responsible for so much; others, of course, have helped flesh out the details in this structuralist approach. The second most potent of Saussure's pairs probably has been his divisions of the sign itself into a two-part entity consisting of *signifier* (the pattern of marks on paper, sounds in the air or even building forms by which the sign itself is made physically manifest) and the *signified* (the concepts, ideas or other thoughts which the signifier actually 'stands for'). Others have detected further components within the sign (see my 'Plain Man's Guide to the Theory of Signs in Architecture', 1978) including, for instance, the *referent*—the object, as it were, to which the sign refers, which may take living, inanimate or rather more abstract forms.

The fundamental question from our point of view of course is: which of these is a building. My view (1969) which shocked many of the semiologists represented in this book is that—according to circumstances—it may be all three. Any existing building obviously can be a *referent*—a physical object which one can actually go and kick. But it can also be a *signifier*—signifying, according to where, when and how it was built, say, belief in the Christian faith (cathedral), the power of bureaucracy (office slab), commitment to self-sufficiency (garden shed) and so on. But it can also be a *signified*—a set of architectural concepts or ideas, signified by words, drawings, photographs, models and so on. Indeed, some buildings, such as the Barcelona Pavilion now exist *only* as *signifieds* in this form.

Useful as it was, in providing a whole new range of insights into how certain things, including buildings, carry meanings, Saussure's sign was by no means adequate for the analysis of all the sign-types we encounter in our day-to-day experience.

Saussure's contemporary, the American philosopher Charles Sanders Peirce, at one time thought that far from there being only one kind of sign, he could detect no less than 59,049 *different* types.

That was a little over-zealous and it arose, in part, because just as Saussure was an inveterate dichotomizer, so Peirce tended to think of things in threes. Eventually, he reduced his excessively complex permutation into a set of 12 trichotomies: these, collectively, still result in a formidable list of sign types, some with even more formidable names. Peirce described each of these several times, in different ways, in the 8 published volumes (with 8 more still to come) of his extraordinarily rich *Collected Papers* (1974). The papers themselves are currently being quarried by all kinds of scholars, in all kinds of fields, to an extent which it makes it seem likely that Peirce himself will become *the* key philosopher of the late 20th century and there seems to be a general consensus (at, for instance, the First Congress of the International Association for Semiotic Studies, held in Milan in 1974) that the theory of signs which Peirce envisaged—he called it Semiotic—promises more, in the long run, even than Saussure's.

So far, the exploration of Peirce's semiotic ideas has been concentrated almost entirely on one of his trichotomies—his division of the sign into the three types: Icon, Index and Symbol. I discussed these in my paper on 'Building Design as an Iconic sign system' included in this volume. Suffice it for now to say that the crucial point about Peirce's Index (such as a pointing finger) is that it has some physical relationship with its object, the meaning of which can be 'read' without any cultural knowledge, that his Symbol (such as a word, a cross or even a whole church) actually *has* to be learned as meaning something within a particular cultural context, whilst his icon *reminds* us of its object by some complex kinds of resemblance—Venturi's poultry-stand looks *like* a duck.

At best, these new concepts from Semiology and Semiotic provide new insights into architecture—as I believe these papers show. In particular, they help us discuss again, in a reasonably tough-minded way, the issues which used to be the province of the most subjective aesthetics.

Most of the papers reprinted in this book are rooted—however vaguely in Saussurean semiology or Peircian semiotic—but a completely different approach to the question of architectural meaning has been developing, in parallel, within that most empirical of sciences, Environmental Psychology.

Having discussed the relationship between these structuralistic and psychological approaches in my 'Plain Man's Guide' and in earlier papers (1975) it seems to me that neither, alone, throws sufficient light on the subject but the two together offer some of the most exciting developments in the whole of architectural research.

Suffice it, for now, to say that more than enough papers have been published within this alternative paradigm for Tomas Llorens, Richard Bunt and I to have edited a second book, which is being published as *Meaning and Behaviour in the Built Environment*.

One final point—the whole field of Meaning in Architecture has been called into question on a number of occasions by certain Anglo-Saxon architects and critics. They see it as far too abstract, too esoteric, too jargon-ridden to be of any interest. Some of it is—we have in fact deliberately included a (small) number of papers in that category on the grounds that without them, the overall flavour of the field would have been lost.

But much of this criticism, I believe, is pure philistinism—evidence of the poverty-stricken intellectual environment in which Anglo-Saxon architects have been operating. The results, of course, are there to be seen all around us; *built* abstractions which, insofar as they 'carry' any meaning at all, convey blank alienation and contempt for humanity. Of course, there are dangers in too much abstraction at any level, but if one has to choose between built abstraction and written abstraction the latter, it seems to me, is far less damaging.

References

Broadbent, G., (1969). 'Meaning into Architecture', in *Meaning in Architecture* (Jencks, C., and Baird, G., eds), Barrie & Rockliffe, London.

Broadbent, G., (1975). 'Function and Symbolism in Architectecture', in *Responding to Social Change* (Honikman, B., ed.), Dowden, Hutchinson & Ross, New York.

Broadbent, G., (1978). 'A Plain Man's Guide to the Theory of Signs in Architecture', *Architectural Design*, July/August.

Pane, R., (1948). 'Architettura e Letteratura', in *Architettura e Arti Figurative*, Ed. di Comunitá, Milan.

Peirce, C. S., (1974). *The Collected Papers of Charles Sanders Peirce*, 8 volumes (Hartshorne, C., and Weiss, P., eds), Harvard University Press, Cambridge, Mass.

Section 1

1.0 Introduction to Section 1

Charles Jencks

Meaning in the environment is inescapable, even for those who would deny or deplore it. Everything that can be seen or thought about takes on a meaning, or position within a signifying system, even the recurrent attempts to escape from this omnipresent signification. 'All is meaningful', even Nihilism, and, what is worse, semiologists have staked out this 'all' as their proper territory: semiology, the theory of signs, the theory of the way anything can take on meaning. With impeccable logic, the logic of imperialism and cannibalism, semiologists have swallowed their ancestors — linguistics, psychology — then literary criticism, anthropology, Little Red Riding Hood, wrestling matches, the brain of Einstein, all of culture and finally all of nature (the codes of planetary rotation, the genetic code etc.).

Always finding similar divisions wherever they look — signifiers/signifieds, metaphor/metonymy — and invariably finding them in pairs, they ultimately get even with the ever present richness of meaning in the universe by making it quite unpalatable and boring. Or if not boring, then trivial or endlessly complex. Such is the sad fate of semiology, or semiotics as it is now officially called, in our time.

Brought into being at the beginning of this century, and made fashionable in the sixties by Claude Lévi-Strauss, Roland Barthes and Umberto Eco, it holds out all the promise of a new science — a physics and logic of culture — with, as yet, few of the rewards of such disciplines. Like psychoanalysis around 1910, it is expanding fast with books, international conferences and inflated pretensions, and it can now generate just about the same amount of excitement, anger and jargon. Should we applaud its temerity, or fault its pedantry? I don't know, but I do think everyone acquainted with the history of semiotics will feel at the same time its ennobling sense of promise, its grand catholic sweep, and some of its exasperating failure.

Semiotics was first introduced into the architectural debate in Italy, very early, when there was a general 'crisis of meaning' during the late fifties, and architects were questioning the International Style—looking for local, regional or historical alternatives to this flaccid Esperanto. Several contributions in this anthology have developed out of and in response to this crisis, notably the work of Umberto Eco and Maria Luisa Scalvini. By the late sixties, in France, Germany and England semiotics was being discussed for its architectural implications and again it was used as a polemical tool, a normative instrument, to attack inadequate theories of functionalism.

So it has remained, partly a neutral discipline like its father, linguistics, and partly a political discipline rooted in a particular historical context, like its mother, rhetoric. Both attitudes will be found recurring throughout this book. In addition, architectural semiotics became in America something like a fashion by the seventies, undergoing all the loosening of thought and precision which this implies, but gaining in breadth and application at the same time. There were Robert Venturi, Denise Scott Brown and their team organizing an exhibition at the Smithsonian—'Signs of Life: Symbols in the American City'—a Bicentennial look at previously disregarded codes of architecture (Schlock and Trad). To give an idea of how loosely the term semiology could be bandied about to mean anything remotely connected with communication, one only has to quote a few Vincent Scullquips (taken from *The Shingle Style Today or The Historian's Revenge*, the revenge that is of Vincent Scully, 1974):

> Clearly, [Venturi's work] its unconcealed focus, its semiological directness as billboard .... Here [in Venturi's Nantucket Houses] semiology approaches its essential, which is the action of people talking to each other .... Still, the chimney and the gable carried Venturi's project beyond Abstract Expression to what might be called the 'Signpost Art', the signaling art, of the following decades. They semaphore (hence 'semiological') what the house means, here roof and fire and taking possession of place ....[1]

1 Vincent Scully, *The Shingle Style Today or The Historian's Revenge*, George Braziller, New York, 1974, pp. 29, 35.

Here, still, clearly, Scully's semiologising to us in his inimitable way, with verbifications of nouns, might distract us from the situation which he is describing—the fact that by the early seventies, semiotics was already having an effect, even if thinly spread, on the leading architects in America. And so it is still today, in Spain, South America and Japan and the other countries I have mentioned. The field has broadened, with over 600 articles and two major international conferences, even if it hasn't yet dug in very deep.[2]

This anthology brings together some of the material which hasn't previously been published in book form. The selection, inevitably, reflects the Anglo-Saxon and Italian bias of the editors. We have included nothing from Germany, where there has been considerable research of an empirical nature, nor anything from the psychological and behaviorist approaches, Environment Design Research Association (EDRA) etc., since this is treated in another anthology—Tomas Llorens, Geoffrey Broadbent and Richard Bunt *Meaning and Behaviour in the Built Enviroment*. But the present collection does bring together the seminal work of Eco and Bonta, to name two contributions which have already had a pronounced effect on the field, as well as theoretical investigations and applications.

This first section explores the general issues raised by architectural semiotics and covers such notions as the codes of architecture and the way it can signify. Most of the key terms and concepts of signification are defined by the authors and the reader will thus find some overlap in these definitions. This redundancy is not necessarily a bad thing since the concepts are complex and need reiteration. Furthermore, as with the question of denotation, the reader will see that authors (in this case Umberto Eco and myself) often take explicitly differing views. Another theme that recurs is the 'aims of functionalism' and the differing codes through which architecutre is read—often opposed as elitist versus populist and modern versus traditional. Thus the reader will find this section like the often quoted musical analogy—a theme with variations—hopefully more like a symphony than a cacophony.

The field is still young and promising to grow, and we may hope that soon we'll have a fully developed theory of archisemiotics and a detailed, critical use of it. As Xavier Rubert de Ventos points out here, the study and construction

2 For the articles up to 1974, see the bibliography published in *Versus* 8/9, Quaderni di Studi Semiotici, Bompiani, Milan, Dec. 1974. This was complied by R. Bunt, T. Llorens and myself. The two large conferences occurred in Casteldefels, Spain, 1972, and Milan, 1974, but there have been many small ones at Ulm and Urbino; and EDRA meetings etc.

of semiotics is itself a form of sign behavior—a form of rhetoric and politics with its own responsibility—so the theory and practice should grow ever more sharp, voluptuous and persuasive.

1.1 Function and Sign: The Semiotics of Architecture

Umberto Eco

This paper is a revision of six chapters of *La struttura assente: Introduzione alla ricerca semiologica*, Bompiani, Milan, 1968. Reprinted from *VIA* Magazine of Graduate School of Fine Arts, University of Pennsylvania, Vol. 1, 1973. A further revised version of this paper will also appear in a collection of essays by the author, to be published by Peter de Ridder Press.

'Since our society produces only standardized, normalized objects, these objects are unavoidably realizations of a model, the speech of a language, the substances of a significant form. To rediscover a non-signifying object, one would have to imagine a utensil absolutely improvised and with no similarity to an existing model . . .. a hypothesis which is virtually impossible to verify in any society.'—Roland Barthes

1 Architecture and Communication

1.1 Semiotics and Architecture

1.1.1   If semiotics, beyond being the science of recognized systems of signs, is really to be a science studying *all* cultural phenomena *as if* they were systems of signs—on the hypothesis that all cultural phenomena *are*, in reality, systems of signs, or that culture can be understood as *communication*—then one of the fields in which it will undoubtedly find itself most challenged is that of architecture.

It should be noted that the term *architecture* will be used in a broad sense here, indicating phenomena of industrial design and urban design as well as phenomena of architecture proper. (We will leave aside, however, the question of whether our notions on these phenomena would be applicable to *any type of design producing three-dimensional constructions destined to permit the fulfillment of some func-*

tion connected with life in society, a definition that would embrace the design of clothing, insofar as clothing is culturalized and a means of participating in society, and even the design of food, not as the production of something for the individual's nourishment, but insofar as it involves the construction of contexts that have social functions and symbolic connotations, such as particular menus, the accessories of a meal, etc.—a definition that would be understood to exclude, on the other hand, the production of three-dimensional objects destined primarily to be *contemplated* rather than utilized in society, such as works of art.)

1.1.2   Why is architecture a particular challenge to semiotics? First of all because apparently most architectural objects do not *communicate* (and are not designed to communicate), but *function*. No one can doubt that a roof fundamentally serves to cover, and a glass to hold liquids in such a way that one can then easily drink them. Indeed, this is so obviously and unquestionably the case that it might seem perverse to insist upon seeing as an act of communication something that is so well, and so easily, characterized as a *possibility of function*. One of the first questions for semiotics to face, then, if it aims to provide keys to the cultural phenomena in this field, is whether it is possible to interpret functions as having something to do with communication; and the point of it is that seeing functions from the semiotic point of view might permit one to understand and define them better, precisely as functions, and thereby to discover other types of functionality, which are just as essential but which a straight functionalist interpretation keeps one from perceiving.[1]

1.2 Architecture as Communication

1.2.1   A phenomenological consideration of our relationship with architectural objects tells us that we commonly do experience architecture as communication, even while recognizing its functionality.

Let us imagine the point of view of the man who started the history of architecture.

Still 'all wonder and ferocity' (to use Vico's phrase), driven by cold and rain and following the example of some animal or obeying an impulse in which instinct and reasoning are mixed in a confused way, this hypothetical Stone Age man takes shelter in a recess, in some hole on the side of a mountain, in a cave.

Sheltered from the wind and rain, he examines the cave that shelters him, by daylight or by the light of a fire (we will assume he has already discovered fire). He notes the amplitude of the vault, and understands this as the limit of an outside space, which is (with its wind and rain) *cut off*, and as the *beginning of an inside space*, which is likely to evoke in him some unclear nostalgia for the womb, imbue him with feelings of protection, and appear still imprecise and ambiguous to him, seen under a play of shadow and light. Once the storm is over, he might leave the cave and reconsider it from the outside: there he would note the entry-way as 'hole that permits passage to the inside', and the entrance would recall to his mind the image of the inside: entrance hole, covering vault, walls (or continuous wall of rock) surrounding a space within. Thus an 'idea of the cave' takes shape, which is useful at least as a mnemonic device, enabling him to think of the cave later on as a possible objective in case of rain; but it also enables him to recognize in another cave the same *possibility of shelter* found in the first one. At the second cave he tries, the idea of *that* cave is soon replaced by the idea of cave *tout court*—a *model*, a *type*, something that does not exist concretely but on the basis of which he can recognize a certain context of phenomena as 'cave'.

The model (or concept) functions so well that he can now recognize from a distance someone else's cave or a cave he does not intend to make use of, independently of whether he wants to take shelter in it or not. The man has learned that the cave can assume various appearances. Now this would still be a matter of an *individual's* realization of an abstract model, but in a sense the model is *already codified*, not yet on a social level but on the level of this individual who proposes and communicates it to himself, within his own mind. And he would probably be able, at this point, to communicate the model of the cave to other men, by means of graphic signs. The *architectural code* would generate an *iconic code*, and the 'cave principle' would become an object of communicative intercourse.

At this point the drawing of a cave or the image of a cave in the distance becomes the communication of a possible function, and such it remains, even when there is neither fulfillment of the function nor a wish to fulfill it.

1.2.2   What has happened, then, is what Roland Barthes is speaking about when he says that 'as soon as there is a society, every usage is converted into a sign of itself'.[2]

To use a spoon to get food to one's mouth is still, of course, the fulfillment of a function, through the use of an artifact that allows and promotes that function; yet to say that it 'promotes' the function indicates that the artifact serves a communicative function as well: it *communicates the function to fulfilled*. Moreover, the fact that someone uses a spoon becomes, in the eyes of the society that observes it, the communication of a conformity by him to certain usages (as opposed to certain others, such as eating with one's hands or sipping food directly from a dish).

The spoon *promotes a certain way of eating* and *signifies that way of eating*, just as the cave promotes the act of shelter and signifies the existence of the possible function; and both objects *signify even when they are not being used*.

1.3 Stimulus and Communication

1.3.1   Still, one might ask whether what we are taking to be communication is simply *stimulation*.

A stimulus is a complex of sensory events that provokes a certain response. The response may be a direct one: a light blinds me—I shut my eyes; there has been a motor response without the sensory stimulus even being perceptually re-solved (certainly, then, without any intellective process tak-ing place). Or the response may be mediated: I see a car coming toward me at high speed and get out of the way: in this case, at the moment of perception, I have perceived the car and the relations between its apparent speed, the distance separating it from me, and what change in my posi-tion could be made in the time that remains—we have passed beyond a simple relation between stimulus and response to an intellective operation in which sign processes have intervened. In fact it may be assumed that the car has been understood as a danger precisely because it has been taken as a sign communicating the 'automobile-moving-at-high-speed situation', a sign that I was able to understand only on the basis of past experiences, on the basis of an ex-perimental code telling me that when a car is coming at a certain speed it constitutes a danger. And if, for that matter, I had inferred the car's impending arrival from a roar some distance up the street, the noise would have been function-ing as an *index* (indices having been characterized by Charles Sanders Peirce as signs that direct one's attention to their ob-jects 'by blind compulsion',[3] but nevertheless depending, it must be assumed, on codes and communicative conventions of some kind in order to be recognized as signs).

There remain, however, stimuli like the blinding light, stimuli that would be difficult to interpret as signs. A brick that falls on my head, provided it does not knock me out, in-itiates a chain of behavioral responses (hands to the head, a cry, swearing, anxious manoeuvres to avoid any more of the same) even when I have no idea *what* hit me.

Does architecture present stimuli of this kind, then?

1.3.2   Undoubtedly a stair acts on me as a compelling stimulus: if I want to pass where there is a stair, I have to raise my feet one after the other, step by step, and I have to do this even if I would rather continue along a level course. *The stair stimulates me to go up*, even when, stumbling over the first step in the dark, I cannot see it.

There are, on the other hand, two factors that cannot be left out of account here, concerning the fact that in all probability I would be going up the stair on the basis of knowing that that is what a stair is for. First, in going up such a structure at some time in the past, I *learn* to go up, and thus I learn to respond to the stimulus; otherwise, the stimulus alone might well fail to produce the expected response. Second, once I have learned that the stair stimulates me to go up (and permits me to pass from one level to another), from that moment on I *recognize* in a stair the stimulus presented and the possibility that is offered of a fulfillment of function.

So from the moment I recognise it as a stair and subsume it under the general concept of 'stair', the individual stairway communicates to me the function it permits; and it communicates this to such an extent that from the type of stair (grand marble staircase, winding stairway, steep and narrow stair, moving staircase) I see, perhaps first of all, whether it would be relatively easy to go up or an effort.

1.3.3   In this sense, *what permits our use of architecture* (passing, entering, pausing, going up, reclining, displaying oneself, shutting oneself off from others, etc.) *is, above and beyond the possible functions of the objects, the meanings connected with these objects, which dispose us to particular functional uses of them*. Indeed, confronted with certain trompe l'oeil phenomena, one may be disposed to a particular use even when the possibility of that function is illusory.

And with regard to some architectural objects—which do not take effect as stimuli in that they do not engage one in a physical response (possibly because having become part of one's immediate environment they function as artifices that eliminate certain stimuli: the vault as shelter from bad weather, for instance)—one may sooner or later fail to even notice a great deal of their functionality (which may be experienced as something 'out of view') while one continues to respond to their communicative effectiveness, as in a sense of security, of spaciousness, and so forth.

2 The Architectural Sign

2.1 Characterization of the Architectural Sign

2.1.1   If architecture can, then, be considered a system of signs, the first order of business would be to characterize these signs.

While inclined to apply here the semiotic schemata we have availed ourselves of elsewhere,[4] perhaps we should first check to what extent architectural phenomena support the application of other semiotic schemata. For instance, if we were to apply to architecture C. K. Ogden and I. A. Richard's well-known semantic triangle,[5] we would come up against some serious difficulties. Suppose, for example, that a door is seen as a symbol to which corresponds, at the vertex of the triangle, the *reference* 'possibility of access', then one would be hard put to define the *referent*, the physical reality to which, it is postulated, the symbol indirectly refers. The only way out would seem to be to take the position either that the door refers to itself, denoting its own reality, or that it refers to the function it permits, in which case, for the purposes of semiotics, the right side of the triangle might as well be lopped off, since the reference replaces the referent. (One might try to salvage the triangle by arguing that the *fulfillment* of the function would constitute the referent; the trouble with this is that, as suggested in 1.2.2, the fulfillment of the function is not at all a necessary condition of the communication of the function, and so to insist it be brought into the characterization of the architectural object as a sign is to insist that semiotics deal with something extraneous to semiotics.) With this schema one would get into even greater difficulties, then, in defining what such a symbol as a triumphal arch refers to: while undoubtedly denoting a possibility of passage, it is, at the same time, clearly connoting 'triumph' and 'celebration'; so here the reference would ramify before replacing the referent, or again the referent would simply be the symbol itself.

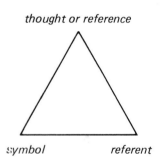

thought or reference

symbol   referent

2.1.2   Another approach, and one that would seem more promising, is that taken by Giovanni Klaus Koenig in trying to define the 'language of architecture'.[6] Koenig goes back to Charles Morris's definition of sign: 'If anything, A, is a preparatory-stimulus which in the absence of stimulus objects initiating response-sequences of a certain behavior-family causes a disposition in some organism to respond under certain conditions by response-sequences of this behavior-family, then A is a sign.'[7] And again 'If something, A, controls behavior towards a goal in a way similar to (but not necessarily identical with) the way something else, B, would control behavior with respect to that goal in a situation in which it were observed, the A is a sign.'[8]

Taking these definitions as a basis for his interpretation of architecture, Koenig observes that if he had ten thousand people living in a district he had designed he would clearly be influencing the behavior of ten thousand people, and that this would be an influence more profound and prolonged than if he had delivered some verbal injunction, such as 'Sit down!' His conclusion is that architecture is a system of 'sign vehicles that promote certain kinds of behavior' *par excellence.*[9] Now we could agree with this in general, but it becomes problematic precisely when read in the light of Morris's definitions. Because while the injunction 'Sit down!' is indeed a preparatory-stimulus that in the absence of the actual stimulus-objects can initiate the same response-sequences, while, that is, this injunction is something, A, that directs the course of behavior toward a goal in a way similar to the way in which another thing, B, would exert control if it were present as a stimulus, *the architectural object is, not at all a preparatory-stimulus that substitutes for a stimulus-object, in its absence, but simply and solely the stimulus-object.* That should be clear from our example of the stair; indeed it is precisely the stair as a sign that defies explanation within the framework of Morris's semiotic theory.

Morris's theory, let us recall, has its own sort of semantic triangle, not unlike the Ogden—Richards one, in that the symbol, or *sign-vehicle*, refers indirectly to a *denotatum* and directly to a *significatum* (for which he earlier used the more confusing term *designatum*); the object of a reference is a denotatum 'where what is referred to actually exists as referred to',[10] and the significatum is what the sign refers to (but in the sense that it is 'the conditions such that whatever meets these conditions is a denotatum of [the] sign').[11] As Max Bense, who has taken up Morris's terms while deriving much from Peirce's semiotic theory,[12] explains, the line spectrum from a black-box emitter may designate (or signify) frequencies of radiation emitted by a particular atom, but it does not necessarily denote the presence of that atom; in other words, a sign may have a significatum without having a denotatum (that 'actually exists as referred to'). And Koenig uses the example of someone stopping a car and warning the driver that a mile ahead the road is blocked by a landslide: the words addressed to the driver are the sign, the denotatum is the landslide blocking the road at the specified place, the significatum is the condition of there being a landslide blocking the road at that place. Clearly the person who spoke to the driver might be lying, and if that were the case the sign constituted by his words would have a significatum but no denotatum. What about architectural signs, then?

Koenig finds the notion of significata 'slippery', and so he has preferred the idea that architectural objects must in fact have, besides significata, denotata. But then let us go back to the example of the triumphal arch and accept Morris's terminology and definitions for the sake of argument: even though, as we have suggested, this sign would have more than one significatum, certainly one of its significata would be the possibility of passage; and if the significatum is 'the conditions such that whatever meets these conditions is a

denotatum' of the sign, then the denotatum, as one might expect from the fact that the architectural object does not
substitute for any stimulus, being itself the stimulus,
becomes the triumphal arch itself.[13] (Note that if we were to
fill in this schema with other types of significata—as Koenig
does in 2.1.4—we would either fail to come up with denotata
or, once again, be introducing something extraneous to
semiotics into the characterization of the sign.)

So with the proposition that the relation of signification
hinges on the existence of a physical denotatum, Koenig is
no closer to a really workable semiotics for architecture than
one would be with the Ogden – Richards schema.

2.1.3   The difficulties of Koenig's position derive from
accepting the presuppositions of a behaviorist approach to
semiotics: the meaning of a sign has to be verified on the
basis of response-sequences or objects that can be observed.

But with the semiotic framework preferred in preceding
sections of this study, one is not obliged to characterize a
sign on the basis of either behavior that it stimulates or
actual objects that would verify its meaning: it is characterized only on the basis of *codified meaning that in a given
cultural context is attributed to the sign-vehicle.* (It is true that
even the processes of codification belong to the realm of
social behavior; but the codes do not admit of empirical
verification either, for although based on constancies inferred from observation of *communicative usages*, they
would always be constructed as *structural models*,
postulated as a *theoretical hypothesis*.)

That a stair has obliged me to go up does not concern a
theory of signification; but that, occurring with certain formal characteristics that determine its nature as a *sign-vehicle*
(just as the verbal sign-vehicle *stairs* occurs as an articulation
of certain 'distinctive units') means that the object communicates to me its possible function—this is a datum of
culture, and can be established *independently of apparent
behavior, and even of a presumed mental reaction, on my
part.* In other words, in the cultural context in which we live
(and this is a model of culture that holds for several millennia of history as far as certain rather stable codes are concerned) there exists an architectural form that might be
defined as 'an inclined progression of rigid horizontal surfaces upward in which the distance between successive surfaces in elevation, r, is set somewhere between 5 and 9
inches, in which the surfaces have a dimension in the direction of the progression in plan, t, set somewhere between 16
and 8 inches, and in which there is little or no distance between, or overlapping of, successive surfaces when pro-
jected orthographically on a horizontal plane, the sum total
(or parts) falling somewhere between 17 and 48 degrees from

the horizontal'. (To this definition could of course be added the formula relating *r* to *t*.) And such a form *denotes* the *meaning* 'stair as a possibility of going up' on the basis of a code that I can work out and recognize as operative even if, in fact, no one is going up that stair at present and even though, in theory, no one might ever go up it again (even if stairs are never used again by anyone, just as no one is ever going to use a truncated pyramid again in making astronomical observations).

Thus what our semiotic framework would recognize in the architectural sign is *the presence of a sign-vehicle whose denoted meaning is the function it makes possible.*

2.1.4   Koenig contends that the denotata of the architectural sign are *existential* ('quanta' of human existence), and says:[14]

> When a school is built, the denotata of this sign complex . . . are the children who go and study in that school, and the significatum is the fact that those children go to school. The denotata of a house are the members of the family that lives there, while the significatum of a dwelling is the fact that people as a rule divide up into families as far as living under the same roof with others is concerned.

It would be impossible, then, to apply his schema to works of the past that have lost their function (ancient temples or arenas, whose denotata could no longer be the people who used to go there, because they no longer exist and a denotatum must exist actually). Nor of course could we apply it to works of the past whose original function is no longer even understood (megalithic temples, where even the significatum would be obscure, because it cannot be 'the fact that someone used to do something or other there').

So it is clear how much is lost by accepting such a perspective. If to characterize a sign one has to have some corresponding observable behavior, one would be unable to consider something a sign when what corresponding observable behavior there may originally have been no longer exists, or for that matter when it is no longer even known what behavior it originally referred to. In that case, we could no longer recognize the elements of the Etruscan language or the statues of Easter Island or the graffiti of some mysterious civilization as signs, and this in spite of the fact that (a) these sign elements still exist, at least as observable and describable physical phenomena, and (b) history tends to see that these observable physical phenomena continue to be filled with meanings, through successive interpretations, in spite of the fact that they continue to be regarded as signs, no matter how ambiguous and mysterious they may appear.

2.1.5 The semiotic perspective that we have pre-ferred—with its distinction between sign vehicles and mean-ings, the former observable and describable apart from the meanings we attribute to them, at least at some stage of the semiotic investigation, and the latter variable but determin-ed by the codes in the light of which we read the sign vehicles—permits us to recognize in architectural signs *sign vehicles capable of being described and catalogued*, which can denote precise functions provided one interprets them in the light of certain codes, and *successive meanings* with which these sign vehicles are capable of being filled, whose attribution can occur, as we will see, not only by way of denotation, but also by way of connotation, on the basis of further codes.

2.1.6 Significative forms, codes worked out on the strength of inferences from usages and proposed as structural models of given communicative relations, denotative and con-notative meanings attached to the sign vehicles on the basis of the codes—this is the semiotic universe in which a reading of architecture as communication becomes viable, a universe in which verification through observable physical behavior and actual objects (whether denotata or referents) would be simply irrelevant and in which the only concrete objects of any relevance are *the architectural objects as significative forms*. Within these bounds one can begin to see the various communicative possibilities of architecture.

2.2 Architectural Denotation

2.2.1 The object of use is, in its communicative capacity, the sign vehicle of a precisely and conventionally denoted meaning—its function. More loosely, it has been said that the first meaning of a building is what one must do in order to inhabit it—the architectural object denotes a 'form of in-habitation'. And it is clear that this denotation occurs even when one is not availing oneself of the denoted inhabit-ability (or, more generally, the denoted utility) of the architectural object. But we must remember from the outset that there is more to architectural communication than this.

When I look at the windows on the facade of a building, for instance, their denoted function may not be uppermost in my mind; my attention may be turned to a window-meaning that is based on the function but in which the func-tion has receded to the extent that I may even forget it, for the moment, concentrating on relationships through which the windows become elements of an architectural rhythm —-

just as someone who is reading a poem may, without entirely disregarding the meanings of the words there, let them recede into the background and thereby enjoy a certain formal play in the sign vehicles' contextual juxtaposition. And thus an architect might present one with some false windows, whose denoted functions would be illusory, and these windows could still function as windows in the architectural context in which they occur and be enjoyed (given the aesthetic function of the architectural message) as windows.[15]

Moreover windows—in their form, their number, their disposition on a façade (portholes, loopholes, curtain walls, etc.)—may, besides denoting a function, refer to a certain conception of inhabitation and use; they may *connote an overall ideology* that has informed the architect's operation. Round arches, pointed arches, and ogee arches all function in the load-bearing sense and denote this function, but they connote diverse ways of conceiving the function: they begin to assume a symbolic function.

2.2.2   Let us return, however to denotation and the primary, utilitarian function. We said that the object of use denotes the function *conventionally*, according to codes.

We will leave the problem of the definition of these codes to part 4 of this chapter, but let us here consider some of the general conditions under which an object denotes its function conventionally.

According to an immemorial architectural codification, a stair or a ramp denotes the possibility of going up. But whether it is a simple set of steps in a garden or a grand staircase by Vanvitelli, the winding stairs of the Eiffel Tower or the spiraling ramp of Frank Lloyd Wright's Guggenheim Museum, one finds oneself before a form whose interpretation involves not only a codified connection between the form and the function but also a conventional conception of how one fulfills the function with the form. Recently, for example, one has been able to go up also by means of an elevator, and the interpretation of the elevator involves, besides the recognition of the possible function—and rather than being disposed to the motor activity of moving one's feet in a certain way—a conception of how to fulfill the function through the various accessory devices at one's disposal in the elevator. Now the 'legibility' of these features of the elevator might be taken for granted, and presumably their design is such that none of us would have any trouble interpreting them. But clearly a primitive man used to stairs or ramps would be at a loss in front of an elevator; the best intentions on the part of the designer would not result in making the thing clear to him. The designer may have had a conception of the push buttons, the graphic arrows indicating whether the elevator is about to go up or down, and the emphatic floor-level indicators, but the primitive, even if he can guess the function, does not know that these forms are the 'key' to the function. He simply has no real grasp of the *code* of the elevator. Likewise he might possess only fragments of the code of the revolving door and be determined to use one of these as if it were a matter of an ordinary door. We can see, then, that an architect's belief in form that 'follows function' would be rather naïve unless it really rested on an understanding of the processes of codification involved.

In other words, the principle that *form follows function* might be restated: *the form of the object must, besides making the function possible, denote that function clearly enough to make it practicable as well as desirable*, clearly enough to dispose one to the actions through which it would be fulfilled.

2.2.3 Then all the ingenuity of an architect or designer cannot make a new form functional (and cannot give form to a new function) *without the support of existing processes of codification*.

There is an amusing but telling anecdote, which we owe to Koenig, concerning some housing units provided for rural populations in Italy by the 'Development Fund for the South'. With modern dwellings complete with bathrooms and toilets at their disposal, the local people, who were accustomed to taking care of bodily functions in the fields and unprepared for the mysterious sanitary fixtures that arrived, took to using the bowls as cleaning tanks for olives: they put the olives on some net they had suspended inside, then flushed and proceeded with the washing. So while we can all see the form of the standard toilet bowl is 'made for' the function it normally suggests and permits, and might be tempted to recognize a profound aesthetic and logical tie between the form and the function, *in fact the form denotes that function only on the basis of a system of established habits and expectations*, and thus on the basis of a code. And when another code (adventitious but not illegitimate) is superimposed upon the object, the bowl denotes another function.

Perhaps an architect could build me a house that would defy every architectural code, and perhaps this house would permit a pleasant and 'functional' form of inhabitation; but it is clear that I will not know how to inhabit it as intended unless I recognize certain 'directions' for its inhabitation built into it, or unless I recognize the house *as a context of signs referable to a known code*. No one has to give me instructions for me to know what to do with a fork, but if I am presented with a new type of mixer, capable of mixing in a way that is more efficient but outside the sphere of established habits, I will need some 'instructions for use'; otherwise the function of the new form would be an unknown.

This does not mean that the architect is necessarily confined to old, already known forms. Here we return to a fundamental semiotic principle that we have discussed elsewhere, apropos of artistic messages, a principle quite well explained in the *Poetics* of Aristotle: *one can institute moments of high information-content, but only when they are supported by a certain amount of redundancy*: every flash of the unlikely rests on articulations of the likely.[16]

2.2.4   A work of art can certainly be something new and highly informative; it can present articulations of elements that correspond to an idiolect of its own and not to pre-existing codes, for it is essentially an object intended to be contemplated, and it can communicate this new code, implicit in its makeup, precisely by fashioning it on the basis of the preexisting codes, evoked and negated. Now an architectural object could likewise be something new and informative; and if intended to promote a new function, it could contain in its form (or in its relation to comparable familiar forms) indications for the 'decoding' of this function. It too would be playing upon elements of preexisting codes, but rather than evoking and negating the codes, as the work of art might, and thus directing attention ultimately to itself, it would have to progressively transform them, progressively deforming already known forms and the functions conventionally referable to these forms. Otherwise the architectural object would become, not a functional object, but indeed a work of art: an ambiguous form, capable of being interpreted in the light of various different codes. Such is the case with 'kinetic' objects that simulate the outward appearance of objects of use; objects of use they are not, in effect, because of the underlying ambiguity that disposes them to any use imaginable and so to none in particular. (It should be noted that the situation of an object open to any use imaginable—and subject to none—is different from that of an object subject to a number of determinate uses, as we will see.)

One might well wish to go further into the nature of architectural denotation (here described only roughly, and with nothing in the way of detailed analysis). But we also mentioned possibilities of architectural connotation, which should be clarified.

2.3 Architectural connotation

2.3.1   We said that besides denoting its function the architectural object could connote a certain ideology of the function. But undoubtedly it can connote other things. The cave in our hypothetical model of the beginning of architecture came to denote a shelter function, but no doubt in time it would have begun to connote 'family' or 'group', 'security', 'familiar surroundings', etc. Then would its connotative nature, this symbolic 'function' of the object, be less *functional* than its first function? In other words, given that the cave denotes a certain basic *utilitas* (to borrow a term from Koenig), there is the question whether, with respect to life in society, the object would be *any less useful* in terms of its ability, as a symbol, to connote such things as closeness and familiarity. (From the semiotic point of view, the connotations would be founded on the denotation of the primary *utilitas*, but that would not diminish their importance.)

A seat tells me first of all that I can sit down on it. But if the seat is a throne, it must do more than seat one: it serves to seat one with a certain dignity, to corroborate its user's 'sitting in dignity' — perhaps through various accessory signs connoting 'regalness' (eagles on the arms, a high, crowned back, etc.). Indeed the connotation of dignity and regalness can become so functionally important that the basic function, to seat one, may even be slighted, or distorted: a throne, to connote regalness, often demands that the person sitting on it sit rigidly and uncomfortably (along with a sceptre in his right hand, a globe in the left, and a crown on his head), and therefore seats one 'poorly' with respect to the primary *utilitas*. Thus to seat one is only one of the functions of the throne — and only one of its meanings, the first but not the most important.

2.3.2   So the title *function* should be extended to all the uses of objects of use (in our perspective, to the various communicative, as well as to the denoted, functions), for with respect to life in society the 'symbolic' capacities of these objects are no less 'useful' than their 'functional' capacities. And it should be clear that we are not being metaphorical in calling the symbolic connotations functional, because they may not be immediately identified with the 'functions' narrowly defined; they do represent (and indeed communicate) in each case a real social utility of the object. It is clear that the most important function of the throne is the 'symbolic' one; and clearly evening dress (which, instead of serving to cover one like most everyday clothing, often 'uncovers' for women and for men covers poorly, lengthening to tails behind while leaving the chest practically bare) is functional because, thanks to the complex of conventions it connotes, it permits certain social relations, confirms them, shows their acceptance on the part of those who are communicating, with it, their social status, their decision to abide by certain rules, and so forth.[17]

3 Architectural Communication and History

3.1 Primary Functions and Secondary Functions

Since it would be awkward from here on to speak of 'functions' on the one hand, when referring to the denoted *utilitas*, and of 'symbolic' connotations on the other, as if the latter did not likewise represent real functions, we will speak of a *'primary'* function (which is denoted) and of a complex of *'secondary'* functions (which are connotative). It should be remembered, and is implied in what has already been said, that the terms *primary* and *secondary* will be used here to convey, not an axiological discrimination (as if the one function were more important than the others), but rather a semiotic mechanism, in the sense that the secondary functions rest on the denotation of the primary function (just as when one has the connotation of 'bad tenor' from the word for 'dog' in Italian, *cane*, it rests on the process of denotation).

3.1.1   Let us take a historical example where we can begin to see the intricacies of these primary and secondary functions, comparing the records of interpretation history has left us. Architectural historians have long debated the code of the Gothic, and particularly the structural value of the ogive. Three major hypotheses have been advanced: (1) the ogive has a structural function, and the entire lofty and elegant structure of a cathedral stands upon it, by virtue of the miracle of equilibrium it allows; (2) the ogive has no structural value, even if it gives the opposite impression; rather, it is the webs of the ogival vault that have the structural value; (3) the ogive had a structural value in the course of construction, functioning as a sort of provisional framework; later, the interplay of thrusts and counterthrusts was picked up by the webs and by other elements of the structure, and in theory the ogives of the cross vaulting could have been eliminated.[18]

No matter which interpretation one might adhere to, no one has ever doubted that the ogives of the cross vaulting *denoted* a structural function—support reduced to the pure interplay of thrusts and counterthrusts along slender, nervous elements; the controversy turns rather on the referent of that denotation: is the denoted function an illusion? Even if it is illusory, then, the communicative value of the ogival ribbing remains unquestionable; indeed if the ribbing had been articulated only to *communicate* the function, and not to *permit* it, that value would, while perhaps appearing more valid, simply be more intentional. (Likewise, it cannot be denied that the word *unicorn* is a sign, even though the unicorn does not exist, and even though its non-existence might have been no surprise to those using the term.)

3.1.2   While they were debating the functional value of ogival ribbing, however, historians and interpreters of all periods realized that the code of the Gothic had also a 'symbolic' dimension (in other words, that the elements of the Gothic cathedral had some complexes of secondary functions to them); one knew that the ogival vault and the walls pierced with great windows had something connotative to communicate. Now what that something might be has been defined time and again, on the basis of elaborate connotative subcodes founded on the cultural conventions and intellectual patrimony of given groups and given periods and determined by particular ideological perspectives with which they are congruent.

There is, for example, the standard romantic and protoromantic interpretation, whereby the structure of the Gothic cathedral was intended to reproduce the vault of Celtic forests, and thus the pre-Roman world, barbaric and primitive, of druidical religiosity.

And in the medieval period, legions of commentators and allegorists set themselves to defining, according to codes of formidable precision and subtlety, the individual meanings of every single architectural element; it will suffice to refer the reader to the catalogue drawn up, centuries later, by Joris Karl Huysmans in his *La Cathédrale*.

3.1.3   But there is, after all, a singular document we could mention — a code's very constitution — and that is the justification Suger gives of the cathedral in his *De rebus in administratione sua gestis*, in the twelfth century.[19] There he lets it be understood, in prose and in verse, that the light that penetrates in streams from the windows into the dark naves (or the structure of the walls that permits the light to be offered such ample access) must represent the very effusiveness of the divine creative energy, a notion quite in keeping with certain Neoplatonic texts and based on a codified equivalence between light and participation in the divine essence.[20]

We could say with some assurance, then, that for men of the twelfth century the Gothic windows and glazing (and in general the space of the naves traversed by streams of light) connoted 'participation' (in the technical sense given the term in medieval Neoplatonism); but the history of the interpretation of the Gothic teaches us that over the centuries the same sign vehicle, in the light of different subcodes, has been able to connote diverse things.

3.1.4 Indeed in the nineteenth century one witnessed a phenomenon typical of the history of art—when in a given period a code in its entirety (an artistic style, a manner, a 'mode of forming', independently of the connotations of its individual manifestations in messages) comes to connote an ideology (with which it was intimately united either at the moment of its birth or at the time of its most characteristic affirmation). One had at that time the identification 'Gothic style = religiosity', an identification that undoubtedly rested on other, preceding connotative identifications, such as 'vertical emphasis = elevation of the soul Godward' or 'contrast of light streaming through great windows and naves in shadow = mysticism'. Now these are connotations so deeply rooted that even today some effort is required to remember that the Greek temple, too, balanced and harmonious in its proportions, could connote, according to another lexicon, the elevation of the spirit to the Gods, and that something like the altar of Abraham, on the top of a mountain, could evoke mystical feelings; thus one connotative lexicon may impose itself over others in the course of time and, for example, the contrast of light and shadows becomes what one most deeply associates with mystic states of mind.

A metropolis like New York is studded with neo-Gothic churches, whose style (whose 'language') was chosen to express the presence of the divine. And the curious fact is that, by convention, these churches still have (for the faithful) the same value today, in spite of the fact that skyscrapers—by which they are now hemmed in on every side, and made to appear very small, almost miniaturized—have rendered the verticality emphasized in this architecture all but indistinguishable. An example like this should be enough to remind us that there are no mysterious 'expressive' values deriving simply from the nature of the forms themselves, and that expressiveness arises instead from a dialectic between significative forms and codes of interpretation; for otherwise the Gothic churches of New York, which are no longer as distinctively attenuated and vertical as they used to be, would no longer express what they used to, while in fact they still do in some respects, precisely because they are 'read' on the basis of codes that permit one to recognize them as distinctly vertical *in spite* of the new formal context (and new code of reading) that the advent of the skyscraper has now brought about.

3.2 Architectural Meanings and History

3.2.1 It would be a mistake, however, to imagine that by their very nature architectural sign-vehicles would denote stable primary functions, with only the secondary functions varying in the course of history. The example of ogival ribbing has already shown us a denoted function undergoing curious fluctuations—it was considered by some effective and essential, but by others provisional or illusory—and there is every reason to believe that in the course of time certain primary functions, no longer effective, would no longer even be denoted, the 'addresses' no longer possessing the requisite codes.

So, in the course of history, both primary and secondary functions might be found undergoing losses, recoveries, and substitutions of various kinds. These losses, recoveries, and substitutions are common to the life of forms in general, and constitute the norm in the course of the reading of works of art proper. If they seem more striking (and paradoxical) in the field of architectural forms, that is only because according to the common view one is dealing there with functional objects of an unequivocally indicated, and thus *univocally* communicative, nature. To give the lie to such a view, there is the story—its very currency puts its authenticity in doubt, but if untrue it is in any case credible—about the native wearing an alarm clock on his chest, an alarm clock interpreted as a pendant (as a kind of 'kinetic jewellery', one might say) rather than as a timepiece; the clock's measurement of time, and indeed the very notion of 'clock time', is the fruit of a codification and comprehensible only on the basis of it.

One type of fluctuation in the life of objects of use can therefore be seen in the variety of readings to which they are subject, regarding both primary and secondary functions. We will here attempt only a rough breakdown, with no pretence at completeness.

3.2.2   In the course of history, or passing from one human group to another, an object of use might be found undergoing one or another of these readings:

1. *(a) The sense of the primary function is lost* and *(b) the secondary functions for the most part remain.* Such is the case with the Parthenon, which is no longer understood as a place of worship, but a number of the original symbolic connotations of which are still grasped, on the strength of an adequate philological familiarity with the Greek sensibility.

2. *(a) The primary function remains* and *(b) the secondary functions are lost.* Antique lamps taken up without regard for their original connotative codes and inserted in different stylistic contexts (a rustic lamp included among sophisticated furnishings): their primary functionality is preserved, as they are still used to illuminate. (Of course

the original secondary functions will in all probability only be replaced by others, or even recovered and deformed, as in some of the following cases.)

3. *(a) The primary function is lost, (b) most secondary functions are lost, and (c) the original secondary functions are replaced by others, through codes of enrichment.* The Pyramids, for example: they may no longer be experienced as a tomb for a monarch, and most of the symbolic code—astrological and geometric—that presided over their connotative effectiveness for the ancient Egyptians has been lost, but the Pyramids now connote other things, from 'tourism' to the portentous 'forty centuries' of Napoleon's exhortations.

4. *The primary function becomes the object of a secondary function.* This is the case with the ready-made: a selected object of use is made an object of contemplation and then ironically connotes its former use. (For an example by way of analogy, the comic strip blown up by Lichtenstein: the woman-in-tears image no longer denotes a woman in tears—it communicates rather 'fragment of comic strip'—and it begins to connote, among other things, 'the way a woman in tears is seen in comic-strip culture'.)

5. *(a) The primary function is lost, (b) another primary function takes its place, and (c) the secondary functions are deformed through codes of enrichment.* A cradle from a Mexican village transformed into a magazine holder, put to a new use; the connotations originally connected with the object and its decorations, the connotations valid for the original users, are deformed, so that something different is connoted, such as affinities with contemporary or primitive art, folksy naivete, 'Latin-Americanness', and so on.

6. *(a) The primary functions are vague and (b) the secondary functions are imprecise and deformable.* Such is the case with Brasilia's 'Plaza of the Three Powers': the concave and convex forms of the amphitheatres of the two houses and the vertical form of the central building do not, except perhaps to their users, denote their primary functions—the amphitheatres seem to us pieces of sculpture—and have not become closely connected with any generally recognized connotative meanings; from the beginning there have been those who would interpret the symbols maliciously, seeing in the concave form of the Cámara a great dish in which the people's representatives are helping themselves to large portions of the public revenues.

3.3 Consumption and Recovery of Forms

3.3.1   The dialectical interplay between forms and history
is an interplay between structures and events, between configurations that are physically stable (and objectively
describable) as significative forms and the constantly changing play of circumstances, which confers new meanings on
them.

Now this process clearly underlies what has been called
consumption of forms, *obsolescence* of values.[21] And in a
period like ours, in which the succession of events is very
rapid—in which technological progress, social mobility, and
the spread of communications combine to change the codes
more frequently and profoundly than before—such consumption becomes, of course, quite evident; this may be
why, even though it is not a new phenomenon (it arises from
the very nature of communication), its theoretical investigation has begun rather recently.

But the same process, while providing the conditions for
this consumption, provides the conditions for the *recovery* of
forms and the *rediscovery* of senses.

3.3.2   A paradoxical aspect of contemporary taste is that
while we seem to be in a period characterized by rapid consumption of forms (because of a rapid succession of codes
and ideological backgrounds), we are also in a period of
history in which forms are recovered relatively quickly, and
for that matter preserved beyond apparent obsolescence.
Ours is a time of cultural awareness and philological agility;
with our special feeling for history and for the relativity of
cultures, it has become almost second nature to
'philologize'. The modern 'consumer' of messages learns,
decade by decade, to rediscover codes of reading for forms
that have become antiquated, to rediscover forgotten
ideological backgrounds and revive them in the process of
trying to understand objects that developed from them. (The
recent vogue of art nouveau is an example.) He learns, it is
true, to 'distort' past forms, to read these expropriated
messages in some 'free' or aberrant fashion, but he also
learns to rediscover the keys to 'correct' readings of them:
his cultural awareness leads him to a philological recovery
of the proper codes, though his agility in recovery frequently results in curious semantic 'shifts'.

Moreover, while the normal growth and obsolescence of
particular communicative systems (or rhetorical apparatus)
followed in the past a sinusoidal pattern—Dante having
disappeared entirely to rationalist readers of the eighteenth
century, then to be revived by the romanticists—today it is
more like a diverging spiral, in the sense that obsolete
systems are often 'shelved', not abandoned, and every

rediscovery is also an accretion of some kind. Our rereading of art nouveau is based not only on what we have rediscovered of the codes and ideologies of the turn-of-the-century bourgeoisie, but also on codes and ideological perspectives peculiar to our times (codes of enrichment), which permit us to insert antiquarian objects in new contexts, to use them both for something of what they meant in the past and for the connotations that we attribute to them on the basis of our present-day subcodes. It is an engrossing and adventurous process, rediscovering, given a form, the original contexts and creating new contexts—like a great pop-art operation, what (discerning its prototype in the technique of the surrealist ready-made) Claude Lévi-Strauss has called *semantic fission*, an abstraction of the sign from its original context and a reinsertion of it in a new context, which charges it with different meanings.[22] So consumption gives way to accretion, with the preservation and rediscovery of codes of the past going hand in hand with the employment of contemporary codes (Lichtenstein charging the comic-strip image with new meaning and at the same time inducing us to recall the denotations and connotations operative for the naïve reader of comics).

3.3.3 That is not to say, however, that this dynamic, part philology and part re-creation, is always 'positive'. In the past as well there were rediscoveries of former rhetorics and ideologies involving a mixture of philology and semantic fission—what else was humanism, and those anticipations of humanism in the vital, if muddled, rediscoveries of classicality of the Carolingian Middle Ages and thirteenth-century Scholasticism? And then, it is true, the rediscovery, pursued rather seriously and over a long period of time, could result in a certain overall restructuring of the contemporary rhetorics and ideologies. But today the dynamics of rediscovery and revival tends to be more contracted and superficial, leaving the underlying cultural system undisturbed; we can see in the present pursuit of rediscoveries a rhetorical technique (now conventionalized) that in fact implies a stable ideology of a sort: a laissez-faire attitude toward values past and present.

We have, besides rapid and conspicuous obsolescence, a stream of recoveries. But our recoveries, in a lightly pulsating alternation of acceptance and rejection, are far from 'revolutionizing' the bases of our culture. It is as if the present rediscoveries of codes and ideologies were the product of an immense rhetorical processor, whose overall operation connotes (and is directed by) the ideology of 'modernity' as *'tolerance' towards the entire past.*

An ideology as indulgent as this puts one in the peculiar position of being able to take up practically anything from the repertory of known forms and read it (or have it read) without ideological repercussions; it permits one to entertain all the ideologies of the past as keys to these modern messages, but these are messages with which even the accretions can fail to make up for a certain loss of significance, because the meanings of the forms are more and more eroded and provisional.

3.3.4   Given this inevitable process, with history voraciously emptying and filling forms, divesting them of meanings and adding new ones, there is perhaps nothing to do but simply resign oneself and rely upon what must be an instinctive wisdom in groups and cultures, which appear to be able, time after time, to find and manipulate forms and significative systems as needed or desired. And yet there is something puzzling and sad about forms that have outlived their usefulness, so to speak, that have lost their original significative power and become rather cumbersome, rather unwieldly and complex, with respect to the uses to which they are finally put. We are surrounded by these relics stripped of sense, or whose sense is now out of proportion with them, relics owing their prolonged life at best to aesthetic or historical interest, but more often to simple momentum or inordinate codes of enrichment that have been found for them (and here one sinks to concoctions of 'rhetoric' in the narrow, negative sense of the term, like the Pyramids as used in Napoleon's exhortations to his troops).

There is also the phenomenon — typical of our period, and sometimes very disappointing — of objects whose primary functions remain intact but whose secondary functions have withered away, certain subcodes having perished long before the basic codes, with slight shifts in taste. This is the case with the automobile that is still good for driving but that no longer connotes the prestige or comfort, or even the 'handleability', it used to. And here we can see the impact of 'styling' operations: periodically providing new symbolic clothing for more or less unchanged primary functions, or enriching with new connotations (or old connotations under new connotative forms) basic functional meanings that remain the same (just as, in the case of the automobile, the ideological background of a culture founded on mechanical devices and their efficiency remains the same).

Indeed a good deal of our manipulation of forms today — employing codes of enrichment with some and putting others aside, or rediscovering one code only to move on to another — is at bottom only a variety of styling. Take the rediscovery of the refectory table: a number of the original connotative subcodes have been restored to the message (there has been some degree of philological accuracy), but in the process these have been complicated with codes of enrichment. The refectory table has been inserted among sophisticated furnishings, semantic fission has had its effect, and the main secondary function of this table, which was to symbolize the frugal repast, has been radically deformed. The end result has been a 'restyled' dining table, for what the refectory table does is provide a new connotative enrichment of the same primary function we had with previous tables, and without ideological repercussions, for it no longer promotes or implies ascetic meals.

So we return to what was suggested earlier: the 'philological' vocation of our time may very well further recoveries of forms, but they are at the same time drained of significance. Perhaps this has something to do with what Nietzsche referred to as the *historical sickness* of the modern world, an excess of awareness, an awareness that, not transformed into renewal, acts as a narcotic.

There might be an alternative, however, a way in which changes in our rhetorical systems *could* mean renewal and changes in our ideological perspectives (whether as consequences of such renewal or as something that promotes it). There might be an alternative to the cycles of rediscovery and oblivion that our world puts *already produced* forms through—and the logic of which belongs really to such special domains as clothing fashions and the antique business.

We are today well aware of the rapid loss of sense to which forms are subject, and their capacity for acquiring new senses. (Whether these new senses seem appropriate or illegitimate at first does not matter, because *use* will determine which of them will be legitmated—imagine that Cossacks are found watering their horses at the stoups of Saint Peter's: there would be something like what was listed as the fifth possibility in 3.2.2, but while the Cossacks' general might find the resemanticization most appropriate, the sacristan of Saint Peter's would no doubt find it unthinkable, and it would remain to be seen which side history would favor.) And thus since the producers of objects of use now presumably *know* that these sign vehicles they articulate will undergo an unpredictable flux of meanings, since the designers of forms are now presumably aware of the process of dissociation between form and meaning and the mechanisms of substitution of meaning, they might undertake to *design for variable primary functions and 'open' secondary functions*.

This would mean that the object would be no victim of obsolescence and consumption, and no passive protagonist of recoveries: it would be instead a continuing stimulus, communicating the possibility of operations through which it could continually be reworked to fit the situations developing in the course of history—operations that would be acts of responsible decision, based on comparisons of the forms with alternative configurations their constitutive elements could assume and comparisons of these with the ideological perspectives that would be their justification.

These would be protean and open objects, implying, with changes in the rhetorical apparatus constituted by them, a restructuring of the ideological apparatus, or, with changes in the way they are used (or in the form they take in use), change in ways of thinking, in how the forms are seen in the broadest context of human activity.

And the ludic activity of repeatedly dicovering meanings for things, no longer turned to dilettantish rummagings into the past, could take the direction of *inventing, not rediscovering, different codes*. The jump backward is replaced by a jump forward. Abandoning oneself to the curiosities of history gives way to a kind of *design of the future*.[23]

The alternatives might be put thus: in 'recovering' fragments of an existing city I might perhaps rediscover antiquated rhetorical codes and forgotten ideological backgrounds, but in the game of recovery, as we said, there will as a rule be only superficial consequences, with my basic codes and ideologies remaining generally the same. But if I had before me an urban macrostructure that would clearly accommodate any number of changes in my basic conception of the city and were prompted to invent a particular disposition of it for my future use, my activity could become anything but superficial, for I might have to restructure my basic codes, in deciding what to make of it, and even my ideological perspective, for clearly in deciding what to make of it I might be prompted to alter my behavior overall.

The use of forms, or rhetorics, that hold within them these possibilities of change in conjunction with restructuring of ideological perspectives would be something quite different from our 'philological' activity. In the latter one can enjoy (but only up to a point) the rediscovery of forms of the past and the insertion of them, with semantic fission, into one's accustomed contexts, but in the former one would be dealing no longer with obsolescent forms: one would be engaged in giving new meanings to forms that are made for transformation, and that will be transformed precisely when one decides they should be and decides what directions the transformations should take.

So against the background of the historical dynamics of death and rebirth of already produced forms—sometimes traumatic and vital (humanism), sometimes tranquil and ludic (the recent rediscovery of art nouveau)—appears the positive possibility of an invention of rhetorics that would provide for different ideological perspectives, or for a continual reworking of the signs and of the contexts in which they would acquire meaning.

4 Architectural Codes

4.1 What is a Code in Architecture?

4.1.1 Architectural signs as denotative and connotative according to codes, the codes and subcodes as making different readings possible in the course of history, the architect's operation as possibly a matter of 'facing' the likelihood of his work being subject to a variety of readings and to the vicissitudes of communication by designing for variable primary functions and open secondary functions (open in the sense that they may be determined by unforeseeable future codes)—everything that has been said so far might suggest that there is little question about what is meant by *code*.

As long as one confines oneself to verbal communication, the notion is fairly clear: there is a code-language, and there are certain connotative subcodes. But when, in another section of this study, we went on to consider visual codes, for example, we found we had to list a number of levels of codification (including, but not limited to, iconic and monographic codes), and in the process to introduce various 'classifications' of the concept of code, and of the different types of articulation a code may provide for.[24] We also saw the importance of the principle that the elements of articulation under a given code can be syntagms of another, more 'analytic' code, or that the syntagms of one code can turn out to be elements of articulation (possibly at either of the levels of a 'double articulation') of another, more 'synthetic' code. This should be kept in mind when considering codes in architecture, for one might be tempted to attribute to an architectural code articulations that belong really to some code, either more analytic or more synthetic, lying outside architecture.

4.1.2 We can expect some problems, then, in the definition of the codes of architecture. First of all, from the attempts there have been to date to spell out aspects of architectural communication, we can see that there is the problem of neglecting to consider whether what one is looking at is referable to a syntactic code rather than a semantic code—that is, to rules concerning, rather than the meanings conventionally attributed to individual sign-vehicles, the articulation of certain significative structures separable from these sign vehicles and their meanings—or for that matter to some underlying technical convention.

Catchwords like 'semantics of architecture' have led some to look for the equivalent of the 'word' of verbal language in architectural signs, for units endowed with definite meaning, indeed for symbols pointing to referents. But since we know there can be conventions governing the semantic reading of architectural signs, it would be appropriate to look also for purely syntactic codifications in architecture. (Finding such codifications, and defining them with precision, we might be in a better position to understand and classify, at least from the point of view of semiotics, objects whose once denoted functions can no longer be ascertained, such as the menhir, the dolmen, the Stonehenge construction).

4.1.3   Then, too, in the case of architecture, codes of reading (and of construction) of the *object* would have to be distinguished from codes of reading (and of construction) of the *design* for the object (admittedly we are considering here only a semiotics of architectural objects, and not a semiotics of architectural designs). Of course the notational codes of the design, while conventionalized independently, are to some extent derivatives of the codes of the object: they provide ways in which to 'transcribe' the object, just as to transcribe spoken language there are conventions for representing such elements as sounds, syllables, or words. But that does not mean a semiotic investigation of the architectural design would be without some interesting problems of its own — there are in a design, for example, various systems of notation (the codes operative in a plan are not quite the same as those operative in a section or in a wiring diagram for a building),[25] and in these systems of notation there can be found iconic signs, diagrams, indices, symbols, qualisigns, sinsigns, etc., perhaps enough to fill the entire gamut of signs proposed by Peirce.

4.1.4   Much of the discussion of architecture as communication has centred on *typological* codes, especially semantic typological codes, those concerning functional and sociological types; it has been pointed out that there are in architecture configurations clearly indicating 'church', 'railroad station', 'palace', etc. We will return to typological codes in 4.2 but it is clear that they constitute only one, if perhaps the most conspicuous, of the levels of codification in architecture.

4.1.5   In attempting to move progressively back from a level at which the codes are so complex and temporal — for it is clear that 'church' has found different articulations at different moments in history — one might be tempted to hypothesize for architecture something like the 'double articulation' found in verbal languages, and assume that the most basic level of articulation (that is, the units constituting the 'second' articulation) would be a matter of geometry.
   If architecure is the art of the articulation of spaces,[26] then perhaps we already have, in Euclid's geometry, a good definition of the rudimentary code of architecture. Let us say that the second articulation is based on the Euclidean

στοιχεια (the 'elements' of classical geometry); then the 'first' articulation would involve certain higher-level spatial units, which could be called *choremes*, with these combining into spatial syntagms of one kind or another.[27] In other words, the angle, the straight line, the various curves, the point, etc., might be elements of a second articulation, a level at which the units are not yet *significant* (endowed with meaning) but are *distinctive* (having differential value); the square, the triangle, the parallelogram, the ellipse—even rather complicated irregular figures, as long as they could be defined with geometric equations of some kind—might be elements of a first articulation, a level at which the units begin to be significant; and one rectangle within another might be an elementary syntagmatic combination (as in some window—wall relationship), with more complex syntagms to be found in such things as space-enclosing combinations of rectangles or articulations based on the Greek-cross plan. Of course solid geometry suggests the possibility of a third level of articulation, and it could be assumed that further articulative possibilities would come to light with the recognition of non-Euclidean geometries.

The trouble is that this geometric code *would not pertain specifically to architecture*. But geometric codes need not be confined to the analysis of abstract, geometric art (Mondrian), because it has long been held that the configurations in representational art can be reduced to an articulation, if perhaps a quite complex one, of primordial geometric elements—this code clearly underlies the formulations of geometry in the etymological sense of the word (surveying) and other types of 'transcription' of terrain (topographic, geodetic, etc.). It might even be identified with a 'gestaltic' code presiding over our perception of all such forms. What we have here, then, is an example of one sort of code one can arrive at when attempting to analyse the elements of articulation of a certain 'language': a code capable of serving as a *metalanguage* for it, and for a number of other more synthetic codes as well.

4.1.6   So it would be better to pass over a code of this kind, just as in linguistics one passes over the possibility of going beyond 'distinctive features' in analysing phonemes. Admittedly such analytic possibilities might have to be explored if one had to compare architectural phenomena with phenomena belonging to some other 'language', and thus had to find a metalanguage capabable of describing them in the same terms. For instance, one might wish to 'code' a certain landscape in such a way as to be able to compare it with certain proposed architectural solutions, to determine what architectural artifacts to insert in the context of that landscape, and if one resorted to elements of the code of solid geometry (pyramid, cone, etc.) in defining the structure of the landscape, then it would make sense to describe the architecture in the light of that geometric code, taken as a metalanguage.[28] *But the fact that architecture can be described in terms of geometry does not indicate that architecture as such is founded on a geometric code.*

After all, that both Chinese and words articulated in the phonemes of the Italian language can be seen as a matter of amplitudes, frequencies, wave forms, etc., in radio acoustics or when converted into grooves on a disc does not indicate that Chinese and Italian rest on one and the same code: it simply shows that the languages admit of that type of analysis, that for certain purposes they can be *reduced* to a common system of transcription. In fact there are few physical phenomena that would not permit analysis in terms of chemistry or physics at the molecular level, and in turn within an atomic code, but that does not lead us to believe the Mona Lisa should be analysed with the same instruments used in analysing a mineral specimen.

Then what more properly architectural codes have emerged in various analyses or, recently, 'semiotic' readings of architecture?

4.2 Varieties of Architectural Code

4.2.1   It would appear, from those that have come to light, that architectural codes could be broken down roughly as follows:

1. *Technical codes*. To this category would belong, to take a ready example, articulations of the kind dealt with in the science of architectural engineering. The architectural form resolves into beams, flooring systems, columns, plates, reinforced concrete elements, insulation, wiring, etc. There is at this level of codification no communicative 'content', except of course in cases where a structural (or technical) function or technique itself becomes such; there is only a structural logic, or structural conditions behind architecture and architectural signification—conditions that might therefore be seen as somewhat analogous to a second articulation in verbal languages, where though one is still short of meanings there are certain formal conditions of signification.[29]

2. *Syntactic codes*. These are exemplified by typological codes concerning articulation into *spatial types* (circular plan, Greek-cross plan, 'open' plan, labyrinth, high-rise, etc.), but there are certainly other syntactic conventions to be considered (a stairway does not as a rule go through a window, a bedroom is generally adjacent to a bathroom, etc.).

3. *Semantic codes*. These concern the significant units of architecture, or the relations established between individual architectural sign-vehicles (even some architectural syntagms) and their denotative and connotative meanings. They might be subdivided as to whether, through them, the units (*a*) denote *primary functions* (roof, stairway, window), (*b*) have connotative *secondary functions* (tympanum, triumphal arch, neo-Gothic arch), (*c*) connote *ideologies of inhabitation* (common room, dining room, parlour), or (*d*) at a larger scale have typological meaning under certain *functional and sociological types* (hospital, villa, school, palace, railway station).[30]

The inventory could of course become quite elaborate—there should, for instance, be a special place for types like 'garden city' and 'new town', and for the codifications emerging from certain recent *modi operandi* (derived from avant-garde aesthetics) that have already created something of a tradition, a *manner*, of their own.

4.2.2   But what stands out about these codes is that on the whole they would appear to be, as communicative systems go, rather limited in operational possibilities. They are, that is, codifications of *already worked-out solutions*, codifications yielding *standardized messages*—this instead of constituting, as would codes truly on the model of those of verbal languages, a system of possible relationships from which countless significantly different messages could be generated.

A verbal language serves the formulation of messages of all kinds, messages connoting the most diverse ideologies (and is inherently neither a class instrument nor the superstructure of a particular economic base).[31] Indeed the diversity of the messages produced under the codes of a verbal language makes it all but impossible to identify any overall ideological connotations in considering broad samplings of them. Of course this characterization might be challenged, for there is some evidence to support the theory that the very way in which a language is articulated obliges one speaking it to see the world in a particular way (there might be, then, ideological bias and connotation of some kind inherent in the language).[32] But even given that, on the most profound, ultimate level, one could take a verbal language as a *field of (nearly absolute) freedom*, in which the speaker is free to improvise novel messages to suit unexpected situations. And in architecture, if the codes are really those indicated above, that does not seem to be the case.

The point is not that in articulating a church, for example, the architect is in the first place obeying a socio-architectural prescription that churches be made and used (about this sort of determinant we will have more to say later). And in the end he would be free to try to find and exploit—playing on the dialectic mentioned in 2.2.3 between information and redundancy—some way in which to make a church that while conforming to its type would be somewhat different from any that had yet appeared, a church that would thereby provide a somewhat unaccustomed, 'refreshing' context in which to worship and imagine the relationship with God. But if at the same time, in order for it to *be* a church, he must un-failingly articulate the building in manifold conformity to a type ('down to the hardware', one might say), if the codes operative in architecture allow only slight deviations from a standardized message, however appealing, then architecture is, not the field of creative freedom some have imagined it to be, but a system of rules for giving society what it *expects* in the way of architecture.

In that case architecture might be considered, not the ser-vice some have imagined it to be—a mission for men of unusual culture and vision, continually readying new pro-positions to put before the social body—but a service in the sense in which waste disposal, water supply, and mass transit are services: an operation that is, even with changes and technical refinements from time to time, the routine satisfac-tion of some preconstituted demand.

It would appear to be rather impoverished as an art, then, also, if it is characteristic of art, as we have suggested elsewhere, to put before the public things they have not yet come to expect.[33]

4.2.3 So the codes that have been mentioned would amount to little more than lexicons on the model of those of iconographic, stylistic, and other specialized systems, or limited repertories of set constructions. They establish not generative possibilities but ready-made solutions, not open forms for extempory 'speech' but fossilized forms—at best 'figures of speech' or schemes providing for formulaic presentation of the unexpected (as a complement to the system of established, identified, and never really disturbed expectations), rather than relationships from which com-munication varying in information content as determined by the 'speaker' could be improvised. The codes of architecture would then constitute a rhetoric in the narrow sense of the word: a store of *tried and true discoursive formulas.*[34]

And this could be said not only of the semantic codes, but also of the syntactic codifications, which clearly confine us to a certain quite specialized 'grammar' of building, and the technical codes, for it is obvious that even this body of 'empty' forms underlying architecture (column, beam, etc.) is too specialized to permit every conceivable architectural message. It permits a kind of architecture to which civilization in its evolving technologies has accustomed us, a kind relating to certain principles of statics and dynamics, certain geometric concepts, many of them from Euclid's geometry, certain elements and systems of construction—the principles, concepts, elements, and systems that, proving relatively stable and resistant to wear and tear, are found codified under the science of architectural engineering.

5 Architecture as Mass Communication?

5.1 Mass Appeal in Architecture

5.1.1   If architecture is a system of rhetorical formulas producing just those messages the community of users has come to expect (seasoned with a judicious measure of the unexpected), what then distinguishes it from the various forms of mass culture? The notion that architecture *is* a form of mass culture has become rather popular,[35] and as a communicative operation directed toward large groups of people and confirming certain widely subscribed to attitudes and ways of life while meeting their expectations, it could certainly be called mass communication loosely, without bothering about any detailed criteria.

5.1.2   But even under more careful consideration,[36] architectural objects seem to have characteristics in common with the messages of mass communication. To mention a few:

> Architectural 'discourse' generally *aims at mass appeal*: it starts with accepted premises, builds upon them well-known or readily acceptable 'arguments', and thereby elicits a certain type of consent. ('This proposition is to our liking; it is in most respects something we are already familiar with, and the differences involved only represent a welcome improvement or variation of some kind.')

> Architectural discourse *is psychologically persuasive*: with a gentle hand (even if one is not aware of this as a form of manipulation) one is prompted to follow the 'instructions' implicit in the architectural message: functions are not only signified but also promoted and induced, just as certain products and attitudes are promoted through 'hidden persuasion', sexual associations, etc.

Architectural discourse *is experienced inattentively*, in the same way in which we experience the discourse of films and television, the comics, or advertising—not, that is, in the way in which one is meant to experience works of art and other more demanding messages, which call for concentration, absorption, wholehearted interest in interpreting the message, interest in the intentions of the 'addressor'.[37]

Architectural messages *can be interpreted in an aberrant way*, and without the 'addressee' being aware of thereby perverting them. Most of us would have some sense of being engaged in a perversion of the object if we were to use the Venus de Milo for erotic purposes or religious vestments as dustcloths, but we use the cover of an elevated roadway for getting out of the rain or hang laundry out to dry over a railing and see no perversion in this.

Thus architecture *fluctuates between being rather coercive*, implying that you will live in such and such a way with it, *and rather indifferent*, letting you use it as you see fit.

Architecture *belongs to the realm of everyday life*, just like pop music and most ready-to-wear clothing, instead of being set apart like 'serious' music and high fashion.

Architecture *is a business*.[38] It is produced under economic conditions very similar to the ones governing much of mass culture, and in this too differs from other forms of culture. Painters may deal with galleries, and writers with publishers, but for the most part that has to do with their livelihood and need not have anything to do with what they find themselves painting and writing. The painter can always pursue painting independently, perhaps while making a living in some other way, and the writer can produce works for which there is no market, perhaps with no thought of having them published, but the architect cannot be engaged in the practice of architecture without inserting himself into a given economy and technology and trying to embrace the logic he finds there, even when he would like to contest it.

5.2 Information Content in Architecture

5.2.1 And yet anyone who pays much attention to architecture can see that there is something more to it, something that would distinguish it from mass communication. Architecture seems to offer messages that have mass appeal, that lend themselves to being taken for granted even when they are not highly conventional, but there are at the same time inventive and heuristic aspects to these messages.

While developing from premises given by the society in which it is produced, an architectural object can become in the end something new or different, something *more informative* than mass communication. (Of course the same might be said of mass-communication messages, for sometimes while clearly originating as mass communication they proceed to set themselves apart from that because of ideological, aesthetic, or other peculiarities they develop, either in their makeup or under special readings—because, that is, of information content exceeding the limits of mass communication.) We can see this when the object is a new *machine à habiter* waiting to be interpreted and accepted and perhaps tending to connote some new ideology of inhabitation, in which case the information content is obviously rather high. But it is also true in another sense, in the sense that even when highly conventional, architectural objects stand as *alternatives* to other architectural objects: besides permitting and promoting certain functions, they permit and promote 'critical' readings, in which one *compares them with prior (and subsequent) means and ideologies of inhabitation*. Now this goes beyond saying that they contrast (or are in free variation) with other 'contemporaneous' architectural objects—that is, with objects to some extent 'distributionally equivalent' in terms of what could be built at the time (however limited in operational possibilities, the codes of architecture do not, of course, exclude paradigmatic relations of various kinds, such as those a stair enters into with other elements that may be used to connect different levels.) For the curious fact is that architectural messages, like works of art, are both subject to rapid obsolescence and long-lived, so that the forms and dispositions produced by architects today are almost inevitably juxtaposed with forms and dispositions 'left over' from former, outmoded codes; in other words, while one can assume with a verbal language that diachronic aspects of the system are more or less irrelevant to its users, who would be dealing only with what would fall under a synchronic description of it, that is not the case with architecture. So while the fact that they are both obsolescent and long-lived may be seen as an argument for the development of more open architectural objects (3.3.4), it may also be seen as a special feature of the system generating increases in information content by promoting comparative readings of its objects, indeed by inducing us to become to some extent architectural critics in reading the architecture, past and present, with which we are living.

Finally there is the phenomenon of technique becoming,

in architecture as in art proper, *self-reflexive*, with the other functions of the message giving way, for the moment at least, to the aesthetic function: besides permitting and promoting certain functions, the object may have one's attention directed *to itself, to the particular way in which it has been decided to 'go about' permitting and promoting them.*

5.2.2   At this point we might consider again the subject of styling. As we said, styling can be seen as the superimpositon of new secondary functions on unchanged primary functions, or as the employment of new rhetorical forms in reiterating conventional messages. Now this can, of course, result in one kind of increase in information content, a kind perfectly consistent with mass communication: there is a slight 'twist' on what one would have expected. The object and its primary function are made to appear, for the moment, fresh and newly appealing, and so this is a rhetorical strategy that can be used to reaffirm something the user already wants and does and knows how to do.

It is conceivable, however, that resemanticization of a conventional object through styling could be directed towards effecting, by means of new secondary functions, a different ideological view of it. The primary function might remain unchanged, as before, but there could be, in the end, a substantial change in the way in which the object is viewed in the overall system of objects, in the overall system of the values held by the objects in relation to one another and in relation to the acts of everyday life.

When a car is redesigned only to provide new rhetorical clothing for the same basic message, there is an increase in information content only with respect to our *rhetorical* expectations, not with respect to our *ideological* expectations.

But if a car that has been a class symbol were redesigned — with the same motor, let us say, and without changing any of the primary functions — to make it a car 'for everyone', then it might well become a substantially different object in use. Styling in this case could result not merely in new surface connotations, but in new connotations that would have ideological repercussions and lead to a comprehensive recodification of the object and its functions.

5.2.3   With these differences and similarities between architecture and mass communication, it is unclear what position the architect is left in with respect to the community of users and their expectations. Can he afford to fly in the face of widely held expectations and confront the users with artifacts that radically challenge their way of life? Or rather, to be effective, must he see that his work is consistent with the expectations prevailing in the society in which he operates, expectations that transcend the terms of architecture and that form systems of the sort that anthropologists study?

An anthropologist faced with a certain community might investigate the codes behind its verbal communications, perhaps reducing them to a general system concerning verbal communications in various societies and languages; he studies kinship structures in the society, perhaps reducing these to a general system having to do with kinship structures in all societies; he might even turn to its 'urbanistic' structures and succeed in reducing them to some system concerning urbanistic dispositions in general. But he ultimately seeks to relate, within the sphere of the particular society being studied, its linguistic forms, the forms of its kinship system, the forms of its village or city layout, etc., integrating all these facts of communication, all these aspects of its culture, into a unitary model, referring them, that is, to an underlying structure that informs them and links them through homology.

Then for the architect who has to build for this same community we could hypothesize three possible approaches, or three possible attitudes with respect to that underlying structure.

First, his attitude could be one of *thoroughly integrating his work into the reigning social system*. Accepting without question the norms governing the society, he tries to satisfy the architectural demands and expectations of the social body as it stands. He designs buildings to permit the way of life to which the members of the society are accustomed, with no thought of upsetting it in any way. In this case the architect would be trying to identify and closely adhere to the technical codes, the lexicons of conventionalized elements, and the 'grammar' of building in use, and if successful, he would at the same time, even without being aware of it, be adhering to that underlying code that transcends the terms of architecture.

Second, taking an approach of 'avant-garde' subversiveness, the architect might decide to *dispense with the conventional architecture and oblige people to live with a totally different architecture*. He contrives designs that would presumably permit, instead of their customary way of life, a way of life having little relation to the existing social patterns, which would have to be abandoned. But is fairly certain that the community would either reject or 'pervert' these new architectural forms, because his work would imply some alien underlying code, a code unrelated to the one governing the community's existing architectural forms, kinship relationships, linguistic communications, artistic productions, etc.

Third, the architect could undertake to *create an architec-*

*ture that would be new but would be intended to answer to
that basic code.* He tries to anticipate the implications, for
the community, of certain new developments (historical,
cultural, technological, etc.), how the needs of the users
might be changing. He tries to determine, on the basis of
various data available to him, what new systems of functions
might have to be permitted and promoted. And only then
—only once he has an idea of what would call for new architectural forms, of what they would answer to, of what
would link them with the basic code of the society and make
them acceptable and comprehensible to its members—does
he attempt to elaborate and introduce the new system of
architectural sign-vehicles. In this case, architecture could
again be considered a *service,* but in another, broader sense:
rather than simply supplying what one has come to expect
from it, it undertakes to provide something one does *not yet*
expect from it, to investigate what new architecture might
eventually be desired and possible within the society, to produce an architecture that would eventually be accepted and
comprehended in the light of prevailing expectations and
related to the whole of the society's systems of cultural communication.[39]

5.2.4   If there is a growing interest in *interdisciplinary* work
as the proper basis for architectural design, then, it could be
explained by the fact that *in the last analysis the architect has
to elaborate his sign vehicles and messages in relation to
systems of meanings that lie outside his province,* even
though these meanings might be signified for the first time in
his work, given their first sign-vehicles in architecture. And
for that reason the architect might find himself in the position of having to *reject the existing architectural codes,* when
rather than providing for the generation of the messages
called for, they hold out only already produced message-
solutions that are no longer relevant.

6 External Codes

6.1 Architecture as Based on Codes External to it

6.1.1   To recapitulate: (a) we began with the premise that
architecture would, to be able to communicate the functions
it permits and promotes, have to be based on codes; (b) we
have seen that the codes that could properly be
called architectural establish rather limited operational
possibilities, that they function not on the model of a
language but as a system of rhetorical formulas and already
produced message-solutions; (c) resting on these codes, the

architectural message becomes something of mass appeal, something that may be taken for granted, something that one would expect; (*d*) yet it seems that architecture may also move in the direction of innovation and higher information-content, going against existing rhetorical and ideological expectations; (*e*) it cannot be the case, however, that when architecture moves in this direction it departs from given codes entirely, for without the basis of a code of some kind, there would be no effective communication.

6.1.2   One might, then, hypothesize some architectural codifications more open, or less limited in operational possibilities, than the codes already mentioned, perhaps something on the order of what Italo Gamberini has proposed with his 'constitutive signs' of architecture.[40]

These matrices of interior spaces would be, according to Gamberini's classification, (1) *floor-plan signs*, which give a 'bottom' to architectural volumes, (2) *connection signs*, which occur between floor-plan elements placed at different elevations and which may be either continuous connection-elements, such as ramps, or stepped ones, such as stairs, (3) *lateral-containment signs*, self-supporting (fixed or movable) or supporting something, (4) *intercommunication signs*, between the spaces established by the lateral-containment elements, (5) *cover signs*, self-supporting or supported, (6) *independent-support signs*, vertical, horizontal, or even inclined, (7) *qualificative-accentuation signs*, and so on.

Clearly a codification of this kind could underlie a very wide range of architectural messages, having none of the rhetorical or typological rigidity of the codes mentioned before. One might consider these 'constitutive signs' elements of a second articulation; however some of them would denote functions, and consequently might be understood as elements of a first articulation.

Of course even more open would be the elements and purely mathematical rules of combination studied in 'metadesign',[41] which is concerned not with what one might actually have to design but with the generative matrices underlying all design (and which indeed is intended to further a kind of design in which the variability of primary and secondary functions is effectively recognized). But here again we would have a code that does not pertain specifically to architecture, though it might well prove fundamentally useful in architecture.

Returning then to the 'constitutive signs' — the freedom of articulation they hold out beyond rhetorical formulas and already produced solutions having been recognized — there remains the question of their adequacy as a code. *What rules for their combination are there for the architect to follow?* If

he rejects as inappropriate the rules implicit in the traditional, rhetorical lexicons, what *then* does he base his combination of them upon? It would appear that the architect is
in the paradoxical position of commanding certain
paradigmatic resources without knowing quite what to do
with them on the axis of the syntagm. He has something of a
vocabulary, or at least an alphabet, but his grammar is yet to
be found. And everything seems to indicate that it is not to
be found within the realm of architecture.

There is only one possible answer. *Architecture must in
fact be based not only upon existing architectural codes, from
which the architect may depart, but also upon other, external
codes* (and it is with reference to these that the users would
identify the meanings of the new architectural message).

6.1.3   It goes without saying, for instance, that an urban
designer could lay out a street on the basis of the lexicon
that embraces and defines the type 'street'; he could even,
with a minor dialectic between redundancy and information,
make it somewhat different from previous ones while still
operating within the traditional urbanistic system. When,
however, Le Corbusier proposes his elevated streets (closer
to the type 'bridge' than to the type 'street'), he moves outside the accepted typology, which has streets at ground level
or, if elevated, elevated in a different fashion and for different reasons—and yet he does so with a certain assurance,
believing that this new sign, along with the rest of his proposed city, would be accepted and comprehended by the
users. Now whether such a belief is justified or not, it would
have to be based on something like this: the architect has
preceded architectural design with an examination of certain
new social exigencies, certain 'existential' desiderata, certain
tendencies in the development of the modern city and life
within it, and has traced out, so to speak, a semantic system
of certain future exigencies (developing from the current
situation) on the basis of which new functions and new
architectural forms might come into being.

In other words, the architect would have identified (a) a
series of social exigencies, presumably as a system of some
kind, (b) a system of functions that would satisfy the exigencies, and that would become sign-vehicles of those exigencies, and (c) a system of forms that would correspond to the
functions, and that would become sign-vehicles of those
functions.

From the point of view of common sense, this means that
to produce the new architecture Le Corbusier was obliged,
before thinking like an architect, to think like a sociologist,
an anthropologist, a psychologist, an ideologist, etc., and
we will return to that shortly. But first we might consider the
peculiarity of the phenomenon from the semiotic point of
view.

6.1.4   Only at the last level, the level of (c), do we find forms that could be understood as 'architecture'. So while the elements of architecture constitute themselves a system, they become a code only when coupled with systems that lie outside architecture.

Now one might argue that the same thing is true of verbal language—and not because of referents of a language lying outside the language, for that would make the argument too naïve; as we have suggested, the question of referents has no bearing on the processes of signification. The argument would be rather that in a verbal language as well a system of sign-vehicles (or a 'plane of expression') is coupled with semantic systems (on the 'plane of content') lying outside it; these semantic systems are systems of cultural units that can transcend particular languages and be designated in different ways in them.

And we could accept this argument as true, in theory. But the point is that it seems to be impossible to demonstrate. One can of course maintain that the union between the sign-vehicle *dog* and the cultural unit 'dog' is entirely arbitrary, that the units are independent, but when one attempts to consider the sign vehicle *dog* independently of its meaning, one finds that one cannot really escape from the fact that it *has that meaning*. Moreover, in order to indicate that meaning as a cultural unit, one is obliged to use another verbal sign-vehicle, and so one never gets outside the circle of the language; the only way one can designate the cultural units is *through* linguistic units, and the only way one can identify the independent linguistic units is by identifying them as *vehicles* of cultural units. Thus (in practice) the verbal language obliges one to see it as a code in which the plane of content is inseparable from the plane of expression. And it is this that led Saussure to compare the sign to a sheet of paper, the two sides of which can be distinguished, it is true, but never split into two independent halves.

What about architecture, then, if we accept the hypotheses of 6.1.3? Let us use *X* for the system of architectural forms, *Y* for the system of functions, and *K* for the system of social exigencies, or the *anthropological* system—an *x* might be a table of certain width, which permits and signifies a certain function *y* (to eat at a considerable distance from one another, let us say), which in turn allows the realization of an anthropological value *k* ('formal' relationship), whose sign-vehicle that function has become.

Then the units in *X*, as spatial forms, admit of several kinds of description—two-dimensional (through a set of drawings or a photograph), verbal (through an oral or written description), mathematical (through a series of equations), etc.; the units in *Y*, as functions, admit of either verbal description or representation in terms of some iconic (cinematographic, for example), kinesic, or other kind of system for 'transcribing' functions; and the units in *K*, as anthropological values, can be described verbally.

Now it is clear that while a form *x* is being used it might seem (to the user) quite closely tied to a function *y* and an anthropological value *k* — just as closely as a meaning seems (to the speaker) tied to a verbal sign-vehicle. But from the point of view of semiotics, it is possible to *describe the units of each of these three systems independently*, without, that is, having recourse to the units of either of the other two.

This is something that was never envisaged by those who have considered the notion of meaning suspect, because up to now studies in semantics have been conducted inside the circle of verbal 'interpretants'. So above and beyond what else it offers, semiotics shows us the possibility of investigating systems of signs where the planes of expression and content are not inseparable — or at least where they can be more successfully separated.

6.2 The Anthropological System

6.2.1   But in introducing this *K*, this anthropological system, have we jeopardized the semiotic framework behind everything we said before?

Having said that architecture has to elaborate its sign-vehicles and messages with reference to something that lies *outside* it, are we forced to admit its sign cannot, after all, be adequately characterized without bringing something like *referents* back into the picture?

We have argued that semiotics must confine itself to the *left side* of the Ogden — Richards triangle — because in semiotics one studies codes as phenomena of culture — and, leaving aside verifiable realities to which the signs may refer, examine only the communicative rules established within a social body: rules of the equivalence between sign-vehicles and meanings (the definition of the latter being possible only through interpretants, or other sign-vehicles by means of which the meanings may be signified), and rules regarding the syntagmatic combination of the elements of the paradigmatic repertories. This means, not that the referent is nonexistent, but that it is the object of *other* sciences (physics, biology, etc.); semiotics can, and must, confine itself to the universe of the cultural conventions governing communicative intercourse.

If for architecture, then, or for any other system of signs, we had to admit that the plane of content involved something that did not belong to the semiotic universe, we would be faced with a phenomenon confounding semiotics, or at any rate confounding all the notions we have put forward here and elsewhere, on semiotics.[42]

So it is not casually that we have been referring to an anthropological 'system': we have been referring, that is, to facts that while belonging to the universe of the social sciences may nevertheless be seen as *already codified*, and thus reduced to a cultural system.

6.2.2   For an indication of what is meant by *K*, we might consider studies in *proxemics*, notably those of Edward T. Hall.[43]

For proxemics, space 'speaks'. The distances one puts between oneself and those with whom one is engaged in social relations of various kinds are charged with cultural meanings, just as such things as perceptions of the warmth of another's body, tactile sensations, and odours take on meanings.

That space has significative value has already been demonstrated in the study of animal behavior. For every animal species there is a 'flight distance' (when this limit is passed—five hundred yards for the antelope, six feet for certain lizards—the animal seeks to avoid the intruder of a different species), a 'critical distance' (a narrow zone between flight distance and attack distance), and an 'attack distance' (within which the animals enter into direct conflict). And when one considers animals that accept physical contact between members of their own species and those that avoid such contact, one finds 'personal distances' (the 'noncontact' animal maintains a certain distance between himself and his fellows) and 'social distances' (beyond a certain distance, which varies from one species to another, the animal 'loses contact' with the group). In short, every animal seems to be surrounded by 'spheres' of great importance to it in terms of its relations with other animals, and these have been measured rather precisely.

The problem of proxemics has been to investigate the codification of such phenomena in human culture, and to investigate the different codifications of them in different human cultures.

6.2.3   Hall distinguishes between 'infracultural manifestations', which are rooted in the biological past of the individual, 'precultural manifestations', which are physiological in nature, and 'microcultural manifestations', which are what proxemics focuses upon and which fall into the following three categories:

1. *Fixed-feature space.* To this category belong many of those spatial configurations commonly recognized as being codified—plans of cities, for example, with the definition of blocks of buildings and their dimensions (think of the plan of New York). And already there are remarkable cultural variations: Hall cites the example of Japanese

cities, where it is the intersections, not the streets, that are defined, and where houses are numbered not according to their order in space but according to their order in time (date of construction); one might also cite the findings from several anthropological studies on the structure of villages, especially Lévi-Strauss's.[44]

2. *Semifixed-feature space.* Configurations belonging to this category are a matter of the arrangement of 'movable' elements of interior or exterior spaces. And here Hall introduces a distinction between 'sociofugal' spaces and 'sociopetal' spaces. The typical seating provisions in the waiting room of a train station make it a sociofugal space, a space that tends to keep people apart, while the arrangement of chairs and tables in an Italian or French bar is sociopetal. As an example of cultural variation, Hall cites the problem caused by the 'open door' policy of a branch of an American firm in Germany:

> In this company the open doors were making the Germans feel exposed and gave the whole operation an unusually relaxed and unbusinesslike air. Closed doors, on the other hand, gave the Americans the feeling that there was a conspiratorial air about the place and that they were being left out. The point is that whether the door is open or shut, it is not going to mean the same thing in the two countries.[45]

3. *Informal space.* Configurations belonging to this category are characterized as 'informal' because they are at the opposite extreme from the more 'formal' configurations of fixed-feature space; they are primarily a matter of the distances maintained between individuals in social situations of one kind or another. One may not as a rule consciously recognize them as codified, but they are nevertheless beginning to be defined and classified as such.

Much of Hall's work has been concerned with those distances occurring in 'informal space'. He has classified them as public, social, personal and intimate distances and subdivided each of these distance zones into a 'close phase' and a 'far phase':

1. *Intimate distances — close phase* (up to 6 inches). To this category belongs, for example, erotic contact, where there is a total involvement. Perception of the physical features of the other person is distorted, and tactile and olfactory sensations are predominant.

2. *Intimate distances — far phase* (from 6 to 18 inches). Here too physical features appear deformed, and such closeness is generally considered neither desirable nor

polite by an American adult — this can be seen on a bus at rush hour — though it is somewhat more acceptable to the young, as for instance in a group of them at the beach. In certain cultures (among Arabs, for example) these distances occur, however, far more commonly, being accepted as appropriately confidential in a wide variety of situations. They might well be considered acceptable at a gathering in a Mediterranean *osteria*, but at an American cocktail party they could, again, appear excessively intimate.

3. *Personal distances* — *close phase* (from 18 to 30 inches). These are distances found acceptable in everyday relations between man and wife, for example, but they might not be acceptable in a discussion between two businessmen.

4. *Personal distances* — *far phase* (from 30 inches to 4 feet). Here one finds oneself at 'arm's length' from other people. This is, according to Hall, 'the limit of physical domination in the very real sense. Beyond it, a person cannot easily "get his hands on" someone else.'[46] One is still inside an 'olfactory bubble' (at least in societies where odours have not been suppressed), and one perceives, if not personal odours, the odours of various cosmetics, perfumes, and lotions — the odour of one's breath may also be perceived, and in certain cultures this odor constitutes a message, though in others one is brought up to direct it away from people.

5. *Social distances* — *close phase* (from 4 to 7 feet). Impersonal business, such as that between people who work together in an office, is conducted at these distances.

6. *Social distances* — *far phase* (from 7 to 12 feet). These are the distances at which, for example, many businessmen and officials keep their visitors, thanks to the size of their desks or the placement of their office furniture — in fact the furniture may be consciously calculated to establish these distances. Hall notes the advantage of social distances of the far phase for receptionists, who when stationed less than ten feet from visitors find themselves forced to make conversation and unable to concentrate on their work.

7. *Public distances* — *close phase* (from 12 to 25 feet). These are typical of 'formal' situations: the speaker at a banquet.

8. *Public distances* — *far phase* (25 feet or more). At these distances a certain inaccessibility of a person is established. An obvious example would be the great distance at which a dictator puts himself from the people: Hitler at

the Nuremberg stadium, Mussolini on the balcony of Palazzo Venezia.

For each of those categories Hall has set out, in an elaborate chart, attendant variations in kinesthesia, thermal and olfactory sensations, visual and oral/aural phenomena, etc.[47]

6.2.4   It is easy to see that these codified distances would be something one would refer to in the design of architectural spaces. And once they have adequately defined and classified, they might seem all the more concrete and important as determinants. Hall has suggested that 'the influence of two bodies on each other is inversely proportional not only to the square of the distance but possibly even the cube of the distance between them'.[48]

But one would, of course, have to bear in mind the often surprising variations from one culture to another. As noted above, the meaning of open and closed doors changes radically when one goes from New York to Berlin: in America when you 'poke your head in the door' you are still thought of as 'outside', and in Germany it would be thought that you have already 'come in'. But there are many other ways in which space is defined differently in the two countries. The German's conception of personal space (reflected in the national anxiety over Lebensraum) implies a somewhat different definition of the limit within which one's privacy is threatened by the presence of others. And to move your chair in order to sit closer to someone who has invited you into his home is considered reasonable in America, and in Italy, but it is nothing short of rude to do so in Germany; indeed Mies van der Rohe's chairs are heavier than those conceived by non-German architects and designers, so that moving them would be difficult. Then compare the disposition of furniture in a German or American house with that in a Japanese house, and even greater differences become apparent. Occidentals generally experience space as a void between objects, but to the Japanese—think of the art of their gardens—it too is a form, capable of figuring as an architectural element in its own right. And our concept of 'privacy' does not exist in Japanese culture, and the Arab's way of 'being alone' consists not in separating himself physically from others but in suspending verbal contact, and so on.

Thus one might question the validity of urbanistic studies determining the number of square feet necessary per person; they might make sense within a given model of culture, but carrying such code data over into the design of spaces for people of other cultures could easily prove to be unfortunate.

6.2.5 So while the distance separating two interacting individuals remains a physical fact, capable of quantitative definition, the fact that this distance has a social meaning—and different meanings in different cultures—means that what we are concerned with here is, rather than a physical event (the distance) per se, *the event is endowed with meaning.* The distance is seen as a significant unit of a proxemic system, and the architect taking it as a parameter in elaborating his architecture would be taking it together with its meaning—it would be taken, that is, as a cultural fact, as part of a system of conventions and significations, as belonging to a code. *Thus we would still be on the left side of the Ogden—Richards triangle.* If there is a physical fact constituting a referent here, it would be no less irrelevant with respect to the processes of signification than the referents considered earlier. The architectural sign is again articulated to signify, not a referent, but a cultural unit. Or better, an architectural form (or spatial configuration) x becomes the sign-vehicle of a possible function y (the possibility of having a certain distance between one another, let us say), which in turn would be the sign-vehicle of a social value k (the value proxemics shows that distance to have).

But then with respect to this K—or with respect to the relation of signification between Y and K—would we not have to characterize architecture as a 'parasitic' language, or as a significative system dependent upon the support of a 'host' system of significations, which in a sense 'gives it meaning'? To put this another way, it appears that the plane of expression constituted by architectural objects has, as its plane of content, another system of significations (consisting of a plane of expression in Y and a plane of content in K).

Now this would in no way be to deny the communicative nature of architecture, or to say that architectural objects are not really sign-vehicles. There are, after all, a number of systems of sign-vehicles elaborated solely to express in their own terms the sign-vehicles of another language (Morse code and the system of semaphor communications, for two).[49] And in fact verbal language itself frequently becomes just such *second-order* language (or 'metalanguage').

We know that in a novel or epic poem, for example, the verbal language employed has to assume the role of conveying certain narrative entities that are distinctive or significant units of a narrative system outside the language. (That the narrative system lies outside the language, and not just as a *plane of content,* can be inferred from the fact that these narrative entities, the elements of the 'story', are often not language-bound and are significative in their own right). Indeed the constitution of the narrative system in question can determine the way in which the second-order—and presumably more analytic — code that is to convey it will be articulated. And if different narrative systems do not seem to require or bring about any change in the constitution of the linguistic code (except perhaps in the case of certain experimental novels), that is both because the linguistic code is flexible enough to allow the analytic decomposition and conveyance of the units of quite a variety of narrative systems and because narrative systems have remained relatively stable and uniform over the centuries — apparently, that is, one has not yet had to face the problem of expressing narrative entities of such novelty that no adequate rules of transformation could be found within the existing linguistic code.

But consider what would happen with a second-order code a good deal weaker analytically — the code of architecture — especially when faced with more 'difficult' external systems to convey — a series of anthropological systems, in continual historical development and continually in opposition from one culture to another. We see the prospect of a frustration of that function, either with the code 'forced' beyond its limits or with it simply articulated in spite of its irrelevance. And if there is the possibility of *revising* the code of architecture, it would seem that one might better, in the end, leave behind the problem of trying to elaborate new rules to suit what appears for the moment to be the external system it has to 'speak', and take up the problem of elaborating generative schemes that would remain viable under any number of unforeseeable anthropological systems to come. (We said something about this in 3.3.4 and will return to it in 6.3.)

6.2.6   Finally, it must be remembered that a code is a structure and *a structure is a system of relations arrived at through successive simplifications with respect to an operational intention of some kind, or from a certain point of view.*[50] So if the architect were to elaborate a code of architecture on the basis of proxemics alone — presumably with the intention of performing certain operations relating to proxemic phenomena — that code would be valid *from that particular point of view*, and not necessarily from another.

To put it differently, leaving proxemics aside for the moment, let us say that the architect has decided to restructure the urban fabric of a city (or the 'shape of landscape' in a certain area) from the point of view of the perceptibility of its 'image'.[51] He might then base his operation upon rules of a code concerned precisely with phenomena of image-recognition and orientation (a code that could be elaborated on the basis of data from interviews and basic research on perception, and perhaps even take into account exigencies of commerce or circulation, medical findings on factors contributing to stress, etc.). But then the validity and significance of the operation, based on that code, would depend upon confining oneself to that particular point of view. As soon as it became necessary for the architect to relate his architecture to some other system of social phenomena as well — the one dealt with in proxemics, let us say — the code concerned with image-recognition and orientation would have to be broken down and integrated with a code concerning proxemic phenomena; and since there would no doubt be more than just these two external systems to relate to, it would become necessary to find the relations between a number of different systems, tracing them all back to an underlying *Ur-code*, common to all of them, on which elaboration of the new architectural solutions would ultimately have to be based.[52]

6.2.7   So the architect, in practice, is continually obliged to be something other than an architect. Time and again he is forced to become something of a sociologist, a psychologist, an anthropologist, a semiotician . . . And that he can rely in this to some extent on *teamwork* — that is, on having experts in the various fields working with him — does not change the situation very much, even if teamwork makes it seem less a matter of guesswork. Forced to find forms that will give form to systems over which *he has no power*, forced to articulate a language that has always to express something external to it — we said there were possibilities of the poetic function and self-reflectiveness in architecture, but the fact remains that because of its very nature (and even though it has traditionally been understood as a matter of pure 'arrangement', regarding only its own forms) these can never 'take over' in it, as they can in other types of discourse, such as in poetry, painting, or music — the architect finds himself obliged in his work to *think in terms of the totality*, and this he must do no matter how much he may seem to have become a technician, a specialist, someone intent on specific operations rather than general questions.

6.3 Conclusion

6.3.1   One might at this point be left with the idea that having the role of supplying 'words' to signify 'things' lying outside its province, architecture is powerless to proceed without a prior determination of exactly what those 'things' are (or are going to be).

Or one might have come to a somewhat different conclusion: that even though the systems of functions and values it is to convey are external to it, architecture has the power, through the operation of its system of stimulative sign-vehicles, to determine what those functions and values are going to be—restricting men to a particular way of life and dictating laws to events.

These both go too far, and they go along with two unfortunate ideas of the role of the architect. According to the first, he has only to find the proper forms to answer to what he can take as 'programmatic' givens; here he may accept on faith certain sociological and ideological determinations made by others, which may not be well founded. According to the second, the architect (and we know what currency this delusion has enjoyed) becomes a demiurge, an artificer of history.

The alternative to these varieties of overconfidence has already been suggested, in 3.3.4: *the architect should be designing for variable primary functions and open secondary functions.*

6.3.2   The problem is only too clear in the light of a famous example of modern architecture—Brasilia.

It was born under circumstances exceptionally 'promising' for architectural design—by political fiat, that is, from nothing, and with practically nothing but its existence having been decided in advance—and so it was possible to conceive of Brasilia as a city that was to institute a new way of life and, at the same time, constitute a complex connotative message, communicating ideals associated with democratic life, with pioneering into the interior of a largely unexplored country, with the triumphal establishment of an identity for itself by a young country still in search of a physiognomy of its own.

Brasilia was to become a city of equals, the city of the future.

In design it was given the form of an aeroplane (or bird), with its wings spread out over the plateau that was to accommodate it. In the central body, secondary functions were to be predominant over primary functions: as the place of public buildings, it was above all to connote symbolic values contributing to the identity desired by the young country. In the two wings, on the other hand, where the residential buildings would be, primary functions were to prevail over secondary functions: great blocks of housing units, the 'superblocks' inspired by Le Corbusier, were to permit government ministers and functionaries of the lowest echelons (it is a bureaucratic city) to live side by side without distinction, availing themselves of the same facilities—a full gamut: supermarket, church, school, 'club' for leisure activities, hospital, police station—provided for the inhabitants in every unit or block of four units.

And around these blocks would run the streets of Brasilia, free, as Le Corbusier wished, from crude intersections, thanks to ample cloverleaves, underpasses, etc.

The architects had, quite correctly, made some study of the systems of functions they were given to believe would be fulfilled in this model city of the future (correlating sociological data, ideological perspectives, information on image-recognition and orientation,, laws of circulation, aesthetic factors, etc.). And in elaborating corresponding systems of architectural sign-vehicles, they were judicious enough to see that these had some relation to the traditional forms (and to allow for a certain amount of reiteration of the latter), which would, in theory, permit novel, unexpected articulations to be taken by the users as something other than 'noise': 'archetypal' symbols (the bird, the obelisk) were woven in with the new forms (the pilotis, the cloverleaves); the cathedral, even while a clear departure from the typological schemes to which one was accustomed, rested on some time-honored iconographic codifications (the flower, the opening of petals, the fingers of one's hands held together in prayer, indeed those images symbolic of a union of various states).

6.3.3   They had also, however, proceeded with both of the unfortunate ideas of the role of the architect mentioned in 6.3.1. They had accepted as givens the functions suggested in the preliminary socio-political study that had been made, concerning themselves with the forms through which these might best be permitted and promoted. And they imagined that simply by being built in a certain way Brasilia would determine its own history.

And what has happened is that in the face of the *structure* Brasilia, *events* have taken an autonomous course; and in the course of events different socio-historical contexts have emerged, with some of the functions anticipated left unfulfilled and other, unanticipated functions taking their place:

The construction workers building the city, who were supposed to live there while they worked, far outnumbered the available accommodations. And so on the periphery of Brasilia the Nũcleo Bandeirante sprang up, and a number of *favelas*, squalid settlements made up (at least from the point of view of many of the inhabitants of the city proper) of shanties, sleazy bars, brothels, etc.

The south superblocks were built before, and better than, the north superblocks, which were put up more hurriedly; so while relatively new, the latter are already marked by wear and tear. As a result, the functionaries of the higher echelons are gravitating toward the southern wing of the city.

The rate of immigration has surpassed all expectations, and—even excluding the people in the surrounding shantytowns and those who prefer to commute from far away—the city of Brasilia has not been able to house all the people who work there. Satellite towns have therefore arisen, with their populations increasing tenfold within a few years.

As one might have expected, the representatives of major industries and businesses have not been housed in the superblocks: nor have they moved into the satellite towns. They live along some 'avenues' that have developed parallel to the two wings of superblocks: these are streets of modest enough dwellings, but here, in contrast to the sociality—the communality—of the superblocks, there is privacy.

For other inhabitants, tracts of little houses have been built on the periphery of the city, though for fear of regimentation many of the people in the shantytowns prefer not to live in these.

One result of the elimination of intersections from the street system was an increase in the distance one would have to travel to get from point to point. This has all but turned circulation into a special privilege, reserved for those who have cars, and given the distances between the superblocks and between the superblocks and the central body of the city, it becomes difficult to maintain a social life beyond one's immediate 'neighborhood', which adds to the process of social differentiation by location.

The disposition of things in space, the form of the city, has indeed become a communicative fact, but now—and the phenomenon is more pronounced here than in perhaps any other city—the particular position an individual occupies, and is more or less confined to, in that disposition communicates his 'status'.

6.3.4 In short, Brasilia has, far from becoming the egalitarian city it was supposed to be, given form to social differentiation. Primary and secondary functions in which the planners and architects had every confidence have been transformed or replaced. The ideology of a community of equals, which was to have become visible in the urban structure and the imagery of the buildings, has given way to other visions of life in society. And this has happened without there having been any gross mistakes in design on the part of the architects, *given the 'programme' they accepted.* The mistake was in accepting that programme, with the social systems identified or implied in it, as definitive and timeless, and in assuming that having been designed *for* that program, the architecture would see it realized. Events have proved the programme to be anything but definitive, and the code under which the architectural forms were conceived is simply not the code under which these forms are being interpreted. So while the architects took a position of passive service with respect to the exigencies set out in the preliminary study they were given, undertaking to invent forms that would answer to these, they might better have oriented their passivity toward the fact that, no matter how valid the programme and no matter how well designed the forms, *no forms created by an architect are going to prevent events from taking an autonomous course around them.*

To try to identify and effect particular social alternatives may not be a senseless pursuit in social engineering or in politics, for there one can reasonably concern oneself with what is going to happen in society within the limits of a more or less 'manageable' span of time. But for the architect the task is to foresee, beyond the limits of any such span of time, the varying of events around his works.

Brasilia might have become more the city of the future it was supposed to be if it had been built on wheels, or with prefabricated, demountable elements—or better than that, along the lines of forms and dispositions flexible enough to provide for different meanings as warranted in the course of events. Instead, it was built as a monument as enduring as any of bronze, and stands there slowly suffering the fate of the great monuments of the past, whose senses history continues to add to or, where that becomes difficult, simply subtract from, which rather than marking a definitive state of events, as intended, continue to be redefined by events.

6.3.5 *While looking outside architecture, then, for the code of architecture, the architect must also fashion his significative forms in such a way that they will remain relevant under different codes of reading.* This is because the historical situation in which his attempts to identify a code would be grounded will be outlived by the significative forms he feeds into this situation. The architect may have to get his bearings to some extent from the sociologist, the economist, the psychologist, the anthropologist, and so on, but he must at the same time acknowledge, in the way he fashions forms to answer to the exigencies they have shown him, the possible failure of their hypotheses and the degree of error and obsolescence to which their work is subject. And he must realize throughout that his work will at best cooperate with, not prescribe, the movements of history.

Notes to the Text

The introductory quotation is from Roland Barthes's *Elements of Semiology*, trans. Annette Lavers and Colin Smith (New York: Hill & Wang, 1968), pp. 41 – 42.

1. See Christian Norberg-Schulz, *Intentions in Architecture* (Cambridge: M.I.T. Press, 1965), chap. 5. Compare Gillo Dorfles, *Il divenire delle arti* (Turin: Einaude, 1959), pt 2,

and idem, *Simbolo, communicazione, consumo* (Turin: Einaudi, 1962), especially chap. 5; Susanne K. Langer, *Feeling and Form* (New York: Charles Scribner & Sons, 1953), the chapters on virtual space; Cesare Brandi, *Elicona*, vol. 4, *Eliante o dell architettura* (Turin: Einaudi, 1956), idem, *Segno e immagine* (Milan: Il Saggiatore, 1960), idem, *Struttura e architettura* (Turin: Einaudi, 1968); Sergio Bettini, 'Semantic Criticism; and the Historical Continuity of European Architecutre', *Zodiac*, no. 2 (1958), pp. 191 – 203; and Francoise Choay, ed., *L'Urbanisme: Utopies et réalités* (Paris: Éditions du Seuil, 1965).

2. Roland Barthes, *Elements of Semiology*, trans. Annette Lavers and Colin Smith (New York: Hill & Wang, 1968), p. 41.

3. Charles Sanders Peirce, *Collected Papers of Charles Sanders Peirce*, vol. 2, *Elements of Logic*, ed. Charles Hartshorne and Paul Weiss (Cambridge, Harvard University Press, Belknap Press, 1932), par. 306.

4. See Umberto Eco, *La struttura assente: Introduzione alla ricerca semiologica* (Milan: Bompiani, 1968), sects. A and B, 'Il segnale e il senso' and 'Lo sguardo discreto'. Generally speaking, we have followed Ferdinand de Saussure's understanding of what a sign is: the coupling of a *signifié* (for which we have used the term *meaning* rather than *signified*) and a *signifiant* (for which we have used the term *sign-vehicle* rather than *signifier*): see Ferdinand de Saussure, *Course in General Linguistics*, ed. Charles Baily and Albert Sechehaye in collaboration with Albert Riedlinger, trans. Wade Baskin (New York: Philosophical Library, 1959), and Barthes, op. cit. in note 2.

5. C. K. Ogden and I. A. Richards, *The Meaning of Meaning*, 5th ed. (New York: Harcourt, Brace and Co., 1938), p. 11.

6. Giovanni Klaus Koenig, *Analisi del linguaggio architettonico* (Florence: Libreria editrice Fiorentina, 1964). This book has been superseded by his *Architettura e comunicazione, preceduta da Elementi di analisi del linguaggio architettonico* (Florence: Libreria editrice Fiorentina, 1970), from which we will now be quoting; the quotations will of course be translations.

7. Charles Morris, *Signs, Language, and Behavior* (1946; reprinted New York: George Braziller, 1955), p. 10.

8. Ibid., p. 7. For comment on Morris's definitions, see Ferruccio Rossi Landi, *Charles Morris* (Rome: Bocca, 1953), chap. 4, 'Il problema della segnita'.

9. Koenig, *Architettura e comunicazione*, cited in note 6, p. 28.

10. Charles Morris, *Foundations of the Theory of Signs*, International Encyclopedia of Unified Science, vol. 1, no. 2 (Chicago: University of Chicago Press, 1938), p. 5.

11. Morris, op. cit. in note 7, p. 354.

12. See Max Bense, *Aesthetica: Einführung in die neue Aesthetik* (Baden-Baden: Agis-Verlag, 1965).

13. In *Architettura e comunicazione*, cited in note 6, pp. 34 – 37, Koenig says that architectural signs are (or at least used to be, before the time of generalized building) *iconic*, since they display directly some properties of the denotata, some properties, that is, of the 'unfoldings' of functions inherent in man's life in society; then he qualifies this, saying that since they represent neither objects nor forms, but rather denote social facts, they are really *prescriptive* signs, requiring specific responses, and that their iconicity must therefore lie in the fact that 'the form expresses the functions through space', 'mirroring' the social fact. He has thus brought in such 'slippery' terms as *mirror* and *express* to characterize an iconicity that might well reduce, given his definition of denotata, to the mere presence, or identity, of the form. Better than this, as a *pis aller*, would be to accept what Cesare Brandi has proposed in his *Le due vie* (Bari: Laterza, 1966): a clear-cut distinction between *semiosis* and *presence (astanza)*, whereby there are aesthetic realities that cannot be reduced to signification, that must be considered in their presence.

14. Koenig, *Architettura e comunicazione*, cited in note 6, p. 30.

15. In this case it is the *aesthetic* function that is predominant in the architectural message, what Roman Jakobson, speaking of acts of verbal communication, has termed the *poetic* function: see his 'Linguistics and Poetics', in *Style in Language*, ed. Thomas A. Sebeok (1960: paperback ed., Cambridge: M.I.T. Press, 1966), pp. 350 – 77. But architectural messages display also the five other communicative functions listed by Jakobson: architecture involves communication that is *conative* (or imperative, making one inhabit it in a certain way), *emotive* (think of the calm of a Greek temple, the turbulence of a baroque church), *phatic* (obviously in the many attention-getting devices of architecture—the phatic function might be found to be predominant, then, in such messages as obelisks, arches, and tympana—but also at the level of urban fabric, where

'channels' are opened and established for architectural messages, as in a piazza's ensuring continued attention to the facades of the buildings that surround it), *metalingual* (where, for one example, to relieve any confusion about the code for interpreting the message architecture assumes a self-explaining, or 'glossing', function—think of the benches built into certain otherwise inhospitable American plazas), and of course *referential* (what we will be concerned with here for the most part—that is, the denotations and connotations of architectural objects).

16. See Eco op. cit. in note 4, chap. A.3, 'Il messaggio estetico'.

17. We should note that the symbolic value of forms was not entirely ignored by the theorists of functionalism: see Louis H. Sullivan's 'The Tall Office Building Artistically Considered', in his *Kindergarten Chats (Revised 1918) and Other Writings* (New York: Wittenborn, Schultz, 1947) pp. 202—13; and Renato de Fusco, *L'idea di architettura: Storia della critica da Viollet-le-Duc a Persico* (Milan: Edizioni di Comunita, 1964), shows that their symbolic value was important not only to Sullivan but also to Le Corbusier. On the connotative value of forms at the level of urban design—turning to the relational forms in the fabric of large urban areas—see Kevin Lynch, *The Image of the City* (1960: paperback ed., Cambridge: M.I.T. Press, 1964), particularly page 91: cities are to be given forms that can stand as symbols for urban life.

18. For a bibliography on this question, see Paul Frankl, *The Gothic: Literary Sources and Interpretations through Eight Centuries* (Princeton: Princeton University Press, 1960).

19. See Suger, abbot of Saint-Denis, *Oeuvres complètes de Suger*, ed. Albert Lecoy de La Marche (Paris, 1867), and idem, *Abbot Suger on the Abbey Church of St.-Denis and Its Art Treasures*, ed. and trans. Erwin Panofsky (Princeton: Princeton University Press, 1946).

20. See Umberto Eco, *Il problema estetico in San Tommaso* (Turin: Edizioni di 'Filosofia', 1956), and idem 'Sviluppo dell'estetica medievale', in *Momenti e problemi di storia dell'estetica*, pt. 1, *Dall'antichita classica al barocco* (Milan: Marzorati, 1968), pp. 115—229.

21. See the works by Dorfles cited in note 1, not to mention his *Le oscillazione del gusto e l'arte moderna* (Milan: C. M. Lerici, 1958).

22. Claude Lévi-Strauss, *Conversations with Claude Lévi-Strauss*, ed. Georges Charbonnier, trans. John and Doreen Weightman (London: Jonathan Cape, 1969), p. 92.

23. See Giulio Carlo Argan, *Progetto e destino* (Milan: Il Saggiatore, 1965), particularly the title essay, where the notion of works that remain 'open' (the *'opera aperta'*) is applied to architectural design. One way of understanding the 'openness' of architectural and urbanistic objects is suggested in Roland Barthes's 'Semiology and Urbanism'. Agreeing with certain views held by Jacques Lacan—discussed in Eco, op. cit. in note 4, chap. D.5, 'La struttura e l'assenza'—Barthes believes that with regard to the city the question of meaning becomes less important than a detailed analysis of abstracted 'signifiers'. Thus, 'in [an] effort to approach the city semantically, we must try to understand the play of the signs, to understand that any city is a structure; but one need never try, or even wish, to fill this structure', for 'semiology at present never posits the existence of a final signified', and 'any cultural (or, for that matter, psychological) complex confronts us with infinite metaphorical chains, in which the signified is always deferred or becomes itself a signifier'. Now it is true that any city confronts us with phenomena of enrichment (and substitution) of meaning, but the semantic value of the city emerges not only when one sees it as a structure that generates meaning: it emerges also when, in experiencing it, one is filling it with concrete significations. Indeed, to oppose to the concrete process of signification—in the light of which the city is designed—the notion of a free play of pure sign-vehicles might be to empty the activity of architecture of much of its creative thrust. For if this notion were carried to an extreme, and the significative power of a city considered really infinite—as infinite as the significative power of verbal languages, which in spite of the fact that man has little say with regard to their constitution and laws still permit them to be adequately 'spoken'—then there would no longer seem to be any point in designing a 'new' city: in any existing city there would already be the elements of an infinite number of possible combinations, permitting every type of life within that form. In reality, the problem of architecture is that of defining the limit beyond which an existing form no longer allows the type of life one has in mind, the limit beyond which the architectural sign-vehicles that pass before one appear no longer as a matrix of freedom but as the very image of a domination, of an ideology that imposes, through the rhetorical forms it has generated, various modes of enslavement.

24. Eco, op. cit. in note 4, chaps. B.1 − 3, 'I codici visivi', 'Il mito della doppia articolazione', and 'Articolazione dei codici visivi'.

25. Through the use of the wrong code, then, a plan might be read as a section or vice versa: see the amusing situation described in Giovanni Klaus Koenig, *L'invecchiamento dell'architettura moderna ed altre dodici note*, 2d ed., rev. and enl. (Florence: Libreria editrice Fiorentina, 1967), p. 107, n. 17, but see also Koenig, *Analisi del linguaggio architettonico*, cited in note 6, chap. 8.

26. See Bruno Zevi, *Architectura in nuce* (Venice and Rome: Istituto per la Collaborazione Culturale, 1960), and his earlier book, *Architecture as Space: How to Look at Architecture*, ed. Joseph A. Barry, trans. Milton Gendel (New York: Horizon Press, 1957).

27. The term *choreme* is derived from χωρός ('space, place'). For a theoretical consideration of the στοιχεια as primary elements of the spatial arts, including architecture, see the remarks by Mondrian discussed in de Fusco, op. cit. in note 17, pp. 143 − 45.

28. See Christian Norberg-Schulz, 'Il paesaggio e l'opera dell'uomo', *Edilizia moderna*, nos. 87 − 88 (1966), pp. 63 − 70: that issue of *Edilizia moderna* is dedicated to 'the shape of landscape'. The entirety of Norberg-Schulz's *Intentions in Architecture*, cited in note 1, is important to the preceding and following remarks, but see in particular the chapters on perception, symbolization, and technics.

29. On these, and on the codes that follow, see Koenig, op. cit. in note 6, pp. 38 − 52 ('L'articolazione del linguaggio architettonico'), and Dorfles, *Simbolo, comunicazione, consumo*, loc. cit. in note 1.

30. On the concept of 'type', see, besides Dorfles and Koenig, the text titled 'Sul concetto di tipologia architettonica' in Argan's work cited in note 23, where the proper parallel is drawn between architectural typology and iconography; type is defined as *progetto di forma*, which comes close to the definition of figures of speech (as *relazioni generali di spettatezza*, or general schemes providing for formulaic presentation of the unexpected) given in Eco, op. cit. in note 4, par. A.4.2.2. See also Bettini, op. cit. in note 1, and Vittorio Gregotti, *Il territorio dell'architettura* (Milan: Feltrinelli, 1966).

31. For Joseph Stalin's well-known view on linguistics, see his *Marxism and Linguistics* (New York: International Publishers, 1951).

32. That language determines the way in which one sees reality is Benjamin Lee Whorf's thesis in his *Language, Thought, and Reality*, ed. John B. Carroll (1956; paperback ed., Cambridge: M.I.T. Press, 1964).

33. See Eco, op. cit. in note 4, chap. A.3.

34. That is, they would constitute a rhetoric in the sense of the term discussed in Eco, op. cit. in note 4, par. A.4.2.2.

35. See Giulio Carlo Argan et al., 'Design e mass media', *Op. Cit.: Selezione della critica d'arte contemporanea*, no. 2 (January 1965), pp. 8 − 30; Renato de Fusco, 'Architettura e cultura di massa', *Op. Cit.*, no. 3 (May 1965), pp. 8 − 21; and Filiberto Menna, 'Design, comunicazione estetica e mass media', *Edilizia moderna*, no. 85 (1965), pp. 32 − 37 (see for that matter the whole of that issue of *Edilizia moderna*, and note the slant of the graphics).

36. For perhaps the most comprehensive study to date, see Renato de Fusco, *Architettura come mass medium: Note per una semiologia architettonica* (Bari: Dedalo libri, 1967).

37. To quote from 'The Work of Art in the Age of Mechanical Reproduction', an essay by Walter Banjamin in his *Il-luminations*, ed. Hannah Arendt, trans. Harry Zohn (New York: Harcourt, Brace & World, 1968), p. 241:

> Distraction and concentration form polar opposites which may be stated as follows: A man who concentrates before a work of art is absorbed by it. He enters into this work of art the way legend tells of the Chinese painter when he viewed his finished painting. In contrast, the distracted mass absorbs the work of art. This is most obvious with regard to buildings. Architecture has always represented the prototype of a work of art the reception of which is consummated by a collectivity in a state of distraction.

38. See the issue of *Edilizia moderna* dedicated to 'design', cited in note 35, and in particular the introduction, 'Problemi del design'.

39. On how significative systems elaborated not by the 'speaking mass' but by a 'deciding group' are subject to the 'determination of the community', see Barthes, op. cit. in note 2, pp. 31 − 32. Reviewing the first version of this text — *Appunti per una semiologia delle comunicazioni visive* (Milan: Bompiani, 1967) — Bruno Zevi, in his 'Alla ricerca di un 'codici' per l'architettura', *L'architettura: Cronache e storia* 13, no. 7 (November 1967): 422 − 23, commented that of our three hypotheses only the second, which seemed to him to be presented as absurd and impossible, would represent the moment of the creative flash, of the 'poetic' utopia that makes history; the first would pertain to purely 'prosaic' works, and the third to a

select body of architectural 'literature'. It seems to me that we have to reach a clear understanding of the nature of the dialectic between fidelity to the code and challenging of the code—which is equivalent to the dialectic between *form* and *openness*, discussed in my *Opera aperta: Forma e indeterminazione* (Milan: Bompiani, 1967). We have to bear in mind the passage from the *Poetics* of Aristotle: there may be a flash of something that does not correspond to the expectations of the public, but these flashes, in order to make an impression, cannot do without the leverage of redundancy, *referring one to the preexisting codes*. The second hypothesis, it seems to me, has to do with subversive operations; formal invention, taking no account of the concrete architectural discourse going on in the society, transforms architecture into purely contemplable forms, and thus at best into a kind of radical sculpture or painting. And what the third hypothesis concerns is rather a possible transformation of the givens, such that the givens one starts with are *transformed* at the very moment they are *recognized and reabsorbed by* the new proposal. The delicate question of how much is to be recognized and *rejected* and how much is to be recognized and 'resumed' is precisely the problem of that 'utopian code' rightly recognized by Zevi as one worth pursuing.

40. See Italo Gamberini, *Introduzione al primo croso di elementi di architettura e rilievo dei monumenti: Gli elementi dell'architettura come 'parole' del linguaggio architettonica* (Florence: Coppini, 1959); idem, *Per una analisi degli elementi dell'architettura* (Florence: Editrice Universitaria, 1953); and idem, *Analisi degli elementi costitutivi dell'architettura* (Florence: Coppini, 1961).

41. See Andries van Onck, 'Metadesign', *Edilizia moderna*, no. 85 (1965), pp. 52 – 57.

42. Reviewing the first version of this text, cited in note 39, Maria Corti commented that in the introduction of the anthropological system into the discussion was 'a trap', one that reopened the problem of the autonomy of semiotics as a science. (Her review appears in *Strumenti critici* 1, no. 4 (October 1967): 447 – 50.) While I acknowledge there might have been some malicious intent to it, I would like to point out that I was really trying to resolve the problem, which would have come up in any case, and that her comments, together with a series of doubts advanced by Vittorio Gregotti in conversation, have driven me to making this point a little clearer, even to me.

43. See in particular Edward T. Hall, *The Hidden Dimension* (Garden City, N.Y.: Doubleday & Co., 1966).

44. Claude Lévi-Strauss, *Structural Anthropology*, trans. Claire Jacobson and Brooke Grundfes Schoepf (New York: Basic Books, 1963), chaps. 7 and 8; see also Paolo Caruso, 'L'analisi antropologica del paesaggio', *Edilizia moderna*, nos. 87 − 88 (1966), pp. 12 − 16, and Vittorio Gregotti's running commentary in the same issue, and English translation of which ('The Shape of Landscape') appears on pages 149 − 52.

45. Hall, op. cit. in note 43, p. 128.

46. Ibid., p. 113.

47. Ibid., pp. 118 − 19.

48. Ibid., p. 122. See also Edward T. Hall, *The Silent Language* (Garden City, N.Y.: Doubleday & Co., 1959), and the various points of view on proxemics in *Current Anthropology* 9, nos. 2 − 3 (April − June 1968): pp. 83 − 108.

49. See Eco, op. cit. in note 4, chap. B.3.

50. Ibid., par. A.2.4.1.

51. K. Lynch, cited in note 17: Juciana de Rosa, 'La Poetica Urbanistica di Lynch' op. cit. No. 2. Jan, 65, pp. 78 − 88; and also in Donald Appleyard, Kevin Lynch, John R. Meyer; *The View from the Road*, Cambridge, M.I.T. Press, 1964.

52. For an example of research into procedures of codification at the level of 'ultimate' structures see Christopher Alexander, *Notes on the Synthesis of Form*. Cambridge, Harvard University Press, 1964.
    For a parallel drawn between Alexander's work and that of structuralists see Maria Bottero, Lo Strutturalismo Funzionale di Christopher Alexander, *Comunità* Nos. 148 − 149, Nov. − Dec. 67, pp. 73 − 82.

1.2 The Architectural Sign

Charles Jencks

1.1 The 'Essence' of Architecture

The nature of architecture is diverse enough to defy all attempts at definition and elastic enough to make them all, partly, correct. Anyone familiar with the recent history of architecture will realise what an excellent opportunity this has created. It obediently follows the definer's wish, evolving like the Bionic woman, in whatever direction the scriptwriter has mapped out. Architecture, like a woman of easy virtue, is highly suggestible.

Twenty years ago, for certain modernists, the essence of architecture was 'space', *Raum*, space concepts, interpenetration of inside and outside, and a hair-splitting form of phenomenal transparency. Ten years ago its essence had become 'place-making', 'identity' and 'personalisation' while more recently it has been defined in terms of the three fashionable 'e's' (energy, environment, ecology) and 's's' (syntax, semantics, sculpture). For every major architect and emergent movement there has been a new definition. Some have lasted as long as an epoch (Le Corbusier, 1923: 'Architecture is the masterly, correct and magnificient play of masses brought together in light'). Others have had periodic revivals (Nikolaus Pevsner, 1943: 'a bicycle shed is a building; Lincoln Cathedral is a piece of architecture . . . the term architecture applies only to buildings designed with a view to aesthetic appeal'), while some depend on multiple qualities (Vitruvius, 1st century B.C.: 'Architecture depends on Order, Arrangement, Eurythmy, Symmetry, Propriety and Economy') or structural relations between different areas ('firmness, commodity and delight' or the Vitruvian triad *Firmitas, Commoditas* and *Venustas* — translated by M. H. Morgan as 'durability, convenience and beauty'). For some writers and philosophers such as Suzanne Langer, architecture is a kind of building which signifies a way of life, or 'ethnic domain'.

For architects in their more lyrical and high-flying moments it is a conveyor of culture and faith (Walter Gropius, 1919: 'What is architecture? The crystalline expression of man's noblest thoughts, his ardour, his humanity, his faith, his religion') while in their lower altitudes it still has a metaphysical role (Christian Norberg-Shulz, 1971: 'Architectural space, therefore, can be defined as a concretization of man's existential space').

So many opposite and sometimes contradictory definitions might, you would think, deter architects from adding still more; or perhaps suggest that they approach their subject with a certain circumspection and humility. But that has not been the case. Where others have succeeded, they too will succeed, because architecture, like life, is essentially polymorphous and malleable. Hence today, it evolves in all sorts of directions — towards sociology, planning, politics, psychology (areas 'outside' the field), or towards construction, rationalism, formalism, grid planning, popular signification (or areas 'inside' architecture). And the schools of architecture follow these discontinuous paths and contradictory definitions.

A sceptic, or simply an intelligent observer of this situation, might claim with some justification, that if architects and theorists cannot locate their field of practice, then there is no hope for architectural semiotics. Imagine linguists trying to define their study, when they can't agree on what constitutes a spoken language (a problem they face every now and then).

With these issues at the front of our mind certain tentative conclusions can be reached: architecture is irreducibly *plural* (it is made up of *discontinuous codes*), its essence is to *change* the referents of its signification as well as its codes (the ideas, social patterns and language can all change) and yet a *various* set of codes come together at any one time to make the practice of architecture recognisable and coherent. Of, say, the fifteen major codes of architecture any five or six will be present to make the artifact distinct from sculpture, engineering and other related constructions.

We might even hazard an historical definition which is 'essentialist' at its centre, but open at its edges to include new codes. 'Architecture is the use of formal signifiers (materials and enclosures) to articulate signifieds (ways of life, values, functions) making use of certain means (structural, economic, technical and mechanical).

The virtue of this definition is twofold: it includes the

Figure 1
Opera as a sign system is essentially hybrid like architecture, which it can include as a signifying element. The notion of the *Gesamkunstwerk*, a total work of art, integrating all the sign systems under a common theme and idea, has been held both by opera writers and architects. The impurity of the systems, their mutual contradictions and discontinuities, make this notion difficult if not impossible to attain

traditional triad of form, function and technic within a signification process and it allows for additional historical meanings to be built upon this essential foundation. To speak metaphorically, architecture occupies an ecological niche with respect to all other practices such as engineering and sociology etc. making use of these practices in a unique combination. Since it is an unstable hybrid based partly on codes external to itself (like film and opera), its practice is more difficult and polymorphous than other fields (painting and poetry) (Figure 1). Furthermore, as we shall argue later, the codes which are most *specific* to architecture (such as habitable space) may not always be the most important to it (as 20th century critics have thought). Following leads in other fields of semiotic study we will attempt a rough approximation at laying out the various codes which make up the architectural sign placing these in a hierarchic order of importance. (See also 3.3.)

1.2. Architectural Signifiers and Signifieds

Clearly the architectural sign like other signs is a twofold entity having a plane of expression (signifier) and plane of content (signified). The *signifiers* tend to be (but needn't always be) forms, spaces, surfaces, volumes which have suprasegmental properties (rhythm, colour, texture, density etc.). In addition there are second level signifiers which often are an important part of the architectural experience, but are yet more significant in other systems of expression (noise, smell, tactility, kinaesthetic quality, heat, etc.). Since there is no clear point where the experience of life leaves off and the experience of architecture and the environment begins, one

could try to formulate a general semiotics of existential action of which archisemiotics would be a part, but such an
endeavour would be premature at this moment. Be that as it
may, the varied and wholistic experience of architecture
must be insisted upon: people react to such large scale and
vague wholes as 'the mood or ambiance' of a building, and
no doubt the obsession with space, as the architectural code
of our century, was an attempt (however reductionist) to
grasp this synthetic, overall experience.

The *signifieds* of architecture can be just about any idea or
set of ideas as long as they aren't too long or complex. (One
can't represent Einstein's equations or complex propositions
with buildings, whereas language, in its way, can form an
adequate if not perfect representation of these things. In
spite of Steinberg's cartoons, buildings do not speak complex volumes of prose with anywhere near the precision of
language. Language dominates all sign systems; hence the
necessity of captions and books to clarify the architectural
message and the fact that most persuasive architects, like
Palladio and Le Corbusier, have always promulgated their
buildings with words.) The signifieds which have recently
dominated architecture are those space concepts and
ideologies I mentioned at the outset, but it is clear there is
another set of unconscious or implicit signifieds which
architecture may articulate (Figure 2). These include social

Figure 2
Signifiers and signifieds

	First level		Second level
Signifiers (expressive codes)	Forms space surface volume etc.	suprasegmental properties: rhythm colour texture etc.	Noise smell tactility kinaesthetic quality etc.
Signifieds (content codes)	Iconography intended meanings aesthetic meanings architectural ideas space concepts social/religious beliefs functions activities way of life commercial goals technical systems etc.		Iconology betrayed meanings latent symbols anthropoligical data implicit functions proxemics land value etc.

customs and anthropological data which have been either
too obvious or obscure to become consciously signified (proxemics, the study of spatial distances which are codified, is
discussed by Umberto Eco, pages 51 — 57) and a whole host

Figure 3
Alison and Peter Smithson, *Robin Hood Gardens*, London, 1968 – 72. The architects intended to symbolise personal 'identity', 'place' and communality, whereas instead, because the codes of the users differ from those of the architects, these forms symbolise 'council housing', 'anonymity', and lack of place. The critic's role is to point out the contradictions between first and second level signifieds, and discontinuities in coding

of possible iconological meanings. In fact, according to Panofsky's famous definition and distinction, iconology must be set off against iconography as the difference between *unconscious* symbols and *symptoms* which are conveyed by an art work versus those *intended* and conventionalised meanings (Panofsky, 1955, pp. 28 – 33).

Obviously the unconscious second level signifieds may become consciously symbolised and therefore first level, intended messages. Team Ten symbolised the 'open society' in the sixties with such devices as the grid plan, the web and the linear growth form. These forms thus conventionally signified 'openness' to these architects, but a critic might come along and show that underlying all their claims was an actual practice of dogmatism, exclusion, rigidity etc. — all the attributes of a 'closed society'. Thus some of the architecture — let us instance the Smithsons' Robin Hood Gardens (Figure 3) — could signify on the first level 'openness', but on the second level 'closedness', lack of pluralism etc. There are many cases where first and second level signifieds are contradictory and obviously a major role of the critic is to decode this opposition (between iconography and iconology if you like). Since architecture like any sign system is open to new interpretations and the decipherment of unintended or betrayed meanings, it is the licence, indeed duty of the critic to unpack these. They are part of what Hjelmslev has defined as the *substance* of content as distinct from its form.

1.3 Signification and Communication

In one sense this distinction between first and second level signification brings up the debate among semioticians as to whether architecture is a semiotic system whose *prime* aim is to communicate. No doubt architecture can always signify something, but is may not be consciously intended to communicate a message. Rather it provides enclosure, or 'works' much the way a machine does, without always attempting to make a comment about that work, or explain itself.

Yet in most cases, and particularly the ones we shall care about (that is the ones which affect people), architecture intends to communicate a message. Furthermore, for a building to work in any rudimentary way, it must be in some code which is comprehensible or, like a new medicine, be accompanied by an instruction booklet (which replaces the code). The 'lesson of the toilet bowl' (see below, 2.2) shows this. Thus all architecture intends at least signification, if not the smaller category within it, conscious communication.

Systems of signfication are built up over time following the adoption and re-use of certain forms and their position with respect to other forms. The white cubic volumes of the International Style signified functionalism and flexibility in 1930 to an elite group of architects, whereas similar forms signified opposite meanings about 100 years previously to a group of architects who followed Pugin's lead into the Gothic revival. For them classical cubic forms were inflexible and not adaptable to different functions. The place of a form with respect to all other forms of an age thus constitutes part of its signification, its value, or its place within a semantic space.

Clearly these semantic fields change both quickly and slowly and for different groups of people. Whereas in 1930 the International Style signified a new society, egalitarianism, progress and hope for the groups like C.I.A.M. (Congress of International Modern Architecture), it also signified inhumanity, barbarism, mechanism and boredom for other groups (not only the Nazis, but such Americans as Lewis Mumford and Frank Lloyd Wright. It is interesting to compare their similar 'misinterpretations' of the International Style).

For C.I.A.M. the International Style was opposed to revivalist styles such as Neo-Gothic and it occupied an antithetical position to such styles in their ideological system. For masses of people however, the Neo-Gothic like the Mock-Tudor, was a humane system of building houses, and any formal system which borrowed images and metaphors from the factory was correspondingly inhumane.

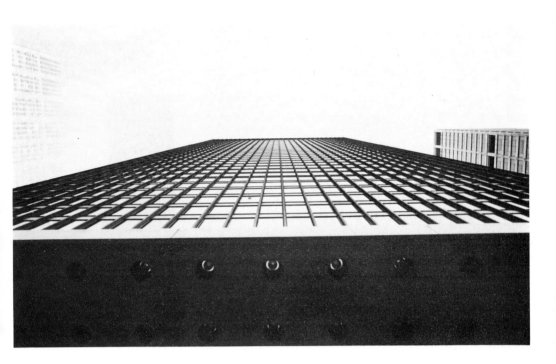

Figure 4
Mies van der Rohe, *Seagram Building*, New York, 1958. The inherent semantic properties of the curtain wall make this signifier appropriate to the inherent properties of office work: that is for our culture. Mies first used this signifier for a domestic function, and when more cool and impersonal systems are invented, it will be semantically shifted once again

From a semiotic point of view it is quite possible to see that while both their systems of signification were opposite, they were nonetheless equally coherent. The further question, which signification system was more valid at the time, is of course political and it is too easy now, with fifty years of hindsight, to dismiss both systems as politically reduced. Neither is a live alternative today.

Systems of signification are built up piecemeal by the introduction of new forms into a previous semantic field. Thus Mies van der Rohe introduced the curtain wall form (Figure 4) in its classic phase on housing in his Lake Shore Drive apartments in 1951. This curtain wall (of glass, steel mullions and infill panels) became by 1960 the sign of office building throughout the world. Why? Because among the formal alternatives at the architect's disposal, it occupied a place in the semantic space which was closest to that also occupied by the function—office building. That is to say the two semantic spaces (one for signifiers, the other for signifieds) placed offices and curtain walls in the same quadrant with respect to other functions and forms. A corollary of this similarity is that they had similar overtones: rationality, order, sobriety, impersonality, rigour, precision etc. It follows, both logically and empirically, that with the introduction of more new forms, the meanings of 'curtain wall' will shift, although it still keeps today its primary signification as 'rational office building'.

The change of meaning of an architectural form can be traced through successive stages starting, perhaps, from a

Object	Meaning	Type of sign
1. 'Real' B—J $8	Strong cover for work transient	Index
2. 'Real' B—J worn by cowboy at home	'I am a cowboy' transient	Intentional Index
3. 'Real' B—J worn by women and children	'The Wild West' transient	Conventional Symbol
4. 'Real' B—J worn by James Dean	Casual and young transient/durable	Conventional Symbol
5. Faded B—J embroidered and worn by youth, $26	Casual aesthetic 'I have had these for ages' transient/durable	Elite Conventional Symbol
6. 'False' B—J tie-dyed, $12	'I am a member of an exclusive group', etc. transient/durable	Elite Conventional Symbol
7. Pre-faded, cotton B—J St Tropez, 1970	'What a joke to think I'm a cowboy' summer set transient	Elite Conventional Symbol
8. Scraps of B—J as coats $185 or bikinis $20	Blue-jean aesthetic transient/durable	Elite Conventional Symbol
9. Suede copy of 7 at $60	'You recognize this expensive joke?' durable	Elite Conventional Symbol of Ersatz
10. B—J in a museum	'Folk-art of urban man' durable	Cultural Symbol

Figure 5
Blue-jean trouser suit with patches worn as a symbol of casualness and as an indicator of tough material. The further opposite cues, 'expensive/cheap', 'chic/proletariat', 'sexual/neutral', make this product one of the most polyvalent in our culture

Figure 6
Blue-jean transformations. Objects are always changing their meanings to become reinvigorated in the consumer process. The type of sign changes incessantly also from index to symbol and back again. Certain objects, like blue jeans, go from a transient state to a durable one, from utility into art

utilitarian base and proceeding to an aesthetic and symbolic level and then back to a functional level. This process, which Juan Pablo Bonta has outlined elsewhere in this book (pages 281 — 283), means that the form changes its nature as a sign (from index to symbol, or in Bonta's terms from indicator to intentional indicator to signal and back to indicator). It also shows that the initial stages of an object's or form's use is not primarily communicative and that a conventional code (such as curtain wall = office) is only one aspect of the architectural sign.

This is what leads Bonta to call his recent book *Expressive Systems in Architecture and Design* rather than the *languages* of architecture (as I would prefer) (Bonta, 1979). He would reserve the term language only for systems of *conventional* signals, arguing that it is misapplied to systems of indication which need not be codified. The term language, however, can be loosely and traditionally applied to systems of indicators (however restricted this language might be) and furthermore every indexical sign has an element of convention, or coded aspect, tied to its interpretation. Otherwise it couldn't be understood or even perceived as relevant.

Furthermore, it is often the economic system which speeds up the cycle of the changing architectural sign. As I have shown elsewhere the blue jean has undergone successive transformations as a sign (most of which are symbolic rather than indexical) to keep its potency as a consumer object (Figures 5 and 6). It has changed from a functional object (a cheap, strong cover for work which is thrown away after use) to a series of symbolic objects. Finally it has become expensive, physically weak and a consumer durable to be preserved in a blue-jean museum.

Thus the symbolic meanings have transformed the utilitarian aspects and certain blue jeans end up signifying

Figure 7
The ad hoc re-use of mannequin parts in a new context reinvigorates clichés. The tendency for all successful usage to exhaust the power of signs can be countered by displacement, distortion and destruction of the habitual context. The pathos of yesterday's meaning and 'dead stock' can be overcome

exactly the opposite thing for which they were originally intended. Most successful products in a consumer society
undergo this transformational reinvigoration (or recoding)
and buildings and architectural signs do also although at a
slower pace. Successive alterations to Gothic Cathedrals,
rehabilitation and changes of use, repainting and sign-
posting—all these are normal urban attempts to reinvigorate
past architectural meanings (Figure 7). The slight recodings
of the curtain wall by the 'Silver' architects Cesar Pelli and
Anthony Lumsden or Norman Foster, Philip Johnson and
John Portman (Figure 8) show the same consumer motivation
within a distinguishable element, a syntagm. These aesthetic
changes have a marginal semantic weight—towards increasing smoothness, sleekness, reflectivity, homogeneity, precision—in short possible analogues of powers. Ultimately it is
potency which is being symbolised, another example of the
precedence of architectural communication over mere
signification. Architecture is a language primarily, not just an
instrument.

2.1 Architecture as Connotative (and Denotative) Semiotics

There are two major semiotic models which have been applied to the architectural sign: the Ogden—Richards
semiotic triangle and Hjelmslev's 'double partition' model.
Both of these models incorporate aspects of Saussure's
definition of the sign as a two part entity—signifier and
signified.

According to the Ogden—Richards model, the signifier
(symbol, word of architectural form) connotes a signified
(concept, thought, content) and may or may not denote a
thing (referent, object, or 'actual function' in architecture)
(Figure 9).

It is the relation (R) between these three entities which is
important for establishing the type of architectural sign,
whether it is mostly indexical, iconic, or symbolic (see below
3.2). In comparison with spoken language, the architectural
language is more 'motivated' and less 'arbitrary', which is to
say that it has a higher ratio of indexical and iconic signs.

Another way of putting this is to say architectural signs
stay closer to their functional base than linguistic ones,
and, in the case of engineering, stay very close.

Umberto Eco has objected to this model for two main
reasons (see above, page 16): because it introduces extra-
semiotic elements (the object or actual function) and
because he cannot see the difference between the signifier
and the object. For him a triumphal arch connotes triumph

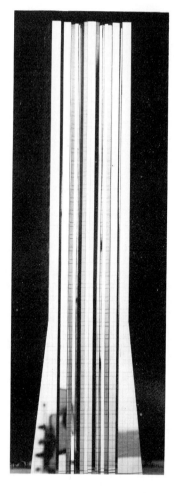

Figure 8
Anthony Lumsden, *Project for Bumi
Daya Bank Hotel.* The 'Silver architects' often produce refined ver-
sions of the curtain wall and
volumetric modelling in an ultra-
sleek, metallic finish that bespeaks
power, affluence, precision and
control—'silver virtues'

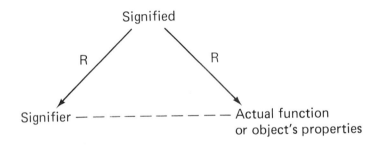

and denotes itself. It is not a *substitute* for the denotation as all signs should be, but the actual thing.

I think this objection rests on a misunderstanding of what the architectural signifier is in this case: an image on the retina, or a mediated percept, mediated by the senses and learned codes. It is not the object itself, or actual function made possible by the object, but rather a set of visual articulations (*figurae*) which are interpreted according to certain conventional codes into a meaning (*sememe*). The virtue of the Ogden—Richards triangle is that, unlike other semiotic models, *it incorporates extra-semiotic elements into the universe of architectural meaning.* Too many semioticians want to exclude these elements as irrelevant or impure, forgetting that 'reality' or 'actual functions' do in fact restrict the codes, or pure semiotic elements, and if the model does not incorporate this level it's going to end up too idealistic in nature.

Another model, Hjelmslev's, divides the sign into two planes similar to the signified/signifier; that is *content/expression.* Furthermore these two planes are subsequently subdivided into *form* and *substance* as shown in Figure 10. The

Figure 10
Hjelmslev's double partition

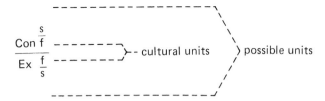

power of this double partition will be apparent shortly, but first let me point up its structure. The architecture of any era will only be concerned with $\dfrac{\text{Con}_f}{\text{Exp}^f}$ (the *form* of content and expression) that is the particular way the culture articulates and conventionalises content and expression. But lying behind these *cultural units* are all possible units, the actual continuum of the plane of content and expression, in a sense the 'ultimate realities' of these two levels. The substances could be, and are, cut up differently, and in that sense form an alternative or critique of the way any particular culture or individual uses them.

Then, as Hjelmslev has pointed out, a sign $\left(\dfrac{Cf}{Ef}\right)$ or semiotic coupling of the two planes can itself form the expression of a more elaborate semiotic $\left(E\ \dfrac{C\ f}{\dfrac{Cf}{Ef}}\right)$ a meta-semiotic or connotative semiotic, and this process can continue indefinitely.

It can be diagrammatically shown as in Figure 11.

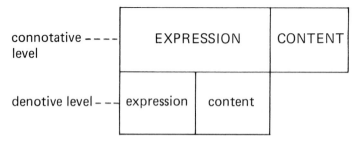

connotative level - - - -	EXPRESSION	CONTENT
denotive level - - -	expression	content

Figure 11
Connotation includes a semiotic system within its plane of expression

To clarify the difference between connotative and denotative levels, I'll cite and criticise the example of the elevator that Umberto Eco brings up in this context (pages 21 – 22). Suppose a Western businessman is confronted with an elevator entrance, or rather its plane of expression — an enclosed box, floor indicators, buttons and a polished aluminium surround. According to the code he knows this total image (Ef_1) denotes the possibility of vertical movement (Cf^1), its 'actual function'. But this utilitarian meaning is invariably a signifier itself (Ef_2) which has another set of contents (speed, uplift, technological sophistication, skyscraper etc.) $(Cf_{1,2,3,4,\ etc.})$ which are commonly called connotations.

Now suppose a 'primitive man' who is accustomed to walking up stairs, is confronted with the polished aluminium box which he hadn't seen before. To him it would denote, say, a wall and connote 'preciousness', 'enclosure', 'hiding', or even denote a mausoleum and connote 'religious relics' etc. He wouldn't know how to use the elevator for vertical circulation and might suppose, at first, that the different passengers who emerged from this box were various reincarnations of some rather stereotyped god in a pin-striped suit.

But as both the businessman and the primitive man continued to observe and then use this object over time, they would become experts about its meaning, and the connotations might become recoded into new denotations. By a jump in logic, or shorthand, it would now denote quick uplift and conformity.

Thus we are led to two immediate conclusions: firstly the difference between connotation and denotation *is a matter of coding, or the order in which meanings are learnt* (and doesn't concern an absolute difference between 'association' and 'function', 'aesthetics' and 'use' or 'vagueness' and 'fact' which is commonly supposed).

Secondly, we can only term denotations, or 'form follows function', that function *which is socially codified to the point where signifiers (E) and signifieds (C) relate as a reflex action*. 'Functionalism', or entirely functional objects, then depend on *how well a code is known* and not on the object's shape or technical qualities alone.

2.2 The Lesson of the Toilet Bowl

The lesson of the toilet bowl, a favourite among architectural semioticians, brings out the coded nature of denotation to a sharper degree. The toilet bowl seems at first a good example of the modern architectural dictum 'form follows function', because its shape, material and surface are determined roughly by its use, and this shape is in some respects beautiful, or at least highly sculptural.

A functionalist architect would admire it (and the bidet and urinal, both of which have been illustrated as exemplary in modern aesthetics by Le Corbusier and Duchamp; (see Figure 12) for its direct response to requirements and because it constitutes a 'word' or 'phrase' of a new, unambiguous language. The hope of modern architects was to build up a complex universal language based on such indexical and iconic words. They believed the 'functions' of these diagrammatic objects would be transparent, or obvious to everyone. This has not proved the case.

In the south of Italy, in a new housing estate for a rural population, the toilet bowl has been used as a cleaning tank for grapes (see page 22). The peasants suspended a net inside the bowl and then flushed water at the grapes until they were clean. In Northern Greece, where peasants also relieved themselves in a customary way in the countryside, the toilet bowl was used as a fireplace to hold burning wood (the shape corresponded to the traditional hole in the ground used for this purpose). To put out the fire and clean up, they also flushed the toilet. Urinals have been used by Africans to take a shower and the bidet is used in so many 'extra-functional' ways that it constitutes a sign of this unconventionality in French farce. It denotes sin, and only connotes washing yourself. The supposedly primary function has been

Maison Pirsoul.

Figure 12
Le Corbusier, *Chapter head to L'Art
décoratif d'aujourd'hui*, 1924. The
curves, purity and surface texture
of toilet fixtures found their way
into the aesthetics of modern
architecture because of such
polemic as this

AUTRES ICONES
LES MUSÉES

displaced by the supposedly secondary function, or connotation.

Umberto Eco and Maria Luisa Scalvini, who discuss these distinctions, thus oversimplify when they place use and denotation *prior to* aesthetics and connotation. As we see, one man's denotation is another man's connotation and it is a kind of cryptic functionalism to claim the priority, or historical genesis, of use over symbol, first function over first idea. Who really knows whether man first invented architecture when he ran into a cave to escape the rain (Eco's version of the origins of the primitive hut myth). He might have had the idea of playing with the beautiful patterns of leaves and conceived this first before realising that it could be used next as an umbrella or building.

Since such functionalism is so ingrained, even among semioticians, we shall give several more examples to dispel this logical monster. As we have argued, the 'actual function' of a building can only be perceived through a code, hence the use of inverted commas which might always surround its

Figure 13

Hamburg Streetscape, 1974. *Trompe l'oeil* at its most witty calls attention to the code of expression and plays on the fact that the viewer sees the double denotation: 'this is a phoney, real street', 'this is a real painting of a non-existent street'. *Trompe l'oeil* then is aesthetic above all in that the language focuses upon pertinent aspects of the language — or makes the form part of the content

use, but which will be henceforward dropped. The actual function can be an idea as well as a use. Thus the cross denotes Christ and Christianity (according to one code) as well as connotes them, and the triumphal arch denotes celebrations and triumph as well as its use — to pass through in procession. We must expand the notion of actual function to include ideas and social customs and only distinguish denotation from connotation as a matter of degree and learning: habituation, stock-response and frequency of use tend to turn connotations into denotations just as they turn metaphors into clichés.

Take the example of the *trompe l'oeil*, or the architectural lie (Eco first pointed out the relation of lying to all sign behaviour; they are both actions of *substitution*) (Eco, 1976, pp. 6 − 7).

Must there always be a real object for there to be denotation? Can we not say the *trompe l'oeil* townscapes (Figure 13) denote conventional objects, i.e. refer to real things? The fact that these things may not exist does not necessarily make them connotations; it can make them a special class of denotata — phonies.

Part of the enjoyment of *trompe l'oeil* consists in the contradiction between the denotation 'this is a real thing' and the connotation 'the thing is an illusion, it doesn't exist'. Aesthetic codes, as Hjelmslev insisted, are pre-eminently connotative semiotics.

2.3 Aesthetic Codes

Maria Luisa Scalvini postulates architecture (as opposed to, say, building) as an area of connotative semiotics, where the basic functional aims ('tectonics') are incorporated, but secondary to the new primary aim of aesthetic significance. A connotative semiotics has as its plane of expression a semiotic system in itself $\left(\dfrac{Cf}{Ef}\right)$. Thus for architecture her model is as shown in Figure 14.

Plane of 'connotators'
    (style, etc.)   Cf   = architecture
                                 (incorporates
                                 the basic
                                 functional aim)
    'tectonics'
    (basic function) E $\dfrac{Cf}{Ef}$
    (first level)

Figure 14
Maria Luisa Scalvini, *Hjelmslevian model*

Now Umberto Eco has criticized her approach saying that an architectural semiotics should start from the first level before going on to the more complex level of spatial and aesthetic articulation.

> To take the poetic functions of architecture as a starting point for an architectural semiotics would be the equivalent of a study of the English language that started from Shakespeare's sonnets and didn't go any further. It would be the equivalent of studying only the ambiguous use (the deviation from the norm) of a code that is not yet known (Eco, 1972).

Scalvini's reply might be the obvious inversion of this criticism: it would be ridiculous to analyse Shakespeare's sonnets with just linguistic tools; we need tools of a more complex or different nature, such as those of literary criticism.

The choice between Eco and Scalvini is probably invidious: to study architecture we need tools that explicate primarily the connotative level, but also (to a lesser degree) the denotative level. The role of actual function is not absolutely essential to architecture, but often it plays some part (and may indeed result in its destruction as with the infamous Pruitt-Igoe scheme in St Louis (Figure 15).

But for the most part this primary level of signification is only relevant to architecture in so far as it is made aesthetically and ideologically pertinent. The tendency is for archi-

Figure 15
Minoru Yamasaki, *Pruitt-Igoe Housing*, St Louis, 1952 – 5. Several blocks in this scheme were blown up in 1972 after they were continuously vandalised. The actual functions—mass housing, long corridors—and the codes they were delineated by—Purism, International Style—were all anathema to the black inhabitants

tecture to dramatize its aesthetic codes, its secondary and tertiary levels, in five major ways.

1. *Fetishism and the self-reflection* of the aesthetic code. Since architecture is a connotative system it can focus on the expressive plane of meaning with such obsession that the expression becomes the content. Architecture, it is often said, is about other architecture, or even about itself. It sets up a small, internal world where forms are heightened and refer back to themselves as forms because of excessive repetition, brightness, an odd texture, an exaggerated window or roof etc. There are key points to an architecture, erogenous zones and pleasure centres, such as the entrance, which I have analysed elsewhere as the usual points of fetishism (Jencks, 1976) (Figure 16).

The work of Michael Graves (Figure 17) is specifically fetishistic in this sense as its meaning consists, as he says, in being about doors, windows and steps. It 'foregrounds' these elements by exploding their size, tilting them sideways, projecting them away from the normal volume of the building. But the popular house, such as the California bungalow, also fetishizes these same elements albeit within the movie star's code rather than Le Corbusier's.

Figure 16
The erogenous zones of a house are accentuated—roof, door, window, planting, statue, light—in this conversion of a white stucco bungalow in West Hollywood.

Figure 17
Michael Graves, *Crooks House*, Fort Wayne, Indiana, 1975. Mouldings are only half finished, layers of the building are peeled back to reveal deeper surfaces, curves are set against centralized elements, the central wall is a mere façade —these distortions of syntax leap out at you because the syntax is largely normalized (classical)

2. *Distortion and disruption* in the aesthetic code. A favourite device of Robert Venturi for calling attention to the scale of his architecture is the ornamental string-course or moulding, which is often placed where it shouldn't be (i.e. half-way up a storey instead of between two storeys). Robert Stern takes this same motif and makes it even more absurd (and therefore relevant) by using it this way and also in a way which recalls the kitsch 'eyebrow' mouldings of Beverley Hills houses. For Olivetti, James Stirling has designed a roof-window-wall element that unites these three conventionally distinct areas. Seeing this building without its gutter and the usual differences calls attention to the elements themselves, their form. In fact distortions and disruptions in the aesthetic code take *extra time* to perceive and this lengthening of the perceptual act could itself be characterised as essential to the aesthetic code (Eco, 1976, pp. 265f).

3. *Redundancy and miniaturization* in the aesthetic text. Another reason reading architecture takes more time than reading building is the redundancy of messages that refer to themselves and even to small messages within the whole. This property, often referred to as 'unity in variety' can make even the smallest perceivable detail important: 'le bon Dieu est dans le detail', the old scholastic dictum taken over by Flaubert and later by Mies van der Rohe might read for us '*architecture* is in the details' because it is the semiotic cross-reference of details which makes a text endlessly decodable. Alberti and Frank Lloyd Wright, among many architects, stressed this aspect of the architectural sign and perhaps over-unified their buildings as a result (Figure 18).

   The repetition and transformation of a pattern at so many different scales casts a kind of hypnotic spell on the viewer (like the patterns of Op Art) and appears to achieve a magical endlessness of signification. Coleridge's classic formulation of the poetic activity stresses this aspect:

   > [the poet] diffuses a tone and spirit of unity, that blends and [as it were] fuses, each into each, by that synthetic and magical power, to which we have exclusively appropriated the name of imagination. This power . . . reveals itself in the balance or reconciliation of opposite or discordant qualities; of sameness, with difference; the individual, with the representative; the sense of novelty and freshness, with old and familiar objects; a more than usual state of emotion, with more than usual order . . . (Coleridge, 1950, pp. 45 − 51).

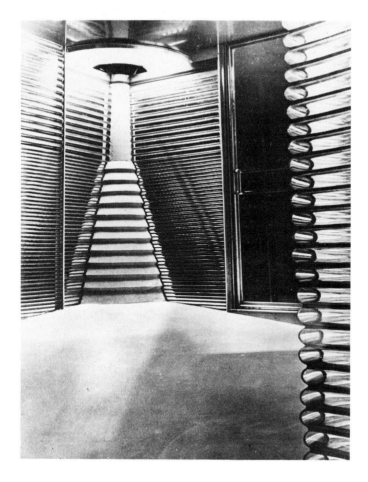

Figure 18
Frank Lloyd *Wright, Johnson Wax Building*, Racine, Wisconsin, 1938. Pyrex tubing, brick and concrete shoot around the whole building complex in a series of horizontal curves. Redundancy and repeating the large pattern in the small are key rhetorical devices, but they work against the message when too exaggerated

It is the imagination of the architect which codes differences to bring out similarity (*discordia concors* and *concordiae violentes*, the forced harmonization of scholastics and Gothic architects (Panofsky, 1957, pp. 64 − 8).

It 'fuses' various parts of the architecture by finding some semiotic link that either hadn't existed before or was unnoticed. This link then relates part to part in such a way that their previous meaning is *modified* and *transformed.*

4. Another way of looking at imaginative transformation, or another aspect of the aesthetic text, is that it is *hermenuetic*, esoteric and, even at its limits, completely *private*. The modern architect, as indeed all artists since the Romantic Age when the theory became understood, invents part of his language, his personal dialect, in order to 'make it strange'. This Tradition of the New, now entirely institutionalized and understood according to theories of information, is of course dependent on the Tradition of the Old for its impact, since one can only

Figure 19
Peter Eisenman, *House VI*, Cornwall, Conn., 1976. Architecture which marks architectural aspects, particularly the wall. The two major axes are emphasised as reference planes which cut the house into four major quadrants, off which bisected boxes are slung (the cuts are picked up as wedges of space or columns). Stairs go upside down, views of nature are blocked, the front door opens into the kitchen, a column with no structural function bisects a bedroom. In other words, pure architecture is signifying its own syntactical meanings to the exclusion of use and semantics, something which that of Terragni and Le Corbusier did in a much more covert way

perceive and understand messages of high information content when they are cued by other, expected redundant messages ('make it strange coherently' would be a more exact injunction). Nevertheless all architecture does in part send new, unexpected messages in a new code which at certain points becomes personal and variable.

The difficulty in decoding these texts, the aesthetic effort and time expended in making up *plausible* meanings as you look at an unfamiliar architecture, are obviously all part of the aesthetic game.

5. Which brings us to the last characteristic of the aesthetic text, and one that has opposite implications to the previous point: it is continuously *open* to new interpretation, *multivalent and plural* in its range of meanings. It is a truism that architecture is reinterpreted anew by each generation and that the history of architecture is an organic unity of traditions where the introduction of a new building, or movement, or style, or set of ideas changes the relation of all the previous buildings in that tradition. The work of the New York Five, or the 'Whites' has forced a reconsideration of the White architecture of the twenties (that of Le Corbusier and Terragni) (Figure 19).

Its elitism, Platonism, and classicism are now becoming even more apparent, as well as its claim to occupy the central throne of 'pure architecture' (architecture about its own 'natural' language).

Yet there is a far more important aspect of multivalence than this: the ability of the aesthetic text to articulate radically different experiences, emotions and values as a whole. The text may never entirely succeed in reconciling the full spectrum of life, but it is always an attempt to do so by analogy, and in that sense a symbol of reconciliation.

The work of Antonio Gaudí is particularly multivalent (as indeed is that of any great architect) and his Casa Batllo is typically made from a plurality of codes (Figures 20 and 21). A series of metaphors, or symbolic signs, can be seen in the elevation. The balconies stare out like so many death masks or skulls. The middle part of the architecture also recalls vegetable and marine metaphors with some people seeing it as a violent blue sea breaking over rocks which, curiously, turn into kelp (the codes of Barcelona are after all sea-weed sensitive).

The bottom two floors adopt a related, organic metaphor of skeletons and bones (the architecture was known as 'the house of bones' when it was finished in 1906) and you can see this exoskeleton go internal in two sides of the third floor. A recent designer has incorporated a wandering, blue neon sign suggesting, if we follow the self-reflexive signs, that the 'legs have varicose veins'. A rather ludicrous example of the way multivalent architecture forces meanings to modify each other.

It is quite possible to see these 'bones' as tendons, a ductile metaphor of wax or lava. The most powerful metaphors are (as aesthetic theories have constantly claimed) *ambiguous, mixed and suggested*. If the metaphors are singular and named (the hot dog stand in the shape of a hot-dog) they become univalent and not open to multiple interpretations. It is Gaudí's virtue that we can find a multiplicity of denotations and connotations for these metaphors.

For instance, they divide the architecture up into three main functional parts (according to classical convention): a base of two floors with the bone/wax metaphor, which can denote shops, entrance and main apartment; a shaft of four floors in the marine/mask metaphor which can denote 'similar apartments of a lesser nature'; a capital roof in the dragon metaphor which can denote 'roof garden, water tanks, skylight, mechanical equipment'. Thus strange hermeneutic codes are used as functional signifiers to break up a large apartment block and give a certain individuality to various parts. This personalisation is entirely appropriate to the domestic function even if

Figures 20 and 21 (previous page) Antonio Gaudí, *Casa Batllo*, Barcelona, 1904–6. Built on a 19th century block with other *Modernista* buildings, the building holds the street facade and distorts, in subtle ways, the normal elements of window, roof and ground floor. The bone, wax and lava metaphors dominate the base; the sea metaphor carried through with undulating ceramic tile and sea-weed balconies (which are also skulls) is on the shaft of the building; and the top is a dragon looking down sleepily, with one eye half open, and a cross stuck in its back it is implausible on an urban scale. The designer's pre-eminent role is to articulate our environment, not only so we can comprehend it literally, but also so we can find it psychologically nourishing, imagine possibilities we hadn't dreamed of before.

In this sense the overall message, or symbol of the Casa Batllo is truly extraordinary; it articulates meanings which are much more profound than the surface metaphors of which it is composed. For a long time I puzzled over the meanings of the roof dragon—that sleeping monster sprawled out at the top who looks down on the passersby with one eye, lazily, half open. The ceramic tiles of its tail (?) (the three-dimensional cross) shade slowly from golden orange on the left to blue green on the right. Gaudí was a very strong Christian and he advertised the fact with the cross and initials of the Holy Family encrusted on the cylinder (Gaudí made use of written signs unlike modern architects)—but what sort of Christianity is this? I had assumed the dragon was a typical Art Nouveau conceit, taken perhaps from Chinese garden walls which undulate this way, but I couldn't see its relation to a religious message. Was it a kind of Tao-Christianity, a form of nature worship akin to pantheism? Not until I returned to Barcelona did I find the conventional reference to these signs.

Saint George is a patron saint of this city, which has always led the separatist, Catalonian movement. Apparently Casa Batllo, represents the dragon of Spain being slain by Barcelona's Saint, while the bones and masks refer to the dead martyrs who have previously been victimised in the struggle. All this in an apartment building, and coded with enough multivalence to be suggested to those who care to read the architecture in depth.

There are other possible meanings and a multivalent architecture, like a multivalent work of art, *Hamlet* for instance, has this power of engaging our mind and opening our imagination to new meanings. It is catalytic, provocative and creative whereas an univalent architecture is reductive and dull. Thus the implication of multivalent architecture is its creative effect on inhabitants and viewers; it, along with other signs, shapes people in a multitude of different ways, articulating their full spectrum of moods, thoughts and behaviours.

3.1 The Significant Units; 'Signs, Words, Sememes'?

The significant units of architecture, the 'words' and 'phrases' of a building, can be thought of, in the first instance, as windows, doors, floors, cornices and so forth.

However, this is only a crude approximation, a rough mapping of linguistic units on to architecture. Consider the case of a column which both Scalvini and Eco bring up in this context (pages 213 – 232). In what way is this distinctive feature a 'word'? A column in a temple is one thing, the column-smoke stack at Battersea Power Station has other meanings, Nelson's column in Trafalgar Square celebrating a sea victory means something quite different, and Adolf Loos' Chicago Tribune project, a skyscraper in the form of a Doric column, is yet another thing. If the column is a word, then the word has become a phrase, sentence and finally a whole novel. Clearly architectural 'words' are more *elastic* and *polymorphous* than the written and spoken variety (and they are relatively more hermeneutic or based on contextual codes).

Yet the linguistic analogy has a certain relevance for there are indeed traditional elements which constitute a lexicon and you can find adequate dictionary meanings for them. Also modern architecture has built up a lexicon of prefabricated details and clichés and these elements have stabilised, symbolic meaning. These 'formulae' are obviously just as necessary for architectural practice as clichés are for language. Any modern building is bound to be made from a combination of traditional formulae and new specific signs but the resultant significant units can only be determined *a posteriori, after the building is completed.* They will concern coding on both the planes of expression and content $\left(\frac{E\,f}{C\,f}\right)$.

Figures 22 and 23
Venturi and Rauch, *Tucker House,* Katonah, New York, 1975. Two codes intersect and are exaggerated: the popular code, based on pitched roof, shingle, picture window etc. and the International Style based on ribbon windows, white flat surfaces and careful asymmetries. Distorted as these codes are, they are still recognisable both on the planes of expression and content: e.g. 'overhanging eave', 'protection' etc. The fireplace is an aedicule, a miniature house

We only understand 'column' as an architectural word because it is already conventionally articulated as a form and set of contents. This can be seen quite clearly when one is confronted with unfamiliar buildings, say those of Robert Venturi, which make distortions in the form and content at the same time (Figures 22 and 23).

Some semioticians argue in favour of *universal* significant units, the fact that all buildings must have something like a floor, roof, enclosure, entrance (sememes) and space, surface, geometry, gravitational direction, up and down (morphemes).

While this may be true at a certain level of generality, no transformational system yet exists for translating one system of usages (the Japanese) into another (the English). Theoretically, however, one can postulate two kinds of universal deep structure based on syntactic and functional properties (see pages 119 – 167).

The history of these units, or 'words', shows another parallel with language. At first, when the unit is invented, it is seen in terms of a *metaphor*. After a few years of usage this metaphor becomes a cliché or, as we have argued, the connotation becomes a denotation (see 2.1).

For instance, the 'glass and steel cage' is now simply 'an office', the 'cheese-grater precast unit' is a sign of 'parking garage', the 'truncated wedge or pie-shape' is codified as 'auditorium' (Figure 24). When people first see unfamiliar units they map them metaphorically onto systems they already know. This metaphorical activity, *by necessity an aspect of all thought that is creative*, is particularly crucial with respect to modern architecture simply because it is unfamiliar. In this century much of it is condemned in

Figure 24
Windowless wedge shape, or a pie-shape with angled base, signifies cinema, theatre or auditorium. The sight and acoustic lines may generate such shapes and the code of modern architects formulated this volume as a 'word'. Melnikov, Le Corbusier and Stirling used the form in its seminal way and it has now entered the vernacular, although there are other 'words' for theatre. The building is in fact the Bristol Country Club Theatre

metaphorical terms ('shoe boxes', 'filing cabinets', 'home as a machine', the 'salad bowls' at Brasilia, the 'battleships' of James Stirling). At least those with predominantly traditional codes (T.C.) tend to dislike these metaphors, whereas those with modern codes (M.C.), especially architects in the Modern Movement, tend to applaud these unexpected associations.

A curious property of the architectural sign is its potential for gathering up *cumulative meaning* over time.* Traditional units such as Georgian doors have gathered more meanings than modern units such as ribbon windows and hence they tend to be favoured by people for the most slow-changing building task, the house.

A well-known irony bears this out. Most modern architects, according to standard jokes in different countries, do not actually live in modern houses, but prefer traditional ones. They rationalise this in economic terms, in terms of the larger space afforded in old buildings (at least Stirling and Safdie do), but there are undoubtedly veiled semantic reasons as well. The feeling being that living functions are best served by richer, historical associations which imply a long and stable time span.

In Houston, Texas, there is an extreme example of this ambivalence. Offices, the NASA Space Centre and new functions are in the International Style, while houses are inevitably in one of four traditional, Ersatz styles (Neo-Tudor, Neo-French Mansard, Neo-Spanish, or Modern Hybrid). When a well known Houston firm constructed a modern housing estate, the youths of the area systematically broke its windows at nightfall because it was un-American (that is, not in an Olde-Worlde style). Such conflicts and double ironies are normal, if less visible, outside of Houston. The discontinuities between different social, or really semiotic, groups can be quite impressive and will lead us, in conclusion, to postulating a grand rift between the *avant-garde* and the profession on the one hand (M.C.) and the rest of society, on the other (T.C.). It doesn't seem possible, or even desirable, to wholly bridge this rift; instead I will plead for a very strong dualism of design, and for architectural semiotics, — a *radical schizophrenia.*

Returning to the question of architectural signs, we might try to find the smallest possible units in the planes of expression and content, the phonemes and morphemes of building. Bricks and pebbles, nails and boards, come naively to mind, the basic stuff of which architecture is built. While these may indeed be basic units of *construction*, they may not in

*For a similar point see Eco (1972, section 8.3) where most of the connotations cluster around the relation /ancient, among ruins/, the patina of meaning that accrues to architectural and art signs, as opposed to, say, musical ones.

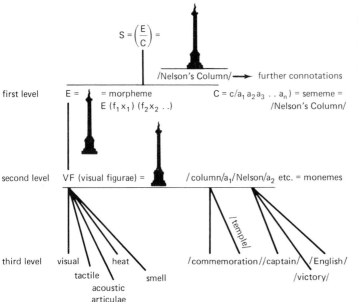

fact be *perceivable* and since we are interested primarily in architecture as communication with inhabitants (not builders) we have to look elsewhere to a more phenomenological description of the sign.

Following the model Umberto Eco has developed in his article 'The Architectural Sign /Column/ (page 213), we may propose several revisions. The architectural sign (s) is a combination of coded elements from the planes of expression (E) and content (C) which have further articulation at a second level (figurae and monemes) which are also coded, and even articulation at a third level, which is uncoded. Thus for 'Nelson's column' (see Figure 25) we have the following (Figure 26). Several points of a general nature should be made about this model, which allows an element by element componential analysis.

a. The total sense experience of the five senses is unified at E under the encompassing guidance of visual expression, which is to say visual elements guide, for instance, the smell of architecture rather than vice versa, and that smell only articulates the prevailing visual code. It would be perverse, if theoretically possible, to experience architecture blindfolded only using the olfactory organ, or by licking it; but on the other hand, blind people *recode* the visual sign in terms of noise and tactile cues. I am only here arguing for the *predominance* of the visual code under normal conditions, not saying that heat, noise, smell and taste don't play some role.

b. The sememe 'Nelson's Column' is constructed from second level monemes, or semic features 'Column' plus

Figures 25 and 26
Nelson's Column, Trafalgar Square, London, 1860s

'Nelson' which are further divisible at a third level into 'commemoration', 'temple', 'against base' etc. and 'naval captain', 'victories', 'English' etc.

Theoretically the subdivisions are infinite and we have unlimited semiosis but practically speaking any sign articulates only a limited, highly structured semantic field. In this case the plane of expression cuts out pertinent features which find their counterpart on the level of content, and we have a series of morphological markers: naval hat/stance/coat /on top of column/ etc. which are further subdivisible into visual figurae and into the articulae of the five senses. All this is quite laborious, but it allows us to see what parts, or else suprasegmental elements of the expression, are articulating which connotations, and thereby see certain areas of great signification. (Eco shows the importance of the morphological markers which articulate time, tradition and history, a peculiar aspect of the architectural sign which is perhaps more atavistic than other signs. It certainly is more a palimpsest and appreciated as such).

c. The main differences of this model from Eco's are that:

1. function and denotation do not take precedence over connotation, they are reversible as noted previously;
2. the syntactic, or morphological, or content markers are thus appreciably enhanced for constructing the stem diagram (see his analysis);
3. non-visual articulae are included at the base level of the sign although guided and unified by the visual code at a higher level.

d. The level at which we take an architectural sign is thus partially dependent on previous coding and the present context. It may be 'Nelson's column' in one case, or the column in Trafalgar Square, or Nelson's hat, or the shaft—all of these are potential signs, depending on one's interest and experience.

A book, *Elements of the Art of Architecture*, brings out this elastic but cultural nature of the sign (Muschenheim, 1965).

William Muschenheim divides his territory into the familiar expressive categories of 'form, surface and space', and mentions the further conventionally defined categories such as mass, volume, plane, line, solid and void, proportion, size, scale, light and shadow (all classed under form); texture, pattern, colour, transparency, reflectivity and translucency (classed under surface); and proportion, scale, rhythm, harmony, contrast, enclosure, height, width, depth, light and extension (classed under space). When he goes on to give architectural examples of these expressive categories, you see how *fluid* and *conventional* at one and the same time are the architectural signs. For instance, he shows photos of the interior of Frank Lloyd Wright's Johnson Wax building and the interior of the mosque at Cordoba under the heading: 'forest of columns with arched or vaulted bracing gives a strong sense of perspective'.

Another page shows a Borromini church, a French chateau and Le Corbusier's Swiss pavilion under the heading 'concave building masses conducive to the play of light and shadow'. Now seeing these kinds of visual correspondences between buldings from different periods became a conventional architectural game in the fifties with the writings of Giedion, Scully and Rowe. They started, or at any rate culminated, the practice of abstracting formal elements from their previous signifieds to compare them as expressive systems. The cultural meanings of church, factory and house were put aside in order to build up new signification systems which emphasised the expressive plane as content (Colin Rowe's 'phenomenal transparency', Giedion's 'space-time concept', Scully's 'stick style' are examples of formal systems which are invested with teleological and other meanings).

Muschenheim, being a man of this time, does the same. His supposedly abstract formal signifiers are always re-attached to new signifieds—'forest of columns . . . gives a strong sense of perspective'. In short, they are new signs, partly conventional ('forest', 'perspective') and partly *hermeneutic* and *private* (his choice of looking at these photos in this way). This is why we say that the architectural sign can only be completely analysed a *posteriori*, in a context.

The architectural sign, in this sense, corresponds, to an utterance, or 'architectural *statement*': 'Nelson's Column', 'concave building-masses conducive to the play of light and shadow'. While perceiving a building on an architectural promenade, one sees a sequence of many such statements, whereas living in, changing and making the building gives rise to entirely different kinds of perceptual categories. These two basic modes of perception are another reason for the schizophrenic aspect of the architectural sign.

3.2 Indexical, Iconic and Symbolic Signs

Returning to the semiotic triangle (2.1), we can classify the main types of architectural sign stemming from the relations (R's in the diagram) between signifiers, signifieds and actual functions. Basically, we will follow Charles Peirce's classification into three main types of sign, but it should be mentioned that no real sign is completely pure (they are all

Figure 27
Indexical Signs in a half-timbered house, Verneys, Crondal, circa 1660. Window, door, roof, structure, wall, chimney are such normalised signs in this language that they mostly just indicate themselves; if you look closely, however, you can see distortions which make the signs more than mere indices

compound signs) and they all have a conventional, coded element (therefore they are all *symbolic* signs at their base).

The indexical sign, or *index*, for Peirce was something which had an *existential relation* between signifier and signified: smoke with fire, footprints with foot etc. In architecture, every sign has an indicative component: a glass door indicates itself and what is behind, arrows indicate circulation, a weathercock indicates the direction of the wind, a window indicates view. These are the *literal* signs and one can imagine a low level significative architecture made up from them such as vernacular, or industrial building, a building of clichés which does not, particularly, refer to metaphors, symbols or aesthetic ideas apart from itself (Figure 27).

The perceiver sees these forms as a matter of fact and generally there has been no intention to communicate on the part of the designer (see above page 76). Indexical signs are learned by the perceiver over time and in this sense really are disguised symbolic signs which have a peculiar quality (the *continual existential* connection of signifier with signified).

Clearly one has to see smoke connected with fire to learn this sign, and if one just sees smoke rising over a hill, he can take it as a sign of fire, tornado, car moving fast, or spring cleaning where a lot of rugs are being beaten.

The indexical sign is important for architecture in as much as many new forms are introduced for pragmatic or func-

Figure 28
Iconic Sign, Los Angeles, circa
1938. The volume is of course only
one formal aspect where the
signifier is mapped to the signified:
the mustard is yellow, the hot-dog
is red, the bun is white and brown.
But iconic relations can concern all
formal articulae

Figure 29
John Nash, *Royal Pavilion*,
Brighton, 1815 – 18. Nash used his
version of the Hindu Style (bulbous
domes, latticework, Gothic tracery)
as a symbol for this royal escape
palace. The convention was
already set by *Kubla Khan* of Coleridge.

tional reasons which then become continuously re-used in
this context until they become symbolic signs.

The iconic signs concern a different set of relations between signifier and signified although, of course, there is
always present an existential and therefore indexical relation
as well: the relations of the iconic sign are *relatively
motivated*. Most 'functional' architecture is of this sort: pie-
shaped, or wedge-shaped auditoria, tube-shaped circulation
corridors, structually-shaped bridges, hot-dog stands in the
shape of hot-dogs (Figure 28), and the use of forms and
materials according to their inherent emotional overtones
(red as aggressive, passionate etc.) (Figure 29). In the twen-

tieth century, many architects such as Le Corbusier and Walter Gropius tried to establish a 'universal' language based on iconic signs, a sort of esperanto which, they hoped, would naturally grow out of the laws of function, structure and perception. 'Purism', Le Corbusier thought, would be transcultural and not dependent on learning, history or symbolism. Nervi believed that architecture was evolving towards 'unchanging forms' based on structural universals.

While the International Style was largely based on these iconic signs and, of course, enjoyed a wide dissemination, it didn't communicate exactly as intended for the simple reason that iconic signs are too restricted and need further symbolic cues to be correctly read.

Peirce defined the icon as 'a sign which refers to the object that it denotes by virtue of certain characters of its own and which it possesses just the same' .... The signifier was 'like' the signified in certain ways such as structural similarity, or analogical constitution.

There are several problems in determining how much similarity constitutes iconicity: five things in common, ten, fifteen? A bridge never looks exactly 'like' the structural forces that go through it: for one thing the signifiers of the bridge are always determined by more things than structure alone (construction for example); for another the structure will act dynamically and partly in an indeterminate way, and lastly, the bridge is like a *conventional representation of these forces* (an abstract, line diagram) and not the forces themselves (forces don't look 'like' anything—have you ever seen a gravity 'wave'?). Such complications, indeed the conventional and coded nature of all perception, have led certain semioticians to dismiss iconicity altogether as hopelessly naive (Eco, 1976), but we may continue to use the concept as long as we realise its conventional nature. It is useful to keep because it refers to that wide range of architecture where there is a *pertinent* mapping between two different conventional codes that is meant to be perceived. Put another way, it refers very nicely to all that architecture which tries to be diagrammatic, from Palladio to Peter Eisenman.

Finally, there is the *symbolic* sign where conventional usage sets the *arbitrary relation* between signifier and signified. Examples of this are the conventional use of three orders of classical architecture (Doric for Banks etc.) (Figure 30); the appropriate use of revival styles (Nash used the classical style for his town house, the Olde English for country retreats); the emblems on pubs, and the great menagerie of animals and Amazons which decorate and hold up buildings (Figure 31) etc. The present-day use of building materials (glass and steel for offices, pneumatic for sports

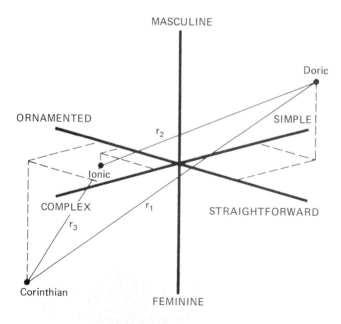

MASCULINE

Doric

ORNAMENTED   SIMPLE

r_2

Ionic

COMPLEX r_1 STRAIGHTFORWARD

r_3

Corinthian   FEMININE

Figure 30
The Three Orders related (r1, r2, r3) on the semantic axes that Vitruvius used to describe them: e.g. the Doric Order is more masculine, simple and straightforward than the other two. If one were to relate different functions, certain of them would fall in similar quadrants (e.g. office work in the Doric quadrant) and the history of the *symbolic sign* might start

Figure 31
Antonio Gaudi, *Guell Palace Entrance*, Barcelona, 1886 – 91. The important distinction between public and private, the act of entry, is signified by parabolic arches, dragons, the family shield and initials (E.G.) which turn into serpents and thence into a collage of ironwork affording one-way views

halls) is also widely symbolic, but there is obviously motivation involved too.

Again the decision to classify a sign as indexical, iconic or symbolic is largely relative. While there is not much in common between the Doric Order and the function 'bank' (except they share overtones of rationality, security, sobriety) you can't say their connection is entirely arbitrary either.

Clearly they occupy the same semantic quadrant with respect to other Orders and other functions, so they have this analogy in common. Yet by and large the Orders are connected to the functions by usage, by feedback, and it is this fact that makes them mostly examples of the symbolic sign.

The architectural sign tends to be more indexical and iconic than the linguistic sign, which is relatively more symbolic, which is another way of saying that architecture is more motivated than language. When we say that language and the symbolic sign are 'arbitrary', we do not mean that the relation between signifier and signified is irrational, but rather that its *initial* use is relatively unmotivated. Of course all subsequent use is motivated as the very slow-changing nature of language indicates.

As I have pointed out, most architectural signs are compound, or indexical; iconic and symbolic all at once, with one of the tendencies dominating. Today the symbolic and metaphorical dimensions have been impoverished and new compound signs are not built up around deeper levels of signification connected with ritual, or metaphysical meaning. The language of modern architecture, unlike that of Art Nouveau, does not suggest either natural metaphors or self transcendence and in that sense has inevitably lent itself to agencies of repression. For in its obsessive concentration on indexical meanings, it promotes a banal and literalist life of simplified functionality.

3.3 Specificity of Codes

Returning to our discussion, at the outset, of the various things architecture can mean, and the various expressive systems with which it can articulate these meanings, we can offer a rough hierarchy of architectural codes. Generally speaking there are codes of expression and codes of content.

The *Codes of content* include, in order of relative importance to the user, architecture as:

1. *a way of life sign*, a sign of ethnic domain, a sign of inhabitation and comfort. This code is almost entirely specific to architecture although it is shared by clothing, personal possessions and other artifacts.

2. a sign of *building activity*, of the historical process of change, personal involvement, buying and selling etc. Although connected with the former sign, this one is distinct enough to warrant separation. When John Turner speaks of 'housing as a verb', he has in mind the existential connection of the inhabitant with his house, the way the latter becomes a sign of personal endeavour and identity, even fulfilment.

3. a sign of *traditional ideas and beliefs*. This is the most commonly known area of signification which traditional architectural history describes as inconography. All sign systems articulate this area, so it is hardly specific to architecture, but no less important for that.

4. a sign of various *functions* including use, social activity, structural capability, environmental servicing, temperature control and building tasks such as church, library, factory etc.

5. a sign of *socio-anthropological meaning*. Proxemics, the study of social spatial dimensions, has revealed how architecture may signify conventional distances between people and groups. Obviously people keep these distances without architecture, so the sign is not specific to building, but may be mostly monopolised by architecture. Many anthropological studies, notably those of Claude Lévi-Strauss, have shown how architecture and village and city patterns articulate social and economic life.

6. Any city can be read as an *economic* class and social icon, in spite of the fact that no one understands how land value and social status really interact as a semiotic system. The fact that people choose their house location according to subtle cues of status and way of life is well observed by real-estate dealers.

7. a sign of *psychological motivation*, sometimes hidden, sometimes betrayed, sometimes overt. Phallic and sexual codes have often been discovered, but rarely signalled (Figure 32).

The *codes of expression* in order of relative importance to the architect, include architecture as:

8. a sign of *spatial manipulation*. Since Renaissance architects began representing space positively as the interval between walls and structural elements shaded darkly, this expressive form has been quite consciously on their minds. Probably the ancient Greeks had a well developed notion of internal space and a topological idea of ordering external space, and no doubt the Romans were highly

Figure 32
Minoru Takeyama, Hotel Beverly Tom, Yomakomai, Hokkaido, 1973. 80 rooms are placed on a form, which is then picked up in other parts of this hotel to quite intentionally signify phallic power—the Shinto symbol 'Tenri'

conscious of their notion of hollowed out, domed space. But in our century space has become fetishised as *the* specific medium of architecture, whereas it is clear that it is shared by other sign systems (landscape, sculpture) and ordinary people notice surface before they understand space.

9. a sign of *surface covering*. What we are continuously looking *at* is the last layer of the constructional meaning, the epidermis, not the deeper architectural meaning. The fact that architects relinquished control of this area, about the same time that interior decoration was born as a modern profession (1925) might be regarded as a coincidence with interesting implications. This expressive plane of meaning is perhaps the most potent in conveying the content 'way of life'. Clearly there are other sign systems which also concentrate on this plane—furniture, sculpture, painting, television, books, film, landscape etc.—but just because it is not specific to architecture, does not make it any less essential. In a hierarchy of

semiotic importance it should probably be placed first in the expressive codes, not only because it is most noticeable but also because it has many levels of articulation—e.g. rhythm, colour, texture, proportion, size, smell, tactility etc.

10. a sign of *formal articulation*. It is difficult to decide how many categories of material articulation one should separate out, as there is a great redundancy of meanings, but three dimensional *shape*—volume, mass, density etc.—seem distinct enough from surface to warrant a separate classification although they both have proportion, scale, texture, smell, acoustic properties etc. In any case it is a question of conventional relevance, and in the West formal articulation has been culturally defined for a long time. Architecture shares this plane of expression with sculpture, landscape, opera etc.

We would probably go on multiplying expressive channels (acoustic, olfactory, tactile etc.), but they seem of secondary relevance to architecture. One area, the *aesthetic sign*, falls through our typology because it is both expression and content at the same time, or rather the meaning of the expressive level is the content (e.g. rhythm accentuated and meaningful for itself, attended to as an end in itself. This was discussed as 'connotative semiotics', 2.1).

We see from these eleven codes that architecture is an impure, pluralistic amalgam rather like opera, and it doesn't make sense to say that a code which is more specific to architecture (space) is necessarily more important than another one. Nor must we believe that all architecture must use all these codes (a bicycle shed doesn't signify a way of life nor articulate aesthetic meaning, but it is still architecture). Those definitions which emphasise one code as the 'essence' of architecture, or exclude certain buildings because of their modesty, display a typical fetishism for specificity. Although such fetishism may be helpful for creativity, it is rather sterile for the theory and criticism of architecture.

3.4 Radical Schizophrenia and Overcoding (Multivalence)

Architectural semiotics grew up in Italy during the fifties, among other reasons because of the crisis in modern architecture, the undeniable sterility of new buildings and their inability to communicate intended meanings to the users. The birth of this field, in action against these semiotic tendencies in the environment, is entirely appropriate since, by its own definition, semiotics is itself a type of sign behaviour located in the social, political and cultural world. It is normative and interventionist by definition. So much the worse then that semiotic study has often been reductive, incomprehensible, or puritanical, a point that Robert de Ventos has emphasised in his paper, 'The Sociology of Semiology'. We cannot practice semiotic activity without producing it, a fact which has been stressed by the Marxist semioticians without, thereby, noticeably improving their style. Nonetheless, they are right: semiotics is a productive activity that changes things and one cannot adopt an Archimedean point outside the world, or value free position, while discussing it with respect to a particular field of signification. This is why we have constantly mentioned the negative semiosis in the modern environment and will conclude with prescriptive ideas.

In this century there has been a recurrent debate going on between the traditionalists and the modernists, or in different terms between the populists and elitists—those who favour a people's architecture and those who value the work of the profession and *avant-garde*. The debate stems from the nature of the architectural sign which is radically schizophrenic in nature; partly rooted in tradition, in the past, indeed in everyone's experience as a child crawling along flat floors and other normalised elements, and partly rooted in a fast changing society with its new functional tasks, new materials, new technologies and ideologies. On the one hand, architecture is as slow-changing as language (we can still understand Renaissance English) and on the other hand, as fast changing as fashion and modern art.

As I have already pointed out many people, including architects, prefer to live in traditional buildings because these buildings have a wealth of appropriate meaning which accrues to old, as opposed to new, form. Many of the inhabitants of Le Corbusier's Pessac felt his stark white cubical forms lacked a proper sense of shelter and protection, so they shortened the ribbon windows, added shutters and more window mullions; they articulated the blank white surfaces with window boxes, cornices and eaves; and some put on the old Bordeaux sign of protection, the pitched roof (Figure 33).

In many quasi-sociological studies—those on high-rise buildings and comprehensive redevelopment—it has been shown again and again that working class and middle class people don't like the humane and artistic solutions of modern architects (Ward, 1973; Newman, 1973).* They find

---

*The writings of Conrad Jameson, Oscar Newman, Phillipe Boudon, Jane Jacobs and Colin Ward are well enough known not to require extensive referencing.

them inhuman and inartistic, to put it charitably, because
they don't have the conventional signs of domesticity, protection and identity and because they do signify 'council
housing', 'social deprivation', 'estate', 'anonymity', 'the
wrong side of the tracks', 'factory' and so forth. In addition
the layout of these estates, the vast open spaces and public
corridors, promote these sorts of signifieds even when they
aren't formally communicated.

   On the other hand, modern architects go on building these
estates with a mixture of good intentions: within the
resources at their disposal, they try to make these large
buildings small in scale, formally inventive and individual.
The problem is (aside from the inhumanity of the building
task itself) one of codes. The modern architect is designing
his meanings of individuality in a code (or semantic space)
which is opposed to that of the inhabitants. His taste and
training place different value on such things as technology,
order, pure form, construction and invention. Not just different, but *opposite* values are often at work. Where he, as a
son of the Enlightenment and Romantic Age, wants to 'make
it new and strange' in order to make it aesthetic, the inhabitant wants to 'have it old and familiar'. Where he wants to
keep pace with new materials and methods, always progress-
ing in the permanent revolution going on down at the patent
office, the inhabitant wants to live more and more like his
ancestors (the more ancient, the more venerable). The
semantic preferences are polarized and will remain so, as
long as there is an architectural profession and *avant-garde*,
because the pressures and training of this elite tend to bring
out a progressivist ideology.

   One could of course do away with the elite and *avant-
garde* (as China has done), or give all the power to the profes-

Figure 33
Le Corbusier, *Pessac Housing,*
1925 – 74, transformed, ruined,
aged and articulated by a traditional language. The signs of personalisation and security have
effectively distorted the purist
language so that it sends out
welcoming messages of domesticity
and 'home' instead of 'factory,
sugar cube and hospital'

Figure 34
James Stirling, *Cambridge University the History Faculty*, 1968. In plan and section the building shows the influence of symmetrical, Palladian planning; the exterior is reminiscent of industrial train sheds, greenhouses and domestic brick buildings as well as a Constructivist articulation of parts. Signs of technology (cleaning booms) and Pop (dayglo paint) accent certain edges. The complex coding had elicited complex reactions

sion (as Russia has done), but in Western pluralist societies these alternatives would be odious.

It remains then to live with our schizophrenia, a dualism I will illustrate with one example taken from the work of a leading British architect James Stirling.

Stirling's Cambridge History Faculty Building has aroused prolonged and widespread praise and hostility. The critics Nikolaus Pevsner and Nicholas Taylor find the building 'anti-architecture' and 'brilliant, if over-antagonistic', the historian Hugh Brogan (one of the users of the building) finds parallels of Stirling with Hitler and Stalin (and he places Stirling among the 'anti-democratic: structural fascists'). A younger critic Gavin Stamp more recently attacked the building for its functional shortcomings finding it 'a sophisticated machine' that failed to work, 'a composition of clichés', and 'aggressive and self-righteous' (Booth and Taylor, 1970).* On the other hand, critics such as Reyner Banham and those from France, Italy, America and Japan have applauded the design finding in it positive meanings of Palladian planning, aerospace technology, the vernacular, industrial tradition and glasshouse building (Figure 34).

As letters to the *Times Literary Supplement* revealed, everyday users of the Cambridge library are equally divided

*See Gavin Stamp, *Building Design*, March 19, 1976 and subsequent weeks for attack, my reply and follow-up letter.

Figure 35
Cambridge History Faculty. The 'waterfall' of glass, the 'goldfish bowl', 'factory' or 'crystalline geometry' and 'clear jewel' etc

on how the building works.* One says it 'works very well indeed' and that 'the library's sweep and light are not only exhilarating but convenient to staff and readers alike' (Figure 35); another says 'I feel worse than the weather' in the building because it is 'cold, the vents draughty' etc.

In twelve interviews I conducted at the library in 1974 I found the same opposite reactions. Those who disliked it said it didn't work for the same kind of reasons that Gavin Stamp mentioned in his attack (noise, leaks, lack of adequate sound insulation between classrooms, heat gain through the glass roof). They also used affective terms and metaphors in describing their feelings. 'It's like a gold-fish bowl' (several girls felt an unusual amount of ogling). 'The glass roof is like a waterfall' (perhaps this was an inadvertent allusion to the well publicized leakage, but clearly it's the busy rush of white and crystalline forms spilling down the slope of the roof that consciously prompted the metaphor). 'It's like a factory, all angles and gawky' (these sorts of people are bored with the pervasive factory metaphor of modern architecture). 'Not cosy' (no gloss needed here). 'You have a sense of being watched everywhere' (again the opinions of two girls who didn't like the central surveillance system, the raised platform from which the custodian keeps watch) (Figure 36). These metaphors expressed very eloquently a commitment to the traditional codes of architecture, and apparently these people were bending the perception of such 'real' or 'functional' things as temperature and leakage. The custodian whose job it was to ventilate the library denied that it ever got too hot and cold *for the thermometer*, contrary to what people experienced (of course it could be his perception which was being bent by his preferences).

Figure 36
Cambridge History Faculty. The raised surveillance desk keeps watch over the reading room. Note how the angles are bent in a gawky way, the roof leans in like a broken back and cuts, visually, through tiers of circulation. This calculated dissonance, an exciting metaphor ('explosion in a glass factory') may explain certain anxieties and impassioned apologias

*See the *Times Literary Supplement,* September 5, 1975.

On the other hand, students who liked the building described its logical layout and crystalline expression. They said 'what a breath of fresh air' it was in Cambridge; what pleasure it was to leave 'the stuffy atmosphere' of the cloistered life and arrive in the 20th century. One student spoke of the 'bookworms' and pedant scholars who crawled around the traditional Cambridge library 'like vermin' and said he came to the Stirling library every day just to experience the 'light-filled space'. It literally 'raised his spirits' to come here and see that Cambridge wasn't all traditional snobbery and well-groomed reticence.

While my interviews and these critical opinions hardly constitute a finely tuned survey of the building, they do, I believe, show the typical balance of response which James Stirling and others have reported. I think they also show (although more research would be needed to confirm this) that the perception of functional inadequacies or perfections is a matter of *more basic ideological codes*.

Many Cambridge dons and undergraduates will happily live and work in cold, dank reverberant buildings which have all the 'functional faults' of Stirling's building, but they won't complain because the architecture is in the classical or Gothic style. These buildings signify the right 'way of life' at Cambridge, and the quasi-Futurist, dramatic use of glass and aluminium signifies the wrong direction to take. To simplify the matter somewhat, the traditional code (T.C.) acts as a restriction on the perception of the building bending its meanings to conform with an ideological interpretation. The modern code (M.C.) equally restricts and warps the incoming architectural signs to fit its semantic preference.

The simplification is, of course, that both codes allow for some opposite meanings to get through and one should really speak of *many* semiotic groups rather than just the two extremes. Indeed I should really refer to 'radical multiphrenia' not schizophrenia, but since the reader is already burdened with his share of ugly neologisms, I will avoid the temptation of adding yet another. The crucial points at issue are that codes based on taste cultures, or semiotic groups, guide the perception of architectural meanings, and that today in a pluralist society we have an inevitable disjunction between these groups.

There are two conceivable ways out of this impasse assuming we do not rule arbitrarily in favour of one group or another. We could design every building at least twice, once by the architect and once by the interior decorator (or craft specialist who is more in tune with traditional codes), or we could teach architects a radical schizophrenia, make them self-conscious of the dual role they find themselves in and train them to design at once in elitist and populist codes. It is, theoretically, possible to overcode a building so that it can be read according to intention. If the modern architect were to make more cogent use of the symbolic sign and were to take an interest in the codes of metaphor which dominate popular perception he could at least be understood, or ambiguous, where he intended to be.

Frankly, many of the modern architects I know don't want to be understood perhaps for the reason that they have

Figure 37
Lucien Kroll, *Medical Faculty Building*, Woluwe, near Brussels, 1969−74. Various functions—living, restaurant, teaching, etc.—articulated with an *ad hoc* aesthetic of different materials. Popular and elitist codes are intermixed in this multivalent work

nothing important to say beyond an aesthetic message. The *avant-garde* seems fairly content to stay within its hermeneutic meanings, shuffling these creatively, as all that is left, it seems, is to be creative (Figure 37). The *avant-garde* in a consumer society seems to have left its previous role as a serious alternative to mass culture and become another adjunct of hedonism. Perhaps no tears will be shed at this departure, since the architectural results of the *avant-garde* have proved so unpopular.

Nonetheless, for those who remain aware of the historical dilemma, of the necessary stratification of semiotic groups, there is no escape from the conclusion that an architecture must be multivalent. Like the buildings of Gaudí it must be overcoded with various signs, redundant with meanings that are vulgar and elitist, conventional and strange, literal and metaphorical. Prediction is hope by another name, but it seems to me we are at a point not unlike that which gave birth to Art Nouveau. Modern architecture as a language is being enriched by popular, vernacular and Ersatz architecture.

Anything can happen and we should make sure that it does.

References

Bonta, J. P. (1979). *Expressive Systems in Architecture and Design*. London, Lund Humphries.

Booth, P., Taylor, N. (1970). *Cambridge New Architecture*. London, Leonard Hill.

Coleridge, S. T. (1950). *Biographia Literaria*, Ch XIV, in *Portable Coleridge*, New York, Viking.

Eco, U. (1972). A Componential Analysis of the Architectural Sign /Column/. *Semiotica*, **5**, 2.

Eco, U. (1976). *A Theory of Semiotics*. Bloomington, Indiana U.P.

Jencks, C. (1976). Fetishism and Architecture. *Architectural Design*, August, 1976.

Mushenheim, W. (1965). *Elements of the Art of Architecture*. London, Thames and Hudson.

Newman, O. (1973). *Defensible Space*. London, Architectural Press.

Panofsky, E. (1955). *Meaning in the Visual Arts*. New York, Doubleday.

Panofsky, E. (1957). *Gothic Architecture and Scholasticism*. New York, Meridian.

Ward, C. (1973). *Vandalism*. London, Architectural Press.

1.3 The Deep Structures of Architecture

Geoffrey Broadbent

Reprinted from Llorens, T. (ed.), *Arquitectura, historia y teoria de los signos,* Barcelona, 1974.

Prologue

For some years now I have been interested in design methods; in the creative, analytical and managerial techniques which architects use within those processes (1966 – 69) and the problems which architects face in designing buildings, that is, reconciling the needs of a particular human group—the clients and users—with the physical environment—a particular site—by means of a physical structure, that is, the building itself (1972). Like most design methodologists, I assumed, tacitly, that if the 'user' was analysed thoroughly enough in physiological, psychological and sociological terms, if the site was analysed thoroughly enough in geological, topographical and climatic terms, if the materials available for building were understood in chemical, physical and mechanical terms, then somehow a 'correct' resolution or reconciliation of all these factors would emerge as the 'optimum' solution to a particular design problem.

Yet something clearly was missing in this view; it simply was not possible for the overall form of a building to be generated in this way. It is true that unlike many methodologists, I had at least been concerned with *Creativity* (1966a) and the *Psychological Background to Design* (1966c), but it seemed illogical to look at the designer of buildings from this point of view without also looking at the user. And when my interests were extended in this direction (1972) it became clear, finally, that architecture could never be strictly 'functional'. Each user brought his own percep-

tions to bear on what the designer had done; there could be
no uniformity of response; what seemed 'functional' to one
was merely 'cold and inhuman' to another. But that led to a
consideration of the ways in which two generations of architects had thought that architecture *could* be functional; I
began, therefore, to analyse the concept of 'functionalism'
itself, as its most vocal advocates had used the term.
Although, as de Zurko shows (1957), it has had a long and
distinguished history, functionalism as we know it was a
tenet of that International Style architecture which Le Corbusier (1923), Gropius (1936, 1956), Mies Van der Rohe (1923,
1924) and others advocated in the first half of this century.

Now, clearly, the functions of a building *can* help determine how it should be designed; the sizes and shapes of the
spaces it contains, the ways in which these spaces are linked
together on plan, the means for moving between them that
ought to be provided, in terms of corridors, staircases,
elevators and so on. If a building fails in any of these ways
we should hardly call it functional. Add to this a particular
set of attitudes to structure, decoration and so on, and the
architecture emerges which everyone *calls* functional. The
architects who advocated it held, in particular, that the
buildings they designed should be free of any reference to
foreign, exotic or native historical styles. Such stylism, they
thought, would actively prevent its efficient functioning.

The ideal of functionalism, in this sense, was firmly
attached by Pevsner (1936) and other critics to a particular
building form, as exemplified by the office building which
Gropius and Meyer had designed for Karl Benscheidt's Fagus
works at Alfeld an der Leine in 1911. Pevsner rhapsodised
over its 'complete facade . . . conceived in glass' with supporting piers 'reduced to narrow bands of steel' and Gropius
himself (1936) did nothing to refute that description in *The
New Architecture and the Bauhaus* of 1936.

And even 50 years after it was built, in the 1960 edition of
his book, Pevsner thought that this building still expressed
'today's reality' in a thoroughly responsible manner; its form
should be recreated, wherever possible, to counter the
resurgent excesses of a new Expressionism, as represented in
the late work of Le Corbusier (Jaoul Houses and Ronchamp),
'the structural acrobatics of the Brazilians' and other wilful
'attempts to satisfy the cravings of architects for individual
expression, the craving of the public for the surprising and
fantastic, and for escape out of reality into a fairy world'.

Yet, curiously enough, Pevsner himself was living in a fairy
world; the Fagus office is not constructed of steel and glass
but of brick, his 'narrow bands of steel' are hefty brick piers,
some 90 cm. × 70 cm. and with entasis like Doric columns
(Figure 1a and b); so Pevsner's 'reality' was actually an illusion of what he *wanted* Gropius's architecture to be like

Figure 1a
The ideal of functionalism was firmly attached by critics such as Giedion and Pevsner to the office building which Gropius and Meyer designed for the Fagus works at Alfeld an der Leine in 1911. Pevsner described its 'complete facade . . . conceived in glass' with supporting piers 'reduced to narrow bands of steel'. Yet as the drawings (b) (page 122) show, the piers were built of brick almost 1 m wide with Entasis like Doric columns, whilst the photograph itself demonstrates that in one respect at least the building was most unfunctional. Karl Benscheidt's own office is shaded from the sun by canvas blinds suggesting that like every other glass-clad building since, this one also suffered from solar overheating

(Weber 1961). He was using the word 'functional' to describe an *appearance* of buildings, a fact which I realised in 1967 when he applied it to the Arts Tower at Sheffield University (Figure 2), in which I was then working, to distinguish it from Stirling's Engineering building at Leicester, which he found 'expressionist' (Figure 3). Neither building clearly, is perfect, but I was suffering from thoroughly inadequate vertical circulation—there were two 40-seater lecture rooms on the roof served by one 10-person lift—from solar heat gain (97°F in my room one day, with snow on the ground outside), glare, noise transmission through floors and partitions, a wind vortex at the base which sometimes made it impossible to enter the front door, and so on. How could Pevsner describe it as 'functional'. It was rectilinear in form and glass curtain-walled, it looked machine made; so, for Pevsner, it must be 'functional'.

Whilst the building was thoroughly inadequate in terms of room size and shape, circulation and so on, its greatest failures, as I have indicated, were environmental; matters of

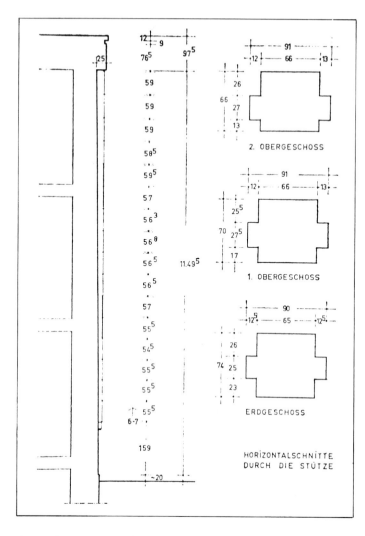

thermal, acoustic and lighting control. Those too are matters
of its functioning and the belief has been growing amongst
certain British researchers that a building's performance in
these terms is even more important than the size and shape
of the spaces it contains. If one assesses even the best
curtain-walled, cubic architecture, of 20th century functionalism against such criteria, it proves to be almost a total
failure in terms of solar heat gain, glare, heat loss, noise
penetration and so on. One *can* pump energy into it, to work
heating, cooling and ventilation plant but that in itself is a
wilful thing to do. It costs money, uses mineral and other
resources which we ought to conserve, whilst the processes
of producing the energy are often themselves polluting. It
may be that before very long, we will see Gropius, Mies and
the other advocates of such architecture as more wilful,
more perverse, more *expressionist* than a Stirling or a Gaudí!
For make no mistake, this architecuture *is* expressive, for like

Figure 2
Pevsner in 1967 described the Arts
Tower at Sheffield as a highly
'functional' building. I was working
there at the time and suffered from
the thoroughly inadequate vertical
circulation, solar heat gain, glare
and noise transmission in my room,
not to mention the wind vortex at
the base which sometimes made it
quite impossible for us to enter the
front of the building

bobbed hair, the bowler hat, traditional jazz, the cocktail
and the Charleston, it now presents some highly potent symbols of 1920's attitudes.

But in architectural terms that is very nearly *all* it does.
Strange that the architecture which set out to be a-stylar and
functional should end up by being some of the most stylish,
but non-functioning, that has ever been built!

Figure 3
Pevsner contrasted the Arts Tower
with Stirling's Engineering Building
at Leicester which he found 'expressionist'. it certainly has its problems but the vertical circulation is
much more sensible than the Art
Tower's with spaces for large
numbers of people, such as Lecture
Rooms, low down in the building
and spaces for fewer people, such
as Research Laboratories and Staff
Rooms higher up

Architecture and Linguistics

The misuse, by architects and critics, of words such as functionalism, is itself sufficient reason for looking more closely
at the language they use; at the relationships between
buildings, the concepts which are used in discussing them,
and the words by which those concepts are defined. This,
clearly, is the province of linguistics, but difficulties arise
when one tries to determine which mode of linguistic
analysis to apply to the language of architecture; the
language, that is, by which architecture is discussed. One has
to make a choice between that which studies language as a
system of signs, such as a Saussurean *semiology*, and that
which sees it as an aspect of communication, as in the
semiotic of Peirce and Morris (1938, 1946, 1964); between

that which seeks to describe language at a particular moment in time, as in certain kinds of *structuralism* which have developed from Saussure, and that which aims to find the rules by which language is generated, as in Chomsky's *generative and transformational grammars* (1957, 1965).

Above all, one must decide whether one's approach is to be fundamentally rationalist—taking innate ideas as the basis for logically-developed, self-consistent theories—or empiricist—holding that everything we know is based on past experience, the residues of our sense perceptions.

The latter view is represented, in extreme form, by the behaviourism of Watson (1924) and Skinner (1957) who took it that all learning was a matter of stimulus and response. The rat in Skinner's laboratory *learned* that if, on hearing the *stimulus* of a bell, he *responded* by pressing a bar, he would be *rewarded* with a food pellet. All learning takes this form, according to Skinner; one's 'correct' responses are rewarded whilst one's incorrect ones will be ignored or even punished. That is how we acquire language; we learn that certain sounds are 'attached' to certain objects, that if we respond to the sounds made, say by our parents, in certain ways, then we too shall be suitably rewarded. We learn to make appropriate sounds with our vocal chords, modifying them by throat, mouth, tongue and teeth. And, according to Watson—the founding-father of behaviourism—thinking itself is nothing more than 'talking to ourselves'—repeating silently the muscular habits thus learned.

Such views are anathema to extreme phenomenologists, such as Chomsky, who believe that our basic knowledge is inborn and whose 58 page review of Skinner's *Verbal Behaviour* is a crucial document in this particular debate (1957). Chomsky believes that our fundamental knowledge is inborn, and that, in particular as human beings, we have an innate capacity for understanding language and for generating sentences which are grammatically 'correct'. So Chomsky is searching, by a deduction from first principles, for a logical theory which will explain the structure of all known—and unknown—human languages, and will enable us to distinguish between *language* proper and all other systems of communication.

It seems to me that neither scheme, on its own, is sufficient to 'explain' language. We once had a cat which, clearly, had no innate capacity for learning the English language; and my attempts to teach him were a dismal failure. On that evidence, certainly, Chomsky is right. But our cat learned many things by stimulus and response, so on that evidence Skinner is right also. An adequate theory of language therefore must embrace both extremes, so the choice of which linguistic model to use is a very complex one. The most popular, by far, is the Saussurean, in its later, struc-

turalist manifestations. Yet that too presents many difficulties. *Any* attempt to describe architecture in linguistic
terms can *only* be achieved at the level of analogy or, more
particularly, of metaphor. Certain early attempts to equate
phoneme (the smallest unit of speech-sound) with, say, brick
(the smallest unit of construction); *morpheme* (the smallest
whole unit of meaning) with, say, window (a small unit of
construction) and so on, were very naive; buildings are *not*
constructed from the elements of language, nor are there
clear, obvious and generally agreed correspondences between the elements of architecture and the elements of
language.

There can be no general agreement even as to what correspondences are appropriate. Scalvini (in this volume)
outlines the conflict between herself (with de Fusco) and Eco
as to the ways in which Saussure's *signifier* and *signified*
apply, metaphorically, to architecture. In Saussure's terms,
the signifier is the *sound image* by which, say, a word is indicated, whilst the signified is the *concept* to which it refers.
For de Fusco and Scalvini, the signifier is a building's exterior, whilst the signified is its interior. Eco, on the other
hand, equates signifier, say, with a staircase and signified
with the act of walking up.

Both parties, clearly, have enriched the range of concepts
against which it is possible to discuss architecture and, just
as one cannot choose between behaviourist and
phenomenologist views as to the nature of language, so one
cannot choose between these. We should hardly expect two
poets to use the same metaphor in the same way; why then
should we expect conformity of usage between architectural
semiologists?

But whilst their metaphors, clearly, give us new ways of
describing architecture and perhaps of understanding it,
their descriptions, finally, are simply new artefacts, to be laid
side by side with the buildings they describe. They do not
change those buildings, nor do they tell us anything specific
about the design of new ones. That is the complaint against
structuralism generally—that it provides descriptive tools of
an exceedingly interesting kind, but is in no way prescriptive
of what one should do next. Naturally, with my deep-seated
interest in the processes by which the design comes about, I
find this finally unsatisfying, which is why, like Eisenman (as
described by Gandelsonas and Morton, 2.3), I have thought it
worthwhile to look at Chomsky's grammars. It seemed possible that these might offer techniques which, by analogy,
could be applied in the *design* of architecture.

Chomsky, as we have seen, is concerned with the capacity,
which each of us possesses, for understanding grammar and
for putting words into sentences which others recognise as

grammatically 'correct'. I had no intention of looking for ways in which 'correct' architecture could be generated, but certain concepts in Chomsky seemed to promise ways of avoiding at least the worst faults of so-called 'functional' architecture.

Deep Structures

Chomsky first sprang to the world's consciousness with the *Syntactic Structures* of 1957, revising his initial thesis, to a considerable extent, in the *Aspects of the Theory of Syntax* of 1965. He suggests that each of us possesses a basic understanding, which may be inborn, of certain fundamental relationships between ourselves and the world outside ourselves which, in *Aspects* particularly, he describes as *deep structures*. He makes no attempt to define these clearly, suggesting merely that they are 'structures generated by the base component'. Base components, in his sense, consist of the words and the rules by which sentences can be generated; we shall consider some examples shortly.

A sentence such as:

The boy sees the girl.

operates at several levels. It indicates that the boy is a sentient being with eyes, that he can perceive the world around him, and that at this moment he can see *a* girl — perhaps the only girl in his field of vision.

The *deep structure*, then, consists of a fundamental relationship between the boy and the girl which, in Chomsky's terms, I have expressed by means of a surface *structure*, consisting, in this case, of five words; a pattern of sounds or letters. According to Chomsky, deep structures are converted into surface structures by *transformational rules*; we understand these instinctively and they give us the *competence* to generate sentences which are grammatically correct. These transformational rules are based on the ways in which sentences are constructed into phrases; Chomsky would write them for the above sentence as follows:

1. Sentence   NP + VP (Noun Phrase + Verb Phrase)
2. NP   T + N (The + Noun)
3. VP   Verb + NP
4. T   the
5. N   boy, girl, etc.
6. Verb   sees, etc.

The relationship between deep structure and surface structure therefore can be represented as follows:

```
        Sentence               Deep structure
      NP      VP               Generative Rules
    T  N   V  NP               (Phrase Markers)
              T  N
    the boy sees the girl      Surface Structure
                               (Basic Strings)
```

The same deep structure naturally can generate a wide range of sentences. To take a simpler example:

```
        NP
       /  \                    phrase marker
      N    V
  He waits  ⎫
  She sits  ⎬
  I speak   ⎭                  basic strings
  You listen
```

Our original sentence expressed a fundamental relationship between 'the boy' and 'the girl'; each of these sentences also expressed a fundamental relationship between some person—He, She, I and You and the world within which we all exist. Charles Fillmore's *Case Grammar* is an attempt to describe a set of concepts, to identify the types of judgement at this fundamental level of which human beings are capable, but for our purposes it will be sufficient to quote C. T. Onions (1904) who believed that only five basic sentences are necessary. Every sentence we generate may be represented by one of these, or by some variation on it:

    He waits
    He is a Frenchman
    He eats ortolans
    He gives me some
    He pleases me

Onions may be right, but if he is, the problem still arises as to *how* we operate transformations on them of the kind which Chomsky describes.

Chomsky's aim, although not clearly stated, was to write *algorithms* for the generation of sentences: fixed sets of instructions which automatically would lead to 'correct' results.

The Theory of Algorithms was worked out in considerable detail by the Soviet mathematician A. A. Markov (1954), in which he defined algorithm as 'an exact prescription, defining a computational process, leading from various initial data to the desired result'. With this end in mind Markov suggested of any algorithm that:

1. It will be *definite* — a precise prescription with no room for arbitrariness: it will also be comprehensive universally.

2. It will be *general*, thus it will be possible to start from any data which falls within certain prescribing limits.

3. It will be *conclusive*; given that the algorithm is orientated towards some desired result, that result will be obtained with certainty, provided that data of the appropriate kind are fed in, after which the algorithm will cease to operate.

Having described the conditions of an effective algorithm, Markov provides an example in which the two numbers 4 and 5 are multiplied together, described in an appendix to this paper.

Chomsky's algorithm is precisely of this kind and its operation in generating our initial sentence is as follows:

	Rule Applied:
Sentence	1
NP + VP	2
T + N + VP	3
the + N + Verb + NP	4
the + boy + Verb + NP	5
the + boy + sees + NP	6
the + boy + sees + T + N	2
the + boy + sees + the + N	4
the + boy + sees + the + girl	5

Having written algorithms for the *generation* of such kernel sentences, Chomsky suggests the possibility of writing further algorithms for *transforming* them into:

the passive:	the girl was seen by the boy
the negative:	the boy did not see the girl
the interrogative:	did the boy see the girl?
the affirming:	the boy did see the girl
the predictive:	the boy will see the girl
and so on.	

These algorithms form his *transformational rules.*

At most, Chomsky's algorithms generate or transform individual sentences; there is no suggestion as far as I know, that they be used to write whole books or even whole paragraphs. And, similarly, algorithms have been written for the design of architecture, or rather for designing parts of architecture with the help of a computer: these include the structural frame, heating, lighting, and ventilation services, and even the drawing of perspectives (see Broadbent 1972). Over half of the algorithms so far written in this field have been concerned with pedestrian, vehicular or services circulation, with pipework and drainage layouts and with space allocation problems; in other words, with the planning of buildings.

Some theorists, such as Gill (1969), would like to see the whole of building design computerised, whilst realising that it cannot be reduced entirely to a set of algorithms. They see a place also for heuristic and adaptive decision procedures. *Heuristic* methods proceed by trial and error, so that each attempt at a solution is evaluated, and used to improve successive attempts, until, finally, an acceptable solution is achieved, whilst in *adaptive* procedures, the computer itself learns by experience; perhaps even gets to know the people it is working with, as in Negroponte's *Architecture Machine* (1969).

Negroponte's aim was to design a machine which could:

> follow your design methodology and at the same time discern and assimilate your conversational idiosyncracies. This same machine, after observing your behaviour, could build a predictive model of your conversational performance. Such a machine could then reinforce the dialogue by using the predictive model to respond to you in a manner that [was] in rhythm with your personal behaviour and conversational idiosyncrasies.
>
> ... The dialogue would be so intimate—even exclusive—that only mutual persuasion and compromise would bring about ideas, ideas unrealisable by either conversant alone.

It would be helpful, obviously, if man and machine are to work together so closely, for them to understand each other at the outset. They will need some clear statement of architectural aims and intention to which both of them can subscribe. In other words, they need an architectural equivalent of Chomsky's deep structures. The majority of architects, who will have to work without such a machine in the foreseeable future, may well be in even greater need of such deep structures. But difficulties arise as soon as we try to find out precisely what such structures can be.

The Deep Structures of Architecture

In 'functional' architecture, the designer started with a preconception about physical structure. The building was to be framed, in steel or concrete, with concrete floors, prefabricated partitions and so on. The structural preconceptions were even stronger in the case of system building. The architect then tried to make spaces within this structure which would 'fit' the functions fairly closely. The 'given' in this case was a physical structure, it was certainly not a 'deep' structure in the Chomskyan sense; Chomsky, as we have seen, is concerned with innate capacities, with man's fundamental relationship with the world outside himself.

Any consideration of structures at this level is bound to raise again the conflict we have already discussed between those such as Chomsky, who *believe* in innate ideas, and those such as Skinner (1957), who hold that everything we know is learned by experience. One important point of dispute between them concerns the nature of those things — such as breathing, hunger, fearing and so on — which the phenomenologist calls *instincts* and the behaviourist, at best, will admit to be *unlearned responses*.

Watson tried specifically to demolish the doctrine of instincts; it was he who called breathing an 'unlearned response' and he noted a number of others: heartbeats, all circulatory phenomena, sucking, swallowing, elimination, smiling, sneezing, hiccoughing, general movement of the trunk, arms, wrist, hand and fingers, climbing movements, movement of legs, ankles and feet. These, he says, may be totally unlearned but certain activities gradually appear which do include a learned component; blinking, reaching, handling, handedness, crawling, standing, sitting up, walking, running, jumping and so on. Primitive man emerged and behaved, presumably in these ways, without *any* benefit from buildings.

We may or may not agree but one essential point emerges; there is nothing in Watson's list of basic, unlearned responses that demands the presence of buildings; he is concerned quite simply with man as an animal, responding physiologically to his environment. So clearly we shall have to take a more compromised view. We might even accept the now suspect doctrine of instincts as described by Fletcher (1957). (See Table 1.)

Some of these clearly are highly speculative and others are by no means as basic as they seem. Wright (1969) suggests that it is perfectly possible for celibate monks and nuns to live rich and full lives without recourse to Fletcher's 'sexual activity'; they possess the necessary mechanisms, but lack, or choose to ignore, the relevant stimuli from their environments. But in spite of this, Fletcher's list is of some value; and the architectural implications it raises fall into three categories:

1. Provision of a comfortable environment in which temperature, humidity, lighting and other conditions can be controlled as necessary.

1. THE INSTINCTS PROPER (PRIMARY IMPULSES)

Table 1
Extract from Fletcher's Table of
Instincts with their Architectural
Implications

Physiological	Instinct	Architectural implications
Respiration	BREATHING	Climate control in terms of temperature, humidity, freedom from smoke, fumes etc.
Contraction of stomach walls	HUNGER	
Parching of various membranes	THIRST	Provide water
Homeostatic mechanisms	MAINTAINING COMFORTABLE TEMPERATURE	Climate control in terms of temperature, humidity
	Keeping warm	Control heating; heat loss
	Keeping cool	Control heat again. Air conditioning
Fatigue	SLEEPING	Darkness, reasonable warmth
Arousal	WAKING	Increased light
Skin receptors	CARING FOR COMFORT OF BODY SURFACE	Protection from insects etc.
Adrenalin flow etc.	FEARING	Protective enclosure, security
Digestive processes	EXCRETION	W.C.s, urinals etc.
	GENERAL STIMULUS SEEKING	Varied and changing environment
	Play, curiosity Hunting	
Hormone flow etc.	SEXUAL ACTIVITY	
	Eroticism and 'courtship'	Privacy
	Sexual fighting	
	Parental activity	Comfortable environment
	Home-making	Protective environment

Table 1
Extract from Fletcher's Table of
Instincts with their Architectural
Implications

Table 1 continued

2. GENERAL INSTINCTIVE TENDENCIES (EGO-TENDENCIES)

Physiological	Instinct	Architectural implications
Overall functioning	PLEASURE – PAIN ATTACHMENT – AVOIDANCE	Warmth, shelter, protection Encouragement of social inter- action. Provision for privacy
	POSITIVE – NEGATIVE EGO- TENDENCIES	Symbols to stimulate the emotions, imaginative, fantastic or religious aspects of life

2. Protection of particular activities from a hostile external environment.

3. Provision of symbols to stimulate the emotional, imaginative, fantastic or religious aspects of life.

They form a reasonable basis for our deep structures, but even *they* hardly require a building. They *could* be satisfied, at a rudimentary level, by moving into a cave, painting its walls with symbols and lighting a fire for warmth. That, in fact, is what seems to have happened when man first decided that the 'natural' environment, as offered by wild nature, was not quite adequate for him.

We might confirm or refute these structures for architecture, by looking at what man did when he actually started to build, at the things he chose to do in transforming the 'raw' environment. It is extremely difficult to identify the first buildings. Leakey (1954) claims that a pile of stones in the Olduvai Gorge, dated to 2 million years ago, is in fact a windbreak (Figure 4), evidence that *Australopithecus africanus* — the 'Southern Ape of Africa' wanted physically to modify the given climate. Leakey's claims clearly are open to dispute; even if it could be proved beyond reasonable doubt that his dating is correct, others might attribute different functions to his pile of stones and, quite specifically, it could be argued that they serve some symbolic purpose, that they 'marked' an apes' meeting place, or even a place of worship. There is no evidence whatever that these apes had a capacity for abstract thought but some, no doubt, will still *want* the first buildings to have been symbolic in function.

Evidence of more sophisticated structures dated to

Figure 4
The Leakeys (1954) claimed this
heap of stones in the Olduvai
Gorge of East Africa as the earliest
structure ever to have been made
by man-like creatures. They
described it as a windbreak and
dated it to 2 million years ago

Figure 5
De Lumley's excavations at Terra
Amata in Nice revealed holes in
the ground evidently formed by
close packed stakes some 13 m
long which he dated to 300,000
B.C. His reconstruction shows them
arched over to form a hut

300,000 BC has been found at Terra Amata, a street at Nice
in the South of France. Here too there were stone wind-
breaks, evidently intended to protect fires from the north
west wind, but they were surrounded by 'huts'—oval structures averaging 13 m long by 5 m wide—marked in the
ground by holes evidently formed by close-packed stakes
some 7 cm in diameter. Larger posts were driven into the
ground down the centre line of each 'hut', and stones were
piled outside the oval of stakes; it is thus conjectured by de
Lumley (1969) that these formed a 'palisade' bent towards
the centre line of the hut where they could be supported by a
'ridge' on the larger posts (Figure 5). Whether this is correct
or not—and the reconstruction clearly involves a good deal

of speculation—it is evident that the palisade served some protective purpose, if only to keep out wild animals. Other 'huts' have been found at Tolabra and Ambrona in northern Spain; these (Cole 1962) may have been conical like tepees, and they have been dated to 250,000 years ago. Three elephant bones were found at Ambrona laid end to end in line: they *may* have marked a boundary or formed a path through a swamp, but alternatively they *could* have been laid in this way for symbolic reasons, no one really knows.

So these early buildings clearly served a protective purpose; evidence that they also served a symbolic function is very scanty indeed. It is generally supposed that man's first awareness of symbolism is bound up with his first obvious use of ritual in burial ceremonies. At Le Moustier (near La Chappelle-aux-Saints) a boy of 15 or so was laid in a trench (some 75,000 years ago) in a sleep-like attitude, with a pile of flints laid carefully to form a pillow. This is the earliest paleolithic burial to have been found so far, but others from slightly later suggest that new attitudes to life and death, to symbolism and ritual had been developing (Pfeiffer, 1970). A human skull surrounded by a circle of stones was found at Monte Circeo, between Rome and Naples, whilst at Shanidar in the Zagros Mountains of Iraq, a man with crushed skull was buried on a bed of flowers, the pollen of which affords an accurate dating to some 60,000 years ago (Solecki 1957).

No real evidence of a capacity for abstract thinking has been found pre-dating these burials, whilst the earliest identifiable art dates from the appearance of *Homo sapiens* in the upper Paleolithic period, some 30,000 years ago. The transition from lower to upper Paleolithic cultures is *marked* by the appearance of new methods in stoneworking, by the earliest known carving, engraving and painting. These may have been practised earlier on perishable, organic materials such as skin, bark-cloth or wood but the earliest that can be dated (to 25,000 or 30,000 years ago) are stone blocks from La Ferrassie, Arcy sur Cure and other sites, with engraved outlines of animals and geometric figures which may be sexual symbols (Ucko and Rosenfield, 1967). As for building of this period, Mongait (1955) illustrates an early example: a mammoth hunter's tent excavated at Pushkari near Novgorod-Seversk. A shallow depression was found in the ground, some 12 m by 4 m with three hearths spaced equally on the long axis. The available building materials were some rather spindly trees, some small stones, and after that the bones, tusks and skins of the mammoths; all that was left after the meat had been eaten. The site as excavated suggested to the archaeologists that the mammoth hunters had built three interlocking tepee-like frames from the available timbers and perhaps from the mammoth tusks. They had then laid mammoth skins over this framework, weighing

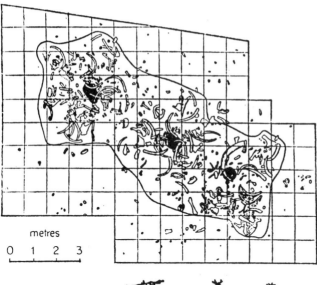

Figure 6
Pragmatic Design—Mongait
reconstructed his excavations at
Pushkari into this mammoth
hunters tent, in which archways
were formed from the mammoth
tusks to which tree branches were
tied to make frameworks after
which the mammoth skins were
laid on the top and weighted down
at the edges by the bones of the
mammoths and small stones

down the edges with stones and the bones (Figure 6). So the
most improbable of materials were used to form a very effective shelter; thus the available resources were allowed to
determine the form.

It seems fairly certain then, that man's first impulses to
build were purely utilitarian and that attempts to 'prove' his
first buildings were symbolic are so much wishful-
thinking—which is not to deny in any way the importance of
buildings as symbols once a capacity for abstract thought
had developed.

Fletcher's instincts helped us identify three deep structures for architecture but these, on their own, are not
enough. In addition to satisfying human 'needs', the form of
a building is also conditioned, to some extent at least, by the
available resources—in terms of materials, manpower and
so on. Forde (1934) describes 'primitive' building forms from
many parts of the world which show differing relationships
between pattern of life, climate to be controlled, available
materials and so on. Rapoport (1969) shows that these relationships are by no means causal, that certain cultures have

built house forms which, in terms of fitness for purpose, really do not perform very well. Function is overridden by symbolism.

We can thus detect four deep structures at the roots of architecture: (see Hillier, Musgrove and O'Sullivan, 1973)

1. The building as container for human activities.

2. The building as modifier of the given climate.

3. The building as cultural symbol.

4. The building as consumer of resources.

Each of these can be elaborated so that a full theory of architecture begins to emerge:

1. The building as container for human activities implies that it will have internal spaces which in size and shape are adequate for the activities it is to house. These internal spaces will exist in physical relationship with each other which may facilitate, or inhibit, patterns of movement between activities both within the building, and from that building to others.

2. The building as climatic modifier implies that its surfaces, particularly the external walls and roof, act as barriers or filters between the enclosed spaces and the external environment. It must perform this filtering task effectively in terms of heat, light and sound control.

3. The building as cultural symbol operates even when the architect — or critic — has pretended it would not, as in the case, say, of so-called 'functional' architecture.

4. The building as consumer of resources; all building material has to be located, extracted, transported, worked, transported again, assembled and so on. Each operation adds to its value; the fact of building new also adds to the value of a site.

These four deep structures are inter-related. One cannot separate out, say, a building's economic function from its symbolic value — as the tax authorities are all too well aware (see for example Collins (1971) on the taxing of the Seagram building).

Transformations

Clearly it is one thing to define deep structures for architecture and quite another to suggest how they might be realised in practice. Chomsky, as we have seen, limited the generative possibilities of his grammars to the use of algorithms. But it is unlikely, as we have also seen, that architecture will ever be generated exclusively by the use of algorithms. It so happens that Saussure (1916) described certain ways in which new forms of language are generated. His *diachronic* linguistics includes four of these modes of change, which he calls *phonetic, analogical,* changes by *folk etymology* and changes by *agglutination*.

Phonetic changes occur whenever phonemes (individual speech sounds) are 'run together' by Saussure's law of least effort (the Scottish pronunciation of Colquhoun is Co'houn); because pronunciation changes when a word is borrowed from one language and used in another (the English *week-end* becomes the French *veekend*); certain habits of speech become fashionable (see for example Steiner's discussion (1959) of changes in German speech during the Nazi era) because populations migrate, and so on. Phonetic changes therefore are brought about by changes in the 'raw material'—sounds—of which speech is made.

Analogical changes occur when concepts which are new to the speaker must be put into words. A child extends his vocabulary by drawing analogies with existing usage. He knows that in English the plural of cat is cats and thus assumes that the plural of sheep is sheeps—although, in fact it is *sheep*. Adults also find it necessary to coin new words by analogy with old ones, as with telephone, television, video-phone drawing, in this case using Latin and Greek roots. Analogy also serves to 'correct' usages which have been straying from accepted patterns. In Saussure's folk-etymology, unfamiliar words are changed in pronunciation or spelling so that they look, or sound, like known ones, thus the French *chaise-longue* becomes chaise-lounge in vulgar English, whilst in his agglutination, two or more words are 'run together', so the Latin *hanc horam* becomes the French *encore*.

Architectural parallels can be found for each of these; thus Baroque architecture displays, often magnificently, the agglutination of classical forms; folk etymology is seen whenever, say, the conventions of classical architecture are adapted into the vernacular or even when Beaux-Arts-trained architects tried to build 'functional' architecture—they insisted on keeping, say, the vestiges of a classical cornice. But these two have had less general application in the development of architectural form than Saussure's two other modes of change—changes in the raw material itself—that is, phonetic changes—and the use of analogy in generating new forms. These parallel two changes—pragmatic and analogical—which I have detected in the development of architecture. I have described these elsewhere (Broadbent 1969(c), 1972) with two others which I will merely summarise here.

Figure 7
We still use Pragmatic Design in such structures as the Munich Olympic Stadium. A great many developments in suspension structures and inflatables have taken place by trial and error, either full size or at model scale

1. Pragmatic design—in which materials are used, by trial-and-error, until a form emerges which seems to serve the designer's purpose. Most forms of building seem to have started in this way—the mammoth hunter's tent is a splendid example, and we still tend to use this mode of designing whenever we have to use new materials, as in the case, say, of plastic air houses and suspension structures (Figure 7). It is only very recently, after two decades of pragmatic design, that theoretical bases for the design of such structures are beginning to emerge.

2. Typologic design—in which the members of a particular culture share a fixed mental image of what the design should be 'like'. Often encouraged in 'primitive' cultures by legend, tradition, work-songs which describe the design process (see Alexander 1964), by the mutual adaptation which has taken place between way of life and building form—as with the Eskimo's igloo or the Indian tepee (Figure 8)—and by the conventions of craftsmanship which take a long time to learn but, once learned, are difficult to abandon. We still set up 'types'—such as Bunshaft's Lever House in New York (1952) which become the fixed mental image for a generation of architects and clients as to what office buildings should be like (Figure 9).

3. Analogical design—the drawing of analogies (usually visual) into the solution of one's design problems. This

seems to have started with Imhotep (c. 2,800 BC) in designing the Step Pyramid complex at Sakkara (Figure 10); given
the problem of building, for the first time, in large blocks
of stone, he drew visual analogies with existing brick
tomb-forms, timber-framed and reed-mat houses, for the
overall building forms, with lotus buds or flowers and
snakes' heads for the decoration, and so on. The prototypes of Greek Doric architecture also were to be found

Figure 8 (left)
Typologic Design—Primitive and vernacular forms survived in many parts of the world on the repetition of a known type, as with the Indian tepee shown in this painting by George Catlin

Figure 9 (right)
We still use Typologic Design; Gordon Bunshaft's Lever House in New York became *the* type for city centre office buildings in the 1950s and 1960s. In many cases clients insisted that their architects built in this way to match their mental image of what a smart, new office building ought to be like

Figure 10 (left)
Analogic Design—a great deal of creative design has consisted of drawing visual or other analogies into one's design problem. The step pyramid complex at Sakkara (2,800 B.C.) is the first large-scale architectural construction in stone and the form of the temple in the foreground was derived by carving onto solid stone the posts, lintels, roof form and other features of existing buildings made from light timbers or reed bundles. The complex as a whole contains some twenty visual analogies of this kind

Figure 11a, b
Frank Lloyd Wright described at
the opening service the way he had
derived the roof form of this
church at Madison, Wisconsin from
the shape of his own hands at
prayer

in timber structures with their forms translated into stone.
There may well have been symbolic reasons for this, and
we still tend to print, say, plastic facing materials with the
textures of timber or woven fabrics. Analogy also seems
to be the mechanism of 'creative' architecture, as with
Wright's use of water-lily forms in the Johnson Wax fac-

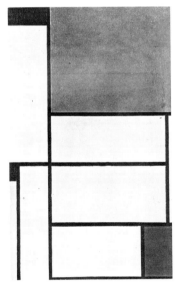

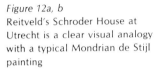

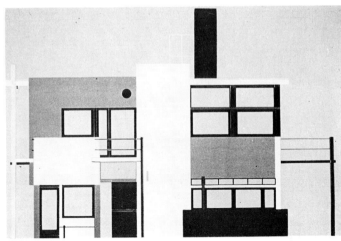

Figure 12a, b
Reitveld's Schroder House at Utrecht is a clear visual analogy with a typical Mondrian de Stijl painting

tory office (1936), his own hands at prayer in the Madison, Wisconsin, Chapel (1950) (Figure 11, (a), (b)) not to mention Le Corbusier's crab-shell roof at Ronchamp. These are direct analogies (see Gordon, 1961). Much 20th century architecture has drawn on painting and sculpture as sources of analogies (Constructivism, Purism, de Stijl, (Figure 12, (a), (b)); but analogies can also be drawn with one's body (personal analogy) and with abstract philosophical concepts (as in the present preoccupation with indeterminacy).

Analogical design requires the use of some medium such as a drawing, for translating the original into its new form. The first Egyptian design drawings date from the same period as Imhotep's pyramid complex and the drawing itself begins to suggest possibilities to the designer. He sets up grids and/or axes to make sure that his drawing will fit on to the available surface; these 'suggest' regularities—symmetries and rhythms—which had not appeared previously in architecture. Any design *analogue*—a drawing, model, or even a computer program, will 'take over' from the designer and influence the way he designs.

4. Canonic (Geometric) design; the grids and axes of these early design drawings took on a life of their own. It became clear that the second-rate artists could emulate the work of a master by abstracting from it the underlying systems of proportion. Once this view had been formed—that art and design could be underpinned by abstract proportional systems—it received a massive boost from the Greek geometers (Pythagoras) and Classical philosophers (Plato, etc.) who believed that the

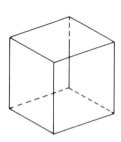

THE CUBE
formed of 6 squares
(24 isosceles triangles)
representing the
element EARTH

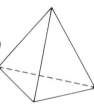

THE TETRAHEDRON
formed of 4 equilateral
triangles representing the
element FIRE

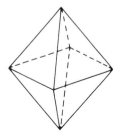

THE OCTAHEDRON
formed of 8
equilateral triangles
representing the
element AIR

THE ICOSAHEDRON
formed of 20
equilateral triangles
representing the element
WATER

Figure 13a, b
Syntactic (Geometric)
Design—Plato believed the entire
universe was constructed from
earth, fire, air and water and that
these in their turn were constructed
from cubes, tetrahedra, octahedra
and icosahedra which themselves
could be made from
triangles—isoceles triangles in the
case of the cube, equilateral
triangles in the case of the three
other figures

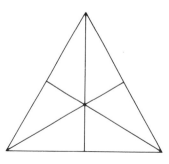

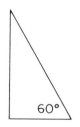

Plato's tetrahedron, octahedron
and dodecahedron are formed
from equilateral triangles. The
60° angle of medieval ad
triangulorum proportion derives
from these.

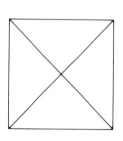

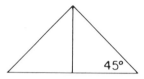

Plato's cube is formed from
isoceles triangles. The 45°
angle of medieval ad
quadratum proportion derives
from these.

LIBER   PRIMVS

Figure 14
The whole of the Medieval Gothic cathedral design was permeated by Plato's system of triangles as Cesaraiono's diagram of Milan Cathedral shows

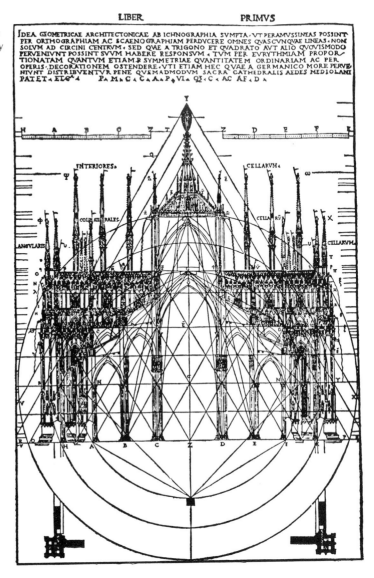

universe itself was constructed of cubes, tetrahedra, octahedra and icosahedra, and that these in turn were made up of triangles (Figures 13(a)(b)). The Platonic triangles underlay medieval Gothic design (Frankl, 1945) (Figure 14). Much 20th century design has been based on similar precepts; they are the basis of all modular systems, dimensional co-ordination, prefabricated system building and so on. New mathematical techniques are likely to boost even further this interest in the abstract *Geometry of Environment*. (See March and Steadman 1971.)

Those four modes of designing: pragmatic, iconic, analogical and canonic, either separately or in combination, seem to underlie all the ways in which architectural form has been, or

Figure 15
Ribart's design for a Palace in Paris
is a clear visual analogy for an
elephant—a grotesque idea which
would make a most inconvenient
palace. That is the difference
between Ribart's analogy and
Frank Lloyd Wright's; Wright's
hands (Figure 11) at prayer make a
rather good roof, easy to construct
with slender timber sections and
rather good also for the rain and
snow of Wisconsin

can be generated. Of the four, iconic and analogic design
seem to be of particular importance to the *meaning* of architecture. Iconic design clearly enshrines a set of values
which will be understood by every member of the culture or
sub-culture for which it is built; i.e. the members of a particular tribe, the architectural profession as distinct from the
general public, a particular fraternity of architects and
critics within that profession, whilst the analogies one uses in
generating form clearly are fraught with meaning.

Yet these also present certain difficulties. Wright's hands
in prayer have obvious symbolic value in the design of a
chapel—yet how many people at the inaugural service
would have 'read' this into the building's form if Wright had
not told them to do so? Few of us on seeing Ribart's Elephant
(Figure 15) can really take it seriously. This palace, complete
with grand staircases, fountains, cascades, a ballroom (top

Figure 16a, b
Eiffel's Tower at the entrance to New York Harbour is no less exciting as an engineering structure than his rather larger tower in Paris, but the symbolisation of Liberty by visual analogy with a female figure clad in copper sheets is almost as ludicrous as Ribart's elephant

left) and an internal garden—all contained within this direct analogy—strikes us as faintly ludicrous, not to say grotesque.

Yet the Statue of Liberty, in many ways, is just as ludicrous—a tower by Eiffel (1883) no less exciting as a piece of engineering structure than his other tower in Paris. It is clad in its copper sheets to make it *look* like a woman, with tourists peering down from her coronet and itching to climb into her torch (Figure 16).

But for many Americans still she *symbolises* Liberty; they have learned to associate that concept with her form, much in the way that Skinner thinks we learn to associate particular words with specific concepts.

Application

In conclusion, I want to present a series of annotated images showing the application of analogies—fraught with meaning—to a design. My first example is the Faculty Club at Santa Barbara, California, by Moore and Turnbull (1968) (Figure 17), which is the kind of complex and ambiguous architecture which Venturi describes so well (1966) but—in my view—designs rather less successfully. Whereas to 'read' Venturi's design one needs a thorough knowledge of classical architecture—in its Beaux Arts iconology—to understand just what rules he is deliberately breaking, Moore and Turnbull draw on visual analogies familiar to all users of their building from the environment into which it is built. As Moore says (1969): 'Santa Barbara is a resort city on the Southern California coast which owes its considerable charm equally to a magnificent site and to a building idiom which has been consistently employed over the past 40 years; a white, stuccoed Spanish supercolonial of simultaneous simplicity and flamboyant verve.'

Similar attempts to build meaning into their architecture have been made by the Taller de Arquitectura in Barcelona which was set up in the mid 1960's by Ricardo Bofill. (See Broadbent 1973b, 1975a and 1975b.) Their first buildings were of small white painted International Style holiday houses at Calpe on the Spanish Mediterranean coast (Figure 27) but they were not satisfied with these and their next development on the same site—which is now called La Manzanera—was an attempt to give people a much stronger sense of identity, a sense of place. They took the line which so many others have taken since (see, for instance, the January 1976 preview issue of the *Architectural Review*)—they reproduced the flavour of the local vernacular still with white painted walls but with pantiled ridge and lean-to roofs. They added certain features to this; decorative shutters and swooping Gaudí-esque walls to tie

Figure 17
The Faculty Club at Santa Barbara
by Moore and Turnbull (1962) is a
fascinating exercise in visual
analogy. They draw on the conventions of Spanish Colonial—the
white stuccoed courtyard house
with a pantiled roof—to generate
the overall form of their club. But
the courtyard contains a swimming
pool and is surrounded by changing
rooms, squash courts, and so on

Figure 18
William Randolph Hearst, the
original Citizen Kane, also drew on
this vernacular at San Simeon, his
castle museum 100 miles from
Santa Barbara which, among other
things, has a repository for the
thousands of works of art—
paintings, sculptures, well heads,
whole rooms, which he looted from
all over Europe

Figure 19
Given the basic courtyard analogy, Moore and Turnbull seem to have planned their building along the route one takes on going into it from reception (top left), along a first-floor deck to the entry, across an elaborate series of bridges and stairs down into the three-storey dining room (top right). Parts of this plan are organized *canonically*, e.g. the basically symmetrical courtyard with its fountain, not to mention the highly complex geometry of the dining room itself, the guest rooms, meeting rooms and so on

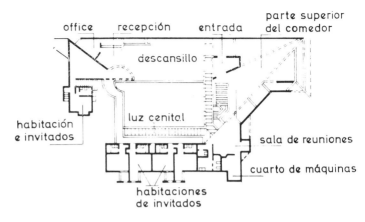

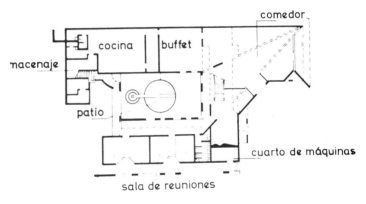

FIRST FLOOR

GROUND FLOOR

Figure 20
The forms as one crosses the first floor deck present clear analogies with cubic, white walled international style, or even art-decor, another Santa Barbara convention

Figure 21
The first thing one sees, at the entry, is this visual cue that one is indeed in a *club*

Figure 22
The baronial hall at San Simeon with its serried ranks of banners

Figure 23
The dining room at Santa Barbara
which also has its banners both
corduroy—halfway up the
wall—and neon, which clearly
bring in connotations of Las Vegas,
although as Tom Wolfe says (1969)
these are rather feeble

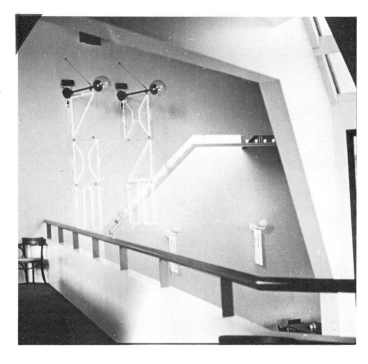

Figure 24
The buffet off the dining room—an
actual Spanish Renaissance room,
taken from San Simeon

Figure 25
Portraits—to remind one, once again, that this is a *club*. But these are local pop heroes

Figure 26
The locker room—another essential concomitant of the American club but with connotations this time of packaging

Figure 27
Ricardo Bofill and the Taller de Arquitectura of Barcelona decided in the early 1960s that they would break away from the 'cemetery suburbs' of typical International style mass housing. yet their first buildings were small, white painted holiday houses at Calpe on the Spanish Mediterranean coast

Figure 28
In their first attempts at giving their architecture a stronger sense of identity, a human scale and a sense of place they took the line which so many others have taken since of drawing visual analogies with the local vernacular. These villas also at Calpe have the pitched pantiled roofs and other features of the local vernacular, but with decorative shutters and swooping Gaudiesque walls which tie them into the site in an interesting combination of the familiar with the new

Figure 29a, b
This strange Pagoda-like building Xanadu consists of holiday apartments each square in plan which could have been clustered together in many ways, such as an inverted pyramid rather like Boston City Hall. Instead of that the Taller looked across at the Penon de Ifach in the distance and derived the silhouette by building up visual analogy with it. They also took the local vernacular roof forms and then painted the exterior of it that brownish green to which the Spanish countryside burns at the height of the summer. These three visual analogies root this building at a specific place on the earth's surface which is why it looks so strange out of context

the houses to the site so that whole thing is an interesting combination of the familiar and the new (Figure 28).

Their next building on this same site, Xanadu, combines this approach with a way of developing house forms which has become basic to the Taller's methodology. Briefly, this consists of taking individual activities, cooking, eating, sleeping and so on, and designing the 3-dimensional space needed for these by one, two, three or more people. Over the years they have developed an extraordinary vocabulary of activity spaces which can be clustered together in an infinity of ways to provide actual dwelling forms. In the early stages, they tended to deal with these as 2-dimensional geometry so that once dwelling forms had been achieved they could be clustered together in a variety of ways. Four of the basic Xanadu dwellings could be clustered in the form of a square or alternatively in the form of a cross. Eight could also be clustered to form a double armed cross. Once these had been worked out in detail they could be stacked vertically, but, given a basic frame structure, there were no particular reasons as to why they should be sandwiched together in any particular order. So the Taller looked across Calpe Bay at the Penon de Ifach, a Gibraltar-like rock, and drew a massive visual analogy with it for the form of Xanadu. They then repeated the vernacular-like forms of El Castillo for the roofs and windows and painted the whole lot in that brownish-green to which the countryside burns at the height of the summer. Here, then, is a building designed for a specific place on the earth's surface which grows right out of the landscape there, but would look thoroughly out of place anywhere else (Figure 29).

This extraordinary combination of geometrical manipulation to achieve individual dwelling form, and visual analogy to give overall building shape, has recurred many times since, in the Taller's work. Barrio Gaudí at Reus for instance, some of the lowest cost housing to be built anywhere in Europe during the 1960's, was developed in exactly this way to produce the grain and texture of the ancient parts of the city and covered with pantiled roofs, because to those who were going to move in, these, more than anything, represented the concept of 'home' (Figure 30).

The clustering processes which have been developed by the Taller, of course, encourage a certain complexity of building form which extends not just to the exterior but also to the interior courtyards. In the case of Los Tres Coronas at Sitges these become high, narrow, intricate spaces which possess an almost cathedral-like aspect (Figure 31). That is true also of the internal courtyards at Walden 7, a massive apartment block on the outskirts of Barcelona (Figure 32), and finally it has emerged in the exterior of their design for a complex of housing, shops, offices, schools, a supermarket

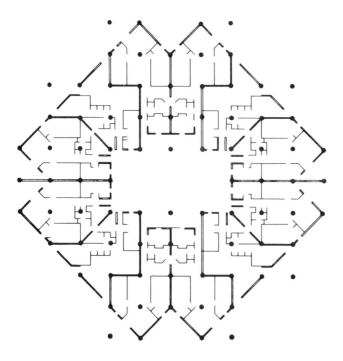

Figure 30a, b
The Barrio Gaudí represents a
much more complex exercise in the
clustering of apartments, but here
too, roof forms etc., were derived
from the local vernacular, thus providing the most potent possible
symbol for 'home'

Figure 31a, b
Kafka's Castle (Los Tres Coronas) at Sitges is a further example of clustering apartments together. In this case they are grouped in spiral formations against vertical service towers containing lifts, staircases and services. The spaces between these towers and apartments are high, narrow and intricate, thus possessing an almost cathedral-like quality

Figure 32a, b
Walden 7—This large complex of
apartments at San Justo d'Esvern
outside Barcelona also was planned around internal courtyards, intended for music, dancing and
other indoor activities

and so on, at Cergy Pontoise, a new town outside Paris
(Figure 33). From Barcelona, the climate of Northern France
looks comparatively hostile so that the Taller's first instinct
was to group this whole building around a vast covered shopping mall, like the great Galleria in Milan. But gradually the
cathedral imagery began to take over, partly for the reasons
I have described and partly because for 600 years the chief
architectural glory of Northern France, of course, has been
its great Gothic Cathedrals. Unfortunately, the original
grandeur of this particular conception, was compromised to
take the form of three Walden 7-like blocks linked by open
square cloisters and finally it was abandoned altogether.

It can be argued, in fact it has been, that the deliberate
building of meaning on this scale represents a megalomaniac
indulgence on the part of the architects, that responsible
designers simply do not behave in this way. That is hardly the
point. They are designing for cultures where high rise, high
density, have become a way of life; asked if they would do
the same for Britain their reply was no. They would look at
the dwelling forms which the British enjoy such as the
Garden suburb and rework this for the last third of the 20th
century. But there is more to it than that. An earlier generation of architects such as Mies had pursued the search for architectural abstraction to such an illogical extreme that their
buildings finally became quite uninhabitable by real people

Figure 33
The ultimate in clustering apartments around an interior space was
to have been La Petite Cathédrale
at Cergy Pontoise outside Paris.
The Taller conceived this as a vast
shopping mall like a great Galleria
Vittorio Emanuelle in Milan with
apartments arching over the top.
They then decided that to give it a
real sense of place they should
build in visual analogies with the
great French Gothic cathedrals.
Eventually the concept was eroded
away into three Walden 7-like
blocks linked by open cloisters and
finally it was abandoned altogether

Figure 34
La Maison d'Abraxas for Fort St Cyr outside Paris is to be a typical Taller apartment block but with these huge sculptural objects in the courtyards. They are meant to symbolise 'the fundamental transitions in man's life from the nothingness before birth, through life, "life a breath of air", to the nothingness after death'

with real sensory needs. So in reaction to that pursuit of perfection, abstract society now demands that buildings shall have interest, intricacy, and a sense of place again. To make this point, therefore, it is necessary that a few pioneers will carry this search for meaning to an extreme so as to demonstrate what they are trying to do with absolute clarity. In one recent project, the Maison d'Abraxas (House of Magic) at Fort St Cyr outside Paris, they actually will try to symbolise the fundamental transitions in man's life from the nothingness before birth, through life 'life a breath of air', to the nothingness after death by means of vast sculptural devices within the inevitable courtyards; such as a sphere to symbolise the harmony that is only possible in dreams, a cube to symbolise that flight towards reason by which man tries to protect himself from the hostile world, a great staircase which symbolises his ascent towards perfection but does not actually get anywhere, and the window, open to the Cosmos, symbolising his yearning for contact with nature to which he constantly aspires but which he always finds hostile when he achieves it (Figure 34). As I have noted elsewhere, (1975):

> Fantasy? Of course, and why not? The apartments themselves are very well planned, economical, flexible, and truly functional. The sphere, cube, staircase, and window are unnecessary; they will make the project more expensive than it would otherwise have been. In

that respect they fall into the same category as those steel, aluminium, or in the case of Seagram, bronze, I sections clipped to the exterior of the typical 'functional' mode for no other purpose than to give it vertical emphasis. (Figure 35)

Figure 35
Contrast this with the bronze I-sections which Mies clipped to the facades of the Seagram Building. These serve no useful purpose, they are simply meant to 'symbolise' structure. The building itself is held up by a completely separate steel frame clad in concrete and Mies's I-sections are not even broad enough to protect the windows from the sun

Moore, the Venturis, the Taller and others represented the beginning of what promises to be a rising tide of architecture which undoubtedly will engulf that bleak, sterile and hostile kind which has been in the ascendant for the past 50 years. They recognise that whatever the designers' intentions, buildings do act as cultural symbols and they attempt therefore, to build symbols deliberately, which can be read with enjoyment by those who use them. This is only the beginning, but they have already demonstrated it to us beyond reasonable doubt that meaning can be built consciously into architecture.

Gebhart (1969) detects further visual analogies in the design of the Faculty Club but the essential point in each case is that members of the club understand their meaning immediately because they are drawn largely from the environment into which the club is built, or based on conventions which are familiar to everyone who could become a club member.

So having satisfied the deeper structures of architecture

by designing a building to contain human activities, modify the rather splendid climate of the California coast and change the value of the land on which it stands, Moore and Turnbull satisfied the remaining condition—that the building should act as a cultural symbol—by intentionally building in a cultural reference which the users could read. It may be, finally, that this is the only way in which one can consciously build meaning into architecture.

Appendix
Markov's Algorithm for
Multiplying Two Numbers

Markov first sets up an *alphabet*, consisting of the letters, I, *
and +, such that his initial problem (multiply 4 × 3) is written IIII * III. He then writes a set of rules for operating his
algorithm: each *step* consists of rewriting the given sentence
according to the first rule in Markov's list which can actually
be applied to it.

1. If an asterisk occurs in a word more than once, it is
   reproduced without change.

2. If an asterisk occurs in a word exactly once and is preceded by at least one occurrence of a line then instead of
   the first occurrence of the line one substitutes a +.

3. If an asterisk occurs in a word exactly once and is not
   preceded by any lines, but lines occur following the
   asterisk, then the line occurring first is replaced by the left
   delimiter of the asterisk.

4. If an asterisk occurs in a word exactly once and no lines
   occur, the first letter of the word is struck out.

5. If the asterisk does not occur in a word but the plus sign
   does, then the first occurrence of the plus sign is replaced
   by a line.

6. If neither asterisk nor plus sign occurs in a word, then a
   step is impossible.

Only one of these rules may be applied at a time, so starting with the given word one applies the appropriate rule,
and performs successive steps until one reaches a word to
which none of the rules apply. Then one stops.

Word:	Application of appropriate rule:
I I I I * I I I	2
+ I I I * I I I	2
+ + I I * I I I	2
+ + + I * I I I	2
+ + + + * I I I	3
+ + + + * + + + I I	3
+ + + + * + + + + + + I	3
+ + + + * + + + + + + + + +	4
+ + + * + + + + + + + + + + +	4
+ + * + + + + + + + + + + + +	4
+ * + + + + + + + + + + + +	4
* + + + + + + + + + + + +	4
+ + + + + + + + + + + +	5
I + + + + + + + + + + +	5
I I + + + + + + + + + +	5
I I I + + + + + + + + +	5
I I I I + + + + + + + +	5
I I I I I + + + + + + +	5
I I I I I I + + + + + +	5
I I I I I I I + + + + +	5
I I I I I I I I + + + +	5
I I I I I I I I I + + +	5
I I I I I I I I I I + +	5
I I I I I I I I I I I +	5
I I I I I I I I I I I I	6

Bibliography

Alexander, C. (1964). *Notes on the Synthesis of Form*, Cambridge, Mass., Harvard UP.

Broadbent, G. (1966a). Creativity, in Gregory, S. A. (ed.), *The Design Method*, London, Butterworth.

Broadbent, G. (1966b). Design Methods in Architecture, in *Architects' Journal*, 14 September, 1966.

Broadbent, G. (1966c). The Psychological Background to Design, in *Conference on Design Methods; the Teaching of Design*, ULM, April 1966, London, Ministry of Education.

Broadbent, G. (1968a). A Plain Man's Guide to Systematic Design Methods, in *RIBA Journal*, May 1968.

Broadbent, G. (1968b). Portsmouth Symposium on Design Methods, in *Arena/Interbuild*, February 1968.

Broadbent, G. (1969a). Design Method in Architecture, in Broadbent, G. and Ward, A., 1969.

Broadbent, G. (1969b). Informe Sobre el Simposio de Metodos de Diseno, Portsmouth, in Bonta, J. P. (ed.), *El Simposio de Portsmouth*, Buenos Aires, EUDIBA.

Broadbent, G. (1969c). Meaning into Architecture, in Jencks, C. and Baird, G. (eds), *Meaning in Architecture*, London, Barrie and Rockliff.

Broadbent, G. (1969d). El Proceso de Diseno, in *La Creatividad en el Diseno Arquitectonico y otros Ensayos*, Cordoba, Argentina, Universidad Nacional.

Broadbent, G. (1973a). *Design in Architecture*, London, Wiley.

Broadbent, G. (1973b). The Taller of Bofill, in *Architectural Review*, November 1973.

Broadbent, G. (1975a). Bofill Taller de Arquitectura, in *Architectural Design*, XLV, July 1975.

Broadbent, G. (1975b). The Road to Xanadu and Beyond, in *Progressive Architecture*, September 1975.

Broadbent, G. and Ward, A. (eds) (1969). *Design Methods in Architecture*, Architectural Association Paper No. 4, London, Lund Humphries for the Architectural Association.

Chomsky, N. (1957). *Syntactic Structures*, The Hague, Mouton.

Chomsky, N. (1959). Review of B. F. Skinner: *Verbal Behaviour*, in *Language*, 35, January — March 1959.

Chomsky, N. (1965). *Aspects of the Theory of Syntax*, Cambridge, Mass. MIT.

Cole, S. (1962). A Spanish Camp of Stone Age Elephant Hunters, in *New Scientist*, 18 October 1962.

Collins, P. (1971). *Architectural Judgement*, London, Faber.

de Lumley, H. (1969). A Palaeolithic Camp Site in *Scientific American*, May 1969.

de Zurko, E. R. (1957). *Origins of Functionalist Theory*, New York, Columbia UP.

Fillimore, C. Quoted in Crystal, D.S., 1971 *Linguistics*, Harmondsworth, Penguin.

Fletcher, R. (1957). *Instinct in Man*, London, Unwin.

Forde, C. D. (1934). *Habitat, Economy and Society*, London, Methuen.

Frankl, P. (1945). Secrets of the Mediaeval Masons, in *Art Bulletin*, XXVII, March 1945.

Gebhart, D. (1969). Pop Scene for the Profs, in *Architectural Forum*, March 1969.

Gill, R. (1969). A Tentative Taxonomy of Design Decision Techniques, in *Computer-aided Architectural Design*, Ministry of Public Buildings and Works, Research and Development Paper, London, HMSO.

Gordon, W. J. J. (1961). *Synectics — the Development of Creative Capacity*, New York, Harper.

Gropius, W. (1910). Programme for the establishment of a company for the provision of housing on aesthetically consistent principles (Memo to AEG), in *Architectural Review*, July 1961.

Gropius, W. (1936). *The New Architecture and the Bauhaus*, London, Faber.

Gropius, W. (1956). *The Scope of Total Architecture*, London, Allen and Unwin.

Hillier, W., Musgrove, J. E. and O'Sullivan, P. (1972). Knowledge and Design, in *EDRA3* (ed. Mitchell). New York, Dowden, Hutchinson and Ross.

Johnson, P. (1953). *Mies van der Rohe*, New York, Museum of Modern Art.

Leakey, L. S. B. (1954). Olduvai Gorge, in *Scientific American*, January 1954.

Le Corbusier (1923). *Vers une architecture*, Paris, Editions Cres.

March, L. and Steadman, P. (1971). *The Geometry of Environment*, London, RIBA.

Markov, A. A. (1954). *The Theory of Algorithms* (trans. J. J. Schorr-Kon, 1962), Jerusalem, Israel Programme for Scientific Translations.

Mies van der Rohe, L. (1923). Bürohaus, in 9 (Berlin), June 1923. In Johnson, 1953.

Mies van der Rohe, L. (1924). Industrialles Baven, in 9 (Berlin), no. 3. In Johnson, 1953.

Mongait, A. L. (1955). *Archaeology in the U.S.S.R.* (trans. M. W. Thompson, 1961), Harmondsworth, Penguin.

Moore, C. W. (1969). Quoted in Gebhart, 1969.

Morris, C. W. (1938). Foundations of the Theory of Signs, in Neurath, D., Carnap, R. and Morris, C. W. (eds), *International Encyclopeadia of Unified Science*, Chicago, Chicago UP.

Morris, C. W. (1946). *Signs, Language and Behaviour*, New Jersey, Prentice-Hall.

Morris, C. W. (1964). *Signification and Significance*, Cambridge, Mass., MIT.

Negroponte, N. (1969). Architecture Machine, in *Architectural Design*, XXXIX, September 1969.

Onions, C. T. (1904). *An Advanced English Syntax*, London.

Pevsner, N. (1936). *Pioneers of the Modern Movement*, London, Faber; reprinted as *Pioneers of Modern Design*, Harmondsworth, Penguin, 1960, 1964.

Pevsner, N. (1967). Architecture of our Time: The Anti-Pioneers, in *Listener*, 5 January 1967.

Pfeiffer, J. E. (1970). *The Emergence of Man*. London, Nelson.

Rapoport, A. (1969). *House Form and Culture*, Englewood Cliffs: Prentice-Hall.

Saussure, F. de (1916). *Cours de linguistique générale*, trans. W. Baskin, 1960, London, Peter Owen.

Skinner, B. F. (1957). *Verbal Behaviour*, New York, Appleton, Century, Crofts.

Solecki, R. S. (1957). Shanidar Cave, in *Scientific American*, November 1957.

Steiner, G. (1959). The Hollow Miracle, in *Language and Silence*, 1967, London, Faber.

Ucko, P. J. and Rosenfield, A. (1967). *Palaeolithic Cave Art*, London, Weidenfeld and Nicolson.

Venturi, R. (1966). *Complexity and Contradiction in Architecture*, New York, Museum of Modern Art.

Watson, J. B. (1924). *Behaviourism* (1958 edition consulted), Chicago, Chicago UP.

Weber, H. (1961). *Walter Gropius und das Faguswerk*, Munich, Gallwey.

Wolfe, T. (1969). Electrographic Architecture, in *Architectural Design*, July 1969.

Wright, D. (1969). Sex: Instinct or Appetite?, in *New Society*, 22 May 1969.

1.4 The Sociology of Semiology

Xavier Rubert de Ventos

This is a revised and edited version of Part Two of *Utopias de la Sensuidad y Methodos del Sentido*. Barcelona, Anagrama.

Abstract

This paper contains, in the first place, a summarized description and a sociological analysis of two attitudes which are nowadays usual in the study of signs. This presentation is followed by a hypothesis about the social and psychological background to which the current inflation of sciences related to information, communication, signs, and signifiers correspond. It ends with the consideration of the signifiers, not only as indicators, but also as provocators of what they signify—which I call semiology-action.

1 Introduction

Two preliminary remarks.

First, in speaking about semiology in Spain there is little innovation and even less arbitrariness. Spain is, we should remember, a deeply semiological country, at least at a consumer level.

The romantics, who, as the first tourists to visit us, invented Spain, consumed us as a sign. We were the 'sign' of everything that the emerging capitalist society, based on normalization, rational exploitation, and foresight, could no longer permit itself. The sign of adventure, passion, danger, and exoticism.

But, if they consumed us—and they still do—as signs of 'nature', we have nowadays begun to consume their signs as 'culture'. As Aranguren observed, we live too far removed politically, scientifically, and culturally from where 'things' happen to be able to participate in them, but also too close to be able to ignore them and permit our reality to produce its own independent superstructures. Thus, we do not know what the 'things that happen' *are*, but we are perfectly aware of what they *mean*. We know what cybernetics, ecology, or counter-culture mean. We even know whether they are reactionary or progressive, and whether they are still valid or already surpassed. What we hardly ever know is what they are. We do not have the opportunity to touch them or practise them; only that of consuming the news of their birth and death. We *live*, as the football fans do with their teams, the birth and overcoming of cultural myths; what is certain, however, is that we cannot get our hands on the ball.

As you may thus see, Spain is, actively or passively, a deeply semiological country: a country in which semiology appears in a 'practical state', precisely because we do not practise the effective contents to which these cultural formations correspond.

Second, to construct a 'sociology of semiology' may seem, in a certain respect, perverse since semiological analysis, at least in one of the two aspects we will discuss, is characterized precisely by the rejection of a sociological perspective. We are thus going to apply a sociological approach to a method that defines itself, among other things, by the rejection of such a point of view.

We should remember, however, that a similar perversion is responsible for the most suggestive of the so-called structuralist methods. And since the cleverness of the structuralists was to analyse historical phenomena from a systematic and ahistorical perspective, we can give them a taste of their own medicine by sociologically studying their own approach. I have argued somewhere else that to construct a sociology of sociological theories is not a redundant activity. I hope I will show now that to fashion a sociology of anti-sociological theories is not a gratuitous perversion either.

Having made those points clear, now, before doing a sociological analysis, I must describe the core of the methodological utopia in question.

1. From a *formal* point of view, structuralism is a method that insists upon the *immanent, systematic, classificatory* aspects of its subject-matter. It does not authorize us to leave the study of the relations within a given level, except for the purpose of penetrating in search of the *code*, of which these relations are an actualization. And this is precisely that which distinguishes this approach from the classical positivist one. One has not to take the *phenomena* one is studying — religion, suicide rates, or

marriage systems — as *things* but as *words*, that is, as the result of a language or basic code, of which these things are products; the language *from which* we speak, the unconscious *from which* we think, the system of kinship *from which* we marry one another. As in linguistics, one has to aim towards the codes we use without expressly thinking about them. The structuralist will then attempt to describe and discover these codes, and, if possible, formalize them by means of a model. The discussion as to whether these 'deep rules' which the structuralist intends to reproduce are ontological realities or simple methodological instruments, may have given philosophers entertainment, an occasion to declare themselves more or less metaphysical or operational, but it is irrelevant in our context.

2. From a *material* point of view, this systematic attitude does not apply to systems of *objects* — such as systems for building, political systems, etc. — worked out in the Enlightenment in the eighteenth century, but to systems of *signifiers*.

Thus, we could provisionally define our method as: *an immanent and systematic study of the signifiers in the search for their code.*

Because of their different sociological significance, I shall analyse these two aspects separately; (a) the *formal* character of the plan that defines what has come to be called structuralism, and (b) the *semic* character of its object of study, to which the specifically semiological studies refer.

2 The Chaste Study of the Signifiers

To summarize the culturalist European trend of structuralism, I am going to coin two new terms — 'positionalism' and 'espeleologism' — whose first virtue, it must be said, is not elegance.

Positionalism   'It's the position that decides the victory', wrote Jean Paul, 'whether we consider battles or phrases'. The meaning of something lies, above all, in the position it occupies within the system where it is found. Faced with a rite, a form of interchange, an architectural form, a myth, a belief, a menu, what the researcher should *not* do is to attempt a sociological-functionalist interpretation of its meaning (i.e. deer-hunting has become ritualized because it concerns a scarce animal, vital for the survival of the group. . .), nor should he give us an explanation of the phenomenon's supposed historical origin (e.g. it is a degeneration of the cult of the god of fertility. . .). What he *should* do, instead, is to make a general outline of the system (of beliefs, foods, etc.), where this particular formation is inserted and of which it is one of the possibilities. The deer cult should be studied, for example, in a systematic relation to the cult of the jaguar and in symmetrical opposition to the corn (maize)/peyote pair in the Huicholes ritual. Raw food should be studied in relation to the 'system' it forms together with cooked, boiled, fried, smoked, rotten, etc., food.

In this way, taking a witch-doctor from a primitive society (or an everyday doctor), I can immediately interpret what his role and social function are, but I would certainly be mistaken if, as Bourdieu pointed out, I did not place him between the prophet and the priest and study him in relation to them. The *Prophet* as a bearer of new subversive charismatic messages; the *Priest* as the natural enemy of the prophet, conserver of the established spiritual order; the *Witch-doctor* as an ally of the first one whose 'signs' he interprets. And, what is more, this system of relation-oppositions, inasmuch as it is 'structural', is transportable and can give an account of the system which, in the restricted world of the arts and culture, the *Artist* (prophet), the *Professor* (priest) as conserver of the 'established culture', and the *Avant-garde critic* (witch-doctor) maintain nowadays.

Whether we speak, then, about the witch-doctor, about the critic, or about the rite of deer-hunting, to try to interpret correctly their function means to discover their position in a system. The first lesson we can get out of this is that signifiers cannot be taken and interpreted separately, but only have meaning from and within a system.

In architecture, design, or urbanism, it is easy to find examples of this necessity for a systematic study. Not long ago, R. Barthes insisted that the concept and function of what we call periphery or *suburb* should be understood in relation to its opposition with the *centre*, with the famous 'heart of the city'. So, apart from its opposition at the level of social classes, it is evident that the periphery is the place for individuality, intimacy, the home; the centre is that for management, movement, anonymity. At the time of the emergence of cities, the Germans said that *Die Staadtluft macht frei*—the air of the city makes free. This is a well-known truth for the inhabitants of small villages, who find in the city a paradise of liberty which can only exist on the basis of a loss of individual identity.

Espeleologism.   A family isolated and without friends inevitably reinforces its internal ties (whether these are positive or negative is another question). If, faced with a significant piece of information, I stop myself, for methodological reasons, from studying its external aspects (*historical*: where does it come from; *sociological*: what relation does it have with the social structure; *psychological*: with what intention is this information emitted), the only thing left for me to study will be the relationship of this piece of information to other pieces of the same family, and this study will simply direct my attention to the common root—the father, the code—where they all originate. Since it is not permitted for data or facts to walk, or swim, or fly, it is clear that the only recourse left to them is to become part of the search for the system of forms, beliefs, objects, etc., *from which* (or *out of which*) we behave, think, or speak.

In other words, it was inevitable that the rejection of historical-social-psychological approaches would point to the only non-obstructed way out: that of the codes or archaeological origins; that of the places where thinking or doing produce themselves. It can hardly be surprising, then, if we find a natural sympathy between late structuralist philosophers and Heidegger—the constant and fastidious searcher for the unsaid *in* what is said, for the unthought *in* what is thought.

It was for the same reason, on the other hand, that methodological inspiration was sought in *linguistics*. Linguistics, and especially syntactical and phonetical studies, made it possible to define a language according to a reduced number of relationships, and it is precisely that which is attempted now in other social phenomena. Grammar was, furthermore, along with logic, a theoretical body developed in order to *mention** and analyse that very same thing which we *use* in speaking: language itself. Linguistics thus offered a model to refer to the code, or message generator, without having to get out of the system itself.

It is precisely this possibility of speaking about a theme 'from within' which initiated the move to find the 'source' in linguistics. In linguistics it seemed possible to be faithful to the notorious 'principle of immanence'—a principle of methodological 'chastity' or 'continence'—which satisfied the profoundly puritanical aspirations of the so-called structuralists. And this is what those who criticized the 'extrapolation' of linguistic methods into their disciplines—psychology, theory of architecture, etc.—have failed to see. They did not understand that when calling for a formal linguistic—or mathematical—method, one is always hoping to be able to analyse one's own field without stepping out of it. On the other hand, critics of the 'linguistic extrapolation' themselves use equally 'imported' concepts—they speak about the 'function' of an institution or about social 'organism' as though these terms have become so normal as to be considered autochthonous products. More popish than the Pope, they still insist that architectural

*Translator's note: 'mention' here is used in the Wittgensteinian sense.

theory, for instance, should not draw on the concept of *function* (which is an organic or mathematical concept) or on that of *form* (which is an aesthetic concept) but on the very strictly architectural one of *type*. I imagine that, with the same kind of logic, a physicist would be able to say: 'The starting-point of physics must be internally physical, not mathematical. We must cement the foundations of our building from really autonomous bases.'

And you will observe that I am not, in the least, defending the 'structural method' or the use of linguistic models, but rather, criticizing the near-sightedness of those who had wished to consider themselves purer than the very method whose first axiom was the principle of chastity (purity).

2.1 Criticism of Sociologism, Historicism, and Intuitive Empiricism

The structuralist method thus opposes other methodologies that seek to understand things from external principles of intelligibility. Let us now look at three examples of such methodologies and the arguments which have been used against them.

1. From a sociologist's point of view, to understand a phenomenon means to understand the social context out of which it comes, and of which it is a product. The structuralists would not deny these facts, but would like to insist that the influence of this social context over the phenomenon is neither purely causal nor linear; that, in any case, its effects can only be understood from what we know about the system through which it operates. The knowledge or understanding of the social 'humus' of a phenomenon is not, in itself, a sufficient 'principle of intelligibility' of that phenomenon.

Let us choose a striking example. A punch has different effects according to the system of tissue to which it is applied: in the eye, the shock results in a haematoma (bruise); in the stomach, it becomes asphyxiation. The structure of the 'receptor' system — eye or stomach — changes the effect radically. It is not enough, then, to explain something by the fist that caused it; one has to pay attention to the systems which the punch effected.

And, in the same way, one could argue about any other external factor ('punch factor') by means of which a phenomenon wants to be explained. It is clear, for example, that the social transformations that took place during the Renaissance influenced painting, but they influenced it only insofar as they were assimilated by the *system* of painting; that is, transforming altar paintings into canvas paintings, working out (the) linear perspective in order to express an anthropocentric vision of the world in art, or discovering oil paint in order to express the little, domestic, everyday things of which the budding Dutch middle class was so proud. Of course, the social crisis of the sixteenth century influenced architecture, but only so far as to incite and transform the architectural language of the Renaissance. The 'unitarian' tendencies noticeable in political life may be observed in architecture through the use (and, obviously, abuse) that Michelangelo makes of the classic rules: using for the buildings in the Piazza del Capitolino Ionic columns on each floor and a Doric column linking the two levels. With this, the elementarism of Renaissance construction began to be substituted by the more global and unitarian concept of architecture we find in Sant' Andrea del Quirinale or Sant' Ivo alla Sapienza.

2. The criticism of *historicism* is not very different from this. It is not enough to appeal to the Counter-Reformation or to the Holy Alliance in order to explain the baroque style, just as it is not enough to refer to just one variable to explain a revolution or a historical 'take-off'. Even within the Marxist tradition, Althusser has had to acknowledge that the dependence of the political superstructure on the relationships of production is not so simple or linear.

Only by understanding the system as a whole is it possible to explain such phenomena as the surprising triumph of Marxist revolution, against all 'classical' prognostication, in such an industrially underdeveloped country as Russia. This was due, according to Althusser, to the coincidence of a series of factors (a capitalist economy based on the maximization of benefits—itself based upon a still agrarian, feudal structure— the oppressive effects of the two systems being added together; an intellectual class uprooted from the rest of society and vulnerable to modern ideas proceeding from Europe; an ecclesiastical class removed from its function of caring for spiritual health and social immobility in each parish, etc.) which made Russia the weakest 'link' within the capitalist countries. In the second place, the working together of this series of factors is not linear, either. Its efficiency has to be understood as 'metonymical causality'; that is to say, it does not affect, as L. Goldman has shown, any given superstructural formation alone, but the entire system jointly, thus requiring a new organization of that system.

And it is here that the structuralist approach performs its most spectacular pirouette in arguing that not only does history not explain the systematic historical phenomena, but that history itself needs to be understood—and is, in fact, always understood—as a system.[1] It is not only that history does not explain things, but that history itself is to be explained and justified from outside. Thus, we should think that there are *many* histories: *informative* histories that give us a lot of facts about kings or battles, and *comprehensive* histories, weaker in facts, but which convey to us the 'meaning', either real or supposed, of the American revolution or the dictatorship of Pisistrato.

And, what is more, when just barely forced towards one or another of the two extremes, history becomes something else. If we study historical events hour after hour, they will end up seeming to be *psychological* processes of the individuals who made decisions; if we study them by every 10 000 years, they will end up seeming like *geological* processes — movements of peoples, in effect, do not seem (nor are they) very different from movements of icebergs or the receding of the glaciers.

Max Weber, Joan Robinson, and Lévi-Strauss have explained the neolithic and bourgeois revolutions on the assumption that, *in order to understand a historical 'change', it is necessary to understand the structure of the situation from which it springs as a historic 'cut' or section.* According to the latter, in order to understand the two great 'jumps' that have happened in history — the neolithic revolution and the Industrial Revolution — one must analyse the synergy implying: (a) scientific knowledge, (b) technological progress, (c) ecological balance, (d) availability of labour, etc. The economist Joan Robinson tries in the same way to explain the bourgeois revolution as an incidence of factors (not independent but neither absolutely interdependent) such as: (a) industrial development, (b) capitalization, (c) instruments of political control, etc. But it was Max Weber who first explained how the development of capitalism had been possible only by the concurrence, at a given moment, of a series of factors, among them: (a) technological progress, (b) existence of 'free' labour, (c) modern State, (d) puritan ethic, (e) traffic security, (f) rational law, (g) rational accounting based on the use of arabic digits (numbers), etc. The appearance of arabic digits, e.g. 4, 5, 6, 7, 8, instead of the classical numbers IV, V, VI, VII, VIII, was a decisive factor in favouring the cost — benefit calculations that the new system demanded. (Try, for instance, to add DCCLXIX and DLCLCIIX.) To such a degree were these cyphers a new and useful instrument that the residual medieval gremia considered their use as 'unfair competition', prohibiting and severely punishing it.

And why not indulge in some 'past-fiction' making in the face of the current inflation of 'futurology'? One could give a tempting explanation of Columbus's discovery of America as the result of a happy conjunction of 'gastronomic', scientific, political, and religious factors:

(a) The *gastronomic* need to obtain spices — which were vital at a time when there were no other means of preserving food—made access to the Far East urgent, while migrations and political changes in the Near East blocked a route that the Crusades (essentially 'gastronomic' in themselves) had failed to clear.

(b) The development of *scientific* knowledge—Copernicus—allowed for the emergence of the idea that it was possible to reach the Far East the other way around the Earth.

(c) The *religious* and *political* ideology of the Catholic kings of Spain fostered a project which implied a response to the challenge of the Turkish Empire.

However this might be, it is only the interdependent and 'synergetic' arrangement of the factors which has explanatory force. Egyptian land-measuring would never have become geometry without the incidence of the Greek *theoria* that gave rise to speculative formulations of the Pythagorean type. Lacking the technologically appropriate instruments, the Alexandrians were not able to produce a true scientific revolution, in the sense of Kuhn, out of their knowledge of 'Copernican' astronomy. Because of the lack of labour, the knowledge of the wheel by the Aztecs—or of the steam engine by the Greeks—was only used in the construction of toys.

3. But this criticism of sociological profundities and historical transcendencies does not imply a defence of the immediate and perceptible world. The true reality of a code is not seen from the points of view of sociology or of history alone, but neither can you perceive it at first sight, as the defendants of the primacy of sensible intuition would like us to believe.

A clear example of this argument (without any connection whatsoever, for the rest, with the structuralist ideology) is that of the famous article by Alexander, *A City is not a Tree*. We are told, in it, that the determining factors of the grace, charm, and spirit of classical cities cannot be recovered in modern town planning either (a) by optimization studies of accessibility, visibility, and so on, or (b), as Jane Jacobs and many inspired urbanists would have us believe, by proposing cities that would have to be a mixture of Greenwich Village and Italian *piazza*, Calle Mayor and casbah.

No. What gave charms to those cities was not their rational structure nor their 'typism', which obviously is a product of our melancholic regarding of them. Those qualities must be discovered on the level of the 'profound structure' of a city. The elements of each stratum—residential zone, commercial zone, administrative zone—were not separated and related only through the intervention of a superior hierarchy as in our modern cities, but they were related among themselves and overlapped with the domains of a superior or inferior range in the hierarchy. Only by understanding the structure of the classical city as a formal system of relationships — like a 'semi-lattice' in contrast with the 'arbor' (tree-like) system of current cities — will we be able to understand the visual and sensual charm of its volumes and spaces. It is in this sense that a structural analysis suggests that in order to understand the visual and sensorial qualities we cannot limit ourselves to the level of the *effects*, but must rather look for the code that makes them possible. The emulation of free picturesque and folkloric qualities are urbanistic practices that, while attempting to overcome the schematicism of the rationalists' plan, are, in fact, just the other side of the coin.

2.2 The Sociological Approach to Structuralist 'Ideology': Metaphysical Naturalism and Superstructuralism

What does this positionalist-speleological thinking mean, and to what principles does it respond?

Michael Foucault has suggested that it is a way of thinking characterizing a certain period of time; a way of understanding what understanding is; an 'epistemological framework' within which we are placed, as in the sixteenth century people thought from and within 'analogy', and in the eighteenth century from and within 'taxonomy'.

In the sixteenth century, to understand something was to percieve its analogy with something else. Art was symbolic-analogical; economic value was understood in relationship to the land. The eighteenth century substituted order for analogy; to know something was, then, to put it into a classification, just as Linnaeus did with biological species. Art was also orderly and academic. Value was understood as a universal sign and mercantilist economists attempted to 'order' the national economy by establishing a favourable commercial balance. The nineteenth century brought with it another radical change: thought was not based now on 'analogy' nor on 'ordering' but on the concepts of *life* and *history*: to understand something was to comprehend its origin and its 'organic' evolution. Thus, classical 'Natural History' became 'Biology', 'General Grammar' 'Philology', and the 'Theory of Wealth' 'Economics'. Ricardo and Marx, Dilthey and Nietzsche are all typical exponents of this break. Today, at last, we are entering the stage of the *System*: to understand something is to find out the system within which it acquires sense. And this stage, obviously, must contain the crisis of historicism and the 'death of man' who, from now on, is no longer a privileged and transparent reality but a phenomenon to be explained, as any other, within the system of relationships from which it has emerged. According to this line of thought, Foucault himself in his *Archaeology of Knowledge* defines his discourse not as an expression of himself as a subject, but as grafted 'into the field of enunciation . . . determined by the dispersion and discontinuity of its subject'.

I have limited myself to noting the 'interpretation' of Foucault: his obsession for synchrony ('the history of knowledge can only be written in the terms of its contemporary context'), his disguised Hegelianism, in which the notion of 'dialectical progress' is substituted by a sort of 'jerking epiphanism' just as wholistic as Hegel's was. But a critical consideration of his view of historical 'dynamics', and of his 'metaphysics', deserve a separate study.[2]

Instead of doing this criticism, I will put forth what I understand to be the meaning of the epistemological and ontological 'systematism' of the structuralist's approach.

The structuralist revolt against existentialisms, historicisms, and vitalisms seems to me to be analogous, on a formal level, to the reaction of literary naturalism against romanticism.

In a country wedding, for example, a romantic would talk about the spirit of the people who sing and dance, who are linked to their land by very ancient roots, who put on their 'Sunday best' especially for today, etc. If, besides being a romantic, he is German or Catalan, he would certainly speak to us of the 'community' (*Gemeinschaft*) that these people make up, so distinct from mere society (*Gesellschaft*); of their common 'spirit' (*Volkgeist*), etc. If he is modern and French, like Sartre, he will try to show the difference between mere aggregation and inert seriality (as in the bus queue) on the one hand, and a group defined by a common and shared purpose (the popular wedding party, or, for Sartre, the revolutionary squad).

Confronted with the same wedding, a naturalist like Flaubert simply wrote: 'their ears appeared more separated from their heads than usually'. This is, at first sight, a very unsettling remark, something like a surrealist 'boutade', but soon we discover that it encompasses a literal description of the observed reality. On Sundays and holidays, actually, it always seems as if people in villages have their ears bigger and more separated from the head, because they have been to the barber's on Saturday. What Flaubert and the naturalists intended—and later, even more radically, the authors of the Nouveau Roman—was to raise a notarial act or bill of what was seen, putting in parentheses whatever considerations concerned the sense, origin, or transcendence of it. 'To achieve what is real', we are reminded, again by Lévi-Strauss, 'one must repudiate, above all, that which has been lived, with the aim of reintegrating it in an objective synthesis drained of all sentimentality.' This is true, however, Sartre replies in his last book about Flaubert, only if we do not forget that this 'putting between brackets that which has been lived' for the benefit of an 'objective' description, this denial to project one's own emotions, is itself understood as a deliberate purpose, and responds as well to a certain *parti pris*.

Structuralism implied, therefore, the same sort of reaction as that of naturalism against romanticism. Looking at any conduct or phenomenon, existentialism or Teilhard-Marxism told us about the vital 'project' to which it responded, about the historical alternative or psychological alienation which it showed, etc. As far as the same social or human phenomenon goes, the structuralist would be much colder, sceptical, and prudent. The existentialists were 'easy triggers': they interpreted and discovered immediately the profound meanings of the phenomena. The new naturalists will insist, to begin with, that one must remain on the descriptive level about the 'ears and heads': that these signifiers, that these 'superficial' realities, have their explanation in the connected system which joins them with other superficial realities. The ears should be noted, therefore, as in a relationship with the noses and the eyes, forming a system of 'members' whose relationship with the clothing system (caps, scarfs, vests, etc.) will give us a new system that, perhaps, will relate us then to the toponymics, or the girlfriends' names, or the system of holidays.

It is easy to see, however, that this defence of the signifiers (of appearances, of names) and the rejection of every 'profound' interpretation (historical, psychological, sociological) is not to be credited on the belief that the matter ends with them. The defence of the epistemological primacy of the signifiers — which are to be, not 'interpreted', but respectfully 'situated' — is due, on the contrary, to the belief in the ontological primacy of a reality much more profound than history, society or man, and of which all these formations are no more than 'manifestations'.

Putting aside this ideological pretension to arrive at the profound roots of being, I would argue that the structuralist claim to study the superstructural systems (religion, gastronomy, ceremonial, etc.) *from within* corresponds profoundly with the fact that these superstructures have gained in our society an enormous importance and autonomy. No longer are they *nothing more*, but, rather, *nothing less* than superstructures. I do not think it necessary to dwell upon this point. It is sufficient to observe the importance that religious superstructures have acquired, channelling a civil war in Ireland and a political crisis in Italy over divorce; transforming Asiatic Marxism into Mao-Marxism or inspiring theatrical forms of social behaviour in the marginal groups of technologically advanced societies.

In this sense, I believe that the structural method was responding to (and was able to better realize) the dynamics of today's superstructures, which do not limit themselves to *reflecting* the 'determining factors in the ultimate instance', but which actually modify or *refract* them.

2.3 From Code to Competence

Contrasting with classical structuralist grammar, generative linguistics approaches the psychological infrastructure of language, not as a *code* or *corpus* with a fixed amount of elements susceptible to diverse orders, but as linguistic *competence*: as a combinatory human 'faculty' always susceptible of new creations; as a capacity to produce an unlimited number of forms from a limited number of elements.

The use of one or other model, I understand to be a purely operative question. It would probably be better to understand as a *code* the five elements (carbon, oxygen, hydrogen, sulphur, and ozone) from whose distinct combinations we get the whole series of flavours and smells; or the four elements of the molecular chain whose distinctive distribution and periodicity enters into the synthesis of proteins, accounting for the differences among the more than two million types of different living species.

What I am very much convinced about, however, is that precisely because the concept of *competence* is 'much more dynamic and open' than that of *code*, it is much less useful for the understanding of processes of formal stylistic changes. Only if we start from the code or repertoire of existing forms can we understand the viscous character of the transformations of art forms: the fact that the first paintings were still, structurally, altar panels; that the first ornaments in bronze were still following the laws of ornament in stone, or that the first motorcars still kept the engine apart from the cabin in accordance with the 'model' provided by horse-drawn carriages.

To consider tradition as that scientific or artistic code which the artist, the writer, or the scientist finds, and from which he has to operate, helps us to understand the fundamental *ambiguity* which presides over the relationship between creation and its frame of reference. It is no longer a matter (see the diagram on p.182) of using the code in an *orthodox* manner (which amounts to trivializing and wearing it out) (U1); and it is no longer a matter of ignoring it (U2), since it is not enough to be an eccentric in order to be a creator. In science, as in art, 'novelty emerges only with difficulty, contrasting against the background of common expectations' but 'novelty can only be seen by him who, knowing exactly what may be expected, is able to recognize that something anomalous has taken place',[3] or who, in art, is able to create by himself the anomaly. The innovatory use of the code is a very delicate operation, therefore—discovering in it possible variations which have not yet been used, never heard of before, but still pertinent; transformations able to enlarge the primitive code (C), which by means of this creative use (U3), is enlarged and becomes a new code (C2), from which the new scientists, artists, or writers will begin, and from which the people will perceive their works.

From the point of view of creativity, therefore, the scheme is as follows:

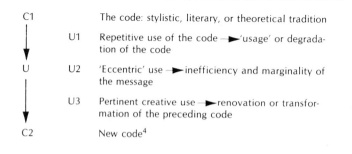

C1   The code: stylistic, literary, or theoretical tradition

      U1   Repetitive use of the code ➤ 'usage' or degradation of the code

U   U2   'Eccentric' use ➤ inefficiency and marginality of the message

      U3   Pertinent creative use ➤ renovation or transformation of the preceding code

C2   New code[4]

The scheme can also be seen 'par l'autre but de la chaine' *from the consumer's point of view*, and so the ambiguity of the reception given to new works is also explained. For the spectator:

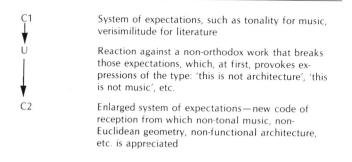

C1   System of expectations, such as tonality for music, verisimilitude for literature

U   Reaction against a non-orthodox work that breaks those expectations, which, at first, provokes expressions of the type: 'this is not architecture', 'this is not music', etc.

C2   Enlarged system of expectations—new code of reception from which non-tonal music, non-Euclidean geometry, non-functional architecture, etc. is appreciated

In this way and only in this way can we account for the phenomena of innovation and creation without falling into structuralist Manicheism and monism: to attribute to human discourse an infinite potential of fluidity and unlimited competence (the monistic approach of transformational grammar), or to explain away creativity as due to a *parole* defined simply as the exception to code (the Manicheistic approach of Saussurean structuralism).

I have dealt, up to here, with this formal and systematic aspect of the semiological perspective because it is that which, by itself, opposes traditional criticism or historical interpretation. Only from this basis is it pertinent to establish the counterposition of semiological criticism and historical criticism, which was the theme of the Castelldefels Symposium on Architecture and Semiotics. I am going now to consider the second, and more properly 'semilogical', aspect to which I referred at the beginning of this essay.

3 The Voluptuous Study of the Signifieds

I have already said that the characteristic of structuralism was the application of formal models to the study, not of material systems, but of systems of signifiers and even, in structural semantics, to systems of meanings. Structuralism, therefore, does not deal with the study of what a seat, a staircase, or a fashionable beach *are*, but with what they signify: the meaningful connections that their experience provokes in those who watch or use them.

Studies or suggestions of a more or less intuitive nature about the 'semiological' value of such things are not, on the other hand, so recent: what is significantly new, as we will see farther on, is the inflation of these types of studies and their adoption of systematic methods. S. Giedion had already emphasized that the difference between the Greek Agora and the Roman Forum was not only topological or functional, but also symbolical. The irregular design of the Greek Agora and its exclusively pedestrian character; the lack of monuments of a religious-funerary nature (exiled into the Acropolis), or of a political representative nature (like the Bolouterios and other public buildings which respectfully present their back to the square)—everything suggests the image of a civic *Trefpunkt* made to the physical and symbolic measure of the free citizen. The spatial structure of the Roman Forum, on the contrary, indicates clearly that it is not a civic but a political administrative centre: its great scale and regular design suggest—as in the unitary, baroque 'plazas' against the mere empty space among Renaissance 'palazzi'—that it is a political centre with its public buildings, the jail, the podium, etc. The Forum tells us, with its scale, symmetry, and structure, that it is the administration or the *imperium*—no longer the free citizen—which polarizes public life.

Eugenio d'Ors also knew how to read the meaning of the domes of Brunelleschi. The ribbed structure of the dome was the symbol of the crown, of the central unifying power, which still permitted the residual existence of medieval parliamentary institutions, here symbolized by the ribbons. It is not necessary to insist on the originally symbolic character of the buildings and urban centres (a Hegelian intuition confirmed, then, by the ethnologists upon analysing the ostentative channelling of the first agricultural surpluses). Alberti already insisted that each type of building corresponds to certain forms which point out their function: the perfect Platonic forms (the circle, etc.) for religious buildings, the regular forms or shapes for the public buildings, and irregular for homes.

Awareness of this symbolic dimension of objects or buildings is not, then, really new—why, this renewed and almost obsessive interest in it? Why this metastasis of the study of the sign-functions besides, or even independently of, the utility-functions?

3.1 Social Practice and Theoretical Models

My thesis, which I shall later attempt to justify, is that theoretical interest in semiology—information, theory, linguistics, symbolic logic, mass mediology, etc.—as well as practical emphasis—in modern design, on symbolic non-utilitarian elements—responds to the importance that specifically *informative* aspects of reality have acquired in our society. As McLuhan argued, 'communication has emerged as a necessary object of attention in the 20th century, not because it's new, but because it's a part of the social organism which is now undergoing elephantiasis'.[5]

In the same way that, in a mercantile society, the economy develops and even tends to interpret archaic periods from the point of view of competition (Darwin explaining the evolution of the species by the struggle for life), and in the same way that ornithology would develop in a society which had many birds, in a society in which an inflation of 'animals' of another species—that is, of 'informations'—appears, it is very logical that:

1. sciences and theories related to this aspect of the emerging reality develop, and that

2. a tendency appears for the understanding of other societies or historical periods from these theoretical frameworks; extrapolating, thus, in space and in time the new perspective that these theories offer.

The process, as I understand it, would follow three stages:

1. Quantitative increase in certain 'objects'.

2. Development of sciences able to handle them.

3. Application of the models of these sciences to other areas.

In our context, the *objects* which are proliferating are those strange and intangible realities that we call 'news' or 'information'; the *sciences* for their treatment are semiology or information theory; and the *application* of those models to other realities would be represented by the attempts to understand behaviour, the evolution of species, social systems, architecture, etc., from a semiological perspective.

I will begin by dealing with this last point in order to pose the most difficult problem of the sociological causes of this increase in 'information stuff'—which is the basis of the development of these sciences, as well as of its imperialistic tendency to colonize, with its methods, neighbouring regions.

In this saturated context of signs in which information has, most of the time, more importance than things—where the main news may be precisely the fact that something is news, even where things or actions are made in order for them to be spoken about—it is very natural for our ethnologists and anthropologists to want to understand the past, employing categories that only this social situation has permitted awareness of.

It is not strange, therefore, that students of animal behaviour with a certain speculative proclivity tend to speak more about *ritual dance* or *symbolic stylization of the behaviours*, than about *struggle for life* or *survival of the fittest*. That they should start to think that the human *smile* is not an immediate expression or a reflection of a corporal state, as much as a *signic instrument* with which the human animal can keep his mother close at hand, and that, throughout his life, it works as a message which says: 'What you're doing to me, or this situation in which I am with you, would make me afraid if you were somebody else, but not being *you*' (Desmond Morris). That they should think, along the same line, that the lips and the protruding breasts of the females of our species have no other function than that of symbolizing, respectively, the genital labia and buttocks, both of them developing themselves from the moment that our species walks erect and there is no longer direct showing of them. Lips and breasts, then, may be understood as corporal 'metaphors'.

For the same reason, it is not surprising that Deleuze discovers that the *Recherche* of Proust is not a sequence of 'memories' but an accumulation of 'signs'; tha Lacan finds in the 'signifying structure of symptoms, imprinted upon the flesh, the omnipresence, for the human being, of symbolic functions'; that Lévi-Strauss and Juri Lotman generalize

Marcel Mauss's notions of 'exchange' and 'gift' and refor-
mulate sociology as a general theory of communication.
Marriage, economics, and language can be considered as
three systems of interchange of increasing rapidity and
decreasing formalization.

> Marriage   Slow communication of *objects*
>   (women) of the same nature and size as
>   the subjects that perform the exchange.
>
> Economics   Faster and easier communication of
>   *goods and services* that reqiure signs or
>   symbols in order to allow for the ex-
>   change.
>
> Language   Very fast communication of *pure signs.*

The formal common denominator of social transactions
and institutions is, therefore, for Lévi-Strauss, communication: 'the study of kinship relationships, economics and
linguistics handle, therefore, formally analogous problems,
although at different levels'.
These ethnological or anthropological theories are
manifestations of the phenomenon mentioned in the third
place in our scheme: the tendency to interpret far removed
realities in terms of a theory which emerged—and, as I
understand, only became possible—from a modern social
practice embedded in the informative value of things.

3.2 Sociological Interpretation

What concerns us now is to discover the factors that favour,
in a given social context, the transformation of
forms—which were originally of an *objective* nature—into
explicitly communicative *images* or symbols.
In my view, the *objective* consideration of reality—the
valuation and appreciation of forms as physical entities that
speak for themselves and not as mere vehicles of information—is only possible within certain *thresholds* of socio-
economic organization and territorial scale. I am referring to
the 'bourgeois scale' that, in Athens, made possible the
speculative discovery of reality as an autonomous object, independent of personal drives or projections, precisely as a
result of a projection in the physical world of the categories
of balance, order, and hierarchy experienced in the
microcosms of the bourgeois city. The scale of the *polis*, in
which it was still possible for art not to be a creation of
'images' on one hand, or a 'spectacular consumption' on the
other; of an art 'linked with the internal communication
of an élite which had a semi-independent social foundation

in the partially ludic structure still being lived by the last aristocrats' (Guy Debord).

Once we have outgrown the boundaries of this bourgeois environment, which literally segregated 'objectivity':

1. communication becomes problematic in such a way that every object is understood in its strict, functional-informative value, and, therefore,

2. the emphasis shifts from the creation or *production* of objects, to their *consumption, communication,* or *propagation.*

We are now going to test (a) how these two factors are the ones that historically explain the periods in which *symbols* dominate over things, in order to conclude by observing how (b) both factors get together in order to favour nowadays this transubstantiation of the social reality into a symbolic reality.

(a) Prehistory and Theory of 'Informativism'

From a historical point of view, the exchange of objects seems to have filled a brief period preceded and followed by the exchange of symbols. In the beginning and at the end, in primitive or in developed societies, the exchange is mainly one of signs or information.

In primitive societies, in fact, it looks as if every form of exchange or interaction among its members is an excuse to exchange the more special and necessary commodity: information, contact with others. The Kula of the Trobriande, described by Malinowski, is a system of symbolic exchange in which people give each other necklaces, bracelets, baubles, etc. objects specially designed to carry out this function of symbolic exchange. In the same way, the Potlach, or conspicuous destruction, calls for the principle of 'I shall burn all my goods and you burn all of yours' with which the rice-growers of Borneo assure a periodical social level-placing, avoiding the establishment of a hierarchy of class differences.

It makes little difference whether they exchange necklaces or bracelets, whether they burn food or tools: in both cases they attempt to keep communicating, to reaffirm or reinforce the contact and the fact of belonging to one circle rather than to another. *That which is exchanged is communication itself.* These rituals of exchange work like *phatic* elements do in verbal language (the 'I say, can you hear me?' 'Yes, yes, fine', on the telephone) or *regulators* in the corporal language (to nod with the head, to 'look around', etc.): as elements which assure or reinforce the duration of the interaction. They are, very exactly, 'maintenance costs' in societies in which communication is difficult or problematic and in which the lack of them can cause death.

Lévi-Strauss understood the essential rule of the 'incest taboo'—the law which obliges one to go in search of a girlfriend in the neighbouring village—as a cunning strategy for the maintenance of communication with which the tribe widens its environment and develops culturally, importing new techniques or contacting other markets.

But, most surprisingly, this primacy of sign exchange over object exchange appears in opposite situations: both in primitive, dispersed, and subsistence-level economies, where the maintenance of contact is a vital necessity, and in societies in which urban crowdedness and economic affluence once again make information into a product of primary necessity. Starting from this, I suggest the hypothesis that only in the medium scale or threshold of the city and the bourgeois system of exchange—when, in the terminology of Poulanzas, the areas of hegemony and domination of a social class coincide—does a concern for objects and their creation exist more than for their effects and their consumption.[6] The proliferation of images in our society is an unmistakable symptom of the fact that both the scale of and the emphasis on production, characteristic of bourgeois societies, have changed. The process would be rather of the following nature:

1. Use of a given medium of communication in accordance with a certain domain: pulpit in the church, rostrum in the city, radio for the nation.

2. Enlargement of the domain and appearance of concurrent media and messages which put the habitual channels of communication in crisis: transformation of the Greek polis into a Roman Empire, or the American nation into a watchdog of the free world.

3. Transformation of all the objects that this society produces into emphatically—if not exclusively—informative ones.

Objects and messages incorporate, then, a certain phatic metalinguistic dimension which ensures and reinforces its transmission—a dimension one could represent as an arrow pointing to and calling attention towards the message itself:

In art history, this process of 'emphatization' can be followed in the transformation of the objective-idealistic Hellenic or Renaissance style into the effectivist, illusionist Roman or baroque style. In Rome, in fact, the formal Greek repertory is used but its syntactical organization varies. Its elements are no longer used for their objective value, but for the *effect* they are able to create in the observer. They think now in terms of the *consumption* of monuments: monuments that are able to be perceived from a great distance. And the

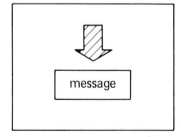

reason, as we have seen, is obvious. Roman buildings and banners have to speak now, not only to a *polis* of *cives* who share its code, but to the barbarians in Gallia or in Hispania, who are controlled by the *ius gentium*, who are entertained by the spectacles and who are impressed with the imperial 'image'. Its style has to be, then, more clearly decodable, more effectivist, and more symbolic. Since its message must travel very far away, classical *forms* are transformed into Roman *symbols*. The quantity—distance, in this case—makes the quality.

Something similar happens with the transformation of Renaissance stylistic language—objective, idealistic, private, civic language—into baroque illusionism. Baroque buildings do not have to talk to the citizens of Florence or Bruges any more, but to the nation or to the Christian world. They have to give, for example, the *image* of a Church—One, Catholic, Apostolic, and Roman. The Church no longer *produces* spirituality as in the times of Eckhardt or of Romanesque churches, but *promotes* eternal salvation and *sells* spirituality. The first known case of a systematic *marketing* of something is that of the baroque commercialization of Faith. It was not by chance, in fact, that it was then when the expression *propaganda fide* was made up and used. The will or necessity of *propagating* a message transforms it immediately into *propaganda*. From there it is a short step to the verbosity of the baroque façades and the theatricality of their images that must carry the message of Redemption rapidly and to the most remote places.

I think that Roman and baroque precedents clearly illustrate the thesis that when the audience enlarges, or when there are 'noises' which make reception of language difficult for the traditional audience (Protestant 'competition' for the baroque Catholic Church, commercial or industrial 'competition' nowadays), it becomes necessary to concentrate forces to get messages across, and, therefore, *forms* develop into concrete *images*, which above all ensure that their messages are well received, understood, assumed, and consumed.[6]

(b) Determining Factors in Modern 'Informatism': Modes of Production, Sales, Consumption, Payment, and Territoriality

Now, we have to turn our attention to specific factors which have brought about this increase of symbols in our society, with the corresponding development of sciences devoted to its study. As has already been pointed out, while in primitive societies it was the *low frequency* of informative contacts due to physical dispersion and cultural fragmentation which made information the most valued merchandise, in modern societies it is the *high frequency* of information (due to urban overcrowding, commercial competition, communication networks on an international scale) that now makes information purposefully produced merchandise. But let us look at these factors one at a time.

1. *Production*   Since the development of a capitalism, no longer based on competition, but organized, technical, and planned, information ceases to be a *luxury* that industrial society allows itself, a surplus in its development or a simple by-product of its activity. In advanced capitalist societies, information becomes a first-rate *working tool*. Being better informed is as much or more important than having more available capital, cheaper labour, etc.

   Industrial information is even sold as 'know-how'. 'Industrial espionage' tries to find out formulae and techniques used by the competition. Universities are no longer considered as that speculative luxury that middle-class society prides itself on; they appear instead as the producers and transmitters of that knowledge whose worth is not only cultural but economic as well. It was this direct instrumentalization of knowledge in universities (knowledge once considered free and critical) which gave virulence and revolutionary content to an old, time-honoured bourgeois tradition of revolt in universities.

2. *Sale*   From the very moment at which several brands can equally satisfy basic or induced necessities, the battle to sell can no longer be fought at the traditional level which based its sales pitch on higher quality or longer life of the product. It is now necessary to create positive symbolic connections with the product to be sold in order to make it desirable. The progressive extinction of differences between products generates the need to manufacture those differences. Each product is now promoted as dif-fer-ent precisely because it is made un-differentiated. Not only must products, or better products, be manfactured, but also *images* of these products. And not only images of these products, but images of the manufacturing company. The shape of a cigarette-lighter, for instance, has to promote a 'daring-masculine-dynamic' image of its owner, and the manufacturer of the lighter will take to bringing out a corporate image of an 'imaginative, up-to-date' business, or, on the other hand, it may opt for an image of being 'confident in a tradition of responsible nobility'. This proliferation of 'images' of products or companies first makes it imperative to tackle the problem of the informative or semantic value of forms and, second, creates an environment of symbols or images which give an increasingly spiritual character to our *Umwelt*.

3. *Consumption*   Correlative with this production of 'images', consumption is being increasingly transformed into

the consumption of symbols: into *semiophagics* (symbol eating).

Calvin discovered the *sign-function of wealth*: being rich was not only useful in order to live better, but it was also a sign of predestination. Later Veblen discovered the *sign-function of consumption*: consumption was aimed not only at the satisfaction of biological needs, but also at the ostentation of acquisitive power. Today, what is more, we are discovering the taste or flavour in *the consumption of the signs themselves*. And this is what our naïve critics of 'consumer society' have not seen: that consumption is today the *only* authentically *spiritual* practice of our time. Advertising does not propose the acquisition of objects, but of ideals, aspirations, sensations. The object for consumption—soap, institutionalized culture, a car, or a drink—is nothing but 'a medium' by means of which we accede to *virility, status, intimacy,* or *power of attraction*. We do not consume objects, but ideals. They are not selling us *stimuli*—an x for the necessity y—but the sensations themselves ('feel younger, more exotic . . . '). They sell to us and we consume not food, but its very flavour; not sex, but the result of its purification: that which is sexy. We do not acquire Christmas decorations for the house, but *gemutlichkeit* itself.

Propaganda works more or less like drugs. One accedes directly to the sensations without the bothersome *duty* of becoming interested in their stimuli: the 'philosophical' advertiser of advanced capitalism is becoming able to *inject* into us the sensation or the information itself, and it is not at all absurd to imagine that the perfection of this society will be the disappearance of the very objects of consumption: the transformation of all market relationships into an authentic *commerce and consumption of universals*.

Each age, one must remember, has the spiritualism it deserves. The only non-traumatic spiritualism that can be made out on the horizon of post-industrial society is this *autophagic* spiritualism by which we acquire and consume—by means of objects—the ideal of ourselves: our originality—*it is different*—our autonomy, our youth. The authentically desired and consumed thing is the Ideal: manufactured objects are nothing more than the sign of this.

4. *Payment*   But not only do the forms of production, sales, and consumption tend to transubstantiate all reality into signs. Also the forms of payment are progressively becoming more immaterial, more symbolic and, in the end, more intimate and spiritual. McLuhan saw the first step when emphasizing that the *credit card* is transforming *product-money* into *information-money*. But it is more than that. As Enzensberger observed, it turns out that the more expensive the product is, the less probable it is that we have

to pay for it: that it is 'free'. We must pay for a packet of cigarettes or a book, but we do not pay materially for services infinitely more expensive, such as travelling on a highway or watching, live on TV, something that is happening on the other side of the world.

Does it turn out that we only pay for cheap things? No. Evidently, what happens is that we pay for the more expensive things by alienating ourselves; by lending ourselves as subjects capable of being 'informed'; by offering ourselves as objects—subjects of publicity manipulation in the intervals between spectacles that television gives us; by giving ourselves in exchange for the services that the system offers us. In an unconscious but sure way, forms of payment are also becoming day by day more spiritual, more symbolic, more 'personal'.

5. *Territoriality*   As we have seen, the extension of external markets, and the competitive character of the internal ones, forced the association of products with the *brand image* which makes them easily decodable within different cultural systems. Which is the shape of the bottle, the figure, or the initials which will immediately suggest the 'refreshing drink' to a lower-middle-class Catalan, to a Turkish peasant, and to a Tuareg. Also, the fact that the information is received from far away or at great speed (on highways, for instance) has made necessary a special study of the way signs are perceived.

Symbols—the huge hamburger, the big boy, the giant glass of champagne—abound, thus, along the strip, substituted for written messages which it would be impossible to read. Venturi's proposal of substituting architecture right away by symbols and advertisement along the highway is not so surrealistic as it might seem. But there is still another way in which the urban forms of territorial organization favour—practically force—the proliferation of signs and the transformation of any reality into significant material.

Starting from the study of animal behaviour, ethologists have showed that living species have certain needs of *spatial structuration*, which they satisfy by means of one of two ways: (a) the *territorialization*, or centrifugal organization, by which each family and group (and among men, subculture) looks for an area where it can project its identity and recognize itself; and (b) the *hierarchy* or centripetal structuration, by means of which individuals belonging to different groups, families, etc., try to share and live together in the same space, avoiding aggressiveness and latent tensions, accepting certain priorities among the individuals permitting this non-conflictive use of the same space. In crowded and 'democratic' modern urban societies, the need for spatial structuration cannot be easily satisfied by those mechanisms, except in a residual and insufficient way (and even with bad conscience; by means of racial ghettos, ways of showing off power, etc.). The modern metropolis, as M. Weber saw, is no longer the culmination of the ancient city or the medieval community—where the bourgeois is the bourgeois *of* a certain city—but the result of its rationalization and conversion into an impersonal instrument for the reproduction of capital. That is why that basic need of differentiation seeks even more sophisticated and symbolic strategies. It is almost impossible to have something or some place distinct since mass production has made both consumption and territory into a homogeneous medium—but even then the recourse of knowing how to use the same place, or to be in the same place, in a different way, remains. Small changes in tone, in rhythm, in tempo are then transformed into status or power symbols. Precisely because material differences are becoming more and more rare, the symbolic ones multiply and blossom. For certain groups, thus, there will be a decisive differentiation value, in *not* wearing blazers *any more*, or in *still* liking Tchaikovsky, or in *coming back* to an interest for neo-classicism, or in *not* driving a Renault 4/4 *any more* . . . .

There is still another reason why the artificiality of the urban medium helps or favours the substitution of natural stimuli by signs. Orientation in traditional cities or establishments is not exclusively visual. Orientating hints reach us through different senses: *touch* or feel of the objects, *texture* of the walls, the *smell* of the shops, the *noise* of the busy craftsmen. *New town* designers, on the contrary, seem obsessed with the idea of eliminating smells, tastes, and wrinkles. They short-circuit our rich orientation system and they bring us, as a substitute, a beautiful 'semiological' design.

They divide the environment into soundproof compartments: they antisepticize the medium in such a way that we can no longer discover 'naturally'—by the smell of coffee, the noise of the spoons in the cups, etc. —where the cafeteria is, and they give us, in substitution, an overstudied sign—'Cafeteria'—created by an experimental team of an American university according to criteria concerned with 'optimization of information', 'legibility', and other niceties. It is something too similar to cutting off our legs and then running to bring us some crutches in accordance with the most modern prosthetic criteria. Semiology as the prosthetics of communication—we have here a suggestive theme for analysis.

Be that as it may, what is sure is that we live in our cities with these symbolic crutches which the technological development of the media and the impotence of architects and designers to organize it in a human way have transformed into a macabre dance of signs without objects, of signs acting like things, of crutch signs instead of stimuli. . . .

Now, while the majority of us (Europeans especially) willingly accept that such phenomena as *marketing, styling, packaging,* or *'image creation'* are practices induced by the forms of production, promotion, consumption, and territoriality of a neo-capitalist society, we reject the assumption that some apparently more scientific or cultural phenomena might be touched and affected by the same factors.

Here we have, I think, the most aggressive and controversial aspect of my thesis.

I believe that the effect of this production system is as much *marketing* as Lacan's psychology or structuralist 'philosophy'; as much *American styling* as the more 'cultural' European 'styling' which has come to be called neo-historicism, neo-liberty, neo-rationalism, or neo-academicism; as much the proliferation of studies concerning acquisitive preferences as that of studies in semiology. With these pages I intended to demonstrate that these are two sides—the 'theoretically cultivated' one and the 'pragmatic/philistine' one—of the same coin; two aspects of the same social reality.

3.3 Semiology-action

Up to this point I have concerned myself with the features of social reality that provoke semiology, but I would not like to conclude without making reference to the complementary aspect of the social efficiency of signs. I have spoken about semiology as 'effect', and now I am going to talk about it as 'cause'.

It is usually assumed that 'saying' is the external expression of something one 'thinks', or that the sign is the expression of a content already existing beforehand. But, it has already been quite a while since Hegel said that there is nothing 'behind' the act, the gesture, or the word. It is usual to assume that every act is loaded with signification; it is a good time to insist on the reverse as well: that every signification is also an action. Linguistic behaviour, as Malinowski saw, is of a basically pragmatic nature: to see it as an embodiment of thought is to 'take a one-sided vision of what constitutes one of the more derivative and specialized functions of language'. Language is a form of behaviour which may be used to communicate, or to avoid communication: to manifest or to hide one's own mind, to make a relationship more intimate, or, on the contrary, more conventional. And it is equally multifunctional as a social institution: it has served, and serves, in Europe or amongst the Hopi Terva, as a tool of unification and adhesion to the group, or, on the contrary (as it happened with secret cults and sects, in ancient Egypt and Greece, or in the Middle Ages), as a tool of social differentiation and segregation.

Austin and the later Wittgenstein based their philosophies upon this principle of semiology-action: to say or signify something is not only to *express* but also to *do* something. It is not difficult to discover situations in which to 'say' presupposes something more than 'giving notice' of something. When I say 'yes' to a girl, while facing a priest in a given ceremonial context, I am not only—or not fundamentally—giving notice of a feeling: I am pledging myself, I am getting married. The word 'yes' does not *say* anything, it *does* it. Words, then, not only say things, but they 'promise', 'pledge', 'institute', 'sanction', etc. At a different level, the declaration by a delegate of the British opposition to a state of precarious stability in exchange rate did not *say* the devaluation, but *made* it.

In *Die Fröhliche Wissenschaft*, Nietzsche carries this point even further:

> Name, reputation and appearance of the thing, all that, as it is believed and transmitted from generation to generation, progressively adheres itself to the thing, wedging itself in it, finally becoming, being converted into, the substance itself. . . . It is enough, thus, to create new names, evaluations, or signs in order to create, in the long run, new things.

Signs, therefore, not only represent a situation, but provoke this situation: they are, in good measure, charismatic, self-fulfilling prophecies of the situation they must signify. And, since signs call for reality, it might be advisable, at a given moment, to feed the market with habits in order to have the production of monks increased. The very existence of signs favours the appearance of the realities they signify. The process of social and cultural evolution can, in this sense, be understood as a process of the 'filling in' or 'completion' of originally empty signs.

The sign, in other words, not only means (signifies) but creates its meaning—or consolidates it if it happens to exist already. The incest taboo in primitive societies is a *sign* of culture—of the imposition of rules on behaviour—but, at the same time, as I have already indicated, it is a *provoker* of culture in increasing the contacts of the group or clan.

And we can observe the same thing in everyday 'signs'. To be seated on a rostrum is a sign of superiority, status, but a *reinforcer*, too, of this status, since he who is higher sees better than the rest of the group and can control it better. In the same way, to go painted yellow in a group where everybody is red is a sign of leadership, but it is also a consolidator of leadership, since, for example, the stranger who approaches the group will be directed, in all probability, to the one painted yellow, and so he would be able to control and channel all the external contacts.

A dramatic example of this fact in education can be found in *Inequality*, by Jencks. An 'intelligent' child, who starts with a small genetic advantage, attracts attention and dedication from parents and teachers, for whom it is more pleasant to teach and educate that child than other, less-favoured classmates. From this a 'cumulative effect of initial differences in capacity' follows. Those who have more capacity and skill find more opportunity to develop them in the environment propitiated by the first signs of their superiority, while those who lack such capacity—or its appearance—tend to be dissuaded. Individual genetic differences start as signs for the environment, but they end up by influencing that same environment.

A confirmation of this is the well-known experiment of the teacher to whom 20 randomly selected children were allocated, telling him that it was a group specially selected for their exceptional intelligence. At the end of the year their level of achievement and qualifications were clearly higher than that of other groups. *Expectation created thus that which was expected: signs that which they proclaimed.*

To live in an exclusive residential area, to give an example on an urban level, is a sign of the economic status of its inhabitants, but this character is reinforced by the sign itself, since the speculators will buy land in this area and they will pay higher prices for it due to the incorporation of the sign of social prestige in the land. *The fact that it is a significative space makes it, then, even more significative.*

This is one reason why, as Hoyt pointed out, territorial growth and the increase in land value in development areas is not homogeneous, as in Figure 1.

Town growth usually follows sectorial patterns as in Figure 2.

But if the signs provoke the reality which they are said to express, it is not absurd to attempt, for example, to create urban zones of a determined character by means of the promotion of a series of sign-elements that will act like a bait. And in the same way that traders and professionals in the media have studied and developed much more sophisticated symbolic techniques than have architects (which is why Venturi proposes the latter should learn from the former), in respect of semiology-action also the merchants have gone ahead of the urban designers. It is obvious, for instance, that the

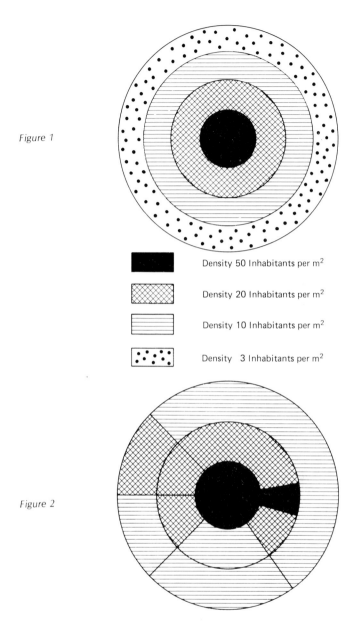

Figure 1

Density 50 Inhabitants per m^2

Density 20 Inhabitants per m^2

Density 10 Inhabitants per m^2

Density 3 Inhabitants per m^2

Figure 2

existence of a young, fashionable, commercial zone—London's Kings Road, Tuset in Barcelona, the pink or golden zones of Mexico City, Ghirardelli in San Francisco—interests businesses as an invigorating pole for sales by means of the creation of a physical framework in which the leadership of youth, in the form of consumption, is evident to the highest degree. And the trained noses of the merchants have not ceased to search for certain places—nor to create certain new places—in which a few spatial signs *produce* this ambiance which they seem to signify. These areas must be, for instance, rather crowded, more easily visible than accessible; several different domains must overlap (cafeteria—exhibition hall—boutique) so that the *spectator group* (which is also *consumer*) may watch the *show group* (hippy, young, etc.) without really feeling alien to it, arriving at the feeling that they are really integrated into what is happening. One, at least, of the more attractive shops must be placed at the end of the route, provoking in this way the walk which keeps people in circulation and attracts outsiders. The client turns into the very show that attracts the next client. . . .

The fact that businessmen have been able to create 'qualified' spaces by means of signs suggests the possibility that artists and architects also learn not only to use signs, but to *make* with signs. When architects start thinking that good spaces are not those which are designed but which have gradually 'grown', when people build following the course of their needs, when artists prefer to be considered as *provokers* of new situations rather than as *creators*—when all this happens there is little doubt that the possibility of favouring a certain development by using signs is one of the new avenues open to them. A possibility which, I personally think, should be used to give people back the eye and the taste for the singular in an environment where everything tends to become more and more archetypal and ideal, intangible and spiritual.

Signs, which are the product of a social and territorial structure, have also an effect in changing it. They are the *result*, but also the *cause* of the situations they signify. Personally, I feel this revival of the power of signs over things is a rather frightening experience; it seems to me an irrefutable proof of the fact that *conflict* and *unrest* in modern culture—the loss of any hope of balance between emotional and intellectual life—have only been increasing. It is, I suppose, a fear similar to that of Tolstoy's horse when he considered the fetishism of human language and concluded: 'What they [men] seek is not so much the possibility of doing or not doing something as the possibility of uttering, with respect to certain things, certain words which they have agreed amongst themselves.' But, be that as it may, the prophetic and charismatic force of signs—their power to cause the sale, the revolution, or the feeling they appear only to represent—is there. And, in the end, the last one to learn to take advantage of this is most likely to come out as the loser in the game.

Notes to the Text

1. A similar criticism of 'genesis' or 'evolution' as a model of explanation has been made by Chomsky as to its use as an instrument of analysis of mental and verbal processes. He says:

   > in order to understand how language is used and acquired we have to isolate, for its separate study, a cognitive system, a system of beliefs and thoughts. . . . We must isolate and study the system of *linguistic competence* which underlies our behaviour. . . . We must describe the different systems of knowledge and beliefs which characterise man according to their internal organisation and *only then* start the study of how these systems may have been generated.

   In this quotation we find the same defence of synchronicity and the same stress on the need for an 'espeleological' approach that we have been discussing so far.

2. Criticism of structuralist positions has been frequent in France. According to T. de Quenetain, when France is no longer the leader of history, she invents an ideology denying history, and debases philosophy into an activity of *bricolage* and of discussion of matters such as fashion or menus. According to Lefebvre, structuralism amounts to a sort of technocratic Hegelianism that no longer puts into question the origins and social function of codes and assumes that every possible transformation is *already* 'written' in a code which determines beforehand every 'pertinent' change. In the same vein, Jean Pouillon argues that it is a theory of order unable to account for disorder. Other critics refer to structuralism as a 'substitute for the ontological aspirations' of traditional metaphysics; as 'Kantism without the transcendental subject' or as 'neo-Parmenideism'.

   Criticisms which refer to structuralism as an 'extrapolation' are of more intrinsic interest. Ricoeur says that the structuralist method can only obtain interesting results when applied to 'primitive' societies—the field of study where it first emerged; that is, to societies where cultural specialization does not exist, as it does in 'hot', or more advanced societies. *The 'material logic' of structuralism would apply to the study of those societies where logic and nature, rules and affective behaviour occur at the same*

level, but it would not apply to those situations, as for instance in the Hebrew tradition, where knowledge and
rules are 'stored' in Books. In these situations a *structural
schematization of the significant elements of behaviour* (as
signifiers) would be insufficient, and it is necessary to
develop a *proper hermeneutic of the meanings* (as
signifieds) and interpretations of the Books. The naïve
assertion by Lévi-Strauss that primitive societies are more
'authentic' would confirm Ricoeur's opinion: Lévi-Strauss
would call 'non-authentic' those societies and cultural formations to the study of which his analysis cannot be properly applied, and 'authentic' those to which it can be applied.

Garaudy criticized structuralism for its lack of 'opportunity'. The happy marriage between theory and practice
propitiated by 'humanist Marxism', Garaudy says, was put
into danger when, with Althusser, Marxism attempted to
become a 'science', just as technical and esoteric as the
study of macromolecules, for instance. What Garaudy
forgets to discuss, however, is the validity of that supposed 'unity between theory and practice' achieved under
the auspices of his favourite version of Teilhard-Marxism.

Contrary to Garaudy, it is my belief that the influence
of structuralism over Marxism has been as beneficial as
the influence of existentialism was, with Sartre's *Critique
de la raison dialectique*. Existentialism brought the notion
that the 'new society' did not exist ideally and that,
therefore, revolution did not consist of carrying out the
revolution but of *inventing* it. Structuralism, on the other
hand, pointed out that the reality to be transformed was
more complex than the orthodox economicist tradition
had assumed it to be. In both cases, theoretical and
ideological Marxism has been revised: with existentialism,
by dissolving its ideological component into *action*; with
structuralism, by trying to bring its ideology closer to
scientific knowledge.

Be that as it may, the sharpest possible criticism of
structuralism, as the endeavour of discovering the systems
from which we operate, is still Sartre's: 'It is not that which
makes us which matters, but rather what we make with
that which makes us.'

3. T. Kuhn, *The Structure of Scientific Revolutions*, Chicago,
University of Chicago Press, 1962.

4. Evidently, one can, in Saussurean terms, understand C as
language and U as *parole*. My diagram, however, differs
fundamentally from Saussure in that I am attempting to
encompass within it the creative role of *parole* acts which
Saussure considered as lying outside the scope of
linguistic analysis. It is precisely this which Chomsky

critized in *Language and Mind*. According to my diagram, we need a structural study of *parole* or creative competence (which Chomsky only postulates as the very 'substance' of language, without ever analysing its viscous relationship with preexisting cultural residua).

5. Sociologists tell us that in our time almost every kind of communication is growing faster than economic production itself; information, economists tell us, is the only commodity not subject to the law of decreasing benefits, and futurologists boast about information and knowledge as future substitutes for scarce commodities (oil, etc.). We seem to have discovered a new species of quite a 'fabulous' nature.

6. In those conditions problems are more or less of a domestic scale, and moral and intellectual models, suitable and useful for that scale, develop—secular religions like Christianity, Humanism, and Scientism. When the scale or the size of problems go beyond these thresholds, these models become useless, and have to be provided for by religions or sciences of a more cosmic nature. When, as happens with primitive societies, or with American contemporary society, problems are of a global nature—problems of power, danger, and responsibility for the survival of the species—the ideologies of scientism and/or humanism are unsuited, and only witchcraft applies. The new spiritualism and orientalism of American youth (which I was completely unable to *share*) was made finally *intelligible* to me when I realized the radicality of the problems and the size of forces and powers one experiences there: racial confrontation, the extinction of a defenceless nation, violence. In the primitive man's jungle nothing can be taken for granted, 'everything is possible'—and the same applies to the streets of an American city; everybody was aware, in the jungle, of the relationship between the limpness of the daughter and the spell cast over her mother, and everybody is aware, in the USA, of the relationship betwen the limpness of the daughter and her mother's schizophrenia. . . . The former do not need yet, and the latter no longer need, our priests, humanists, and rationalists of the 'political'-domestic scale. They need the shaman, or the prophet, who may bring them illumination, salvation, who may bring them back, purified, that very external power and force they fear and that internal power and force which chills them. . . .

Towards the end of the nineteenth century Santayana wrote:

Mythological and animistic habits of thought hold their

force beyond the boundaries of knowledge, where
scientific explanation does not reach. Within ourselves,
amidst the intricate chaos of animal and human life,
we appeal to the efficiency of will and spirit. But in the
intermediate domain of modern life, where mechanical
sciences have progressed, the inclusion of personal and
emotional elements in the conception of reality would
only be eccentricity.

If something can be learned from recent developments it
is the fact that Santayana was very wise in calling the domain of scientific ideology 'intermediate' and not 'last';
since that 'remote night' is reappearing and the 'boundaries of knowledge' seem to reunite again, distressingly,
once we have stepped out from certain thresholds. The
future of religion—'the future of an illusion'—is not quite
as simple as Freud saw it. What the crisis now affects is
not illusion—the Great Illusion in capitals—but rather the
petite monnaie, sensible and humanist, which our Western
culture made out of that illusion.

7. The Japanese, because of their lack of balance between
domain and power, between economic development and
political control, have recently felt the need to control the
image they offer to the outside world—an image which,
like the American one, tended to deteriorate. An institute
has been recently formed in Tokyo with the sole purpose
of manufacturing and propagating this image.

Section 2

2.0 Introduction to Section 2

Geoffrey Broadbent

This section is concerned with the application of semiotic methods into the analysis, not merely of architecture, but of architects, ideologies (Blau), the ways in which architects work when they are actually designing (Bonta, Broadbent and Gandelsonas), the individual components of building (Eco's analysis of the architectural sign/column) and, of course, whole buildings (Jencks on Stirling's Olivetti building). The methods employed fall into all three areas of semiotic studies—the pragmatic, concerned with the effects of signs on human behaviour (Blau); the semantic, which of course, is concerned with *meaning* (Bonta, Broadbent, Eco, Gandelsonas and Jencks) and the syntactic, concerned with the *structure* of language, as distinct from its meaning (Broadbent and Gandelsonas).

Blau looks at the structure of architects' opinions, of architecture itself and, more particularly, of other architects. She finds how principals in architectural practice define a successful project (some 69 per cent of them mention managerial successes, including financial ones, against the 65 per cent who mention user-satisfaction). She also finds some interesting relationships between the degree to which certain architects are known and the extent to which their work is admired. 95 per cent of those who knew of Le Corbusier also admired his work. The equivalent for Stirling was 92, for Mies 87, and for Venturi 49 (for Archigram 61) whilst the lowest percentage of 'liking' for any architect was Albert Speer with only 9 per cent. She further classifies her architects according to whether they were thought of as bureaucratic, Purist, Avant-Garde or Camp and again, against Wotton's three conditions for 'well building': commoditie, firmness and delight. She also found that of some 36 typical statements concerning attitudes to architecture, the most popular by far (agreed by 95 per cent) was 'good buildings must relate to their environment'.

Such work, of course, helps us pinpoint—at a particular moment in time—the ideas by which a particular group of architects find motivation for their work. Its real value will emerge when different groups are sampled in the same way at different places and at different times, but even such a limited study provides us with something rather more than vague feelings as to what architects seem to be thinking.

Eco in his classic paper tries to define just what the basic unit of meaning in architecture might be, concluding that it probably will be found at the level of an individual, identifiable, separable component such as a column. He discusses the ways in which such a component might be analysed according to various theories of signification—including his own analysis of the various levels at which signification may take place, Hjelmslev's division of all sign-systems into a plane of content and a plane of expression—each with form and substance and a 'theory of settings' derived from Katz, Fodor and Postal in various permutations. He then moves into what probably is the most spectacular analysis of a written passage in the entire literature of semiotic—taking as his subject a highly evocative, highly romantic essay on the *Eternity of the Column* by Dora Isella Russell.

He dissects this phrase by phrase, finding that some of her statements, have connotations which are specifically architectural, others are historical whilst others again have aesthetic connotations. Eco then analyses relationships by which words fit together in sentences—he is concerned with their structure or syntax, their syntagmatic dimension. In Eco's syntax—capital stands on column stands on base, whilst in those relationships of association which are now called paradigmatic—a Doric column is different from, but reminds us of an Ionic one, a Corinthian one and so on. Eco then submits the column itself to an equivalent analysis, concerning its vertical and its horizontal relationships with other components.

Of course, a semiotic analysis of this kind confirms certain home truths, but it also provides us with a vehicle for the *detailed* contemplation say of a column, its parts and its relationships with other parts of the building, thus forcing us to think about a column with all its connotations much more profoundly, thus encouraging our own deeper personal insights into the nature of a column.

Bonta's interests also lie firmly in the semantic dimension. He points out that, whilst most English readers have drawn on Roland Barthes's interpretations of Saussure—thanks to its availability, there are alternatives, such as those of

Buyssens and Prieto who, among other things, make a useful distinction between *indicators* — directly perceptible facts of nature and *signals* — indicators which are recognised by the interpreter as having been set up in human beings deliberately for the purposes of communication. He also shows how the same form — in this case that of a bar door, will mean quite different things in different contexts.

But in spite of his insistence that the examples he shows are of less importance than the theoretical basis which underlies them, many readers will find that the former are so well chosen that they not only vindicate Bonta's own theoretical approach; they also show that in certain circumstances meaning can be built deliberately into designed objects. The most eloquent of these examples is the chess set, which Bonta has used in many places with many groups of students — rather as Eco has used his column example — to show semiotic analysis can indeed draw our attention, in very great detail, to those attributes of an object which actually 'carry' its meaning.

Having encouraged this kind of analysis, however, Bonta has gone much further by encouraging students to use their semiotic analyses of existing chess sets in the design of new — and hopefully — even more meaningful ones. With chess sets, of course, there is, or can be, a direct one-to-one relationship between function — that is movement over one, two or more squares up the board, laterally or diagonally across it — and form. The rules which govern the movement of various pieces can be expressed in a one-for-one relationship with the forms they actually take. In Peirce's terms, Bonta is dealing with indices and the principle obviously can be extended to any kind of index — such as a designed object in which indication is important to expression, whether alone or in combination with icon and symbol.

Broadbent, in his piece tries to sort out from Peirce's turgid writing just what he meant by Icon, Index and Symbol — using Peirce's own words, wherever possible and amplifying these with reference to more recent work in the psychology of perception by Piaget, Bruner, Goodnow and Austin, and others. He finds that Peirce's categories can be greatly sharpened by these references and having quoted Peirce's various definitions, he then analyses architectural examples in each category. He also finds certain correspondences — and certain differences — between Peirce's three major categories of signs and the four modes which he (Broadbent) has detected — Pragmatic, Typologic, Analogic and Canonic — as underlying the thought processes by which architects actually *generate* architectural form (Broadbent, 1973).

Mario Gandelsonas — in collaboration with David Morton — is also concerned with how design comes about. He discusses the work of two architects, Michael Graves and Peter Eisenman from that extraordinary group of 1920's survivalists, the *New York Five*, including also Richard Meier, Charles Gwathmey and John Hejduk who have developed most of their architectural ideas by designing white-walled, post-Le Corbusian villas for New York based patrons of The Arts. To the casual observer, their houses are more notable for their similarities than for their differences, but Gandelsonas detects some interesting contrast in their working methods. For given Charles Morris's crucial distinction between Pragmatic, Semantic and Syntactic semiotics, he sees Graves as a subtle semanticist and Eisenman as a rigorous Syntactician.

Graves's stock in trade as a semanticist, of course, is analogy, in various specialised forms such as metaphor—that is the transfer of a signifier from its proper signified to another, thus throwing light on the meaning of the latter—and metonymy in which a particular attribute of the signified (e.g. 'crown' for 'king') is used instead of the usual signifier. Graves's analogies are drawn from Classical art and architecture, Cubist painting, from Modern architecture (specifically the International Style of the 1920's) and from nature. Unfortunately the clarity of his semantic intentions is somewhat blurred against certain syntactic preoccupations. Unlike, say, Charles Moore, the Venturi's or the Taller de Arquitectura (see my 'Deep Structures' paper in this volume) who tend to use their (somewhat different) analogies in a fairly straightforward way, which makes their *intended* meanings comparatively clear, Graves places his within a syntactic structure which is almost as complex as Eisenman's. Graves believes that meaning results, not from our reading of objects in themselves but from our perception of *relationships* between objects. He also thinks that these relationships can best be expressed in terms of oppositions; thus he sees the orders of architecture as related to each other by a complex binary code, involving simple/complex; rude/elegant; male/female and so on. The design of his actual buildings therefore is based on a further set of oppositions, such as architecture/nature; ideal/real; in/out and so on.

Of course, it is perfectly true that symbols generally—in the Peircian sense—such as words, *do* derive their meanings from relationships of this kind, but Graves's visual analogies by definition are icons in Peircian terms. Their sources be they in Classical architecture, Cubist painting, Modern architecture or elsewhere, already have their own inherent meanings before he draws on them. Indeed, if they did not there would be no point in his drawing on them! There is a certain redundancy therefore—not to mention a source of confusion—in treating icons as if they were symbols, that is in taking objects which already have meaning and trying to give them further meanings by these syntactic relationships. How much better to cross-fertilise them, as the other semanticists tend to do, thus encouraging the observer to read whatever *new* meanings he wants to read from the assemblages thus formed. For all the sophistication of Graves's working methods, his models still look 'like' Le Corbusier Villas. And so do Eisenman's. In terms of working methods, however, Eisenman is much more consistent; like the Italian Rationalists, he is trying to develop an architecture of pure syntax based on its own internal logic, an intellectual structure in which all such physical banalities as building construction, user comfort, convenience and the meanings which people read are seen as unfortunate, by-products of building in physical reality. Eisenman's syntax—like Graves's semantics—is based on the relationship of opposites real/virtual; space/form; solid/void and so on. Eisenman personally is not so much interested in the processes by which actual buildings come about—he sees close analogies between these processes and the ways in which language is formed, according to the Generative and Transformational grammars of Noam Chomsky. His generative processes also are based on oppositions, such as those between column and wall; volume/column and volume/wall. He sees the structural grid 'provided' by modern technology as a basic framework within which spatial syntaxes can be developed and in a typical case, such as House II he starts with two square volumes, shifted against each other diagonally as the basic generators of such a grid. The first volume is then 'marked' by a grid of columns, three bays by three, with 'open' spaces between them, whilst the second is 'marked' by four parallel walls running from east to west across the plan towards the diagonal, so that whilst the northern most wall runs full width, the others stop short, successively, against this diagonal.

Having set up two geometric systems, a columnar grid and a set of parallel walls, Eisenman then combines them and begins to consider the volumes contained between them. These generally step down in height from the south east corner to the north west thus a set of interlocking spaces is defined within which the house can then be planned.

Eisenman's syntax obviously is much purer then Graves's semantics but still his overall aim, 'The elimination of semantic considerations and the focus on syntactics', inevitably proves self-defeating. For the architecture of columns, white walls and large windows inevitably 'reads' as post-Le Corbusian International Style to anyone with the slightest familiarity with the history of architecture in the 20th Century.

Jencks's piece on the Olivetti building indeed is a potent demonstration of that central, inescapable fact that every sign we make—and for sign in this case read building—*will* carry meaning, in spite of our intentions. Of course, it was the 'functionalist' myth that buildings could be designed which merely fulfilled their functions, clearly and efficiently, doing so because they simply 'worked' with no kind of meaning or symbolic connotation whatever. But what a forlorn and misguided hope. People looked at the simple, rectangular slabs called functional and talked of 'matchboxes', 'cornflake packets' or made other (pejorative) comparisons. If a building had standard industrialised glazing, then, of course, it 'looked like' a factory; if it was faced with white tiles then it 'looked like' a public lavatory and so on. How could it be otherwise?

It is a fact of human existence, as demonstrated by psychologists such as Bruner, Goodnow and Austin —described in Broadbent's piece—that we survive in this world by putting things into categories. We have to do that because otherwise, we should have to think out afresh each time what to do in every situation in which we found ourselves; how to talk to a person we meet in the street, how to enter a building, how to open a door, to sit down in a chair and so on. Of course, that would be quite intolerable, so we categorise our experience after which we *know* what to do every time we meet a new situation in any of those known categories. We know what matchboxes, cornflake packets, factories, public lavatories and so on 'look like' so when we meet a new and strange building which 'looks like' one of those, we naturally put it into that category.

Jencks—like Graves—calls such comparisons 'metaphors' (I prefer analogy; Broadbent, 1977) and being fascinated by the way in which different people read different metaphors into the same strange building form, he looks at the variety of their response. He confronted his students with Stirling's Olivetti building which, of course, was quite unlike any other building they knew. They had to encompass it within their understanding and in order to do so, they had to make comparisons with forms they knew. The comparisons they drew naturally were conditioned by whether they liked the building or not, so it's hardly surprising that they ranged from 'plastic trash cans' (pejorative) through caravans (neutral) to train/bus (examples of 'good' design).

Stirling (1972) himself reacted somewhat naively to Jencks's similar analysis of what people read into his residence at St Andrews. Jencks (1972) had found various connotations—greenhouses, ships and so on. Stirling objected violently on the grounds that his St Andrews Residence was no more designed to 'look like' a ship than the Leicester Engineering building like a waterworks: the Cambridge History Faculty a glasshouse and so on. In doing so he quite missed the point—which Jencks himself makes so eloquently in *The Language of Post Modern Architecture* (Jencks, 1977) that unless the building looks *specifically* and only like a matchbox (e.g. any building by Mies), a duck (e.g. the poultry stand on Long Island to which Venturi—and Peter Blake—have drawn to our attention) or something equally simple and banal, other people will read into his building what they want to read, what their experience tells them, quite irrespective of what the architect consciously or unconsciously did, or did not, intend.

So in this section, above all, there is variety but whilst the papers vary in intention from clear objective analysis to poetic evocation, they are all informed by a care for buildings as objects which 'carry' meaning, and with a concern for just how that meaning *is* carried.

References

Broadbent, G. (1973) *Design in Architecture*, John Wiley & Sons, London.

Broadbent, G. (1977) 'The Language of Post Modern Architecture, A Review', *Architectural Design*, April 1977.

Jencks, C. (1972) 'Rhetoric & Architecture', *Architectural Association Quarterly*, vol. 4, no. 3, Summer 1972.

Jencks, C. (1977) *The Language of Post Modern Architecture*, Academy Editions, London.

Stirling, James (1972) Letter to the Editor, *Architectural Association Quarterly*, vol. 4, no. 4, Autumn 1972.

2.1 A Componential Analysis of the Architectural Sign /Column/

Umberto Eco

Reprinted from *Semiotica*, Vol 5:2, 1972. Translated by David Osmond-Smith. Also to be published in a collection of essays by Eco published by the Peter de Ridder press.

0.1   One of the main tasks of semiotics consists in arriving at a study of all aspects of culture as communicative processes. This does not mean that all aspects of culture are only communicative processes but that (a) they can be regarded as communicative processes; (b) they have a cultural function precisely because they are ALSO communicative processes.

It is obvious that—in this sense—a semiotics of architecture represents one of the crucial points in semiotic research.

0.2   Architecture is composed of artifacts, which delimit spaces (outside or inside them) so as to permit functions: going up or down, coming in or out, sheltering from the weather; gathering together, sleeping, eating, praying, celebrating events, instilling reverence . . . .

0.3   In my book *La struttura assente* I tried to define architectural signs generically (and it remains to be seen what is meant by /sign/ as 'unit of an architectural code') as a system of manufactured objects and circumscribed spaces that communicate possible functions, on the basis of systems of conventions (CODES). I distinguish simple PROCESSES OF STIMULATION (a step that I stumble over in the dark, forcing me to raise my leg) from PROCESSES OF SIGNIFICATION: a /staircase/ consists of the articulation of a few morphological elements that are together recognized as a 'machine for ascending'. If the staircase is recognized as such, it is used. It can be recognized without being used. It can even communicate the possible function of 'ascent' without in fact allowing it (as in cases of *trompe-l'oeil*). This means that in architecture the communicative aspect predominates over the functional aspect, and precedes it.

0.4   So from this point of view the signified functions of architecture are not necessarily REFERENTS—they are not necessarily functions that may be carried out, and they are not functions that have been carried out. They are not TOKENS (*my* concrete act of climbing THESE stairs HERE AND NOW) but TYPES. They are classes of possible functions. They are thus CULTURAL UNITS, before being practical acts. An architectural object is therefore a sign-vehicle (*un signifiant*, according to Saussure's definition) that denotes a meaning (*un signifié*).

0.5   Still referring to *La struttura assente*, I had also distinguished two types of function: PRIMARY FUNCTIONS, those that the functionalist tradition recognizes as functions in the true sense of the word (going upstairs, standing at the window, taking the air, enjoying the sunlight, living together, etc.); and SECONDARY FUNCTIONS, those that art-historians and iconologists have preferred to classify as the 'symbolical values' of architecture: a Gothic cathedral makes possible several primary functions such as 'gathering together', but at the same time it communicates a number of 'ideological' values such as 'mystic atmosphere', 'diffusion of light as symbol of the divine presence', or else 'concentration', 'deference', and so on, I thus distinguished in the architectural sign a process of DENOTATION of primary functions and a process of CONNOTATION of secondary functions. Naturally, for many architectural objects communication of the secondary functions is more important (socially and ideologically) than communication of the primary functions. Therefore the term 'function' is not to be understood in the restricted sense assigned to it by classical functionalism.

0.6   But several problems were left unsolved in *La struttura assente*. One of the most important of these is: what are the levels of articulation of architectural signs and what is the significative unit in architecture?

1.1   The first problem is extensive and rather awkward, because one runs the risk of making out elements of secondary articulation in architecture (figurae according to Hjelmslev) that are not exclusively architectural. For example the elements of Euclidean geometry, which I have called 'stoicheia' differential, codified elements, undoubtedly without meaning but not belonging exclusively to the architectural language (they could be elements of secondary articulation in a painting by Mondrian or in the printed reproduction of an image seen through a raster).[1] At the mo-

---

[1]Cf. M. Krampen and P. Seitz ed., *Design and Planning* (New York, Hasting House Publishers, 1967); and my contribution to the proceedings of the conference on 'Stato e tendenze attuali della ricerca sulle communicazioni di massa con particolare riferimento di linguaggio iconico' (Milano, Istituto 'Gemelli', October 1970).

ment this problem is being examined in several places, and perhaps the most interesting approach up to now is the one adopted in the course in architectural semiology in the Faculty of Architecture at Buenos Aires.[2]

1.2   The second problem, with which I shall be explicitly concerned from now on is: what are the *significative units* in architecture? If it were valid (which it is not) to transpose linguistic concepts into the terminology of architectural semiotics, one would have to ask: 'what is an architectural "word"'? But one can ask: 'what is an architectural SEMEME', and thus 'what sign-vehicles in architecture communicate a specifically architectural meaning?'

1.3   A further problem will be that once one has identified the sememes, one will have to try to carry out a componential analysis (or semic analysis) to show that the meaning of the architectural sign-vehicle is composed of other, smaller significative units, not necessarily architectural, which together form the sememe.

1.4   It should be clear that the sememe is a cultural unit, and that it is the object of a structural semantics of architecture. The architectural sign-vehicle will instead be called a 'morpheme'. The analogy with linguistic terminology is etymologically justified this time, since an architectural morpheme is a complex of formal qualities. It is the object of study of a morphology of architecture. The classic treatises on architecture that identified the architectural orders, for example, were morphological treatises and identified morphemes or complex syntagmatic chains composed of morphemes.

2.1   Before proceeding with such an analysis one must however eliminate a dangerous ambiguity that prevails in many current attempts to elaborate a semiotic of architecture (most of which, moreover, are being carried out by Italian schools of architecture).[3] This ambiguity derives from an aesthetic fallacy held in common by critics and historians of architecture, who almost always make a distinction between building and architecture. Building is thus the construction of manufactured objects that circumscribe spaces set aside to foster practical functions (a hen-house, a hangar, an 'unsightly' block of flats). On the other hand, architecture

---

[2]Cf. in particular Roberto Doberti's study, as yet unpublished, *Sistema de figuras* (Universidad de Buenos Aires).

[3]Cf. in particular the studies of R. De Fusco and M.L. Scalvini, 'Significanti e significati della rotonda palladiana', and of Gillo Dorfles, 'Valori iconologici e semiotici in architettura', both in *op. cit.*, 16 (September 1969); Urbano Cardarelli, 'Lettura storia-semiologica di Palmanova', in *op. cit.*, 17 (January, 1970).

consists of articulating spaces that, although they can also permit practical functions, are valued above all for their aesthetic auto-reflectiveness. According to this theory, architectural work primarily signifies its own structures. This means that one identifies the architectural language with its poetic function (as defined by Jakobson). To take the poetic functions of architecture as a starting-point for an architectural semiotics would be the equivalent of a study of the structure of the English language that started from Shakespeare's sonnets and didn't go any further. It would be the equivalent of studying only the ambiguous use (the deviation from the norm) of a code that is not yet known.

2.2   One of the aesthetic fallacies of architectural semiotics lies in the affirmation that architectural objects are sign-vehicles whose meanings are spaces. Space (or rather an abstract notion of space as 'spatiality') then becomes the object of architectural communication.

2.3   It is easy to understand that, from this point of view, it becomes irrelevant to establish what the significative units in architecture are. An architectural work, such as Palladio's Rotonda, communicates 'that particular space that is the space conceived by Palladio'.

To ask oneself what the steps or the columns that mark out that space mean becomes useless. They are intermediate elements[4] that serve to signify an aesthetic conception of space. It is not by chance that this type of architectural semiotic is based upon works explicitly constructed to provide aesthetic experiences above all else, rich in 'secondary functions' and poor in 'primary functions' (or rather, that entirely sacrifice primary functions to secondary functions).

2.4   To solve this problem one must turn to a useful distinction, made by Hjelmslev, between LEVEL OF EXPRESSION and LEVEL OF CONTENT, which are in turn divided into SUBSTANCE OF EXPRESSION and FORM OF EXPRESSION, SUBSTANCE OF CONTENT and FORM OF CONTENT, as in the following scheme:

$$\frac{C \ \dfrac{s}{f}}{E \ \dfrac{f}{s}}$$

2.5   Studying architecture as the communication of a particular conception of space is the equivalent of studying language as a means of expressing syntactic relationships. But the syntactic relationships, in the arrangement that they

---

[4]De Fusco (cit.) would call 'symbols' those elements of architectural articulation that can have a semantic value (for example a column, or the Doric order) but are 'without that internal spatiality which I have proposed as the true meaning of architecture' (p. 11 – 12).

immediately assume, constitute an aspect of the form of expression signifying a content that is in turn subdivided into relevant units (organized in semantic systems). So that in architecture the fact of articulating a certain space in a certain way signifies the subdivision of all possible spatial articulations and dispositions (substance of expression) according to a system of oppositions (forms of expression) in order to communicate, among all the possible functions that man may perform within his cultural context (substance of content), a series of functions that are specified and defined by a system of cultural units (the system of sememes) that represents the form of the content.

2.6   A man thrusts a stick into the ground. He may do it to measure the position of the sun, to fix a point of no return, to indicate a point of reference. The stick is an object that does not enclose an internal space (another aesthetic fallacy is that by which it is believed that 'architectural = aesthetic' space is what is delimited WITHIN an architectural object), but gives a new meaning to the space around it (which becomes 'space around the stick, space near the stick, and space far away from the stick', etc.).

Now, the space thus marked out by the stick is not the meaning that the stick communicates — it is, along with the stick, one of the elements of the sign-vehicle that serves to communicate the several possible functions permitted by that point of reference.[5]

2.7   It must furthermore be added that space (or rather spatial relationships, distances, as elements of the indeterminate substance 'space' that are already formalized), represents a pre-architectural material, already charged with its meanings, as we are taught by proxemics.[6] This expressive material, with the meanings that it conveys, is re-utilized by

[5]This function of space as sign-vehicle has been very well covered by Giovanni Klaus Koenig, *Architettura e comunicazione* (Florence, Libreria editrice fiorentina, 1970), which takes up and develops several of my proposals from the first edition of *La struttura assente*, (which in turn is indebted to previous studies by Koenig for a number of ideas). But even Koenig tends to think that an architectural unit such as the column cannot be considered a *choreme* because (a) occupies a place without creating a space; (b) it does not denote anything and it takes no function 'other than a static function (and therefore syntactic rather than semantic) of supporting something' (p. 162). Apart from the fact that the column may also, for example, connote 'leaning against', apart from the fact that simply denoting support is no trifling communication, I have tried to demonstrate in the new edition of *La struttura assente* (sec. A), that even what are called syncategorematic terms in language denote something — that is, precisely, their syntactic function (which permits the articulation of contextual meanings). In this way Koenig makes the same mistake as the other Italian researchers I have mentioned, and only attributes the value of a significative unit to complex syntagms, which create an articulated spatiality.

[6]Cf. Edward T. Hall, *The Hidden Dimension* (New York, Doubleday, 1966).

architecture as a sign-vehicle to signify new meanings, new cultural units. the sememes.

3.1   Let us therefore imagine a significative process of the type:

in which x^1 is the relevant unit of a system of pre-architectural spatial configurations (for example the linear distance of 12 feet). In *La struttura assente* these spatial units are called 'choremes'—from the Greek *chora*, 'space'.
    Y is the unit of an anthropological (rather than spatial) system of physical functions: as Hall explains, at 12 feet it is possible to perceive skin texture, hair, the condition of clothes, but not the finest details of the face;
    K is the unit of a system of socio-anthropological functions, in this case, for example, 'social distance—far phase'.

3.2   The process of signification presumes a spatial sign-vehicle that denotes a physical function. Choreme x_1 and function Y (insofar as together they constitute a sign) in turn become the sign-vehicle of a connotated, socio-anthropological function K. As one can see, architecture is not involved at this stage; a relationship of this type could be established between two human beings in a desert.

3.3   Architecture becomes involved when a physical object (for example a table-top) incorporates (realizes) as the form of its own expressive substance the distance of 6 feet. Space in this sense is not a meaning of the architectural object—it is one of its morphological characteristics, one of its morphological markers (thus in lexicology the lexeme /desk/ possesses the grammatical marker 'singular'). It is at this point that a significative process of the type is realized:

in which m_1 is the relevant unit of a morphological system and Y is the unit of a system of physical functions, already examined in proxemics, but not signified this time by a spatial distance, but by an object that imposes (as a stimulus) a spatial distance and that does not communicate the spatial distance but the physical function Y. K is the unit of a socio-anthropological system (e.g., 'social distance—far phase').

3.4   Yet one cannot assert that m_1, as a morphological element, is the sign-vehicle of a possible sememe 'desk in the office of important person' (cf. Hall, p.115). In order to realize the meaning 'desk', the presence of the morphological feature m_1 is not enough. There must be other morphological features, for instance four vertical supports (the legs of the table), which in turn communicate physical functions of the category Y (such as 'support'). m_1 is therefore an element (with morphological marker x_1) of a more complex architectural morpheme M to which corresponds, as a semantic unit, a sememe A, which is 'desk in the office of important person'.

3.5   So that, given a morpheme M possessing morphological features m with spatial features x:

$$M [m_1 (x_1), m_2 (x_2, x_3), \ldots m_n (x_n)]$$

the morpheme M expresses an architectural sememe A with semic features $a_1, a_2, \ldots a_n$.

3.6   Each of these semantic markers may directly belong to the Y category (denoted physical functions) or to the K category (connotated socio-anthropological functions). Each of the features of the K group will in turn connote, with reference to precise architectural conventions, other socio-anthropological functions (and thus secondary functions) such as 'power', 'respect', 'manager', etc. Each of the connotated secondary functions must base itself upon a morphological feature of the M group (for example 'luxury' will be a semic feature a_n expressed by a morphological feature x_n that could be the use of a valuable wood).

3.7   These theoretical hypotheses, which, as may be seen, imply the possibility of a componential analysis of architectural objects, were tested out in the course of an experiment conducted during a seminar that I directed for the Instituto Interuniversitario de Especialisacion en Historia de la Arquitectura, held at La Plata (Argentina) in July — August 1970, in which students interested in the semiotic approach to architecture, critics and historians of architecture, and architects took part.[7]

4.1   As will be seen, in order to attempt a componential analysis of an architectural morpheme, a method of stem-

[7]The research work that follows was discussed by everyone taking part in the seminar but in particular, was developed with the help of the architects Andrés Garcia, Mariana Uzielli and Evelia Peralta of the Universidad de Tucuman. I must, in any case, thank Professor Marina Waisman, president of the Instituto Interuniversitario, who organised the seminar at La Plata and made possible the discussions with which this research originated.

ming was used which brings to mind the one put forward by Katz and Fodor and by Katz and Postal.[8] I criticized this method on several points in *La struttura assente* because I thought it excessively schematic. However, in the absence of more elaborate systems of notation and representation it may, I think, prove didactically effective as a first approach to the problems of componential analysis.

4.2   But it should be made clear that in the stems that follow some nodes are introduced that are excluded from the hypothesis of Katz — Fodor — Postal. They in fact consider that it is not possible to elaborate a THEORY OF SETTINGS, and thus that it is not possible to include among the semantic components of an item the possible contextual events that will assign to the sememe one path (reading) rather than another. The argument asserts that a theory of settings would imply the consideration of all possible contexts and therefore of every event in the universe. I, on the other hand, would maintain that in the semantic representation of an element, privileged events, which is to say the contextual connections among which it habitually recurs, may be taken into consideration. In this sense it is valid to consider that these contextual connections are codified and recognized as 'canonical', and that they may therefore find a place in a componential analysis.

4.3   Neither does the Katz — Fodor — Postal hypothesis consider as semantic components of a lexical item its possible connotations, for the same reason it rejects a settings theory. In fact the possible connotations of a semantic unit are, in theory, infinite. But if one may take into account contextual circumstances (privileged in relation to the others, because more likely to recur) it will then also be possible to include in the componential description of a unit the connotations it is most likely to generate — and which therefore appear to be already codified.

4.4   These particulars only serve to explain (a) why a system of componential description that resembles Katz — Fodor — Postal's in several respects is adopted, (b) why the present system diverges from it, and (c) why, all things considered, I would regard this system of description as entirely provisory and simplistic.

5.1   The Argentinian experiment was the fruit of a series of

[8]Cf. J.J. Katz and J.A. Fodor, 'The Structure of a Semantic Theory', in Katz and Fodor eds., *The Structure of Language* (Englewood Cliffs, Prentice-Hall, 1964); J.J. Katz and P.M. Postal, *An Integrated Theory of Linguistic Description* (Research Monograph, n. 26) (Cambridge, M.I.T., 1964). As for a general sense of 'semic analysis', I am greatly indebted to A.J. Greimas, *Semantique Structurale* (Paris, Larousse, 1966).

discussions in which several architects—who held views similar to those of Italian sociologists of architecture—tended to fall into the trap of an aesthetic fallacy, maintaining that the meaning of an architectural unit was its over-all aesthetic signification in terms of Space. The fact that they tended to analyze works of art (those of Frank Lloyd Wright for example) rather than ordinary constructions, revealed the architectural critics' aversion to 'building'. In these cases, potential elementary significative units lost their powers of signification because they had to be viewed as elements of a more extensive syntagm. To check this temptation, it was even decided to conduct an enquiry among children (free from aesthetic-cultural prejudices), asking them what a door or a window was. It was in fact a question of finding out whether, for an 'uncultured' recipient—lacking an academic degree—there existed minimum units endowed with sense, such as a step, an architrave, or a stair.

5.2   At times, the project took the form of a paradoxical proposition: what instructions ought I to give a Martian in order to get him to construct a door? Would I necessarily have to make him construct the whole building, or city, or could I provide him with inputs such that in output (considering the Martian as a black box) they would supply a 'door' or 'window' object that the Martian could recognize as such semantically? The most frequent objection was: 'one thing that is not clear is the meaning of a column; in itself a column doesn't mean anything; it is the complex of columns called the Parthenon that acquires architectural meaning; a column does not communicate possible functions, it is a neutral element that combines to form more complex morphological chains which do have an architectural meaning'.

5.3   During the discussions I happened to come across an article, 'Eternidad de la columna', by Dora Isella Russell, in the daily paper *La Prensa*, 26 July 1970. I translate it in full, emphasizing the phrases whose semantic units are then to be subjected to analysis:

The Eternal Column
Around it blow the winds of time. The winds embrace the *uplifted, time-defying shaft.* Centuries have passed without touching its *slim body,* and *towering among the ruins,* the column *affirms its timeless destiny.*

A glance back through the ages reveals to us the vast panorama, studded with *venerable ruins,* from which emerge *solitary* columns, the *last remaining witnesses of vanished greatness.* Amongst them *wanders the shadow of melancholy.* The mighty civilisations that lighted the awakening of human consciousness were ground into the dust, and other men and other ways of life raised above their exhausted cultures the hope of resurrection. Phantoms of India, shadows of Babylon, Chaldean shepherds consulting the stars, priests of Heliopolis filing invisibly past, wandering Phoenicians hoisting the first sails in our seas, grave pharaohs submerged in death, luminous memories of Hellas as the sun of the Peloponnese sinks, soldiers of Gaul extending the frontiers, all were consigned to oblivion before the uncontainable onrush of new ages. And the flood swept down upon men as upon things, blotting out peoples, burying buildings, shattering temples, destroying statues, wiping out all trace of the work of individual men. And yet here and there in remote corners of the Orient, and along the roads of Europe, menhirs and dolmens remained standing, hinting at reconstruction, and in Egypt as in Greece, at Rome as at Palmyra or among the remotest oceanic islands, something was able to escape from the inexorable massacre—the *aristocratic upthrust* of the column, an object of wonder, a *sacred relic*, an *unscathed document*.

The first *tree-trunk*, the first lopped branch that some distant inhabitant of this planet hammered into the ground in front of his cave, were its most distant forerunners. From the tree was born the column. The imagination arrives at such an idea *without effort*, and so simply, so logically that there is no race that has not concerned itself with the column, as *support* and as *ornament*. *It sustains, yet nothing sustains it*, and it may possess the *patina of millennia*. It *allegorizes the miracle of survival*, belying the *apparent fragility* of a *single point of contact* with the earth.

Rare were the Egyptian monuments that lacked imposing internal colonnades. Generally, a *stiff plume of palm, lotus,* or *papyrus* fronds *twined around the capital*, taking over its place, which in itself constituted no mean *imaginative audacity* for a people of such grave and hieratic formulae. India, on the other hand, was to allow leaves, flowers, allegories, and legendary figures to climb around her columns; the imaginative exuberance of her mythology found intricate expression in decorations that *reached to the roofs* of her colossal sanctuaries.

But at the height of Greece's glory the artists of Hellas trimmed away *all foliage*, leaving naked the *smooth, scarcely tapered body* of the *Doric* column, or else, later, adding the *nimble volutes* that embellish the *Ionic* order. The column became *channelled with grooves*, with *flutings* that enhanced its weightlessness in a crystalline, open-air exaltation that *lent harmony to their constructions.* When the *Corinthian* column became burdened with *acanthus and olive leaves;* when *griffons, pegasi* and *sphinxes* were added; when the *capital blossomed into a profusion of interwoven forms,* the end was near. These baroque mannerisms, for all their beauty, heralded the sunset—a glorious but finally inescapable twilight that brought to an end the 'Grecian miracle'.

In Asia Minor the *bodies of fantastic animals* replaced the traditional column on many occasions. In Persia there were kneeling camels; in India the *pachyderms* of Ellora, carved in the stone of the mountain, served as the base for prodigious temples, while at the palace of Susa *bull-heads* crowned the columns. The Egyptians, even earlier than the Greeks, had revealed the sumptuous majesty of hypostyles such as those at the temple of Karnak, and had arrived at the stage of sculpting *human forms on the capitals* of Denderah that reproduced the masks of Isis. Yet it was the Greeks of Pericles' time that dared to entirely *replace the column by making the human body* assume its functions, supporting the architecture of their temples now upon the *male statues* (talamoni), now upon *female bodies* that graciously and effortlessly carry the building's weight without losing their feminine delicacy. The caryatids raise their graceful forms and fluttering robes, and have for centuries borne their *heavy task* with that diaphanous limpidity with which the Grecian sky lends nobility to the sacred relics of its history.

In every latitude and in every age the column has *enriched monuments, giving to façades solidity and sumptuousness,* to *interiors grandeur,* and above it *have risen towers and cupolas* that re-echo its *upward-aspiring intentions with that verticality* so characteristic of Gothic art. The Gothic column *has no modulus,* is not independent of the building—*it inter-reacts with other columns* to form groups which *mount vertiginously upwards,* pointing towards heaven, as if by their means the faith of men rose towards mystic regions inhabited by saints and angels, that have been metamorphosed into finely-wrought stained-glass. The mediaeval cathedral absorbs the column in its obsession with upward-climbing masonry that *sprouts architraves,* branching forms, spears of stone, dominated by the *impulse to rise.* Ogives, arches and columns do not belong to Gothic art alone—while mediaeval Europe was constructing her cities, with their prodigious, steepled bell-towers, Muslim art gave birth to the Mosque of Omar at Jerusalem, the Mosques of Amru and of Touloun at Cairo, and in Spain the famous

Mosque of Cordova and the Palace of Zara, built upon four thousand, three hundred columns.

A lyrical raptus renders it poetical. Its *suggestive power* renders it subtle. The anonymous Arab poets celebrate it, identifying it with the *palm-tree*, 'the column of the desert'. 'Slender as a column and with eyes like stars', they say of *their beloved.* Her *neck* is an 'alabaster column'; the litany of beauty employs it as a likeness for the delicate *throat*, the smoothly shaped *arm*, the perfectly formed *leg*. 'Her legs are columns of marble upon bases of fine gold', one reads in the Song of Songs. Nations raise columns *in commemoration* of their great feasts, events, and heroes—the Trajan column, the column of Place Vendôme, the column of Trafalgar Square, recalling Nelson . . .

Since they *are not easily thrown down*, men erect them *as memorials.* An aesthetic mission, a historical mission, both devolve upon these *obstinate, airy, arrogant* columns raised above the passing hours.

For time is a sharp-keeled ship that leaves in its wake all that is transient. And the column that spans the centuries appears as *the mast* of this mighty vessel.

5.4   At first sight, the article would appear to be a collection of exceedingly obvious reflections upon the rhetorical theme of the column, an inventory of banalities with pseudo-poetical intentions. Any cultivated reader would be tempted to dismiss it as a sample of critical kitsch.

But rereading the article, one realizes that these 'obvious reflections' correspond precisely to an inventory of the current tradition of thought about the column. It represents the astonishing record of an imaginary survey that collects from a sample of everyday users of architecture all the meanings that they associate with the unit 'column'.

5.5   These meanings may be viewed as 'endoxa' in the Aristotelian sense of the term (that is: general opinions or socially codified acquired habits). Society, that is, recognizes several obvious morphological features in the column, such as presence of shaft, base, the capital, and so forth. One may also extrapolate from a number of 'pseudo-poetic' statements several semantic features such as 'verticality', 'support', etc.

5.6   In the second place, it is possible to compile an inventory of connotations of the unit column that sets out in three columns an analysis of the article's connotative content (see Table I). All these connotations could be summarised in more precise formulae, but at present it seems more convenient to keep to the ones employed in the article.

To explain points (I) and (J) better I should add that the first case refers to colonnades in which identical columns follow one another, the second to colonnades of the Gothic type in which rhythms such as AB−AB, or ABC−ABC may be established.

Table I

architectural connotations	historical connotations	aesthetic connotations
A. tree-trunk	1. the winds of time blow around it	a. affirms its timeless destiny
B. apparent fragility	2. venerable	b. amongst them wanders the shadow of melancholy
C. supports without being supported	3. last relic left standing of vanished grandeur	c. it rises aristocratically
D. effortless	4. unscathed document	d. universal
E. enriches monuments	5. commemoration of events, great deeds, heroes	e. pure
F. gives solidity to façade	6. mast of ship of time	f. legendary
G. gives sumptuousness to façade	7. has the patina of millennia	g. audacity of imagination
H. gives grandeur to interior	8. allegory of the miracle of survival	h. mounts vertiginously upwards, pointing towards heaven
I. unity in repetitive variety	9. time-defying	i. poeticized by lyrical raptus
J. unity in modulating variety		j. neck of beloved
K. irremovable		k. slender body
L. mast of ship		l. shapely arm
M. airy		m. perfectly formed leg
N. gives harmony to building		n. obstinate
		o. arrogant
		p. solitary
		q. sacred remains
		r. Greek miracle
		s. prodigious

6.1   At this point 3 problems arise:

(a) the provision of a morphological description of the column; this must be composed of morphological markers and constructive operations similar to those that one would supply a Martian (or a robot) with if one had to make him construct a column; the possibility of such an operation will demonstrate the possibility of construction of (and therefore of defining) an isolated architectural object furnished with autonomous meaning.

(b) the provision of a semantic description of this isolated column; seeing whether the various semantic markers are based upon precise morphological markers, and thus which morphological markers are necessary in order to single out a semantic marker.

(c) the insertion of the isolated column within a context, so as to see whether this insertion will charge the object with new meanings. This operation poses a series of problems of description, granted that the contexts in which the architectural object may be included are various. The context may be seen (i) in ELEVATION, as the façade (or one side) of the building in both vertical and horizontal relation; (ii) in a VERTICAL SECTION of the building; (iii) in OTHER SECTIONS, which give account of the depth of the building; (iv) in GROUND-PLAN. For analytical convenience, and for reasons of didactic clarity, I have decided to limit myself to a laboratory situation, and to examine possibility (i) alone.

In the diagrams that follow, the following graphic rules must be kept in mind:

(A) The sign in isolation is represented by a horizontal stem, the sign in context by vertical stems.

(B) The terms in brackets represent morphological markers; those in inverted commas represent semantic markers; Arabic numerals, Roman numerals and letters of the alphabet refer to the inventory of connotations listed in 5.6. It seems to me, that is, that the primary function denotated in a particular morphological node becomes the sign-vehicle of a connotated secondary function only in that particular node.

(C) The symbol ┌──┴──┐ and the symbol ⌐ are used when a given node generates a series of possibilities that are not mutually exclusive but can co-exist (the shaft can possess height, diameter, and weight just as a lexical item can simultaneously possess morphological and semantic markers such as masculine, singular, animate, etc.). The symbol ⟋⟍ or the symbol ●◁ is only used when the markers are exclusive and in mutual opposition, implying a binary selection between different paths or readings. These binary exclusions could be similar to those that in Katz — Fodor — Postal's lexical models are defined as 'distinguishers'.

(D) The representation by means of stems possesses an analogical aspect in that the vertical and horizontal succession of elements also suggests the order of their succession. In other words, the fact that in the first scheme the shaft is BELOW the capital and ABOVE the base, furnishes the robot with instructions as to how to combine the pieces. It is obvious that with a robot that functions digitally, such instructions could be given in another way, and for this reason, once again, the scheme has been simplified for didactic purposes.

7.1   For the componential analysis model of the sign /*column*/ out of context see Table II.

7.2   The semantic marker is placed in a particular node if

TABLE II

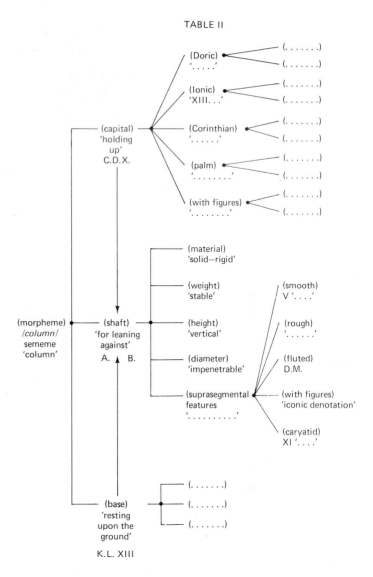

and when the connected meaning is only recognized in the presence of the corresponding morphological marker. Thus the semantic marker 'holding up' is only assigned to a column when the shaft supports a capital. A column without a capital does not give the impression of holding up anything. The same may be said of the shaft—base relationship with regard to the marker 'resting upon'.

This scheme is full of analogical elements that have been used for the sake of speed. In fact, distinguishing (Doric) between the morphological features of the capital simply means that in place of this verbal category there ought to be other instructions. Probably these instructions would also be of the analogical type (an iconic representation to be reproduced on the pantograph), but there is nothing to prevent one from arriving at a system of digital notation capable of making the robot construct a standard Doric capital. The same is true of morphological instructions such as (smooth) or (rough) or (with figures) or (caryatid). The last two are indeed cases of an iconic code superposing upon the architectural one. Naturally the componential spectrum could be more complex here as well.

7.3   It may be objected that many of the semantic markers denoted by the morphological markers are not amongst those that would be called 'functions' in architecture. 'Resting upon' and 'holding up' are certainly functions, but are 'vertical' or 'impenetrable' functions in the same sense? Here one has to establish whether the functions communicated by architecture are only bio-physiological (leaning against, going out) or also constructive (holding up, rising vertically, etc.). One would be tempted to call the second ones syntactic functions and the first, roughly, semantic functions. But, apart from the fact that the so-called semantic functions are instead bio-physical functions, the so-called syntactic functions, while undoubtedly playing a part in the way the building, or single object (cf. column) supports itself, are also perceived by the observer as semantic communication of cultural units. The column communicates (as Miss Russell's article demonstrates) semantic markers such as 'verticality' and 'impenetrability'. One therefore has to consider as irrelevant the distinction between bio-physiological and constructive functions at the present, preliminary stage of analysis. But a more accurate description ought to be able to distinguish between these two aspects.

7.4   One also notices that, of the connotations or secondary functions singled out in Miss Russell's article, very few would appear to associate themselves with the morphemes and sememes of this scheme. As will be seen, the greater part of these connotations are instead associated with the column placed in its spatial and temporal context. Associated with the single column are the connotations C ('supports without being supported': a typical poetico-kitsch connotation, which is applied to the shaft — capital relationship without taking into account the shaft — base relationship). D ('effortless'), and consequently X ('neck of beloved', for clear analogical reasons). The shaft — base relationship generates the analogical connotation XIII ('leg'). D and M ('effortless' and 'airy') seem to me to apply to the morphological feature (fluting), as indeed the context of Miss Russell's article would give one to understand. And it is obvious that the presence of a caryatid will arouse associations of XI ('slender body'), which may however be associated with the whole column. In any case, the association of connotations has been undertaken on the basis of common sense. One would have to carry out an examination of this field by means of interviews

TABLE III

A Componential Analysis of the Sign /column/ in a Vertical and Horizontal Content

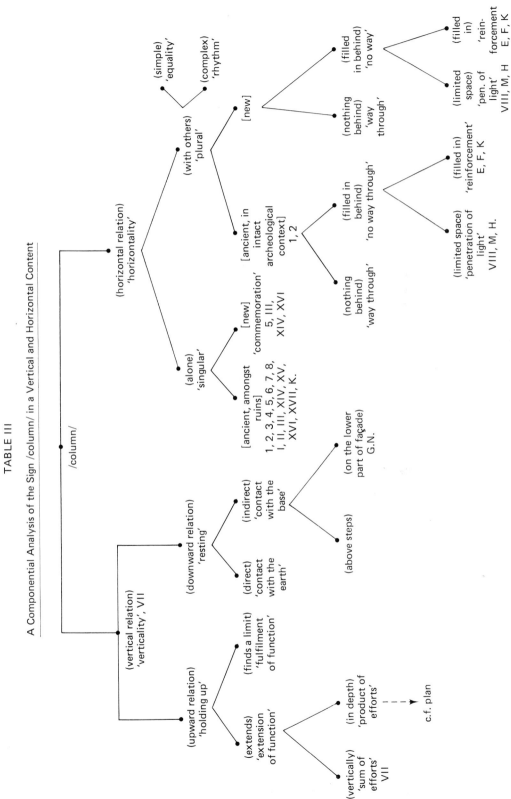

to be able to establish with precision the average psycho-semantic response.

8.1   For the componential analyis model of the sign /*column*/ in context see Table III.

8.2   In this second scheme, which is undoubtedly more complex than the first, certain details require further definition, which will be given by reference to individual morphological relations:
—(*Vertical relation*): the column considered in connection with what is above and what is below.
—(*Horizontal relation*): the column considered in connection with lateral architectural signs.
—(*Upward relation*): the column may support a tympanum or other columns; in such cases the function (extends), that is, the 'holding up' is transmitted to other columns placed above which in turn hold up something else, or else the function (finds a limit) in the tympanum or in some other architectural element which, as it were, finishes the process off. The function may be extended (vertically) when the column is supporting other columns, as in a façade with colonnades at several levels, or else (in depth)—this latter expression has been used to indicate the typical extension of function that one finds in the Gothic column of an ogival vault, which curves back to join with other columns in the *clef-de-voûte*, adding its own sustaining power to that of others. It is for this reason that one is referred to the plan, since a representation in elevation cannot give an account of this morphological feature.
—(*Downward relation*) places the column in direct contact either with the earth, or with other elements of the base (steps) or else with other columns standing beneath it on the façade.
—(*Horizontal relation*): the column may be at a horizontal relation of zero, and therefore (alone), or else (with others). In the first case this single column may be an ancient one, standing alone [amongst ruins], or a [new] one erected for commemorative ends. It should be noted that in this group of nodes the morphological features have been put in square brackets. These are in fact *morpho*-HISTORICAL features, and are thus SYNCHRO—DIACHRONIC at one and the same time. That a column seems ancient and appears amongst ruins is undoubtedly one of its morphological characteristics; but to define this one has to make reference to time. These morpho-historical features are typical of architecture, and probably also of other forms of visual communication in which the sign-vehicles are not consumed in the moment of emission, as with the *flatus vocis* of verbal language, but persist in time. These observations are equally valid for markers such as [ancient, in intact archaeological context].

—(*Nothing behind*) means that a column, associated with at least one other column, circumscribes an empty space, thus permitting and communicating the function 'way through'. (Filled in behind) means that the column functions as a reinforcement to the wall. In such a case it communicates 'no way through', but it can accompany a (limited space), and thus frame a window, communicating a possible or actual 'penetration of light', or else circumscribe a filled-in space, in which case it will communicate the function of 'reinforcing' the wall itself, even if structurally this is not the case.

The two markers (simple) and (complex) which laterally distinguish two possible ways of linking (with others) several columns, refer to the fact, already mentioned in 5.6., that the columns may succeed one another identically, or according to a rhythmic modulus of alternation, of the type AB — AB or ABC — ABC, etc.

This stem summarizes practically all possible uses of a column in context, or at least those that have been codified by tradition. Every use of the column not mentioned above must be considered as deviating from the norm and therefore as giving out an ambiguous message with the aim of using architecture poetically.

8.3   As for the connotations, I shall dispense with an extended commentary on the reasons for their being arranged in the morphological nodes indicated. They should be clear to the reader. It is worth noting that the connotations of an aesthetic type are concentrated around the relation [ancient, among ruins], further evidence that the aesthetic appreciation of architecture and of art in general is due to what Walter Benjamin called *aura*, that is, the halo of fetishistic respect that is connected to the past, time, and the price that venerable age confers upon an object.

8.4   One last note. The morphological features are expressed in verbal terms for the sake of convenience, but they could be expressed in iconic terms by means of some other symbolical notation. As for the semantic features, they are expressed in verbal language, but they refer not to linguistic entities, but to cultural units that may be translated into linguistic sign-vehicles of various types. In this way a new function, and a very useful one, may be found for semantic analysis in architecture. While at the level of verbal language both the definition of sign-vehicles and the definition of meanings as cultural units must be carried out by means of verbal language, in architecture both architectural sign-vehicles and meanings are expressed by linguistic and other types of notation that are not architectural. One is thus faced with a system of communication that needs to be represented by extremely complex diagrams (of which the ones given above are merely minor and imperfect examples), but that does all the same permit an analysis of the gap between sign-vehicles and meanings without falling a victim to the particular semantic illusion of verbal language, where both entities must be indicated by means of other linguistic sign-vehicles. For this reason, a semiotics of architecture may also turn out to be useful for semiotic studies in general.

8.5   In *La struttura assente* I adopt Peirce's notion of 'interpretant' in order to underline the fact that every semantic marker of a sememe is itself a sememe that in turn calls for its own componential analysis. A componential analysis of architecture proves that every semantic marker of a sign is a verbal interpretant (or an interpretant of some other type) and demonstrates that semic analysis never comes to an end, but must continually return to the problem of semantically defining its own instruments, thus realizing an UNLIMITED SEMIOSIS.

This does not prevent the unlimited process of semiosis from being provisionally halted, in certain experimental situations. It has been done in this instance in order to demonstrate that certain architectural objects, either out of context or in context, but always as single objects, can be the bearers of meaning, and are thus considered as the pertinent units of an architectural semantics—the sememes that culture recognizes and organizes in a structured system. But if and how the system is structured has yet to be demonstrated.

2.2 A Semantic Analysis of Stirling's Olivetti Centre Wing

Charles Jencks

Reprinted from *Architectural Association Quarterly*, September 1970.

We experience and classify architecture roughly in terms of metaphors. At least laymen tend to do this before they go on to any deeper perception or use of a building. They say, perhaps without verbalizing it, 'this building looks like an X', 'it feels like Y', and 'reminds me of Z'; 'I like it, it makes me feel good', 'I never noticed it'. These crude metaphors and affective judgements are, as I have argued elsewhere, the primary average classifiers and the modern architect disregards them at his peril (Jencks, 1972).

But one can sympathize with him: they seem literary and vague, idiosyncratic and superficial — nothing he can control or take responsibility for. As Umberto Eco has suggested, architecture is often experienced inattentively, the way one listens to background music, and is used in aberrant ways (Eco, 1973), so why should the architect care about this most general and malleable level of meaning? It seems to me because this level is actually quite coherent and influential in the way people use buildings. These metaphors and connotations of form are socially shared subcodes which have a fair amount of stabiliy in any one time or place. They guide a deeper reading of the architecture: its actual use, denotation and overall signification.

In terms of malleability and change, the architectural code is located roughly between that of painting and language. Like spoken language, architecture makes use of slow-changing subcodes where the relations between signifiers and signifieds is stable (door = passage etc., Gothic style = Age of Faith etc.), but like abstract art it can also reinvent these relations with each building (new technologies, borrowing from other fields such as painting

etc.). This curious position of architecture as a sign
system—half traditional and known to everyone from the
day he is born and half historical and 'new'-creates a corresponding schizophrenia in its interpretation. Generally
speaking, there are two architectural subcodes: a popular,
traditional one (T.S.) which like spoken language is full of
clichés and a modern one (M.S.) full of neologisms and
disruptions between conventional signifiers and signifieds.
Rather than taking up a position on one side or the other as is
common today, it seems to me that architectural semiotics
ought to follow the inherent dual nature of this sign system
and incorporate the polarities of elitist/popular, avant-
garde/traditional, and explicate both subcodes. Ideally of
course it should explain the *many* subcodes existing between
the two extremes, but let it start, at least, with the necessary
duality.

I will show some of the issues involved here with a semantic analysis of James Stirling's New Training Centre for
Olivetti at Haslemere, located in the stockbroker belt of
England's rolling southland. One approaches this new
building on a carefully controlled route. You drive into a
forty-two acre estate past exotic trees and up to an Edwardian mansion—the former country house of Lord Aberconway
(now the residence for Olivetti trainees). The new building is
tacked onto the old in an awkward and rambling way recalling the traditional Picturesque aesthetic, but in material,
form and scale it breaks with conventional usage. It is divided into four main, distinguishable units: two plastic wings,
one plastic box-like element with cruciform clerestories and
a flared glass and steel link (see Figures 1, 2 and 3). Only this
link is a conventional sign: its construction signifies greenhouse, its linear shape signifies circulation, its transparency
literally indicates plants, ramps, radiators and so forth.

The plastic units are however unconventional—except for
the repetition of windows. Since plastic curves over roof and
wall the conventional syntax is broken (gutter, cornice, joint,
change of material) and we have a new syntagm 'wall-roof'
(which connotes 'strangeness', 'missing roof' etc.). The profile
of the wings is also strange: double-pitched, curved and
depressed at the centre. At most these wings conventionally
denote 'repeated rooms' and the plastic box denotes
'assembly'—but beyond this nothing in terms of common
usage. However, if one knew the four main functions
(classrooms, auditorium, transition, residence) one could
easily map them with the four material-forms (plastic wings,
plastic box, glass and steel link, Edwardian mansion),
because the conventional and natural signs are being used
appropriately.* The problem arises after this level of denota-

---

*I am aware that 'appropriately' begs some important issues here which there
is no space to argue.

Figure 1
Axonometric drawing—isolated
from considerations of material,
texture, activity contained or
existing context

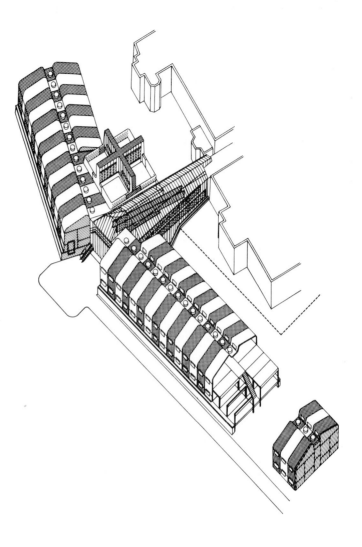

tion: because the modern subcode (M.S.) and traditional subcode (T.S.) interpret the values of the forms in opposite ways
(if we may speak of subcodes interpreting rather than individuals). Schematically, the M.S. approves of new
technologies for building, round plate glass windows, strange
shapes, glass and steel, repeated forms signifying 'equality'
and disapproves of eclecticism, rambling composition,
idiosyncratic domesticity and so on. The T.S. inverts these
judgements almost completely, except for the glass and steel
greenhouse, the sign of conservatory. Thus one would expect
to find, as I have in brief empirical research, that opinion is
divided over what these forms 'look like' and how they are to
be valued.

From the side approach, the two plastic wings look—to
the M.S.—like trains or double-decker buses with their
rounded windows and repetitive modules. If one likes the
idea of plastic (or GRP, Glass-reinforced-polyester) being in-

troduced into a building context of an Edwardian country house and rolling English landscape — or even if one is amused by this idea — then he might follow a semantic chain like this: 'The wings look like a train or bus made from curved plastic or metal, the definition of which (a vehicle to move

Figure 2
Interior view

Figure 3
The glass wing flaring out from the existing Edwardian country house. Teaching rooms and offices to either side and the auditorium, with its movable walls, under the cruciform arrangement. Maximum contrasts are achieved in terms of material and geometric juxtaposition (odd angles, 'broken' pure forms, intersecting volumes etc.) These contrasts heighten the perception of opposed meanings

people fast) is appropriate to the building by association with 1930s notions of "futurism" and the "machine aesthetic".' This is a rather unwieldy sequence and no doubt the actual semantic chain proceeds faster and unconsciously, but it is still guided by affective routes which run through categorical levels from the general aesthetic to the specific function. Another positive metaphor: 'The wings look like an Olivetti machine made from curved plastic with clipped joints, the definition of which (an operative, miniaturized instrument) is appropriate to the building because it is for training Olivetti salesmen and technicians and because these machines connote 'contemporaneity', 'modernity' etc.' Not surprisingly, it is this last metaphor which James Stirling intended people to see.

Yet since a building is above all a mixed metaphor, there are other possible readings and in several lectures and inter-

views I have discovered other coherent semantic chains.*
The most negative concerns seeing the classroom wing as a
series of stacked, plastic trash-cans. This reading is guided
not only by the context and subsigns (the windows pivot like
lids for refuse) but more by the subcode of the viewer. One
person interviewed, who lived in a traditional Regency house
and disliked the idea of a plastic building attached to an
Edwardian mansion immediately saw the wing this way and
as a caravan (before I even asked her what it looked like).
Other people, perhaps politically motivated or just sceptical
of Olivetti's cultural salesmanship, also saw this at
once—and primarily. The implicit value guiding these interpretations was that the wing (or metaphor) was 'banal and
grubby' or 'petit bourgeois and sprawling like a park for
mobile homes'.

Using a method of analysis adapted from Katz and Fodor
(Eco, 1971; Katz and Postal 1964), I have constructed the
semantic chains shown in Figure 4.*

Naturally, many more metaphors than those shown here
could be found, but in fact most people saw the wing in
terms of two or three most plausible metaphors: train/bus =
12, Olivetti machine/washer drier = 8, trash-can/letterbox =
8. The reasons for this consensus are the context and code
restrictions which immediately limit and guide the choice of
a path.

Surprisingly, no one said that the wing looked like a plastic
building, or another example of architecture, a metaphor
which invariably occurs in such analyses. Perhaps this is
caused by the unfamiliarity of plastic buildings in Britain and
the fact that two strong 'plastic' conventions already exist
(use on machines and caravans).

The analysis also shows a difference between architec-

Figure 4
Metaphorical analysis—Four major
metaphorical types were seen by
students at the Architectural
Association, and similar types were
noted by students in Norway and
California—thus demonstrating the
predominance of these 'codes' in
different cultures today. The
'chains of association' implicit in
these types were analysed with
their 'code restrictions' showing
that those who tended to dislike
the building also tended to see
pejorative metaphors. Because the
building was unusual when it was
built, no-one saw it as a 'plastic
building', or as being like other,
comparable, works—a result which
is rare in such studies

*Lectures in January 1974 at the Architectural Association and Thames
Polytechnic in London. See Figure 4 for the results of the votes on the
metaphors. The audience was asked 'what does the building wing look like?'
They were shown slides of a wing *out of context* and 95% didn't know the
buiding. After no more metaphors were seen, the audience was asked to vote
on which two metaphors they found most plausible among their list. If
debate is allowed and if the context is shown a much greater consensus is obtained. Using the same method on other buildings, I have invariably found
that some people see them as buildings they know: 'like La Tourette' etc. The
Olivetti wing is only marginally like one other building in Britain and that one
is not well known.

*For their 'semantic markers', I have substituted aesthetic-material
categories as these, I believe, are primary classifiers leading to functional
categories (or their 'distinguishers' or 'definitional meanings'). For their 'selection restrictions', I have used context *and* code restrictions, because, I
believe, architectural reading is highly determined by the code of the viewer.
Umberto Eco has modified the KF Tree in a different way (Eco, 1972, pp
97-117). His analysis is morphological-semantic and more elaborate than the
one attempted here.

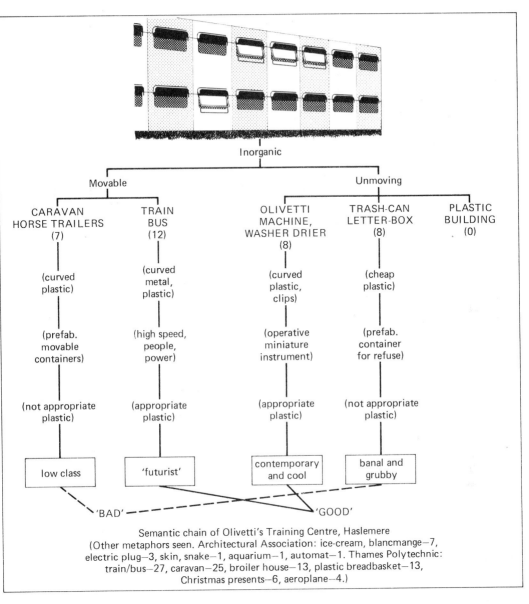

Semantic chain of Olivetti's Training Centre, Haslemere
(Other metaphors seen. Architectural Association: ice-cream, blancmange—7,
electric plug—3, skin, snake—1, aquarium—1, automat—1. Thames Polytechnic:
train/bus—27, caravan—25, broiler house—13, plastic breadbasket—13,
Christmas presents—6, aeroplane—4.)

tural and linguistic semantics. in language, the choice of a reading is more influenced by the context of the sentence and the subcode of the reader, whereas in architecture the reverse, I believe, is true. Architecture is hence a less precise means of communication than language and more subject to mutation, fashion or whim of the interpreter. It is true that when two readings clash (Olivetti machine versus trash-can), one can appeal to the context and see which has the more appropriate mapping thus making a reading more 'correct'. In this case, it would consist of seeing whether the metaphor is or is not appropriate to the Olivetti context, is or is not plastic, made from clipped parts, the right colour, curved, with pivot windows, stacking, etc—in short, a point by point morphological-semantic mapping.

Also it is inevitable that mixed metaphors will generate major and minor interpretations to be held in the mind at the same time. Most architects (M.S.) saw the wing as a train/bus first and liked it, but they acknowledged unpleasant overtones; many laymen (T.S.) might invert this relationship. In any case, semantic subcodes in architecture are subject to quicker shifts than, say, phonetic or kinship codes. If more plastic buildings are constructed in England and certain aesthetic and functional conventions become established (plastics for schools may emerge) one will see the meaning of this wing change radically; it will be seen in terms of other architecture prior to other artefacts or vehicles. 'It looks like a school' may be the response; common usage turns surprising metaphors into ordinary clichés, unlikely connotations into functional denotations.

Despite semantic change, this analysis shows that architectural metaphors work in coherent ways, which suggests in turn that architects could take responsibility for how people will see them; a fact of considerable importance if modern architecture is grasped first, by the public, through metaphor. Le Corbusier's 'house as a machine for living in', Niemeyer's 'salad bowls' at Brasilia, Stirling's 'battleship' at Saint Andrews, Scotland—countless examples show the public accepting or rejecting modern buildings as metaphors which the architect has either consciously controlled or unconsciously betrayed. There are obviously more dimensions to communication than this rather crude level—the syntactic, aesthetic, technical, social to name but a few—but it often serves to classify and permeate these other levels.

References

Eco, U. (1971) 'A Semiotic Approach to Semantics' in *Versus*, Milan, 1, September 1971.

Eco, U. (1972) 'A Componential Analysis of the Architectural Sign /Column/. Semiotica S:2, The Hague; Mouton.

Eco, U. (1973) 'Function and Sign: Semiotics of Architecture', in Bryan, J. and Sauer, R. *Structures Implicit and Explicit*, VIA, Graduate School of Fine Arts, University of Pennsylvania, Philadelphia, 1973, p.143.

Jencks, C. (1972) 'Rhetoric and Architecture', *Architectural Association Quarterly*, London, **4,** 3, Summer 1972, pp. 4—17.

Katz, J.J., and Postal, P.M. (1964) *An Integrated Theory of Linguistic Descriptions*. M.I.T., Cambridge, Mass., 1964.

Postscript

Since this paper was written, I have had further confirmation of several points. First, the schizophrenia of reactions. Those who like it see positive metaphors, those who don't are reminded of alien objects; in both cases the metaphors are partially guided by the codes of the viewers.

Second, the metaphors seen in the wing remain relatively consistent with the previous interviews and tests even though one test was carried out in Norway where codes might have been different.

The result of these further tests:

1. *Students at the A.A.* November, 1974—*Metaphors seen in the Wing Section*: Double-decker Bus 7, Industrial Design object 7, Vehicle (Tube Train) 6, Machine 3, Cow Shed 2, Blancmange Mould 2, Arm of Propeller 1.

2. *Students at Trondheim, Norway*, February 27 1975—Alien Object 24, Train 23, Camping Wagon or Trailer (Caravan) 23, Aquarium 7, Outside of a Boat 5, Thermal device 5, Plastic Cover 3, Machine 3, Four faces (suggested by a section of four windows) 2, Octopus arm 2, Meccano toy 1, Worm becoming a butterfly 1.

3. *Students at the University of California at Los Angeles*, May 1976. Double decker train 29, Plastic bathroom 15, Neapolitan Ice Cream 9, Plastic Caterpillar 7, Dog Kennel 2, Airstream trailer 2, Cyronic mausoleum 2, Submarine 1, Blinkered Argus 1, Sliced Bread 0, Filing Cabinet 0.

Thus in all the analyses (see Figure 4) trains, buses and caravans are in the top categories with things like machines and industrial objects coming next. The fact that most students in Norway thought it looked like an 'alien object' led them to vote 23 to 10 that it was a 'bad' rather than 'good' building. Of course, this last vote was meaningless with respect to the actual merits of the building, but it did correlate with their attitude towards the metaphors.

On the other hand, the students at UCLA who saw relatively more organic and friendly metaphors (e.g. Neapolitan Ice-Cream 9) gave an opposite verdict; 26 said they thought it was 'good', 11 'bad'. Stirling's work very clearly articulates polar reactions (see 'The Architectural Sign'. this volume, Section 1.2).

2.3 On Reading Architecture

Mario Gandelsonas and David Morton

Reprinted from *Progressive Architecture*, March 1972.

Figure 1
Graves: Benacerraf Residence

Working independently, architects Peter Eisenman and Michael Graves* are exploring the application of theories of communication to the problem of generating architectural form. Presented here are their works and ideas, based on an analysis by architect Mario Gandelsonas, and written in collaboration with Progressive Architecture *associate editor, David Morton.*

In recent years, there has been a reexamination of the functionalist tradition, in which two opposing tendencies can be recognized. The system's approach attempts to cope with today's complex world by linking architecture to computer technology and to sophisticated mathematical models; it tends to shift architecture further toward the realm of engineering. In contrast, there is an emerging tendency that views the system of architecture as a system of cultural meaning; it attempts to explain the nature of form itself, through viewing the generation of form as a specific manipulation of meaning within a culture. It is within this approach that the work of Eisenman and Graves belongs.

In the pages that follow, the work of these two architects is presented for the first time. While they work independently, their approaches are related to certain shared concerns. Their work can be viewed as complementary possibilities within the general perspective of signification (meaning) in relation to architecture.

Figure 2
Eisenman: House II

*Peter Eisenman is Director of the Institute for Architecture and Urban Studies in New York. Michael Graves is Associate Professor of Architecture, and Director of the Visual Arts Program, at Princeton University.

Systems of Signification

Meaning can be transmitted through language—a system of agreed-upon rules to communicate. It can be seen as the product of certain operations performed on language, or as the operation of language itself (Greimas, 1970).

Meaning becomes a problem only when access to it is difficult. When one encounters an unfamiliar language, for instance, the first communication problem is that of meaning. For any message to acquire meaning, it must be submitted to translation. Meaning, then, is linked to language, to communication, and to message. But the term 'meaning', which is so evidently linked to language, can be extended to other cultural systems; for example, while there are certain paintings or music one may not 'understand', or which seem without meaning, they are recognized as cultural systems of signification; each is related, in a different way, through a specific form, to the problem of meaning in a given society or culture.

Figure 3
Graves: Benacerraf Residence—
Addition

Architecture as a System of Signification

Important investigation has been done in relation to cultural systems as systems of signification in a-literate societies (Lévi-Strauss, 1967), but little has been done in relation to our own culture—very little specifically in relation to architecture, which usually has been concerned with direct function rather than with the problem of meaning. That architecture is indeed a system of signification is suggested by the fact that function represents a relation between architectural products and their use, which is a recognized and understood cultural fact; in addition, the known set of architectural forms is limited and has systematic characteristics.

Architecture has been implicitly concerned with the problem of signification since the Renaissance when architects such as Alberti and Palladio resystematized Vitruvius' *Ten Books of Architecture*, thus marking the constitution of architecture as a specific mode of organizing notions and concepts (a system of rules: prescriptions and interdictions) related to the manipulation of significant forms in the design and construction of 'buildings'. (Agrest and Gandelsonas, 1972). While in most architects' work the systematic characteristics are *implicit*, they become necessarily *explicit* in Eisenman's and Graves's exploration of architecture as a system of signification. By comparing their work to that of others dealing, apparently, with similar problems of meaning, their position can be clarified.

Figure 4
Eisenman: House II

There are many buildings that cannot be explained in terms of a functionalist approach alone. For example, the new 'Parthenons'—certain public buildings and cultural centers—might be defined as symbols in that they stand for, represent or denote something else, not by exact resemblance, but by suggestion. As Saussure notes, 'one characteristic of the symbol is that it is never wholly arbitrary; it is not empty, for there is a rudiment of a natural bond between the signifier (the building) and the signified (its meaning) (Saussure, 1959). For these buildings to symbolize something else, such as a Greek temple, they must establish and maintain a relationship to the thing being symbolized. Because some of their formal patterns strongly suggest the Greek stylobate, colonnade, and entablature, they can be read 'as temples' immediately. Usually, there is not a direct and obvious relationship between form and meaning in architecture because, in architecture, this relationship is much more complicated and systematized. It is usually simplified however, when it appears as a direct relationship between architectural form and something that embodies conventional meaning.

Because there is no direct relationship between form and conventional meaning in Eisenman's and Graves's work, it may appear unintelligible at first. Although they work within the system of architecture (as a system of notions or a set of rules), they attempt to separate themselves from this system in order to view some aspects of it more objectively. Architecture can become, in their terms, a process of its own examination, through which they hope to understand something of its intrinsic nature.

Semantics and Syntactics

Both Eisenman and Graves approach architecture as a system of signification. Within this general approach, however, their works represent two completely divergent positions. While Graves indicates the relationships between architecture and context, as shown through his interest in the history of architecture and painting and his concern with architecture and nature, Eisenman disregards all relationships between architecture and any cultural meaning. The position of each is concentrated on one of the main and specific aspects particular to architecture as a system of signification. Although Charles Morris indicates that every system of signification has three characteristic dimensions—semantic, syntactic, and pragmatic—it is only the first two that are of primary concern to Eisenman and Graves. 'Semantics', according to Morris, 'deals with the relation of signs (something that refers to something), to their designata (what is taken account of) and so to the objects which they may or may not denote . . . . Syntactics (is) the study of the . . . relations of signs to one another in abstraction from the relation of signs to objects or to interpreters' (Morris, 1970).

The general distinction between semantic and syntactic can be seen in architecture. Architectural form, as conceived by the architect through internalized thought, has always been related to an external problem. Because of this, architecture has developed essentially along semantic lines. However, since the basis of architecture lies within its function as a system of problem solving, it would seem important for architecture to construct a body of syntactic concepts to guide it in this activity. While there are certain prescriptions for possible relationships among different architectural elements, or combinations of groups of elements, these prescriptions relate mainly to the solution of external problems, and ultimately only reinforce dependence upon external requirements.

The unique characteristic of Eisenman's work lies in the attempt to separate his work from this general attitude. In his houses, the semantic aspects have been absorbed in 'marks' that interrelate without dependence on external references; they are not substitutions of something absent. Consequently, his work exists primarily within the syntactic dimension of architecture. Although Graves's work remains within the semantic level of architecture, it is distinct from architecture that relates forms to external requirements, because his main concern is to show the linkages that exist between the actual form and the complex system of architectural notions or ideas that generate it.

Their work is not fully explained, however, by comparing their similarities and differences. Therefore, a different communication model is used to analyze the work of each.

For Graves, a first model is used to show the differences between direct communication (function or use in architecture), and the system of signification (the system of notions that allows that communication). A second model shows the specific nature of signification through the two aspects of the semantic dimension.

For Eisenman, his own general model of the syntactic dimension is enlarged and considered within a dialectic relation between the 'writing' of architectural form (as the generation or transformation of form), and the 'reading' of architectural form (for relating implicit and explicit relationships) through the design as a device allowing these readings. Following these models, Graves's work is presented through various aspects, or parts, of several buildings, while Eisenman's work is presented as one complete building.

Michael Graves: The Semantic Dimension

In analyzing some of Graves's buildings realized between 1966 and 1971, it will be helpful to consider the ways he organizes slide lectures in which he discusses aspects of his work. His lectures are divided into segments dealing with pairs of contradictory notions illustrated by paired images representing natural landscapes, Classical art and architecture, and Cubist painting, and concluding with the presentation of various aspects of his own work. In shifting from external forms to his own architectural forms, he never shows buildings as whole units, but only as fragmented elements or focused parts taken out of context, with meaning concentrated solely in intersecting or in dominant elements. Order emerges though, when his organization is seen as reflecting essential characteristics within his work that are considered as messages within the semantic dimension of architecture.

Communication and Signification

If architectural form is considered as a message, then what is the role of this message? In language, its role is to transmit signification (meaning). However, any individual act of communication, whether language or not, is defined by a set of factors comprising sender, receiver, channel, code, referent, and the message itself. The presence of these factors is indispensable to any communication, whether it be language or another system of signification, such as painting, music, film, or architecture.

With this definition, any object, architectural or not, has the possibility of communicating a message, as Umberto Eco suggests (Eco, 1968). For example, the use of a door as a movable barrier to open or close a passage both allows this function and promotes it. To state that a device promotes a function indicates that the device performs the function of communication, or that the device itself communicates its own function. Indeed, the dictionary usually defines an object (signifier) by describing it, as well as by indicating its function (signified).

Primary Meaning and Secondary Meaning

To consider an object in its direct communicational aspect results in its definition only in terms of its primary meaning, that is, in terms of its function. In this context, architectural form can be analyzed as a message referring only to the referent (use) and to the channel (physical support). But, as noted above, the complete communicational circuit also includes the sender, receiver, and code. These six communicational factors are, according to Roman Jakobson's model of the communicational act (Jakobson, 1962), related to six complementary areas of signification within any system of signification—for instance, within the system of architecture. Although this model only classifies areas of signification without explaining them, its application allows one to isolate areas related to the primary meaning in architecture, or the notion of function, from other areas related to secondary meanings. The primary meaning in architectural messages is 'buildings' (as messages) 'representing' their use (referents) or their physical structure (channels). Secondary meanings 'represent' and emphasize the areas related to sender, receiver, and code—rarely conscient and explicit parts of architectural design.

The concern of modern architecture has been mainly within the area of primary meaning, the functional area. And important to the functionalists' concern within this area was the replacement of one set of rules with another set of rules—with the replacement, for example, of Classical, symmetrical, architectonic compositions by asymmetrical compositions determined by the building's use, as in Le Corbusier's Pavillon Suisse. Graves's main concern lies in the area of secondary meanings: his interest is not in replacing rules, but in showing the rules, that is, as prescriptions or prohibitions. He does this by paraphrasing or quoting the vocabulary of modern architecture. For example, his 'idealized window', a quotation drawn from Corbu's garden in the Petite Maison, indicates a series of opposite architectonic notions, such as architecture/nature, ideal/real, in/out, which are within the area of secondary meaning that is related to the code (the system that interrelates elements to make a message understandable).

In Graves's work, each of the areas of secondary meaning is structured in the same way. Pairs of notions are related to each other according to their similarities and differences. A horizontal plane, read as 'romantic' or perceptual, is opposed to a vertical plane, read as abstract or conceptual. By postulating these pairs of oppositions, Graves is demonstrating the principle that anything acquires meaning when opposed to something else, since oppositions represent the basis of any meaning (Figure 5) (Greimas, 1970).

Some characteristic oppositions can be abstracted from Graves's work to demonstrate their ability to indicate signification. The opposition between horizontal plane and vertical plane represents the opposition of architect versus user. It is a 'double program' that comprises the architectural rules plus the user's requirements. These are not only different, but contradictory to each other. Within an architec-

Figure 5
Benacerraf Residence

tural rule system, however, the means of resolving the contradiction may be provided. The opposition between *in* and *out* represents the opposition of the real use of the building as a scene for one's action versus the symbolic use, or the reading and interpretation of the building by others. The opposition of plan to internal elevation represents the opposition between the plan as designed and the elevation as read. The idealized window or the sky supported by a column represents the opposition of nature versus architecture.

Graves emphasizes areas related to secondary meanings only to show that secondary meanings exist. But to show their function as areas of signification in architecture, other elements of his work should be considered.

Signification in Architecture

In architecture, signification might be described in terms of two interrelated aspects; the first, a set of possibilities for structuring the components, subcomponents, systems, and subsystems of a building; the second, a repertory of ideas, images, and notions from an architectural repository. With this model, the semantic dimensions of the architectural system can be seen as a synthesis between the first, specifically architectonic aspect, and the second, repository aspect, which can draw its formal patterns from architecture itself or from anywhere else, such as painting, music, etc. The architectonic aspect does not provide form but only the possibility for structuring form; the repository aspect provides the sources of actual formal patterns.

The Architectonic Aspect

The architectonic aspect could be described as composed of codes (organized architectonic ideas or sets of rules for their organization), and the operations of metaphor and metonymy, which enable selection and combination of architectonic ideas or rules to form complex architectonic units.

The notion of code refers to the organization, or system, that interrelates the elements, or units, of any message and makes possible its understanding (Jakobson, 1962). The basic elements of a code should not be seen as singular elements, but as pairs of oppositions interrelated in infinitely complex ways. Each pair embodies two notions that have something in common in conjunction with something that separates them, such as *in* and *out* (Figure 6).

In architecture, code has traditionally been seen as a body of architectonic ideas structured within a fixed framework. This understanding of architectural code, however, is restric-

Figure 6
Benacerraf Residence

ting; it does not explain the complexity of architecture. To suggest this complexity, architectonic code could be seen rather as a field of dynamic tensions, based on oppositions, which only provide an empty framework of possible architectonic relationships. It is through this framework that the sets of ideas, images, and notions of buildings drawn from the architectural repository must pass, in order to create the synthesis that underlies architectural form (Figure 7).

Figure 7
Doctor's Residence

Metaphor refers to an operation that links a message, by the selection or substitution of its elements, to a code. It also establishes, by relating elements through a code, a connection between elements present in the message and elements absent from the message, which could be substituted for them. Metonymy refers, on the other hand, to an operation that interrelates the elements present in the message itself, by their internal combinations (Jakobson, 1962).

In architecture, metaphor and metonymy operate within a logic predicted on architectonic rules. For example, in Classical architecture the relationship between the five orders is based on a complex code involving oppositions such as simple/complex, rude/elegant, male/female, etc. Even when the orders have a similar code in a building, the substitution of one order for another constitutes a metaphorical operation that provokes a change in the meaning of a building as a message according to certain rules. But there are also rules for the combination of order—the way one must be placed under another—which govern the metonymic operation.

In the work of Graves, the architectonic order is upset through a particular use of metaphor. Instead of combining architectonic ideas according to the traditional architectural rules, which prescribe the selection of one element from a pair of oppositions, he shows, through expressing both elements of the opposition, the opposition itself.

In doing so, he upsets the normal syntactic relationships for the purpose of showing the different sets of architectural codes as codes in themselves. Because attention is focused on oppositions, the building is initially seen more as a grouping of apparently unrelated components, than as a cohesively organized unit in itself; on further inspection, however, order is revealed (Figure 8). This emphasis on metaphorical operations, revealed through the way Graves structures components as manifestations of architectonic codes, can be illustrated by two examples, an interior wall and an entrance.

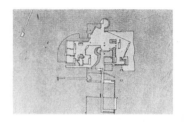

Figure 8
Drezner Residence

In the Hanselmann House, an idealization of the plan of the building is superimposed on an interior wall (elevation), thus juxtaposing contradictory elements representative of a

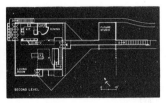

Figure 9
Hanselmann Residence

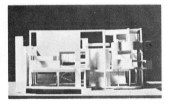

Figure 10
Hanselmann Residence

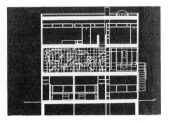

Figure 11
Doctor's Residence

Figure 12
Hanselmann Residence

chain of oppositions. The contrast between the drawing (in this case as a painting) and the wall is equivalent to the opposition between the horizontal plane where the drawing is 'written' and the vertical plane where the façade is 'read' (Figure 9). It is also equivalent to the opposition between the architect's vertical line of vision while making the drawing and the client's horizontal line of vision when perceiving the wall. Each of these pairs of oppositions represents a specific arrangement of one set of ideas specific to architecture — the opposition between architect and client. This series of oppositions is also representative of one of the possible architectural codes, in this case, the writing/reading code (Figure 10).

This code is based on the differences between the complexities of creating (writing) a design and the apparently simple interpretation of the built space (reading); between the paper drawing and the existing building; between the plan as generating an elevation, section, or perspective, and the wall as the material from which the building is read (Figure 11). While the code is representative of oppositions, its own essence lies in contradiction, that is, in the fact that the building itself only partially manifests the operations, or drawings, that generate its architectural form.

Another illustration of a component representing contrasting elements is shown in Graves's treatment of the entrance to the Hanselmann House, where he has literally removed a component (a complete, positive, cubic volume that normally would be the entrance area), and reestablished it as a separate, but connected, component of the building. Here the removed volume and its resultant void also represent a chain of oppositions. In this case, a building section has been extended to the external façade, thus revealing internal aspects of the building. The terms of opposition are, on one side, internal, positive solid volume, private and real use, and on the other side, external, negative or voided volume, public and symbolic use (Figure 12).

This uniting/separating, or delimiting code, represents a second possible architectural code based on the differences between the building as a 'transparent' mediator between man and function (real use), and the building as a material and opaque object where the line of vision stops (symbolic use); or between the use of a private system (inside) that is radically different and separated from the public use (outside). The interpretation of a building as a double system (inside/outside) depends upon a delimitation in which skin is interpreted as form, and where the entrance connects and interrelates the internal and external forms and spaces.

Figure 13 (above)
Hanselmann House from South

Figure 14 (above left)
Hanselmann House

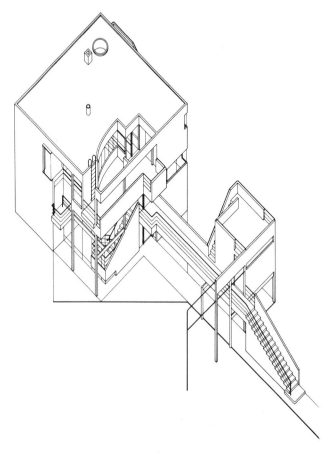

Figure 15
Hanselmann House

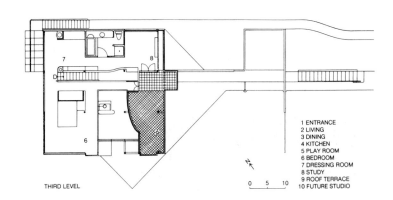

1 ENTRANCE
2 LIVING
3 DINING
4 KITCHEN
5 PLAY ROOM
6 BEDROOM
7 DRESSING ROOM
8 STUDY
9 ROOF TERRACE
10 FUTURE STUDIO

THIRD LEVEL

0   5   10

Figure 16
Hanselmann House—Third Level

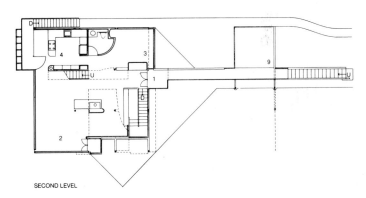

SECOND LEVEL

Figure 17
Hanselmann House—Second Level

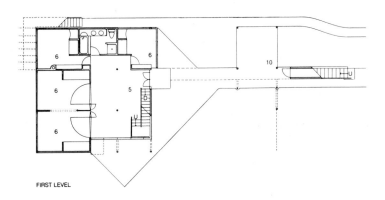

FIRST LEVEL

Figure 18
Hanselmann House—First Level

Figure 19
Hanselmann House—South-West
corner

Figure 20
Hanselmann House—South-West
corner

The Repository Aspect

Architectural form can be seen as the manifestations of the codes, plus 'quotations' drawn from the architectural repository.* These quotations are sets of ideas, images in general, and notations about buildings in particular. In drawing from this repository, the architect can select any form or idea in its original state; he can use formal patterns directly from the five orders of Classical architecture, for instance, or he can use aspects of Mediterranean popular architecture as found in Le Corbusier. Alternatively, the architect can use the opposite of an original form or idea, as occurred with the use of asymmetrical order in modern architecture in contrast to the Classical rule of symmetry. Finally, the architect can modify or transform earlier ideas or forms to generate new ones, such as occurred with the invention of new orders in Classical architecture.

In Graves's case, there are four areas of primary interest: Classical art and architecture, Cubist painting, Modern architecture, and nature. His isolation of these four areas, which are crucial to an understanding of his work, relates to his intention to indicate the oppositions comprising architectonic codes, and to his exclusive use of metaphor, that is, with the operation that links a message to a code. He believes these four areas hold material pertinent to the notion of code in architecture.

During the Renaissance, architectural codes were constituted and institutionalized; the notion of nature played an important role in this constitution. To the Classical architect, the implicit opposition between nature and architectural form was resolved through the assimilation of the underlying laws of nature, which possessed, for Alberti, the essence of beauty. The designation of a building as architectural meant that it was beautiful, and since beauty was obtained through the understanding of nature, the primary essence of architecture was its relationship to nature. The Modern Movement, with its self-conscious synthesis of art and architecture, represented an important historical change where some codes were abandoned, others were maintained, and, finally, new codes were incorporated into architecture.

In relation to Classical art and architecture, Graves feels that Modern architecture offered a new conception of space as cubic volume contrasted to that seen, for example, in a Piero della Francesca painting, where space is defined by frontal planes arranged to form the background of narrative settings. Furthermore, be believes that the Modern concept of architectural space has never been fully developed, and in

---

*This notion is related to J. Kristeva's notion called 'Intertextualite', see *Recherches pour une semanalyse*, Éditions Seuil, Paris, 1969.

Figure 21
Gunwyn Office

an attempt to understand it, he has based his investigation upon a contrast between Classical and Modern architectural space, as well as upon certain similarities he finds in the two. This investigation is also concerned with the relationship between architecture and classical painting—an area where Graves finds highly developed concepts of spatiality, such as the notion of delimitation, of layering of planes within space, and of light as a coordinate of structuring space.

In Modern painting, and in Cubist painting in particular, Graves feels that notions such as duality and plurality are more highly developed than in architecture. For instance, in the work of Juan Gris, objects are not seen only as formal pieces, but as problems to be manipulated for the purpose of providing an expanded sense of pictorial form. Gris accomplished this through the manipulation of notions such as inside/outside, real/ideal, male/female, etc. Such pairs of notions represent, to Graves, the idea of duality, while their appearance together represents his idea of plurality. This idea of duality can be compared to the notion of oppositions which, in acting as sets or combining together, are the bases of the code. To Graves, the difference between the ideas of duality and plurality is significant. In duality, concern is with elements in relation to one another on a one-to-one basis; in plurality, concern is with relationships among relationships.

As suggested earlier, the virtue of Classical architecture was derived from its 'imitation of nature' (Alberti, Palladio), its transposition of 'natural' laws for the purpose of giving order to architectural form. Architecture continues to be related to this concept of nature, but on a different level where the opposition is between nature and culture, between needs seen as 'natural', or without order, and the program which transforms them into architectural order (Alexander, 1971) Graves's interest in nature is more closely aligned to a Classical position, though perhaps not for the same reasons as those of the Classical architect. Graves relates the notion of nature to architectural form in different ways. He develops the new conception of space in Modern art and architecture by jointly analyzing the relationships between plane (surface) and volume (depth), and between nature and architecture. An example in his work shows the sky as a plane supported by a column as a tree, while a beam represents an arbor and clouds define transitory areas in a ceiling (Figure 21).

This substitution of elements cannot be explained only in terms of the relationships between architecture and nature. In relating architectural forms to 'natural' forms, Graves introduces an additional use of metaphor, which sees metaphor as an operation that may constitute the basis of architectonics itself, that is, how any architectural system is established as a closed entity.

Hypothetically, if man's primordial home could be understood in architectural terms as 'shelter', then an arbor could be seen as a 'ceiling' sustained by trunks of trees as 'supports'. In terms of signification, the tree (signifier) is seen as a support (signified):

$$\frac{|}{support} = \frac{signifier}{signified}$$

With man's ability to consciously construct shelter, a transformation of signification took place; in this example it occurs within the operation of giving form to the support. In shaping a material to make a support, a column was created to substitute for the known support, the tree:

$$\frac{\square}{|} \quad \frac{column}{tree}$$

The entire operation could be symbolized in the following way:

$$\frac{\square}{|} \times \frac{|}{support} = \frac{\square}{support}$$

By thus joining the old and new significations, the tree is cancelled, or repressed, and becomes a latent signifier. The operation described by this formula is the operation known as metaphor, (Lacan, 1966) and it is precisely this operation that forms the beginning of any architecture. In his use of a tree as a support, Graves reverses the architectural metaphor and brings it out of its latent position to return it to its position as original signifier:

$$\frac{|}{\square} \times \frac{\square}{support} = \frac{|}{support}$$

By means of this kind of gesture, Graves might be providing important elements for understanding the basis of architecture as a system of primary operations that is still present, although usually repressed, in any gesture of the architect. Usually, the primary operation, or the original metaphor, like the subconscious, remains hidden and is only perceptible in certain moments, such as dreams, where poetic plays a fundamental role.

The crucial aspect of Graves's work is its indication of the notion of code in architecture, showing that the direct or apparent manifestations of architecture represent only a primary level of understanding, and that a second level, organized in a specific way, underlies the first level. The recognition of this underlying organization has two consequences: it implies a definition of the limits of the architectural system (the describable set of rules); it also implies the repression of certain basic operations that separate entities belonging to the system from those that remain outside. While Graves indicates this operation of original metaphor, the actual thing represented by the metaphor remains, in reality, a latent and 'repressed' problem within the definition of the generation of architectural form.

Figure 22
Benacerraf Residence. Second Level: 11 Bedroom, 12 Bath, 13 Terrace, 14 Void

In contrast, just the opposite situation is represented in the work of Peter Eisenman; his approach to architecture places special emphasis on the generation of form, while the relationships between architectural form and context, which are characteristic of the semantic dimension, are suppressed or absent from his work.

Peter Eisenman: The Syntactic Dimension

The key to Peter Eisenman's work lies in his concern for the architectural system itself, *unrelated to any exterior reference*. In this respect, he works exclusively within the syntactic dimension of architecture, where syntactics is independent of semantics. If his work is compared to other architecture, one is immediately aware of certain differences, without necessarily realizing that these differences are due to his exclusion of the semantic dimension.

An architecture that suppresses syntactic operations and emphasizes the semantic dimension, such as Graves's, is a logical contrast to Eisenman's syntactic approach. Compared to Graves's work, Eisenman's may seem almost impossible to approach on any known level; the reason for this is that a 'known level', or context, is precisely what is absent from his architecture. Communication is inimical in Eisenman's work; he attempts to eliminate all factors at the communicational level except the message itself (a house is ac-

Figure 23
Benacerraf Residence. First Level: 1 Bedroom, 2 Foyer, 3 Living Room, 4 Screened porch, 5 Dining, 6 Bar, 7 Kitchen, 8 Breakfast 9 Terrace, 10 Playroom

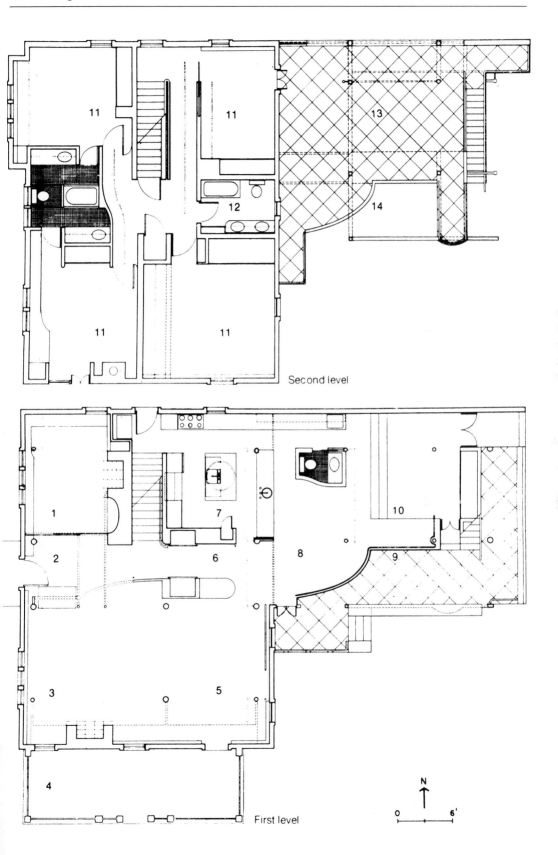

Second level

First level

N
0   6'

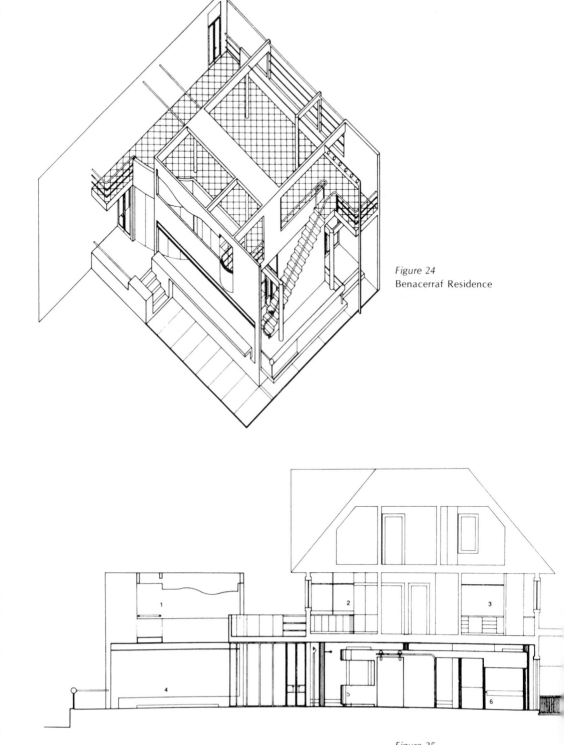

Figure 24
Benacerraf Residence

Figure 25
Benacerraf Residence—Section
looking south

tually there). Consequently, there seem to be few or no references to client, to user, to technical structure, or to symbolism. The message is as unresponsive to existing communication models as it is to the semantic model used to analyze Graves's work. Thus, a new model must be sought.

There are three links to external reality that are helpful in an initial appraisal of Eisenman's work. The first is the notion of use. His structures are only incidentally houses; that is, they are determined as such by their name and use. At a more basic level, the program of the house is welcomed by Eisenman because, as he notes, 'in a sense, its program is known; there is an infinite set of combinations for its solution in physical terms; therefore, its importance to me is that it allows the concern for function to be reduced ... there is little polemic or new meaning available in the particular arrangement of its functions'.

The second link to reality is the use of a certain technical structure. Eisenman's use of a structural grid is based upon his belief that

> modern technology provided architecture with a new means for conceiving space ... in a sense, space was no longer necessarily limited or defined by structure, and this was specially true with respect to the use of the load-bearing wall; the column became both the primary structural and the primary formal element. With a diminishing of these structural constraints, it was possible to examine the column and the wall in a capacity other than in the solution of pragmatic problems .... Le Corbusier's Maison Domino was paradigmatic in this respect.

The third link to external reality is Eisenman's use of a vocabulary based on Modern architecture.

> For me, 'Cardboard' architecture is not an aesthetic, not a style, not an eclecticism. 'Cardboard' architecture is not a pejorative term but a rather precise metaphor describing two aspects of my work. First, it is an attempt to unload the existing semantic. While in itself it may be semantically charged, it might be considered syntactically neutral, and thus lead to a new semantic. Second, 'Cardboard' is connotative of less mass, less texture, less color, and ultimately less concern for these, it is closest to the abstract idea of plane.

On the basis of these three notions alone, it is impossible to say anything about this architecture other than it is, at least, architecture. (Similarly, one could recognize Chinese as a language, yet have no understanding of its meaning.) For the implications of Eisenman's work to be seen, one must suspend concern with normal external references, and consider a framework where architectural form is related only to architectural form. Within such a framework, a building can only be seen as a complex of interacting relational units where it is impossible to perceive or separate components, because there are no components as such.

Usually, an architect concerns himself with combining components in order to design a building, or, as in the case of Graves, with a dialectic relationship between components and the building. Eisenman's concern, on the other hand, is with the building as the manifestation of a system of relationships; that is, with the architectural system as the generator of architectural form as well as its meaning.

If Graves's lectures were important to analyzing his work, Eisenman's writings are equally integral and fundamental to any comprehension of his buildings, since he considers his writings as essential to the architectural process as his drawings and models.* Their mutual function is to make explicit the architectural problems he attempts to explore in each project, where the project is considered as research into the nature of architecture itself or, more specifically, into the syntactic dimension of architecture. With this attitude, he separates himself from the tradition in which writing is concerned with descriptive and prescriptive aspects of architecture and attempts to explain architecture as a system of signification.

Syntactic Structure

A second aspect, which further separates his work from the traditional conception of architecture, is seen through comparison with Graves, for example, who is providing data for understanding the semantic dimension. Eisenman, through exploring the syntactic dimension itself, is inventing data.

To define, in architectural terms, the relationship between semantics and syntactics, Eisenman has introduced an important idea from generative, or transformational grammar, in which language is seen as a generative activity rather than as a description of semantic and syntactic relationships. (Chomsky, 1965, 1968). In this view of language, syntactics takes on a new meaning where syntactic structure itself is seen as the primary generator of language. Eisenman incorporates this concept into architecture because it helps him to account for what he sees as a similar process of synthesis in architecture, the process of the generation of architectural form. He replaces the semantic relationship of form to exter-

*The quotations of Peter Eisenman are from his published and unpublished writings of 1967 – 1971.

Figure 26
Eisenman: House II

Figure 27
Eisenman: House II

Figure 28
Eisenman: House II

nal requirement, function, or structure, by a system of internal relationships—that is, function and actual structure are
seen in terms of relationships between relationships, defined
by the three primary physical systems of line, plane, and
volume. In doing so, he sharply separates semantics from
syntactics; the semantic aspects become absorbed, and are
revealed as abstract notations, and not as forms related to
use or to other meaning. Their relevance depends solely on
their combination with each other, rather than on their relationship to external references. They are not substitutions or
signs representing something absent.

The prime consequence of this isolation from external
relationships is the dissolution of the main semantic opposition of form to program (internal/external). This opposition is
replaced by a new internal system of oppositions; the operation moves into an exclusively syntactic level (internal-
internal) where units are only related to each other.

Regional Units and Deep Structure

The relationships between units are based on complex
systems of oppositions which develop from line, plane, and
volume. These elements, meaningless in themselves, become
a system of equally weighted elements (as opposed to the
traditional aesthetic distinction between primary, secondary,

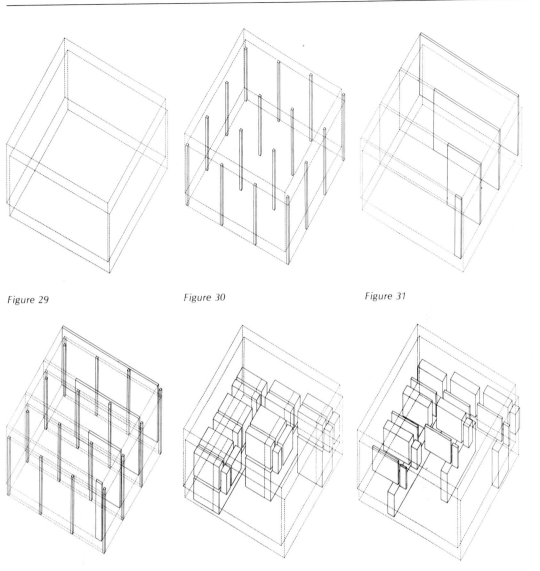

Figure 29

Figure 30

Figure 31

Figure 32

Figure 33   · Figure 34

Figure 29 – 46
Eisenman: House II—Selected
drawings indicating system of
transformations from deep to surface levels

and tertiary systems), or a system of relations defined by a dialectic between elements. In this system, volume can be seen as an extension of the plane, while line or column can be seen as a residue of the plane. This understanding is possible through recognizing what Eisenman calls transformational rules, which mark and link deep structure with the specific column or wall.

In Eisenman's House II, three main relational systems, which he calls deep structure oppositions, are used; column/wall, volume/column, and volume/wall. The complex system of these oppositions influences, or is marked in, the surface structure. As Eisenman says,

In House II the spatial system attempts to provide for a
continuing and countermanding dialectic using the column and the wall. Here the interplay of shear wall and
screen walls provides a formal structure between the
screen wall and the column grid. The articulation of the
column and the volume is an attempt to create a
dialectic between a reticulated grid, i.e. form which is
essentially additive, and walls cut away to reveal columns, i.e., form which is essentially subtractive. This
same idea is involved in the specific articulation of the
columns . . . which can be read either as additive, that
is, as a build-up of planes, or as subtractive, that is, as a
cut-away to reveal a residue of planes.

Layerings

All of these elements represent only the combination of simple, explicit elements in Eisenman's work. These elements
are further conditioned, however, through systems of implied movement linked to the notion of systematic parallel
or diagonal layering, which has a unique role in his architecture.

Layering, as an adjunct to the Classical concept of space
as a dramatic setting, was expected to reinforce the illusion
of perspective from fixed observation points. In Graves's
work, which develops from concepts of space in Modern
architecture, layering is derived from notions of space as exemplified in Cubist painting, where space is perceived not as
a stage setting, from a fixed proscenium or picture plane, but
rather as a dialectic between plane and depth; between frontal and non-frontal planes; between an observer's ability to
make precise readings of frontal planes, and only imprecise
readings of peripheral planes.

Eisenman's use of layering has little in common with that
of either the Classical or Cubist concept, where layering is
only partially systematized and remains partly related to the
physical experience. While Eisenman may use spatial con-
structs that are superficially familiar, they are not used for
their physical implications, he says, but rather as consti-
tuents of a specific architectural system of relations,

> much as a mathematical notation can be used to
> describe a construct in music. Layering in this sense,
> becomes dominantly notational, as well as generative
> of the entire system because it establishes the arrange-
> ment and relationship of elements. It establishes both a
> formational and a transformational structure in that it
> gives order to a base system and generates a system of
> implied spatial oppositions—shear, tension, compres-
> sion, centrifugal or centripetal—which are not actually

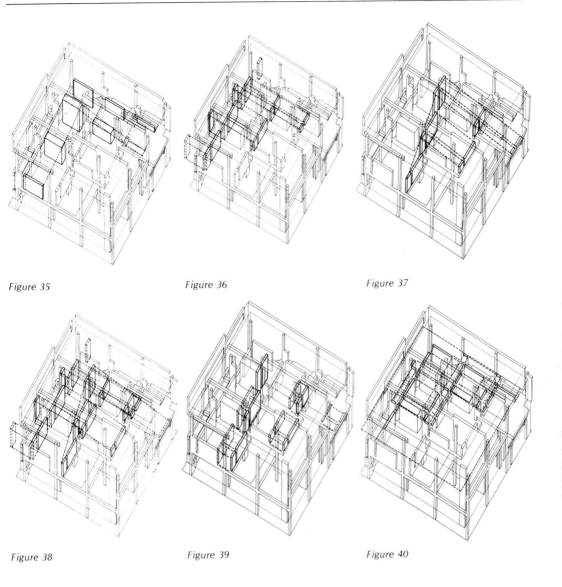

Figure 35

Figure 36

Figure 37

Figure 38

Figure 39

Figure 40

in the specific forms, but which accrue to relationships developed from this layering.

The result is the assembling of complex relations into an ordered series generating from a given plane or point of reference, either actual or conceptual. Within this framework, the implied movement is initiated at a precise point in time in the deep structure. From these relationships of layered spatial systems, all specific form is generated. In this method the notion of layering refers not only to the actual manifestations of explicitly layered elements, but to implicit relationships between relational elements. This form of layering requires neither a single constant 'proscenium' nor a normative plane of reference.

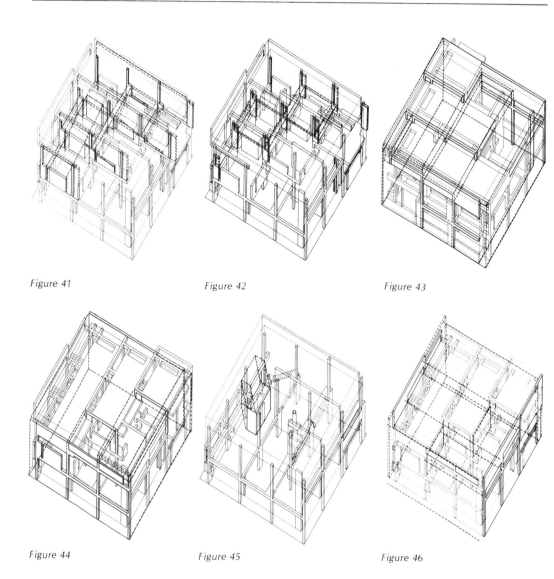

Figure 41   Figure 42   Figure 43

Figure 44   Figure 45   Figure 46

Double-Deep Structure and Surface Level

The final and more specific notion that Eisenman introduces in his definition of the deep, or conceptual, level in his syntactic model is the notion of double-deep structure. Its analysis requires the definition of the surface level and an examination of the interrelationships between deep and surface levels.

For Eisenman, the surface level in architecture has traditionally represented only the appearance of the forms in which architecture manifests itself; the actual building has revealed none of the operations that generated its final form. Eisenman is not concerned with the surface level as a final product in itself, but with its use as a potential structure for revealing, and marking in the building, the operations and the deep structure that generated the architectural form. This represents, he believes, a transformation of the deep level of architecture to the surface level, where reading of the surface level initiates a sequence of continually deepening readings, which reveal the operations that generated the form. This, Eisenman hopes, can give 'the "reader" (myself or anyone else) . . . a greater understanding of architectural form, and perhaps a richer and more precise notion . . . about certain specific qualities of architectural space'.

Based on the similarities and differences he sees between the two, Eisenman compares the reading of a building to the reading of a painting. According to him, both allow multiple spatial readings; architecture as literal space, painting as figurative space. To aid the reading of the deep structure in his architecture, he has borrowed the notion of conceptual ambiguity, as opposed to literal ambiguity, from Modern art, thus, he says 'creating a dialectic between what exists and what is implied'. This dialectic is accomplished by providing, within the object, a *double-deep structure*, which allows two different readings of the object. He notes that

> One way to provide access to a conceptual relationship — to shift the primary intention from the physical object to a formal relationship — might be to provide in the object two conceptual readings, so that the object can never be held in the mind as a single entity, but rather as in a state of tension or as a dialectic between two conceptual notions. In House II, there are two alternatives posited as a neutral referent. The first, marking one of the . . . aspects of the deep level, are the shear walls, which can be read as a datum, especially when seen from the north, whereupon the columns may be read as a residue of these planes, transposed diagonally from them. Alternatively, the columns can be read as neutral, or deep level referents, especially when seen from the south, whereupon the shear wall may be read as having been shifted from the column-wall ambiguity.

Other aspects of the deep level — the dialectic relationship between plane and volume — work in a similar manner.

To Eisenman, then, the notion of transformation in architecture is related to the opposition explicit/implicit, and to the notion of layering, of double-deep structure, and of reading as the mediating operations between deep and surface structure. He observes that 'most transformations are those rules or moves which can take a deep structure and transform it into a surface structure or specific form. At the same time, these transformations provide one with, as it were, the framework for understanding the specific form. These transformations allow one to see the particular forms in a particular or new way.

The most important thing for Eisenman is not the finished product itself, but the operations that gave rise to it. In his desire to understand these operations, he substitutes for the traditional means of representation (plan, elevation, section, and perspective) a generative sequence of axonometric perspectives related to representative cardboard models. He asks,

> What is the reality of architecture? Is it the actual building, which is detailed and planned to look as if it were made of 'nonreal' building material, such as cardboard? Many people see photographs of House II as if they are pictures of the model, rather than the house. Thus, the actual building is, in itself, in one sense, unreal. This, in turn, poses the question, is the cardboard model of the building the reality, or is the ideal of the model and the actual building the reality?

By separating architectural form from external reference, Eisenman is exploring an attitude that produces two complementary notions. The first is the idea of a double-level structure, where the surface or the perceptible manifestation is generated by a deeper conceptual level, through specific transformations. The second is the idea of reading that reveals this mechanism through a deepening play between the explicit and the implicit, provided by the surface level.

Eisenman's approach should be differentiated from research that largely restricts itself to the empirical description of facts, which produces reality rather than explains it, and sometimes concludes with knowledge similar to Ptolemy's knowledge of a sun that turns around the earth. In contrast, Eisenman works through the construction of hypothetical models on the basis of existent means; his intent is to understand, rather than invent form, so he can 'generate more rational form, that is, form designed with more precise control, which ultimately allows more precise understanding'.

Conclusion

Objects in general, and architectural objects in particular, have traditionally been impenetrable to analysis. The tight-fitting relationship of objects to the notion of use accounts for the predominant definition of the form of the object as a representation of use. The definition of form, by its use, appears as a primary meaning in Graves's work, and appears as

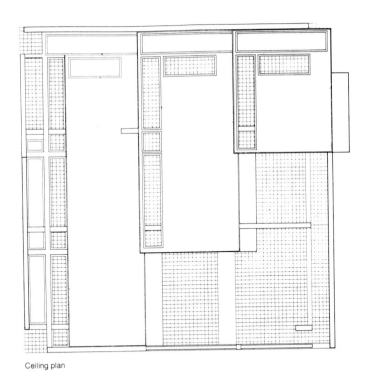

Figure 47
Eisenman House—Ceiling Plan

Ceiling plan

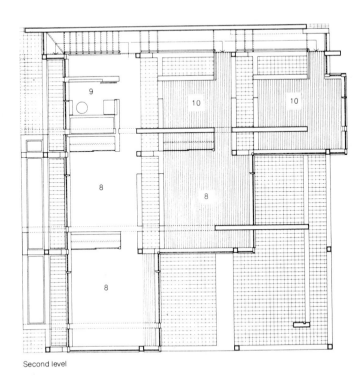

Figure 48
Eisenman House—Second Level. 8
Bedroom, 9 Bathroom, 10 Study

Second level

surface structure in Eisenman's work. This interpretation, however, opens the possibility of a more profound understanding of the essence of architectural form. The first,

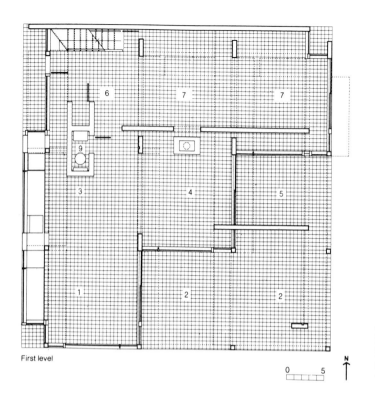

First level

0   5

N

Figure 49
Eisenman House—First level. 1
Playroom, 2 Evening Terrace, 3 Kitchen, 4 Summer Terrace, 5 Morning
Terrace, 6 Entry 7 Winter Wing

explicit aspect of architectural form obscures another, much more complex, implicit aspect. This implicit aspect can be seen, in Graves's case, as the signification of architectural form; in Eisenman's case, it is seen as deep structure. Their acknowledgement of, and further development from, this fact provides a possibility for architecture to be seen as a systematic phenomenon, as a system of prescriptions that appear as 'innocent' forms of descriptions, such as 'this is X'; or of 'explications' such as 'X is because of Y'. With the conscious manipulation of this system of rules, Eisenman and Graves are part of an emerging dialectic field of analysis that is open for approval, refusal, or further transformation.

Notes

Agrest, D. and Gandelsonas, M. (1972) arquitectura/Arquitectura, *Summa*, Buenos Aires, January 1972.

Alexander, C. (1971) *Notes on the Synthesis of Form*, Harvard University Press.

Chomsky, N. (1965), *Aspects of the Theory of Syntax*, Cambridge, Mass., MIT Press.

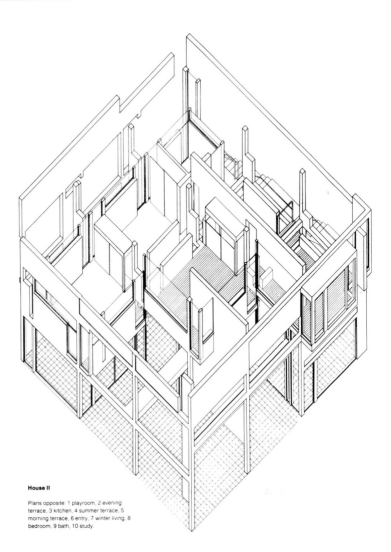

Figure 50
Eisenman: House II

House II

Plans opposite: 1 playroom, 2 evening terrace, 3 kitchen, 4 summer terrace, 5 morning terrace, 6 entry, 7 winter living, 8 bedroom, 9 bath, 10 study.

Chomsky, N. (1965) *Language and Mind*, New York, Harcourt Brace & World, Inc.

Eco, U. (1968), *La Struttura Assente*, Milan, Bompiani.

Greimas. J. (1970) *Du Sens*, Paris, Éditions Seuil.

Jakobson, R. (1962), *Selected Writings*, The Hague, Mouton.

Lacan, J. (1966). *Écrits*, Paris, Éditions Seuil.

Lévi-Strauss, C. (1967) *Structural Anthropology*, New York, Doubleday.

Morris, C. (1970) *Foundations of the Theory of Signs*, University of Chicago Press.

de Saussure, F. (1959) *Course in General Linguistics*, New York, Philosophical Library, Inc.

2.4 Notes for a Theory of Meaning in Design

Juan Bonta

Reprinted from *Versus*, Vol. 6, No. 2, 1973.

Yesterday[1] someone asked to see concrete applications of semiotics to design. I would like to answer positively to this request, but I find myself in a dilemma. I could either show some specific examples, some photographs of objects which were designed applying a design method based on semiotics, or I could present the method itself. In the first case attention would be centered on the results; in the second, on the criteria and hypotheses which guided us in the task.

Apparently curiosity would be better satisfied by showing examples than by developing a theory. Nevertheless I have my doubts about the validity of such an approach. Finally, the values of objects designed with a semiotical method —or, for that matter, with any other method—are not necessarily values of the method itself; there are architectural masterpieces which were designed on scarcely any theoretical grounds, and refined conceptual tools that produced poor results in the hands of an incompetent interpreter. My purpose is to present a theoretical approach and the examples of application will be mere illustrations.

In former sessions of the Symposium, two tendencies in architectural semiotics have been outlined, one of them behaviourist—based principally on Morris—and the other structuralist—based on Saussure and more specifically on Barthes. But these are not the only conceivable orientations. There is also a third one, briefly mentioned yesterday by Dr

[1]This paper was read in the Symposium on 'Architecture, History and the Theory of Signs', organized by the Colegio Official de Arquitectos de Cataluna y Baleares in Castelldefels, Spain, on 16 March 1972. Dates, comments and other details mentioned by the speaker refer to the context of this Symposium.

Krampen: it is in my opinion more promising than either of the other two. I am referring to Eric Buyssens and Luis J. Prieto's approach, and it is this approach which forms the basis of this paper.

I would like to situate Buyssens's school. To speak of a 'Saussurean' semiology is to misuse terms: Saussure anticipated the possibility of the existence of semiology and even coined its name, but he did not constitute it as a discipline. he limited himself to saying that semiology 'had a right to existence, a place staked out in advance'. But several decades would pass before his anticipation was to be embodied into an actual set of principles. Those who have talked about Saussurean semiology in the past few days were referring, on the whole, to Barthes's semiology, formalized at the beginning of the sixties—half a century after Saussure—agreeing with the Genevan master on many points and disagreeing with him on many others.

But there is another semiology apart from that of Barthes, which has the same right to be called Saussurean, because this one too is an attempt to embody Saussure's anticipation. It was conceived at the beginning of the forties when Buyssens's book was first published, and it was further developed by Prieto. I think that the merit of having recognized its relevance to architectural theory corresponds to the Buenos Aires school of architectural semiotics.

1 The Components of Meaning

Indicators and Signals

I shall distinguish three components of the meaning or signification of a designed form. To do this I must begin by defining two concepts—indicator and signal—following Buyssens and Prieto.

An indicator is a directly perceptible fact, by means of which it is possible to learn something about other indirectly perceptible facts. For example: an obstruction in the road, a queue of cars, and people running, are directly perceptible facts; the occurrence of the accident is not. Through the former I can learn something about the latter; consequently, they are indicators.

At least two elements can be distinguished in this situation: the perceptible facts, which constitute the indicators, and the indirectly perceptible ones which compose the meaning of the indicator. (In the context of design, we shall talk about the *form* and the *meaning of the form*.) There are also other elements susceptible of identification, of which I shall mention only one: the *interpreter*, which realizes that the indicator is referring to a meaning (the observer, as in the example). The indicative relationship is thus characterized as a triadic one (form/meaning/interpreter).

Signals are a special class of indicators that fulfill two additional conditions: firstly, they must be deliberately used—or eventually produced—with the purpose of having an act of communication; secondly, they must be recognized by the interpreter as such as having been deliberately used to have a communicative act. If either of these two conditions is not fulfilled, we may be faced with an indicator, but not with a signal.

Taking an example related with the former one, imagine that the police intervene and put a notice at the roadside informing drivers that an accident has occurred. The notice is, in the first place, an indicator, in as much as it is a directly perceptible fact which tells us something about another fact, not directly perceptible, and it is also a signal, because it was deliberately used by someone—the police—to communicate something to somebody—the drivers—and because when they see the notice, drivers realize that the police intend to communicate something to them.

Signals have form, meaning and interpreter, like indicators; and in addition they have an *emitter* (the police, as in the example). The interpreter of a signal can also be called *receiver*.

There is a considerable difference between indicators and signals. Indicators tend to show objective reality, matters of fact; the obstruction in the road reflects that there has *in fact* been an accident. On the other hand, signals communicate what is called by Buyssens *states of consciousness* of the emitter. Faced with the notice left by the police, I do not find myself before the accident as a matter of fact, but as a content of consciousness; there is someone—the police—who knows something and is trying to transfer it to me.

Both in the reading of indicators and of signals there is a possibility of error: I may attribute the queue of cars to an accident when it is in fact due to other causes and I can misread the police notice. But in the case of signals, there is in addition the possibility of deceit: it is possible that the police are lying, to make me believe that there has been an accident when in fact it was something else. Such a presumption is not possible in the face of a mere indicator and it is another proof of the dissimilarity of both entities. The meaning of a signal is different from that of a mere indicator.

Another aspect which distinguishes indicators and signals is the nature of the bond which links the form to its meaning. The obstruction in the road means an accident because it is possible to construct a chain of inferences linking one fact to the other. In the case of indicators, the relationship between form and meaning is natural or factual; the meaning results from the form as the consequence of an act of analysis. In the case of signals, on the other hand, this relationship is conventional and, up to a certain point, arbitrary or not motivated: even though it is possible to limit somewhat the arbitrariness of codes using resources such as iconicity and articulation, the reading of signals always requires the knowledge of some conventions, the learning of a code.

Communication and Indication

Signals *communicate*, indicators *indicate*. Communication theory is concerned with the study of signals; indication theory with the study of indicators. Both are branches of the theory of meaning or signification.

The fact of something being an indicator or a signal does not depend on its nature as an object but on the role it plays within the significative process; on the relations that are established between its parts — form, meaning — and with the other elements of the process — emitter, interpreter. Consequently, objects taking part in more than one process of signification could be indicators and signals at the same time. The police notice mentioned earlier, for example, is a signal which communicates that there has been an accident; but it is also an *indicator* which means that the police have intervened.

Frequently those who are concerned with signals (engineers, communication theorists) are not interested in these in as much as they are indicators and inversely, those who study indicators (doctors, meteorologists, archeologists) ignore the possibility that they also operate as signals. The separation is, nevertheless, somewhat academic and can lead to partial visions in fields where forms frequently act as indicators and signals.

One example is the case of medicine. Medical semiology studies the symptoms of the organism as indicators, that is, as observable conditions by means of which it is possible to know something about other conditions of the organism not directly observable. The symptom is the form, the non-observable condition is the meaning. The relationship between form and meaning is natural, independent of the patient's will. Nevertheless, medical psychology has revealed that in the case of certain disturbances the 'artificial' production of symptoms is possible, which then operate as signals by which the patient *communicates* what he will not or cannot communicate in another way. The best diagnosis will be that which conciliates the meaning of the symptom in its possible roles of indicator and signal.

Another field in which the levels of communication and indication frequently overlap is that of design. A theory of meaning in this area cannot be limited to one level or the other; both must be considered potentially present. It will be convenient to talk about an *indicative component* and a *communicative component* in the meaning of a designed form, thus recognizing beforehand the possible functioning of the form in both ways.

Intentional Indicators

Nevertheless, this range of components is not yet rich enough. I shall define a third component of the meaning of designed forms, situated halfway between indicative and communicative components.

There is an entity which is neither pure indicator nor signal, though it is related to both. I shall call it an *intentional indicator*. Its possibilities were not developed by Buyssens nor by Prieto, but they offer an adequate model for a wide range of signifying processes in design.

An intentional indicator is an indicator which fulfils the first of the conditions of the definition of a signal, but not the second. In other words, it is an indicator deliberately used — or produced — by someone to generate an act of communication, but which must *not* be recognized as such — as deliberately used for communicating — on the part of the interpreter (the user or producer of intentional indicators cannot be properly called *emitter*, since we are not really dealing with communication; it will be better to call him the *producer*.)

For instance, there are certain ways of talking, dressing, or behaving that are associated with certain social classes, professional groups, ages or ideologies. Essentially, they are indicators that naturally reflect the individual's belonging to the group concerned. But it is easy to imagine — and in fact it frequently happens — that people produce these kind of indicators hoping to induce in other people the idea of their belonging to one of these groups. In such cases, the indicator is deliberately produced; but its efficacy depends on the interpreter not recognizing it as such but considering it as natural. Such indicators pretend to reflect a matter of fact while they actually correspond to states of consciousness which are supposed not to be recognized as such.

In design these manipulations are not unusual. They occur each time an office is arranged to produce a certain impression on the visitor; or when a house, factory, or public building is designed in order to reflect a certain image of the client, whether individual or collective.

These examples may suggest that the use of intentional indicators in design is limited to the exhibition — or perhaps affectation — of a certain *status*, but this is not the case. In designing an object it is necessary to make sure that the user will recognize it, that he will read it as what it is. A corkscrew which nobody recognized would be a bad corkscrew however ingenious its mechanism were. It would be possible to put a label on it (in other words, to use a signal) but this would be looked down upon by many people. The alternative is to give it a form such that is recognizable for what it is. The user will then receive the message ('this is a corkscrew') as corresponding to a matter of fact; but the message was actually originated in the designer's consciousness. Intentional indicators are common in design, and there are no reasons for having moral prejudices against them.

I would like to refer to the example so frequently quoted in the last few days, the door of the bar at the back of this room. The distinction between indicators, intentional indicators, and signals is applicable here. When the word BAR was fixed over the door, a signal was used. When one recognizes the bar by its noises, smell or because one watches the interior, one is operating by indicators. Finally, if the designer installs a glass door so that one can see through it (or if he doesn't put a door at all, for the same reason) we have before us an intentional indicator; from the interpreter's point of view, it is equal to an ordinary indicator; the designer does not declare his presence as the emitter of the message; he limits himself to pulling the strings behind the scenes hoping that the information will reach people at the right moment and in the right way.

Talking about this same example, someone made a cunning remark yesterday. It is not necessary, he said, to use the sign BAR nor to let the smell through so that it can be recognized. There are certain doors which are recognized by everyone as bar doors, because they have been seen in Westerns or other places. That is so; I would just like to add that these doors too are signals, no longer verbal but architectural. There is a repertoire of conventionalized architectural forms which behave as signals, like words. Their reading demands the knowledge of a code. Codes can be implicit. Forms in this case do not give direct evidence of matters of fact; they remit to states of consciousness. They can be suspected of deceit: it could be a typical bar door, leading to an ironmonger's.

We have already mentioned the indicative and the communicative components in the meaning of a designed form, corresponding to its roles as indicator and signal. We can now add to the list another component, which I shall call *the expressive component*. It corresponds to the form used as an intentional indicator. A form's meaning may have all three components or just some of them. Indicators, intentional indicators and signals are not three kinds of forms, but roles which a single form may perform in different combinations.

The Dynamics of Stabilization and Changes in Meaning

There is interaction between these components. Pure indicators tend to produce intentional indicators and the latter tend to become signals. We can illustrate this with the example of the bar. Only if people recognize bars by direct vision (pure indicator) can the idea arise in the designer's mind of making a transparent door (intentional indicator). Using it repeatedly—let us assume, for the sake of the argument, that it is not used for other kinds of stores—this door will end up by being associated with the idea of bar; it will denote the existence of the bar without it being necessary any longer to look through it and to actually see it; it will have been converted into a signal.

The repeated use of the signal might finally lead to its obsolescence—its consumption—according to a process which has been studied, among others, by Rupert de Ventos and Dorfles. The form will end up by being desemanticized, losing its original meaning, and it may eventually be resemanticized with supplementary or metaphorical meaning. Actual bars will not have these doors any more, and the 'typical bar doors' may appear again in the entrances to sophisticated shops for men, alluding metaphorically to the masculinity of the Westerner's world. There might also be a bit of humour in this, due to the fact that interpreters and emitters recognize each other as belonging to an elite group which is familiar with a certain restricted code.

In substituting 'masculinity' for 'bar' there is a change in *meaning*, but not a change in the *component* of meaning concerned: in both cases they are signals. But the dynamics of the process will continue in both planes (meaning and component). Those who ignore the code representing the bar doors as a signal of masculinity will finally get used to their use in shops and will recognize them as indicators of, perhaps, 'sophistication'. In this case there is a switch of component; from the communicative (signal) we pass to the indicative. From here onward, the whole cycle of transformations going from indicators to intentional indicators and from there to signals can begin again: less sophisticated shops will use the same doors just because they want to look sophisticated, thus intentional indication takes the place of mere indication and the evolution continues. The various steps of this process are diagrammatically presented in chart no. 1.
Architectural language—no less than verbal language—is in a permanent state of transformation: some forces are driving for change, others for stabilization.

Chart 1. The bar door. Stabilization and changes in meaning

Step Form	Role	Meaning	Component	Comments	Process
1 open bar	indicator	bar	indicative	perceived as a matter of fact	
2 glass door leading to bar	intentional indicator	bar	expressive	perceived as a matter of fact — but result of manipulation	conventionalization (stabilization of meaning)
3 'typical' bar door (same as in 2)	signal	bar	communicative	there is no need to see through the door. Meaning as a state of consciousness	
4 same door in the entrance of a store for men	signal	masculinity	communicative	meaning is metaphoric. The code is sophisticated	change of meaning
5 same as in 4	indicator	sophistication	indicative	sophistication is a matter of fact	
6 same door in any shop	intentional indicator	sophistication	expressive	perceived as a matter of fact — but result of manipulation	stabilization

It is difficult in practice to distinguish the different stages of the process, because the perceptive modalities of the various sections of the community do not always evolve simultaneously. Disparity in reading of the same form by different interpreters is unavoidable. There are what could be called architectural sub-cultures — the strangest of which is that of the architects themselves. A sub-culture is characterized by a certain internal cohesion with regard to their ways of reading forms, and sometimes by a deliberate separation with regard to other people's way of reading. Sociology can throw some light upon this question, and inversely the study of architectural 'dialects' can be relevant to sociological classification.

The difficulties one stumbles against, in practice, when distinguishing between indicators, intentional indicators and signals must not obscure the validity of the distinction itself. They correspond to different phases of the development of architectural language and each of them operates according to its own modality.

The practical consequences of the distinction for

criticism, history and the very art of designing seem obvious; I do not think it necessary to elaborate upon this point.

2 Form and Meaning

Physical Form and Significant Form

I shall call the *physical form* of an object (or place) the set of all its features directly or indirectly perceptible, such as, for example, its shape, colour, texture, smell, sound, temperature, weight, mechanical, chemical, electrical properties and so on.

The *significant form* is an abstraction of physical form which includes some of its features—those which refer to the meaning—and excludes the rest. Frequently I shall say *form* instead of *significant form*; I shall only use the complete expression when otherwise there could be a risk of confusion with physical form.

One single significant form can correspond to diverse physical forms. The previously mentioned police notice can be made of metal or wood, it can measure two feet or three: though the physical form of these diverse objects is different its significant form and its meaning are the same. As Prieto has pointed out, significant forms correspond to *classes* of concrete forms.

What Prieto bypassed (because it was not pertinent to the conventional semiological systems he was studying, though it is pertinent to systems of objects) is the reciprocal affirmation: that various significant forms can correspond to one physical form—each with its meaning—according to which are the features of the physical form to be abstracted. The physical form of the police station is, in each given circumstance, one only; nevertheless at least two significant forms can be abstracted from it: a signal signifying that there has been an accident and an indicator signifying that the police intervened. Objects—in contrast to the signals of the systems studied by Prieto—are naturally polysemic, that is susceptible to acquiring different meanings. Polysemy occurs at the physical form level, not at the significant form level: each object admits various significant forms but each significant form admits—generally—only one meaning. When it is not so—when a significant form admits various meanings—we call it a case of *ambiguity*, which must not be confused with polysemy. Polysemy is proper to physical form; ambiguity—when it exists—is proper to significant forms.

It will be convenient to designate in some way the relationship that exists between physical and significant forms. We can say that physical forms *realize* or *admit* significant forms and that the latter *organize* or *analyze* concrete physical forms.

Morphological and Semantic Questions

When saying that the significant form is an abstraction of physical form which includes those of its features that refer to meaning, two questions are posed: (1) Which are the features of physical form? and (2) How do we know which of them refer to meaning? The first is a morphological problem; the second a semantic one.

The morphological question would be solved from a naïve perspective, simply by approaching the object; once we know the thing, we know its features. Nevertheless we know that a single object can be described, organized or analyzed by its features in more than one way. A certain geometric form, for example, can be read as an oval or as a flattened circle: while in the first case only one feature is recognized, in the second there are two: circularity and flatness. How do we determine then which are the features of the physical form that should be considered?

For the moment I shall limit myself to pointing out the problem, deferring the fixing of a criterion which leads us to its solution until later.

With regard to the semantic problem—how to determine which are the features of the physical form that refer to the meaning and which do not—we can apply the procedure known by linguists as *commutation*. It consists in modifying each feature, observing if the meaning then changes. We shall see some examples immediately.

Form and Meaning

Form is composed of features; meaning is composed of *values*. I am not using the term in the sense which is given to it in axiology, but as a purely conventional name for designating the components of meaning. We can talk about indicative, expressive and communicational values according to our previous classification. Values can also be classified according to other criteria. Form was defined as the set of values that affect meaning: reciprocally, meaning is defined as the set of values susceptible to being modified by changes taking place in the form.

Nobody will miss the circularity of these definitions; each of the notions is defined in terms of the other one. The difficulty is unavoidable because we are not concerned with intrinsic properties of the entities that constitute form and meaning, but only with their relational properties. Everything that satisfies the said properties can legitimately be called *form* and *meaning*. The approach is *structural* in this sense. We shall see later that there is another meaning of the word *structural* which is also applicable here.

Models

Every set of features and values which satisfy the definitions of form and meaning constitute what we shall call a *significant model.*[2]

Analogously other types of models can be defined. A functional model of an object is an abstraction of some of its features, those which confer certain possibilities of function to it. Multiple use objects admit more than one functional model. Visual models abstract features which define the appearance of the object; economic models abstract features that determine economic properties, and so on.

There are features that contribute to various types of models. The shape of a knife, for example, contributes to its functional model inasmuch as it makes a certain type of operation possible, and to its significant model inasmuch as it allows this possibility of operation to be recognized.

Models organize or analyze objects and objects realize or admit models. Each model organizes numerous objects and each object realizes many models.

Our interest is centered on significant models. I shall call them *model*—without any other qualification—and only use the complete expression when otherwise there would be a risk of confusion with other kinds of model.

An Example of Significant Model

I shall illustrate these concepts with the system of chess pieces which we surely all know. The point is to recognize the objects of which this system is composed and to distinguish the various significant models that they admit.

Recognition of the physical forms of objects does not present any difficulties; such recognition includes all their directly or indirectly perceptible features; but what is the significant form and what is the meaning of a chess piece?

The question allows, we said, various answers: there are many points of view from which it is possible to organize a physical form into a significant form. It is a question of finding sets of features and of values amongst which there exists

[2]Scholars use different terms to designate the same or very similar concepts. My ideas are based on Prieto's *sema*. I changed the name for *significant model* because as I explain next, I can see an analogy with other kinds of model. Working with systems of signals and not systems of objects, Prieto could not be aware of nor interested in this analogy.

the relationship established in the definitions.

It is easier to begin by determining the sets of values (the meaning) and then defining the corresponding features (the form).

One of the possible answers originates by considering that the meaning of each piece is what we normally call its *identity*. (Some semiologists consider *identificatory* signs as a special class of signs, particularly relevant.) Let us take any chessman—for example, the white king of an ordinary wooden set. Its identity (or meaning) is the conjunction of a series of observations (or values) such as:

(a) that it is a king and not, say, a queen.

(b) that it is a white piece, not a black.

(c) that it belongs to an ordinary wooden set and not, for example, to a luxurious ivory set.

(d) that it is a chessman and not, for example, a draught.

The features of the physical form that refer to these values could be listed as follows:

(A) its shape

(B) its colour

(C) its material

(D) certain details of its finish

This is not a one-to-one relationship between features and values, but a relationship between the set of values and the set of features; the fact that both sets have the same number of elements is accidental. Each of the values can be modified by varying one or more features, and by means of changes in any of the features it is possible to affect at least one of the values; as a result, these two sets constitute one of the significant models of the chessman we are considering.

The Universe of Discourse

Other significant models related to the one we have just seen can be found by modifying what logicians call the *universe of discourse*. This expression alludes to the totality of the objects taken into consideration in a given circumstance. For a chess player immersed in a game, for instance, the universe of discourse is limited to the pieces in play; the identity of the king is exhausted in the observations—or values—(a) and (b). For the buyer choosing a chess set from several, the universe of discourse is extended to all the possible options; the value (c) of our list becomes relevant. There may ultimately be other games also in consideration and then (d) will have to be taken into account.

In each of these universes of discourse, the object—the chessman—realizes a different significant model. The player only thinks, as we have said, of the values (a) and (b) and the features on which these rest, which are (A) and (B). The other values—the quality of the pieces (wood, ivory and so on) and the nature of the game (chess)—like the features that carry them (material, details of finish, a certain general configuration of the silhouettes) are common to all the elements of the universe of discourse and therefore lack all discriminatory power. They can be called *universal* values and features of the system.

Universal features and values are excluded from the significant model. According to our definitions, the form is composed by the features *whose change* affects the meaning, and the meaning is composed by the values *that change* as a result of the changes there have been in the features. But universal features and values cannot change, at least within the limits of the system in which they are universal.

The possibility of change is a necessary condition but it is not sufficient for a feature or a value to be incorporated in the form or the meaning respectively. If all the chessmen considered in a given circumstance were wooden or if all were of ivory, this feature could not be significant. If some pieces were wooden and some others of ivory, the feature could be significant or not significant: it would be significant if the difference in material affected some value of the meaning, for example, if one player were to play with wooden pieces and the other with ivory pieces; difference in material would thus be equivalent to difference in colour. Differences in material would not be significant if the distribution of wooden and ivory were random, as when pieces of different sets are used because neither of them is complete.

An amplification of the universe of discourse can make values and features become relevant which remain latent, in the form of universals, in the more restricted universe of discourse. Inversely, a reduction in the universe of discourse may turn universal—and thus eliminate from the model —other features and values.

Systems of Models

Significant models tend to constitute systems, such that the system, considered as a whole, exhausts the universe of discourse. There is, for instance, a system constituted by the models of all the men of a given chess set, another constituted by the models of all chessmen, another by the models of pieces that serve for playing games in general. We have already seen that changes in the universe of discourse affect the nature of each model; this is what allows us to say that the set of all the models constitutes, not a mere aggregate, but a system: the introduction of new models—or the suppression of some—has a repercussion on the nature of the rest.

When significant models are conventional, the systems they constitute are usually called codes.

Other Significant Models

It is not only by changing the universe of discourse that new significant models of an object can be generated. There are as many possible models as there are perspectives or areas of interest. For an anthropologist, for example, the significant features of a chess piece are those that allow it to be classified as a cultural object, not a natural one; as an object the function of which is to be used in games, rather than, say, in the production of wealth; a game which is a reflection of a social or military organization, but not of a religious conception; a sublimation of aggressive and competitive impulses, but not of eroticism, and so on. A designer, in his turn, will see other features which will allow him to classify the piece as the result of an act of conscious design, not as an anonymous tribal product; as belonging to an industrial culture, not to one of craftsmanship; as designed—let us say—in the 19th century and not in the 20th. A manufacturer of chess sets, finally, will see in the pieces those features which indicate that they can be turned on the lathe or that they must be carved, and so on.

Generality of the Theory of Signification

Questioning the *real* meaning of chessmen is obviously superfluous. None of the various possible significant models has intrinsic virtues that permit it to be chosen above the rest, within the limits of a theory of signification. Quite the contrary, theory of signification should be general enough to make room for the multiple significant models with which man organizes the objects of his world, according to his changing interests and needs.

It is a waste of time to discuss whether architecture expresses its primary and secondary functions—as Eco maintains—or whether its meaning remits to spatial values—as De Fusco and Scalvini show—or if it constitutes patterns for the identification of urban space—as suggested by Lynch. These diverse models are not mutually exclusive.

Signification theory should not be concerned with the nature of the particular meanings nor the specific formal features that happen to be relevant in each case. Theory should concentrate on the study of the general abstract properties, truly semiological, of all possible models whatever the sphere of interests to which they correspond. The concepts of *significant form, meaning, feature, value, significant model, indicative, expressive* and *communicational components of meaning*—as we have defined them—and those of *articulation* and *context*—which we shall examine next—are independent of the specific nature of the entities to which they are applicable. I hope, as a result, that this scheme will be found useful both by the followers of Eco and by those who work according to Scalvini.

3 Articulation

Articulation in Models

In general terms, each feature of form can affect one or more values of meaning, and each value can be affected by one or more features. We shall say that there is *articulation* or that the model is *articulated* in the special case when there is a bi-univocal correspondence between features and values; in other words, if each feature affected a single value, and each value were affected by a single feature. Features and values would in this case be called *articulating*.

Let us take as an example the first significant model we saw of the white king in chess, the one in which meaning was supposed to be equal to identity. If we confront the lists of features and values and trace lines joining each value with the feature on which it depends, we shall have:

Features	Values
silhouette ———————	king
colour ———————	white
material ———————	ordinary
finish	chess

We observe features as *colour, material* and *finish* which refer to a single value, and also features like *silhouette* that refer to several; and there are values, like *king, white,* and *chess* that depend on a single feature, while others, like *ordinary,* depend on several. This model is not articulated.

On the other hand, if the universe of discourse is restricted to the pieces of a given set, the features *material* and *finish* and the values *ordinary* and *chess* become universal and disappear from the model, which is then articulated:

Articulating features	Articulating Values
silhouette ———————	king
colour ———————	white

Sometimes we shall speak, for convenience, of articulated *forms* or *meanings*; by this we mean the forms or meanings of articulated models. The use of the abbreviated expressions should not make us forget that articulation cannot be established only in the plane of form or meaning, but that it implies a given coordination of both planes.

The features and values of an articulated model can also appear in other models of the same system or code. For example the silhouette of the white king (which corresponds to the value of 'being a king') also appears in the form of the black king with the same value; and something similar applies to the colour white, which not only appears in the king but also the queen or the bishop.

Articulation in Systems

Between each articulating feature and the value which corresponds to it, there exists a relationship of signification similar to the one there is between a form and a meaning. This permits a new system to be defined, hierarchically subordinate to the previous one: its forms are articulating features and its meanings are articulating values of the other system. Systems of this type—whose forms and meanings are respectively articulating features and values of another system—will be called *articulating systems*; and their models will be called *articulating models*.

We shall call *articulated systems* those which have a subordinate articulating system such that by means of the models of the latter it is possible to compose all the models of the former.

It should be noticed that the notions of *articulated* and *articulating* are not absolute but relative; a system can be articulated with regard to a hierarchically subordinate system; and it can be articulating with regard to another one hierarchically superordinate.

The forms of the articulating system—which are features in the articulated one—can appear in more than one form of the articulated system. It is thus possible that the number of forms of the articulating system is inferior to that of the articulated; and the same can be said about the number of meanings. In other words, it is possible that the subordinate system is smaller, when measured in relation to the number of elements it is composed of, than the superordinate one.

The system of chessmen, for instance, comprises twelve forms and meanings (or models): six correspond to white and six to black. All models are articulated as is the white king we have already commented on; and the articulating system has only eight models: six correspond to figures and two to colour (chart no. 2).

Chart 2. Chess. Ordinary Articulation

	Articulated System			Articulating system		
Form	Meaning	Features		Features	Value	Forms
I	white king	1	7	1	king	I VII
II	white queen	2	7	2	queen	II VIII
III	white bishop	3	7	3	bishop	III IX
IV	white knight	4	7	4	knight	IV X
V	white rook	5	7	5	rook	V XI
VI	white pawn	6	7	6	pawn	VI XII
VII	black king	1	8	7	white	I II III
VIII	black queen	2	8			IV V VI
IX	black bishop	3	8	8	black	VII VIII
X	black knight	4	8			IX X XI
XI	black rook	5	8			XII
XII	black pawn	6	8			

Articulation in Language and in Design

Our concept of articulation—based, with great simplifications, on Prieto's work—is analogous to the first articulation of language, studied by Martinet and others. In language, sentences constitute the articulated system and the smallest significant units compose the articulating, subordinate system. Such units are what Martinet called the *monemes* and in a rough approximation they can be considered to be equivalent to words. There is also a certain analogy, though less perfect, with the second articulation of language, where the articulated system is that of monemes or words, and the articulating one is that of phonemes or—roughly—letters.

Nevertheless there exist two differences between articulation in language, as linguists understand it, and articulation in design, as we are presenting it. The first of them consists in the enumerabilty of articulating models, and the second in the necessity of articulation.

Articulating systems in language—both that of monemes and that of phonemes—comprehend a finite repertoire of models the nature of which is known, and they are independent from the sentences in which they occur: both phoneme and the monemes of language are, in principle, enumerable. The same cannot be said about articulating models in design: as we have already said, semiological theory cannot decide *a priori* on the nature of the forms and meanings of the models it studies, nor affirm that their number is finite. Double articulation is, for Martinet, an essential distinctive characteristic of language; a system lacking it would not be a linguistic entity. Once more, this is not the case in design. Articulation in a system or a model is only a contingency, not a necessary property.

The Morphological Question Again

On what does it depend, that a model or a system be articulated? Among other things, on the way in which form and meaning are decomposed into features and values. We said, when talking about this decomposition for the first time, that generally there were different ways of accomplishing it, and that it was necessary to count on some criterion in order to choose one of them. We can now add that the best analysis of form and meaning is that which produces articulation, that is to say, a bi-univocal correspondence between features and values.

Articulation constitutes a paradigm, an ideal pattern to which it is only sometimes possible to adjust in analysing an architectural or designed form. When an articulated reading exists, it is preferable to other possible readings. There are several ways of decomposing the white king's form into features: silhouette and colour, head and body, carved part and part turned on the lathe and so on. But when playing chess the first decomposition has an advantage over the other, because the features correspond one-to-one to values of meaning.

Criticism and Design

Articulation in a system depends on certain intrinsic qualities of the objects that realize it and also on the ways in which the interpreter organizes the objects in the system; in other words, there are objective and subjective factors which affect the existence of articulation. The latter operate in the moment of the object's fruition and as a result, primarily interest those concerned with analysis and criticism of existing works of design. The former, on the other hand, remit to the instances of creation of the objects and consequently interest both designers and design method theorists. We shall examine the usefulness of articulation in the design process.

Degree of Articulation

We shall call *degree of articulation* of a system the number of hierarchically subordinate articulating levels that it admits; for example, we may assume the degree of articulation of one, of the system of chessmen currently in use, because it only admits one subordinate system (chart no. 2).

The degree of articulation of a system is a variable which is, within certain limits, under the designer's control. He can introduce further degrees of articulation or, on the contrary, try to avoid its existence at all.

The articulation of the current sets of chessmen, for instance, is far from being unavoidable. In many ancient designs equivalent men of different colour had different shapes; colour was an articulating feature, shape was not. On the other hand, systems could be constructed that had an ulterior articulation level, in addition to the usual in current design. Let us pause to analyze this possibility.

The six figures of the game (king, queen, bishop, knight, rook and pawn) constitute, together with colour, the articulating system currently used. But this system could be articulated, in its turn, in a lower articulating level.

Chart 3. Chess. Possible Ulterior Levels of Articulation

		Articulating system	*Articulated system* Features		
Feature	*Value*	*Forms*	*Form*	*Rich*	*Poor*
Proposal I					
1	limited movement	K,Kt,P	K	$\overline{1}$ 2 3	$\overline{1}$ 3
2	movement in column	K,Q,R,P	Q	$\overline{1}$ 2 3	$\overline{1}$ 2 3
3	diagonal movement	K,Q,B	B	1 $\overline{2}$ 3	1 $\overline{2}$ or $\overline{2}$ 3
$\overline{1}$	unlimited movement	Q,B,R	Kt	1 $\overline{2}$ 3	1 $\overline{2}$ or $\overline{2}$ 3
$\overline{2}$	without movement in column	B,Kt	R	1 2 3	$\overline{1}$ 3
$\overline{3}$	without diagonal movement	Kt,R,P	P	1 2 $\overline{3}$	1 $\overline{3}$
Proposal II					
4	can begin	Kt,P	K	$\overline{4}$ 5 6	$\overline{5}$ $\overline{6}$
5	can castle	K,R	Q	$\overline{4}$ 5 6	$\overline{5}$ $\overline{6}$
6	are two	B,Kt,R	B	4 $\overline{5}$ 6	$\overline{5}$ $\overline{6}$
$\overline{4}$	cannot begin	K,Q,B,R	Kt	4 $\overline{5}$ 6	4 6
$\overline{5}$	cannot castle	Q,B,Kt,P	R	4 $\overline{5}$ 6	$\overline{5}$ $\overline{6}$
$\overline{6}$	are not two	K,Q,P	P	4 $\overline{5}$ 6	4 6

K = king; Q = queen; B = bishop; Kt = knight, R = rook; P = pawn.

Chart no. 3 presents two possibilities chosen from the many that could be conceived. The values of both systems are here referred to the properties of the figures according to the rules of the game. The list of pieces accompanying each value helps to define what the value is so 'limited movement' corresponds to the king, the knight and the pawn, three men which advance by fixed intervals — in contrast to the queen, the bishop and the rook which can move one or several squares and so on.

The negation (or absence) of the properties has also been considered. The use of affirmative and negative values implies working with binary classification. One could also conceive classificatory criteria that would admit a wider range of possibilities — in other words, that could reflect degrees of manifestations of the value. For the sake of brevity we shall limit our discussion to binary classification.

The features corresponding to each value are expressed in the chart by means of figures — negative in the case of negation — to the meaning of which we shall refer at once.

On the right hand of the chart the combinations of articulating figures corresponding to each form of the articulated system are shown; so, the king is constructed with the combination (1 2 3) in proposal I, or ($\overline{4}$ $\overline{5}$ $\overline{6}$) according to proposal II. One can verify that forms are thus unambiguously identified, since no combination of features is repeated.

Attribution of Features of Values

Each figure of the chart represents a certain concrete formal feature. For example, (1) can be 'short', (2) 'square based' and (3) 'triangular based'.

The attribution of features to each value is a very delicate step in design, which requires special comment.

It is desirable that the relationship feature/value should be as immediate as possible. But relationships that are seen as immediate in one culture could seem strange to another. Designers must perceive with subtlety not only the relationships that are already conventionally established, but also which are *possible* within a given cultural system. We are still far from properly understanding what characterizes a relationship which is perceived as immediate, as opposed to ones which are not. One could say that the relation feature/value must be iconic; but this might only perpetuate the difficulty, necessitating a definition of iconicity, a term which is not easy to define, as Jakobson and Eco have shown.

Another point to be considered is compatibilty of the various features. When two values appear together in a single meaning, their corresponding features must be physically compatible in order to constitute the form. For example, 'movement in column' and 'diagonal movement' both appear as values in men such as the king or the queen. Consequently, features (2) and (3) could not be, for instance, 'with a square base' and 'with a triangular base', except if one can conceive a way for a piece to have a base simultaneously triangular and square (pyramids with a square base, perhaps).

Finally, we must discuss the interpretation of the negative figures of chart no. 3. Three criteria are possible (chart no. 4). According to the first of them, features would be attributed only to positive figures. Negative figures — or no figures at all — would be expressed by the absence of the feature. Proceeding in this way, forms constituted by figures all negative could not be materialized. This would be the case of the queen in proposal II. The problem can be solved by adding

Chart 4. Attribution of Features to Negation and to Absence of Information

	Criterion A	*Criterion B*	*Criterion C*
Affirmation (positive figure)	corresponding feature	corresponding feature	corresponding feature
Negation (negative figure)	absence of feature	opposite feature	opposite feature
Absence of information (no figure)	absence of feature	absence of feature	neutral feature

to all the forms of the system a universal feature, whose meaning would be 'to be an element of the system'. According to another criterion, negative figures could be expressed by features that are opposite to those corresponding to positive figures: if (1) is 'short', (1) would be 'long'; if (2) is 'square based', (2) would be 'round based'. One has to be careful, in this case, not to attribute the features which in one model represent the negative, to any other model, to represent neither positive nor negative figures. Absence of figure, equivalent to absence of information, is expressed by absence of feature, as with the former criterion.

The third possibility is to use series of features such as 'short/middle-sized/long'. The absence of figure (no information) would correspond to a neutral figure ('middle-sized'). Doberti has studied the use of this type of series as signifiers in visual codes. They seem to be particularly appropriate if binary classification is to be substituted by a more sensitive quantification that will take into account a range of intermediate shades.

Articulation and Families of Concrete Designs

It should be noticed that each of the proposals suggested in chart no. 3 leads, not to a concrete design, but to a whole family of different, possible designs. Each concrete design will be distinguished by the particular features selected to represent the values, and also by the criterion followed when attributing features to negative figures. The number of articulatory levels and their particular organization, such as described in chart no. 3 reflect a certain deep structure of each system, which may be common to designs which are formally different.

Significant Richness

Chart no. 3 shows yet another thing. In almost every case, the identification of a form does not require the use of the three features introduced: by giving only two of them (the ones in the extreme right column) the piece is determined. (For this reduction to be possible, it is necessary for the negation of a value to correspond to an observable feature, not just to the absence of another feature.)

Thus a new variable of design is introduced which we shall call *significant richness*. The designer not only defines the articulatory system; he also chooses—within certain limits—the quantity of information that is to be incorporated in the forms. He can minimize information for economy's sake; in the case of the example he could use only features for the design of each man. Or he could maximise significant richness, at the cost of economy, by using not only the three features defined in each proposal but the set of six; the king would then be expressed by the combination (1 2 3 $\overline{4}$ 5 $\overline{6}$).

The values on which the articulating system is based have no reason to be limited to the rules of the game, as in the examples we have seen. Any value can serve as a basis for an articulating model. The only condition is that it must divide the class of models of the articulated system—in this case, the set of six figures—into two non-empty classes. One class is composed by the models for which the value is positive and the other by those for which it is negative. For example, the value 'being important' could serve as a basis for an articulating model, only if we were able to divide the set of chessmen into two classes, one of important and one of non-important men. If we did not know how to make this division, or if all or none of the pieces were important, we should refrain from using this value.

The amount of significant richness that can be included in the design of an articulated system is thus considerably increased. In a design exercise conducted with my students in Buenos Aires, we realized that the variety of values that can be associated with the pieces has no limit other than the designer's sensibility for perceiving differences. We worked with the pieces' supposed masculinity or femininity, their human, animal or inanimate character, and, in general, with any social, historical or military connotation that came to mind. But before commenting on the concrete results of this experiment, I would like to show some other simple examples and to develop yet another chapter of theoretical concepts.

An office chair that has been recently launched onto the market is based on a tractor seat. It shows that models coming from systems that are supposed to be different can nonetheless be combined. The limits of the system are thus broadened and its richness is increased.

There is a typist unit that includes a typewriter, a desk, a seat, a dictaphone and earphones. The case is similar to the former, but more complex.

A video-terminal produced by Olivetti illustrates a different possibility: a very complex instrument, whose functional components do not need to be invididualized by the user, assumes the deceitfully simple form of a screen and a console prepared on a table. The articulation in 'supporting console' and 'supporting table' bears no relation to the actual internal structure of the appliance, but it does make sense in relation to the users' preconceptions about furniture.

In the latter examples the articulating elements correspond to physical, spatial components of the articulated form. Articulation is in this case called spatial or *segmental*. There also exists *non-segmental* articulation, in which the articulating elements are not identified with many spatial components but with different attributes of the same spatial component; for example, chessmen's articulation in shape and colour. The applicability of articulation is thus considerably enhanced.

4 The Context

Lexical and Structural Approaches

In studies on the semantics of language it is usual to distinguish between lexical and structural approaches. The former are characterized by the assumption that the meaning of each term can be studied, in principle, independently from the meaning of all other terms, like in a dictionary. Structuralists, on the contrary, assume that the meaning of a term is influenced by the meaning of all the other terms which, with it, compose a certain system or structure; therefore, semantic analysis must not be done atomically, term by term; it requires instead the consideration of the whole system. In the case of chessmen, for example, white pieces are not *really* white, they are simply clearer than the other which are supposed to be 'black'.

Position and System

In Saussurean structural semantics, two aspects of structure are frequently distinguished: the syntagmatic or *positional*, and the paradigmatic or *systematic*. Position is concerned with the relationships that are established between the term and the other terms which accompany it in a given circumstance. System is connected with the relationships between the term under consideration and the other terms which could have taken its place, its position within the syntagm. Our recent example (white men which are actually only clearer than the black) illustrates the positional aspect of structure; we shall soon see the effect on the identity of chessmen of the systematic aspect.

Tripartite Significant Model

We had defined the significant form as the set of features of the physical form of an object, which refer to its meaning; and the meaning, as the set of values susceptible to modification by changes made in the form. The structural approach brings us now to the consideration of elements proper to the syntagm of the system, which exceed the physical form of the object, but which nevertheless are concerned with its meaning. This compels us to revise our initial ideas, replacing the bipartite notion of significant model (form/meaning) by a tripartite notice (form/context/meaning). The form is the set of features of the object, changes in which are capable of producing changes in meaning; the context is the set of factors independent of the physical form, changes which are also capable of producing changes in meaning; and the meaning is the set of values susceptible to modification by changes made in the form or in context. The elements of context are classified into positional and systematic.

Articulation in the Tripartite Model

Thus a broadening in the signifier's plane is produced, which can now be classified into three areas: form, positional context and systematic context. Each of these areas comprehends certain features, which can be properties or relationships between properties.

This classification on the plane of the signifier could be matched by a parallel classification in the signified's plane: it could happen that some values depended exclusively on the form, others on the positional context and yet others on the systematic context. This would be a special case of articulation. Then one could talk of a *lexical* component of the meaning which would accompany the form wherever it occurred; a *positional* component, proper to the circumstance in which the form is used and relatively independent of the form itself; and of a *systematic* component dependent on the system to which the form belongs and relatively independent both of the form itself and of the circumstance in which it appears. The signification of the *Arc de Triomphe* of the *Place de L'Étoile*, for example, includes certain (lexical) values which would accompany the same form in any other place in which it occurred; as well as other (positional) ones which depend on the peculiar situation of the monument, in that convergence of avenues. The positional values would also be present if instead of an Arc de Triomphe, we were to have an obelisk or a palace. Other values (the systematic ones) depend finally, on the fact that, though it would be possible to have an obelisk or a palace, the form chosen was that of an Arc de Triomphe.

There could also be articulation in a tripartite model without following the classification in these three areas. Lastly, the more general case of non-articulated tripartite models can be admitted.

The most interesting case for theoretical discussion — though not the most frequent — is that of perfect articulation in the three areas, to which we alluded before. It could happen that some value of the meaning occurred in more than one component (lexical, positional or systematic), thus producing redundancy; or that there was a contradiction between the meaning corresponding to two components, in which case it would be possible that the form were contradictory, or ambiguous, or that one of the components dominated the other. In the last case, it can be questioned whether there exists some component which by nature is stronger — or weaker — than the others. We shall call once more on the system of chessmen to illustrate these ideas.

Lexicalization of Contextual Meaning

We have already shown the existence of a positional component in chess when noting that white and black are only recognized as such in comparison with each other. Now it will be convenient to forget this observation, and admit that the yellowish tone that has been recognized, because of its context, as 'white', *is actually white*. The relation 'yellowish = white' becomes established for the interpreter and from then onwards he will recognize the feature as if its meaning were expressed lexically. When contextual signification has a certain stability, it tends to become lexicalized.

Position

Thus considering colour as a lexical feature, it is possible to show the existence of other positional components in the plane of the signifier of chessmen. Note that a chess set consists of thirty-two men, but only twelve different forms (six white and six black), many of which are repeated two or more times. Nevertheless pieces are not confused during the game: nobody moves by mistake, say, one white pawn instead of another. This shows that the men's identity is not limited to the lexical values expressed by the features of the form ('white pawn'), but it also includes positional values ('. . . of the king'). Articulation exists. (As the game advances, men's initial positions become irrelevant; but other positional features appear which go on identifying each piece: a certain pawn will be the one that attacks the opposite knight,

Chart 5. Chess. Lexical and Positional Meaning in Various Systems

	System of 12 forms (Staunton, Hartwig)			System of 32 forms (Charles the Great)			System of 6 forms (new possibilities)		
		meaning			meaning			meaning	
piece	form	lexical	positional	form	lexical	positional	form	lexical	positional
1 wK	1	wK	—	1	wK	—	1	K	w
2 wQ	2	wQ	—	2	wQ	—	2	Q	w
3 wKt(K)	3	wKt	(K)	3	wKt(K)	—	3	Kt	w(K)
4 wKt(Q)	3	wKt	(Q)	4	wKt(Q)	—	3	Kt	w(Q)
. . .	. . .	. . .	. . .	. . .	. . .	. . .	. . .	. . .	. . .
. . .	. . .	. . .	. . .	. . .	. . .	. . .	. . .	. . .	. . .
32 bP(QR)	12	bP	(QR)	32	bP(QR)	—	6	P	b(QR)

K = king; Q = queen; B = bishop; Kt = knight; R = rook; P = pawn; w = white; b = black; (x) = belonging to x.

another the one that defends it, and so on.)

In chart no. 5 we have listed, on the left, the thirty-two men; we registered their correspondences to the twelve forms and the distribution of meaning into the two components: each man's value and its colour are carried by the form, and the distinction between like men is based on their position on the board.

There are two observations for chess players, which could be omitted: first, the positional component registered in the chart refers to men's initial formation; as was already said, as the game goes on the content of this component would vary, but this does not affect the essence of the question. Second, in the initial moment of the game each man occupies a predetermined position on the board, and as a result there is redundancy between lexical and positional meaning; trained players actually do not need to read the form of each man in order to recognize the total configuration. As the game goes on redundancy decreases and it ends up by disappearing. We chose not to register it in the chart, for simplicity's sake.

This distribution of meaning in lexical and positional components occurs in the familiar, Howard Staunton design of chessmen, and in many other possible designs: such as that of Man Ray, the one Joseph Hartwig made in the Bauhaus, or the one recently launched by Cy Endfield in commemoration of the Spassky — Fischer match. Once again we found a deep structure of the system, that can remain invariable though the concrete forms are replaced by others. This structure is concerned with aspects totally different from those studied with regard to articulation.

It must be questioned now whether it is possible to find alternative structure, in other words other distributions of the meaning of chessmen in lexical and positional components. Very soon we shall discover that the answer is affirmative; most ancient sets—for example, the one known as Charles the Great's set—had thirty-two different forms: one for each man. Thus we may register a widening of lexical meaning, destined, nevertheless, to become redundant in the face of its inevitable superposition with positional meaning.

There are, lastly, other possibilities. By giving each piece some directional feature, its pertinence to one player or the other can be indicated by means of its position on the board—pointing in one direction or the other—and habitual differences in colour can be suppressed. Positional meaning takes the place of lexical one, and the system would only have six different physical forms. This type of design would oblige a more careful manipulation of the pieces while playing, but on the other hand it would have an interesting quality: at the end game with a few pieces, a mere glance at the board would enable us to notice which was each player's field, which does not happen with ordinary design.

Finally, there is nothing to prevent us from playing chess with dice that have the image of a figure on each of their six sides; there would only be two physical forms: a white die and a black die. The advantage of such a design—perhaps somewhat academic—would be that the pawn's coronation would loose its uniqueness: instead of involving the substitution of a piece, it would imply like the other moves, only a change in position.

Beyond its repercussions in the design of chessmen, the significance of this analysis lies in the notion that the distribution of meaning between form and positional context on one side, and the redundancy level existing between both on the other, are variables which are, within certain limits, under the designer's control. We shall return to this point later.

System

In addition to positional context, we must consider systematic context, which is constituted by all the forms that compose the system to which a given form belongs, whether positionally present or not.

This aspect is most frequently underestimated by those who approach semantic problems with lexical criteria. It is temptingly easy to maintain, for instance, that in the system of chessmen the form of the knight means *knight* because it iconically reflects some characteristics of his horse.

Figure 1
Various designs of chess sets from the Renaissance to the 19th Century (according to Hans and Siegfried Wichmann)

Analogously, it could be said that the form of the king, while not remitting to a flesh and blood king, alludes nevertheless to a certain conventionally established image, that of the *chess king*. (All lexical meanings of chart no. 5 could be understood in this way.) According to this point of view, any piece would be recognizable even outside the system to which it belongs. A brief examination of different chess sets designed in the last five centuries (cf. Figure 1) would confirm this hypothesis: many of the knights look like horses, rooks like castles; and the other figures oscillate with some variations around certain prototypical images which finally crystallized in Staunton's series. Most students arrive at similar results when asked, without further explanation, to design a chess set; they produce insipid stylizations of the culturally established models.

Creative design is impossible unless one frees oneself from the clichés proper to all lexical approaches. Understanding the realm of contextual meaning and learning its intelligent use are unavoidable steps in the designer's education.

The same collection of historical sets we have just mentioned allows the fragility of lexical meaning to be shown. The pawn of one of the systems can be converted into bishop or queen by merely placing it in Staunton's system in the place occupied by one of these pieces (Figure 2).

It is possible to go even further. The king of any design could be converted into a pawn of a new system, just by producing eight pieces identical to the king, which are smaller than any other figure of the new system. Likewise one could take the form of the pawn and convert it into a king, fitting the rest of the system conveniently to it. Lastly, even the

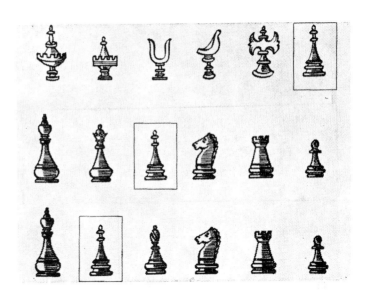

Figure 2
Permutations of elements derived from the systems of chess represented in Figure 1

form of the knight—apparently the most sharply defined figure in lexical terms because of its iconical reference to a horse—could play the part of a king or a pawn: there are sets that use only animal forms, and there is nothing to prevent one conceiving a system in which all pieces were equine, where Staunton's knight could take over the position of the king, the pawn or any other figure. The identification of a form does not depend so much on its intrinsic properties or in its similarity to certain lexical prototypes, as on its relationships with the other forms of the system. Where there is a contradiction between the indication proceeding from the form itself and the one resulting from the place which it occupies in the system, as in the examples we have just seen, the systematic component dominates the lexical one.

Most significant systems used in design have a certain redundancy level which allows any form to be replaced by another completely neutral one, without the system losing legibility. For example, when a chessman is lost we can substitute a coin for it. We can do this with one piece, but probably not with two and certainly not with all those which compose the system at the same time. Each form bears its own identity and contributes to the definition of the others; one piece's form is the other's context.

In the last instance, all attempts fail to separate lexical and contextual meaning in a clear-cut way. Meaning is the result of a complex interaction of indicators which arise from the form of each piece and from its context. The designer's task is to distribute these indicators conveniently between the various elements of the system, thus achieving the desired meaning with an adequate redundancy level.

An interesting example of an extreme situation is that of the doors of the Municipal Library at Stockholm, by

Asplund. The handles are in the form of nude human figures; it is only their position on the doors that gives them the character of handles. The doors, on their part, are huge sheets of glass surrounded by windows of the same size; it is only the presence of the handles that identifies them as doors. Neither doors nor handles are recognized lexically but by their positional context. Each of these forms is the context of the other. As a result they constitute a system where what matters are its relationships; they form an architectural correlation of what we have seen with regard to the king and pawn in chess.

5 Applications

Some of the notions I have presented were applied in an exercise of designing chessmen conducted with first-year students in the School of Architecture of Buenos Aires in 1969. We began by asking them to design a set, without entertaining any theoretical discussion. They produced designs which I do not need to show, based as was to be expected, on small variations of the forms we all know. They modified traits which in their opinion did not alter recognizability, such as proportion or finish. In our terms, we should say that they designed physical forms, adjusting to the known significant forms imposed by their cultural environment. They did not conceive that these could be challenged. Next they were told that significant forms and even meanings themselves were susceptible to redesign. By applying synectics, brain-storming and other techniques, they identified a surprising variety of values that could be taken into account for distinguishing the pieces from one another, chess sets from one another and chess sets from other games.

Finally we pointed out that they could exercise control not only over physical form, signifiers and signifieds but also over what we called the *significant structure* of the system. We defined this by means of three parameters: degree of articulation, quantity of significant richness and use of context. It was shown that each parameter was like a variable whose value could be fixed by the designer, within certain limits. By analysing the significant structure of known systems such as those of Staunton, Hartwig, Ray and others, they proved that all were surprisingly similar and that they only made use of a narrow range of the theoretically conceivable possibilities. Finally the students designed a system for the second time. (cf. Figures 3 — 6)

There is no room here for a detailed explanation of each of the designs, nor of the criteria taken into account for their realization. Let it be enough to say that some students chose

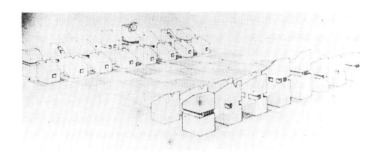

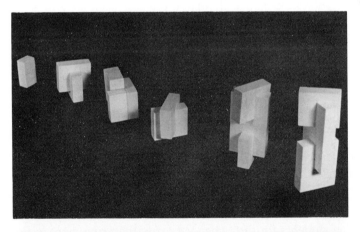

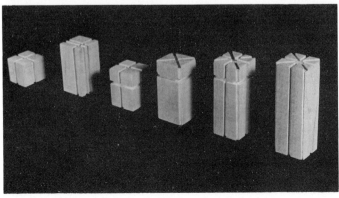

Figures 3–6
Designs of Chessmen produced by
students at the University of
Buenos Aires (Photographs provided by Juan Pablo Bonta)

to found their designs on rigorously defined significant structures, selected by themselves from the range of possibilities opened up by the theory. These projects were characterized by a tendency towards high levels of articulation and of significant richness, and by the limitation, in many of them, to the purely communicative area of meaning: they would require the learning of a conventional code in order to be interpreted. For example, in one of the sets a clear window, if situated on the front of the piece, indicates the possibility of this advancing one square, and if on the edge, a diagonal movement. A small window represents limited movement, a horizontal strip makes prolonged movement. A groove in the upper surface of the piece indicates that one can begin the game with it, and so on. Other systems included a more imaginative range of significant values, not so subject to the contents determined by the rules of the game.

Other students, naturally less inclined towards the type of intellectual gymnastics that the exercise supposed, nevertheless made use of the iconoclast fury generated, and swept away not only its conventional initial images but also the semiological system itself, which from a certain moment on they found too narrow. I would not like to compromise my opinion in favour of one or other attitude. I shall limit myself to pointing out that, though in the first instance almost all new designs seemed to be freer and far more imaginative than the first ones attempted, some of them in fact were the somewhat arid results of the mere application step by step of the design process devised by the professor. Systematic design methods — both those referring to problems of meaning and those orientated towards other areas — raise, in principle, the level of the results; but they also raise the level of expectations and they do not erase, in the last instance, the gap between talented designers and those less fortunate. Whether this is a piece of luck or a shame, I do not know.

The main criticism which, in my opinion, the proposed designs deserve is that they generally require the use of a conventional code in order to be understood. I do not blame the students for this; when we made the experiment, a few years ago, these studies had been begun shortly before and my ideas were not yet clear enough with regard to the communicative, expressive and indicative components of meaning. These notions were not explained to the students. I think a new exercise would today lead to better results.

The critical question with regard to the point we are concerned with is, whether articulation is privative to communicative meaning, that is, to signals. I have no doubts about the fact that indicators, too, can be articulated. For example, certain hoof prints in the mud indicate the recent passing of horses. The prints' silhouette (one of the articulating features) indicates that horses passed, not cows;

the peculiar conformation of their edges (the other feature) indicate that the passing was recent, not distant. The two articulating models (silhouette = horses, clearcut edges = recent passing) could also occur in other models of the articulated system, which would be the complete system of prints of different animals and recency.

If we were to make the exercise again, the point I would pay the most attention to would be the assigning of features to articulating models. A careful study of iconicity and isomorphism could be used in the search for forms which bare the meaning to the sphere of the expressive component, which does not require the intervention of explicit codes.

Almost all our examples referred to the game of chess. I would not like you to think that the validity of the ideas expressed is limited to this system, nor that its only practical application consists in the designing of new pieces. (This task's utility would be, by the way, doubtful: the ruling of the International Chess Federation gives every player the right to refuse to play with men whose design is out of the ordinary.)

The ideas presented could serve as a basis for a general theory of meaning in design; they are applicable, for instance, to the parts of a piece of furniture, the furniture of a living room, the rooms of a building, the buildings of a larger block, the parts of a city; to the units of a set of glasses, cutlery or crockery; to the system of coins or stamps of a country, to the network of road-signs or the controls of a machine-tool; to the identification of the shops of a commercial centre, to the buildings of a civic centre or the areas of a recreational centre; to the redesign of a vehicle, of an artifact for the home or of a container. To prolong this list indefinitely would be easier than to find a counter-example, a case of design in which the problems of meaning were not present.

Let us look briefly at just one of the systems mentioned. The forms and arrangement of the chairs, armchairs, dais-desks and other equipment of a tribunal of justice constitute, as Rapoport has already shown in another context, an implicit description of a country's system of administration of justice. The configuration of furniture in the room would constitute a correlation of the organization of chessmen on the board. The *meaning* of each seat, legible from the form and its context, would be the role or the hierarchy of the person occupying it: the president of the tribunal, the secretary, the members of the jury, the prosecutor, the solicitors, witnesses and scribes, the public and the guards would play the part of the king, the bishops and the pawns. The physical relationships between the seats of honour would express in a certain code the hierarchical and functional relations existing between those who occupy them.

(Other significant models could also be abstracted from

the same physical forms. From the point of view of the *style* of the equipment, for example, a set of 'modern' form would be expressive of a certain conception of the state or of public administration, which would also be reflected in the forms of a 'modern' school or health centre; 'classical' furniture, on the other hand, would be associated with other conceptions. We already said that the variety of significant models pertinent to a certain physical form has no limits other than the interpreter's changing needs or interests.

Correlating its features and values, one proves whether the model is articulated. The seat of honour of the tribunal's president would be articulated if it presented certain features which would distinguish it as presidential. For instance, certain forms or the size of the seat or—more likely—of the back, would be common to all judges' seats of honour, but not, say, to the scribes'. Other features would bear the *presidential* value: for example, the hammer on the desk in front, which not only serves for imposing silence but also for identifying the president who has the authority to use it. (The hammer also appears in front of the presidential seat of honour in the Parliamentary chambers.) Alternatively, the presidential value could be expressed by the national coat of arms on the back of the chair—that we also find on the official paper used by the magistrate and on his car's doors.

It could also happen that the presidential seat of honour were physically identical to the rest, and that its privileged nature would only arise from its position in the context: that it were in the symmetrical axis of the room, possibly on a higher dais. As in chess, the identity of each unit does not depend only on its own lexical characteristics, but also on the relations established with the other forms.

There will be seats of honour that cannot be used except by a single functionary: such is the case of the presidential seat of honour, where, say, the accused cannot sit. Other seats will serve for members of the public, for witnesses, or for orderlies, as suits each circumstance. The greater the flexibility of use, the smaller the significant weight, and vice versa: the more defined the occupant's identity, the greater the form's significant richness. The same is valid for the whole room: the richer its expression as tribunal seat, the less adaptable it would be for other uses; the more flexible, the more limited its specific meaning. There are limits both to the flexibility and to the significant richness possible.

In this example it is not difficult to distinguish between the various components of meaning. There are communicative components, whose comprehension requires the intervention of conventional explicit codes and which appear to the interpreter as contents of other people's consciousness; such is the case, for instance, of the meaning of the national flag or coat of arms, of the signs which possibly appear on some doors, of the red dot on the mouthpiece of the fire hose. There are also indicative components that tend to impose themselves as matters of fact—as when a certain session is seen to be important from the untiring work of photographers, from the presence of a crowd of journalists or from the expectant attitude of the public. Further, there are expressive components that also impose themselves as matters of fact, even if they are the result of a provident design work: such is the case of the preponderance of the tribunal members, situated on a dais, with regard to the relative subordination of the accused, the witnesses, the scribes. As we have already said, intentional indicators tend to be converted into signals—such would be the case of the dais, if it were used exclusively and systematically for contrasting the judge's seat of honour. Signals tend to be converted into indicators—as when the flag or the coat of arms operate independently of their conventional meaning—and then again into intentional indicators—if they are deliberately used to take advantage of this circumstantial semanticization.

The degree of articulation, the significant richness, the use of context and the relative importance of indicative, expressive and communicative components of meaning allow the significant structure of the whole system to be described in a general way; they constitute a *deep structure* by means of which it is possible to establish analogies between superficially different systems. This reminds us of Chomsky's deep structures to which various colleagues have referred in the last few days, but whilst the latter are syntactic, the structures we refer to here are semantic.

The greater or less articulation, significant richness or use of context and the tendency to emphasize one component of meaning or another are not in themselves good or bad in terms of design. It is not a question of ascribing *a priori* in favour of one type of structure or another, but of taking into account during the design process a wide range of possibilities, in order to be able to choose the most appropriate one. The selection must be done according to evaluation criteria which semiology itself does not provide. The discussion of evaluation standards goes beyond the limits of our theme today. Finally I would like to point out that the theory of meaning, of which we are sketching the outlines, must be useful not only for criticism and actual design, but also for the history of architecture. Every time new methods are proposed for architectural analysis, it becomes possible and necessary to explore also its application to the study of past works. The progress made in the analysis of resistent structures during the 19th century, or the development of, say, the visibilist or sociological theories of art produced in the 20th century, to quote only a few examples, allowed aspects of medieval architecture to be put into perspective, which had not been noticed before.

There is no doubt that systems of meaning—like those of resistent structures, or economic or social ones—change in time. (In this respect, the Chess Federation's good sense is noticeable: instead of trying to establish once and for all a certain design of chessmen, for example that of Staunton, it recognises the inevitable dynamics of forms, and limits itself to convalidating the system which the community in each circumstance perceives as normal.) But it is not only a question of the fact that significant systems are subject to dynamic processes, whose origin could be somewhere else, perhaps in social or economic phenomena: there are reasons for supposing that significant facts often constitute the very driving force of change. This is the case in the processes of semantic wearing or 'consumption' of the forms, and in the contrary processes of re-semanticization of those with new meaning arising from new contexts. So we not only have an instrument for casting light on an aspect of architecture which until now was approached with vague generalizations, but the aspect in question is concerned with the very core of stylistic transformation.

Though we can already count on important works based on the application of semiological viewpoints to the study of past architectural works—I am thinking specially of the work conducted in Naples by De Fusco and Scalvini—the general history of the systems of meaning in architecture has still to be written. It is possible that the analysis of significant structures will confirm the validity of traditional historical units, adding a new dimension to its knowledge; renaissance could be characterized by a tendency towards articulation, mannerism by the primacy of communicative meaning, baroque by a rich use of positional context. It is also possible that in some cases semiological analysis could lead to historical material being classified into units different from the traditional ones: for instance, English baroque could be assimilated to mannerism from the significant point of view.

I cannot hide a certain dismay on thinking that I am leaving more questions formulated than those I have been able to answer. But I am comforted by the knowledge that we are not alone in the face of these problems; in the whole world there is a growing interest in these affairs allowing us to hope that, perhaps in a very short time, a radical rearrangement of ideas will take place with regard to architecture and history. No doubt, semiology will play an important role in it.

2.5 Building Design as an Iconic Sign System

Geoffrey Broadbent

This paper was presented at the First Congress of the International Association for Semiotic Studies, Milan (1974) and represents the author's views as developed at that time.
A shortened version of this paper has been published in the proceedings of the Congress (The Hague, Mouton, 1979).

In the book *Design in Architecture* (1973) I argued that, faced with the problem of generating three-dimensional form, the architect resorts to a number of mechanisms or processes which I called 'Types of Design'. These were: Pragmatic, Iconic, Analogic and Canonic; and their characteristics, briefly, were as follows:

Pragmatic Design—originating in pre-history, in which the available materials: earth, stones, tree-trunks, branches, leaves, reeds, bamboos, animal skins, tendons or even snow were put together initially by trial and error until a building form was achieved which actually 'worked'. Pragmatic design is still used in design with new materials—plastic skin inflatables, suspension structures, and so on.

Iconic Design—in which the designer starts with some fixed 'mental image' of a familiar building form as the best possible solution to his problem of using the materials which happen to be available at a particular place, with a particular climate, to house an established life-style—the mechanism of 'primitive' and 'vernacular' architecture but still used by lesser architects in following the designs of the great 'form-givers'. For reasons which will emerge in this paper, I now prefer to call such designing Typologic.

Analogic Design—in which visual analogies are drawn with existing buildings, with forms from nature (Le Corbusier's 'crab-shell' roof at Ronchamp), from painting (de Stijl) and so on; structural analogies with the feeling of tension and compression in the designer's own body; philosophical analogies with principles from physics (indeterminacy), biology (general systems theory) and so on, linked, historically, with the first use of drawings, models,

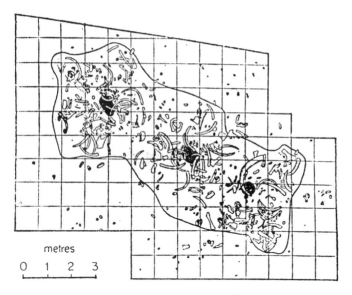

metres

0 1 2 3

Figure 1
Pragmatic Design—an example
from pre-history in which
Mammoth Hunters on the steppes
of Southern Russia (Pushkari, near
Kiev, c. 40,000 B.C.) built
themselves shelters using the
available materials by trial and
error

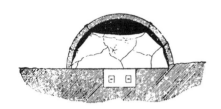

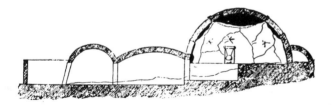

Figure 2
Typologic Design—the Eskimo
would have frozen to death if he
had had to think out each time
how to build a house in snow. He
simply repeated the known
type—the snow house or igloo

Figure 3
Analogic Design—consists of drawing visual or other analogies with existing forms. Le Corbusier says that the crab shell which was lying on his drawing board 'became' the roof of his church at Ronchamp

etc., as *analogues* for the building whilst it was being designed.

Canonic (Geometric) Design—in which the form is generated by some two or three dimensional geometric system. Originated by the Egyptians, given extensive philosophical stiffening by the Greeks (Plato, Aristotle), and utilized in the design of the Gothic cathedrals, Renaissance

Figure 4
Canonic (Geometric)
Design—Throughout recorded
history a great deal of architectural
form has been generated by
geometric systems. The Egyptians
used certain canons of proportion
so did the Gothic cathedral
builders, the Renaissance palace
designers, not to mention many
architects at the present time.
Recent manifestations include Le
Corbusier's Modulor, dimensional
coordination and prefabricated
building systems, not to mention
the work of the New York Five

Figure 5
The Parque Los Caobos in Caracas
by Miguel Galia is a recent example of Canonic Design in which the
same geometric system is used
both for the planning of the park,
including the paths, avenues, pav-
ing and tree planting and for the
elevational systems of the building,
including the board marks on the
concrete and the openings for ventilation

palaces and so on. Current manifestations include Le Corbusier's Modulor, dimensional co-ordination and
prefabricated building systems.

I argued in the book that these are used, singly, or in combination, in the generaton of *any* three-dimensional built
form, and after an extended analysis of how architecture has
been designed in history (now being prepared for publication) I have yet to find any example which could not be explained in these terms.

Now obviously this scheme overlaps but does not match
Peirce's three-part categorization of the *sign* into icon, index
and symbol (Peirce 1897-1903) of which his basic definitions
were as follows:

> 'An *icon* is a sign which refers to the Object that it
> denotes by virtue of certain characters of its own and
> which it possesses just the same, whether any such ob-
> ject actually exists or not.'

Figure 6
March and Steadman's analysis of
three Frank Lloyd Wright houses
shows that even though they were
designed for different clients on
different sites and built from different materials, they are 'like'
each other in terms of the *underlying* relationships between the
various systems. Each is an 'icon'
for the others and also for March
and Steadman's graph

B bedroom
B' sundt bedroom
C car port
E entrance
F family room
J bathroom

K kitchen
L living room
O office
P pool
T terrace
Y yard

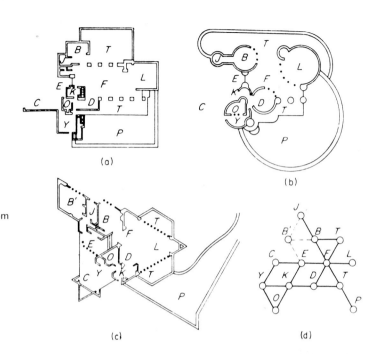

A *symbol* is 'a sign which refers to the object that it
denotes by virtue of a law, usually any association of
general ideas, which operates to cause that symbol to
be interpreted as referring to that object' and

An *index* is a sign, or representation 'which refers to its
object not so much because of any similarity of, or
analogy with it, nor because it is associated with
general characters which that object happens to
possess, and because it is in dynamical (including
spatial) connection, both with the individual object on
the one hand and with the senses or memory of the person for whom it acts as a sign.'

Confusion obviously arises between these two schemes, and
in particular, between Peirce's concept of icon and mine. I
could explain this away initially by suggesting that my
scheme refers to activities which the architect performs or
the tools he uses in the process of designing, whereas
Peirce's categories might apply more appropriately to the
building itself as an actual sign-system. But that would be an
over-simplification. Whilst the part played by the materials
in my pragmatic design, or by geometric systems in my
canonic type may not be detectable in the finished
building—although even that is unlikely—any use of type or
analogy, in my original senses—almost certainly *will* show in

the final design. The building will act as a sign—iconic or analogic—for the object(s) which 'inspired' the designer.

Peirce goes on to say that:

> All words, sentences, books, and other conventional signs are Symbols. We speak of writing or pronouncing the word 'man'; but it is only a *replica*, or embodiment of the word, that is pronounced or written. The word itself has no existence, although it has a real being, *consisting* in the fact that existents *will* confirm to it.

As usual, Peirce is concerned with linguistic examples; all verbs for him are symbols because they incorporate the mental concept of something being done. Clearly the relationship between word and object has to be *learned* and this brings us up against the fundamental problem of representation—how one object comes to 'stand for' another.

In an early paper (1957) Charles Osgood offers a simple, S − R (stimulus/response) model of representation; he suggests that certain stimulus events will have 'wired in' associations with certain response events. Once the hungry infant has experienced the taste and feel of warm milk in its mouth, certain activities such as salivating, swallowing and digesting follow automatically, by reflex. When the baby first perceives, say, a feeding bottle this does not automatically produce such behaviour, but he soon learns to think of the bottle not only as a source of food, but as a *sign* that milk will become available. The milk bottle becomes a sign by straightforward processes of perceptual decoding. Of course there are other sorts of signs: Osgood is interested particularly in the relationship between perceptual and linguistic signs. The child learns to recognise a certain object by its perceivable characteristics: resilience (soft), shape (spherical), weight (light) and so on. It is his ball, and when this object is brought into his presence certain patterns of behaviour will follow: rotary eye-movements, grasping, bouncing, squeezing, and even the pleasurable automatic reactions associated with play-behaviour. So, as Osgood puts it:

> Long before the child begins to use language, most of the sensory signals from its familiar environment have been lifted from their original Jamesian chaos, have become perceptual signs of objects by virtue of association with representational portions of the same behaviour the objects themselves produce.

But when the object is presented to him 'Johnny is likely to hear the noise "ball", a linguistic sign . . . in frequent and close continuity with the visual sign of this object'. And eventually, he will realise that if he stimulates those around him by making that noise, there is a high probability that they will present him with his ball. 'Thus a socially arbitrary noise becomes associated with a representational process and acquires meaning, e.g. *a unit in linguistic decoding.*' The relationship between word and object therefore is a learned one; Osgood has simply described the processes by which the *signifier* and *signified* of Saussure's sign—which is equivalent to Peirce's symbol, come to be associated 'in the mind'.

So we ought to look again at my original design-types in the light of Peirce's categorization, to see what modifications, if any, will be necessary to my scheme if it is to be accommodated within the main stream of semiotic studies. So let us look at Peirce's definitions in rather more detail to see what light they throw on my original design-types.

As a first step we shall plot a 'spectrum' or continuum of possible relationships between signs and their object in Peirce's sense. Peirce's icon is a physical thing, possessing certain 'characters' which it shares with its object. There are 'likenesses' between them and it is these likenesses which enable the one to act as a sign for the other. His symbol on the other hand relates to its object only by an association of ideas, a social contract or 'law' which causes 'that symbol to be interpreted as referring to that object' by the members of a particular society. It is a *de jure* relationship of the kind which Saussure required between the signifier and signified of his two-part sign. There is no identifiable 'likeness' between Peirce's symbol and its object, nor need there be one in the case of his index. His indexal relationship is one of physical, perhaps spatial connection, given the many continua therefore among which it is possible to plot Peirce's signs, we shall choose one which reads as follows:

Likeness . . . . Association

	Physical	Arbitrary
ICON	INDEX	SYMBOL

We shall elaborate this later in our attempt to clarify the relationship between Peirce's categorization and mine (see Figure 12).

Having tentatively explored the relationships between Peirce's signs and their objects, we shall need to look also at the *effects* which these signs might have on their *interpreters*—to use Morris' terminology (1946). In order to do this, we shall have to look at Peirce's definitions in even greater detail, starting with his symbol. A symbol, for Peirce is:

A sign which refers to the Object that it denotes by virtue of a law, usually an association of general ideas, which operates to cause the symbol to be interpreted as referring to that Object.

But symbolization is much more complex than that. Piaget (1969) suggests that initially, a child is unable to distinguish between himself (subject) and the environment around him, including the objects it contains. There is 'no fixed boundary between data given internally and those given externally'. Yet to survive at all in the environment, he has to learn that his body is simply one object among many, a realization which grows as he manipulates the objects around him by simple physical action: grasping, sucking, and so on. Initially, he is unaware even that he initiates these actions. He cannot co-ordinate them and 'each constitutes a small isolable whole which directly relates the body itself to the object, as for each example, in sucking, looking . . . etc.'

But eventually—and Piaget puts the age at eighteen to twenty-four months—the child begins to realise that he himself is the source of these actions. He learns that certain actions will have certain results; he discovers that one of his toys, if shaken, will produce a sound of some kind. It becomes simultaneously something to be looked at and something to be listened to. Having discovered these properties in one of his toys, he will shake all the others to see if they also are 'listen-to' objects in addition to being 'look-at' ones. In this process of dissociating his own body from other objects, the child learns two basic kinds of thinking. On the one hand he learns that his distinguishable, personal actions may be subsumed, interrelated, ordered in a particular sequence of time; in other words, he learns 'those general co-ordinations underlying . . . logico-mathematical structures'. Thus the basis emerges for abstract, structural thinking. At the same time, however, the child learns that the objects themselves also may be subsumed, interrelated, ordered in space and time sequences in ways which are analogous to the structuring of his personal actions upon them. He thus learns that *he* can cause things to happen to the various objects, and on this basis he begins to understand the nature of physical existence and of causality itself. But—and this is his most important insight—Piaget believes that *basic semiotic functions, and representational intelligence, emerge from this interrelating of causal physical action with logico-mathematical structuring.* As we shall see, certain problems arise when one tries to separate them out.

If we take Piaget's child in his original state, however, his first responses to his own body, and to objects in the environment around him are at a direct, physiological level. Other physiologists might call these 'unconditioned reflexes'. He then starts to learn the relationships which exist between himself and those objects in terms of physical/causal actions and logico-mathematical structures. Later still, he learns the (arbitrary) relationships between the objects around him and the 'socially arbitrary noises' used by the particular culture in which he finds himself to signify them. One could plot another continuum relating these events:

De facto. . . . . de jure

Direct physiological response (unconditioned reflex)	Physical causal actions	Logico-mathematical structures	Culturally sanctioned response (learned)

We shall use this continuum also in relating Peirce's system of signs to my types of design (Figure 12).

But *symbolization is even more complex even than that.* Bruner, Goodnow and Austin (1962) point out that if each individual stimulus to the senses had to be considered in isolation, then we could not possibly survive. In order to cope with our complex environment, we have to group things together:

> To categorise is to render discriminably different things equivalent, to group the objects and events and people around us into classes, and to respond to them in terms of their class membership rather than their uniqueness.

Figure 7
Bruner, Goodnow and Austin show how a range of cards can be classified in various ways according to the kinds of symbols: squares, circles or crosses; their number: 1, 2, or 3; their content: solid black, shaded or white; the number of borders and so on

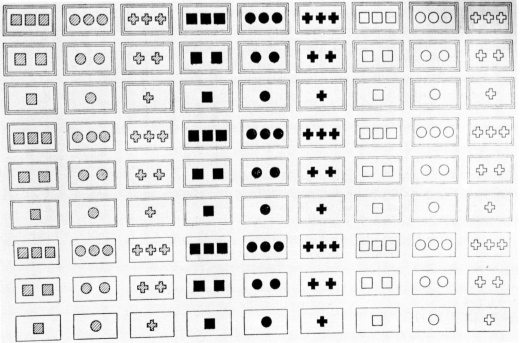

Given it is possible to identify some seven million different colours, we have to categorize them crudely to cope with them at all. We 'get along' with a dozen or so basic names; so that in referring to a particular book on my desk, I can point to the one with the 'blue' cover. But it also has other characteristics—Bruner and his colleagues call them attributes—such as size, shape, texture and so on. I shall name any object which displays those same attributes, a 'book', even though the actual colour, size, shape, texture, and so on will vary from one book to another. The process of categorization therefore consists in recognising that certain objects possess certain similarities—they share the same attributes. One identifies the attributes which *must* be present if an object is to be described as 'book' even though a particular book may possess further attributes which are by no means present in the generality of books. The formation of concepts such as book-table, chair, house, church, in such terms has many advantages, as Bruner and his colleagues point out. In the first place, it reduces the apparent complexity of our environment so that we can cope with it more easily; secondly, it enables us to identify objects and to place them into context; thirdly, it reduces the need for constant learning; fourthly, it provides us with a basis for action by giving direction to our instrumental activities; fifthly, it enables us to order and relate various classes of events.

Bruner and his colleagues distinguish between two kinds of attribute: defining attributes—that is defined by law, by scientific convention and so on, and criterial attributes, which one has learned to identify from one's own observations. Inevitably, these match the two extremes of the continuum against which we plotted possible responses to signs: *de jure* and *de facto*. From our point of view, their most useful distinctions are those between conjunctive, disjunctive and relational categories:

A conjunctive category is determined by the joint presence of certain attributes, each present at an appropriate value. All men have a head, a body, two arms, two legs and so on; an individual can be recognised within the general category of men by his particular height, girth, skin colour, hair colour and so on, but each of these must fall within an acceptable range. We should be most surprised to find even one individual whose skin colour was bright green.

In a disjunctive category the range of attributes may be broader and each member needs to possess only some of them. All mammals have four limbs and a certain amount of fur, but only some of them—including man—walk upright and a few of them—again including man—could hardly be described as 'furry'.

The members of a relational category may have even fewer attributes in common, but they are always in the same rela-

Figure 8
Pugin described in *The True Principles of Pointed or Christian Architecture*, the attributes he thought a building must possess to symbolise the true Christian Church, including a tower, with buttresses, spire and pinnacles, a porch, a nave and aisles, an altar, an east window and so on. If we see the building with *all* the attributes Pugin describes then we certainly identify it as a church. Even a modern church such as Ronchamp (Figure 3) has a porch, a nave, an altar and so on in 'correct' spatial relationship with each other

tionship. A thalidomide child, for instance, lacks certain of the attributes which one would think essential for a human being, or possess them in barely recognisable form. But certain criterial attributes, such as the head and trunk, are still there and in 'correct' relationships.

Between them, Osgood, Piaget and Bruner provide us with a basis for identifying just what it is possible for Peirce's symbol to be. Obviously, to be effective, a symbol must belong to some conjunctive category of signs which we have learned to associate with certain objects, or concepts, in the ways which Osgood thought we should. To take an architectural example, the 19th century Anglo/French architect Auguste Welby Pugin (1841) defined the attributes which any building must possess to symbolise — in his terms — the true Christian Church.

> An old English parish church, as originally used for the ancient worship, was one of the most beautiful and appropriate buildings that the mind of man could conceive; every portion of it answered both a useful and mystical purpose. There stood the tower, not formed of detached and misapplied portions of architectural detail stuck over one another to make up a height, but solid buttresses and walls rising from a massive base, and gradually diminishing and enriching as they rise, till they were terminated in a heaven-pointing spire surrounded by clusters of pinnacles, and forming a beautiful and instructive emblem of a Christian's brightest hopes. These towers served a double purpose,

for in them hung the solemn sounding bells to summon the people to the offices of the church, and by their lofty elevation they served as beacons to direct their footsteps to the sacred spot. Then the southern porch, destined for the performance of many rites, — the spacious nave and aisles for the faithful, — the oaken canopy carved with images of the heavenly host, and painted with quaint and appropriate devices, — the impressive doom or judgement pictured over the great chancel arch, — the fretted screen and roof loft, — the mystical separation between the sacrifice and the people, with the emblem of redemption carried on high and surrounded with glory, — the great altar, rich in hangings, placed far from irreverent gaze, and with the brilliant eastern window terminating this long perspective; while the chantry and guild chapels, pious foundations of families and confraternities, contributed greatly to increase edifices which have been abandoned for pewed and galleried assembly rooms, decorated only with gas fittings and stoves, and without as much as one holy or soul-stirring emblem about them.

Obviously he saw that as a conjunctive category and certainly even now anyone brought up in Northern Europe and faced with a building which possessed all or most of those attributes, would immediately recognise the symbol 'church'.

I could certainly symbolise the concept 'church' by designing a building which incorporated all, or most of Pugin's attributes. If I copied *exactly* the 14th century, Early English Parish Church-type which he illustrates, then the symbolism would be clear, complete and unequivocal. Even a modern church, such as Ronchamp, possesses certain of these attributes — a porch, a nave, an altar — and in the 'correct' spatial relationship with each other. It therefore belongs to a *relational* category of church.

Unfortunately, Peirce also (1897 — 1903) left his *icon* in a thoroughly confused state and it has become something of a major industry since to try to clarify what he actually meant by iconic sign (see, for instance, Eco, 1968, 1972, Volli 1972, and so on). We have looked at Peirce's original definition already: he goes on to say:

It is true that unless there really is such an object, the Icon does not act as a sign, but that has nothing to do with its character as a sign.

Anything, however, be it quality, existent individual or law, is an Icon of anything, *insofar as it is like* that thing and used as a sign of it.

Unfortunately he does not say what he means by 'like' and that is where the problem lies. It is certainly not helped by his next attempts at definition: 'An Icon is a Representation whose representative quality is a Firstness of it as a First. That is, a quality that it has qua thing renders it fit to be a representamen. Thus, anything is fit to be a substitute for anything that it is like.'

But his next paragraph is slightly more helpful: '. . . a sign may be iconic, that is, may represent its object mainly by its similarity, no matter what its mode of being.'

Actually, in presenting examples of iconicity, Peirce takes only one three-dimensional object—a donkey—as an iconic sign for another one—a zebra. He says: 'I surmise that zebras are likely to be obstinate, or otherwise disagreeable animals, because they seem to have a general resemblance to donkeys and donkeys are self-willed . . . Here the donkey serves precisely as a probable likeness of the zebra.' In my terms, he is using his donkey as an *analogy* for his zebra. But most of his examples of iconicity prove to be *man-made* representations of one sort or another: 'Every picture (however conventional its method) is essentially a representation . . . so is every diagram, even although there be no sensuous [perhaps he means sensory] resemblance between it and its object, but only an analogy between the relations of the parts of each.'

Eco (1968/72) and Volli (1972) regard this question of relations between parts as fundamental to the nature of iconicity. They prefer to think of it, not so much as a matter of analogy but as a matter of digital relationships, pointing out that relationships between the parts of *anything*—and particularly between the parts of a drawing or diagram—can be expressed digitally, that is by some system of numerical coordinates. They want to go further, in fact, and to suggest that any form of drawing, diagram and so on can be represented by an on/off binary system of digits. That is true of the black and white dots which form the picture in a screened newspaper photograph, the on/off points of light in a television picture or a computer display, but this leads them to generalise that *all* iconic signs must be digital in structure, rather than analogical. In doing so, of course, they tend to stress one aspect of Piaget's epistemology—that concerned with logico-mathematical structuring—at the expense of the other—that concerned with physical causality. The trouble is that it leads to a confusion between the sign itself and the structure of the sign-vehicle. One can perhaps illustrate this with reference to the crabshell which Le Corbusier used as a *visual* analogy for the roof-form of his Chapel at Ronchamp. The photograph of this crabshell in Le Corbusier's book on the Chapel (1959) is so crudely screened

that one can see the pattern of individual dots as they lie on the page; the sign-vehicle undoubtedly is digital. But that in no way diminishes the analogical properties of the crabshell itself; it merely serves to show that the analogical properties of the sign-vehicle can co-exist with the digital. They are complementary to each other rather than mutually exclusive.

Eco and Volli therefore seem to have fallen into the trap—so common in semiotic studies—of stressing logico-mathematical structures at the expense of causal-physical ones. True iconicity obviously involves both and Peirce certainly seems to support my view that the analogic properties of iconic signs are of fundamental importance:

> . . . a great distinguishing property of the idea is that by direct observation of it other truths concerning its object can be discovered *than those which suffice to determine its construction* as a particular sign (my italics).

So I shall continue to call 'analogic' those aspects of iconicity which depend on 'likenesses' between objects, whilst agreeing with Eco and Volli that those aspects of iconicity which can be expressed digitally, are also of importance. The general term for underlying structures in language is *syntax* and I like to think of such underlying structural relationships as *syntactic*. The architectural equivalent, I believe, lies in

Figure 9
A photograph of Le Corbusier's Crab Shell as printed in his book on the Chapel at Ronchamp demonstrates that an Icon can be *both* a visual analogy for the thing which it is like and a 'binary system of digits' of the kind which Eco and Volli describe. The enlargement of the photograph shows that it is formed from a system of on/off black and white dots

those underlying geometric systems I had in mind when I wrote of canonic design.

In stressing the digital aspects of iconicity, Eco and Volli are particularly concerned with the underlying *structures* of objects — the relationships between their parts which are not necessarily apparent from their surface observation. All mammals, for instance, have a skeleton, not to mention equivalent muscular, digestive and nervous systems. But different kind of mammals may *look* quite different. Each, in Peirce's terms, is an icon for the others, because of the underlying structure which they share. The three Frank Lloyd Wright plans shown in Figure 6 also share an underlying structure of room relationships as indicated by March and Steadman's graph. Each of these therefore is an icon for the others, and also for March and Steadman's graph.

Peirce himself describes the place of iconic signs in the process of design:

> Another example of the use of likeness is in the design an artist draws of a statue, pictorial composition, architectural elevation or piece of decoration, by the contemplation of which he can ascertain whether what he proposes will be beautiful and satisfactory.

But whilst he refers specifically to 'design', I have no doubt that Peirce would recognise the iconic nature of *any* representation — drawings, three-dimensional models, analogues and so on — which the designer uses for this purpose. I suggested in *Design in Architecture* that the 'raw materials' for such representations could be words, numbers, spatial representations or mechanical devices, and that they could exist in 1, 2, 3 or more dimensions. Thus a written description is a one-dimensional, verbal model, a sketch is a two-dimensional, spatial representation, a typical architect's model is a three-dimensional spatial representation, and so on. In my terms, these all are — or could be — design analogues, and the possibilities extend also to computer representations in analogue or digital form (Figure 10).

Peirce suggests further possibilities:

> Particularly deserving of notice are icons in which the likeness is aided by conventional rules. Thus, an algebraic formula is an icon, rendered such by the rules of commutation, association and distribution of the symbols.

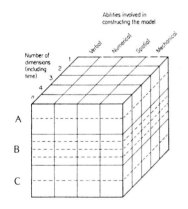

A = descriptive
B = concept structuring
C = exploratory

Figure 10
A classification of models (G. Broadbent, *Design in Architecture,* 1973)

Formulae of course are mathematical models by which *relationships* between various objects are indicated so that the mathematician can manipulate them in certain ways. He suggests that the reasoning of mathematicians is found chiefly on the use of formula as 'likenesses' for things in the real world. He goes on to say: 'this use of likeness to mathematicians consists in their suggesting in a very precise way, new aspects of supposed states of things.' The closest equivalent to this in my design types, of course, is canonic design, in which a two or three dimensional geometric system is used to generate the form. The drawings, models, etc., which are used to develop this are undoubtedly iconic in Peirce's sense and also within the more restricted range of relationships expressed digitally within which Eco and Volli want to constrain iconicity. It seems therefore that my analogic and canonic design types represent different aspects of iconicity whilst my iconic design has little or nothing to do with Peirce's original concept. That is why I now call it Typologic, thus bringing it into that long tradition of design by typology which dates at least, from Laugier (1753), especially as interpreted by Quatremère de Quincy (1825).

As for Peirce's index, that is a sign, or representamen

> which refers to its object not so much because of any similarity of, or analogy with it, nor because it is associated with general characters which that object happens to possess, as because it is in dynamical (including spatial) connection, both with the individual object, on the one hand, and with the senses or memory of the person for whom it serves as a sign . . .

He gives some examples

> . . . A rap on the door is an index. Anything which focuses the attention is an index. Anything which startles us is an index . . . A weathercock is an index of the direction of the wind; because in the first place it really takes the self-same direction as the wind, so in the second place we are to constitute that when we see a weathercock pointing in a certain direction to draw our attention to that direction, and when we see the weathercock veering with the wind, we are forced by the law of mind to think that direction is connected with the wind.

Indices seem to operate entirely at the level of Piaget's causal relationships between objects, their ordering in time and space, and so on. Possibly, from that point of view, they are the most primitive of signs.

Obviously my pragmatic design involves causal relationships between objects, their ordering in time and space: there are 'dynamical' connections between the functions to

Figure 11
This hand indicates the word 'index' by drawing attention to it physically

be served and the materials available for serving them.

But I do not propose to substitute Peirce's term for my own; the meaning of 'pragmatic' in this context is self-evident, whilst the meaning of 'indexal' most certainly is not.

Let us now attempt to summarise. I have suggested already in developing an understanding of signification, one moves along a continuum from direct, physiological response (*de facto*—unconditioned reflex) to the learning of relationships between signifier and signified as agreed by social contract (*de jure*). I have suggested also that the relationship between signifier and signified, between content and expression, exists at a certain position along another continuum, between direct physical likeness and arbitrary association. Let us, following a suggestion of T. Llorens, use these two continua as coordinates of a semantic space, into which Peirce's icon, index and symbol can be plotted, and my pragmatic, typologic, analogic and canonic types of design (Figure 12).

Clearly my scheme can be subsumed into Peirce's without any difficulty. The diagram also suggests why, in spite of Eco and Volli, it is useful to retain the two major aspects of iconicity—the analogic: concerned with physical or other likenesses, and the syntactic: concerned with abstract (possibly digital) structures.

It raises many other implications of which the most interesting perhaps, is the re-ordering into a different sequence of my four design-types. Originally, I plotted them chronologically from pragmatic—first used deep in prehistory via iconic (typologic) and analogic to canonic (geometric), first used by the Egyptian geometers. But the 'observer's response' continuum requires them to the located in quite a different order—from pragmatic—based

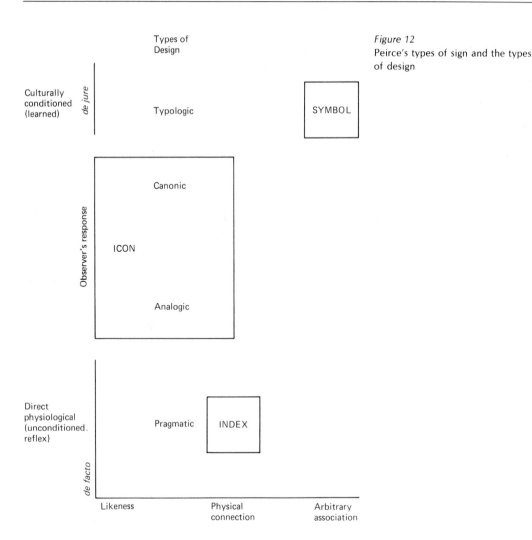

Figure 12
Peirce's types of sign and the types of design

Relationship between content and expression

on the direct physical manipulation of materials—via analogic and syntactic to typologic based on the application of rules or social conventions. On this continuum, obviously, pragmatic design offers the greatest possible opportunity for creative accident, whilst typologic design—by definition—constrains creativity against convention.

These types of design, therefore:

Pragmatic

Analogic

Typologic

Canonic

Figure 13
This Poultry Stand on Long Island which was photographed by Peter Blake—and used to make various points by the Venturis—looks 'like' the ducks which are sold inside it. The building therefore is a visual analogy, an Icon for ducks and vice versa

will be even more useful in describing the *processes* which an architect employs in the act of designing; but the question still arises as to the concepts we ought to use in describing the building itself, once it has been completed. For this purpose it seems to me Peirce's icon, index and symbol offer some interesting possibilities.

There is no doubt in my mind that a building *can* be an icon.

One thinks of the poultry stand on Long Island, which excited Venturi so much (1972), shaped 'like' a duck. It certainly

> refers to the object that it denotes . . . by virtue of certain characteristics of its own, and which it possesses, just the same, whether any such object actually exists or not.

Well, no, that is not quite true. The poultry stand would *not* have existed in its present form if the designer in the first place had been ignorant of ducks. My term —analogy—seems more appropriate here. Nor could one say, conversely, that a real, live duck was an iconic sign of Venturi's poultry stand. Given the entire population of those who have seen ducks, it would only be 'like' a poultry stand for those who have seen that particular esoteric example on

Long Island, or Venturi's pictures of it. At this level therefore, I believe that my original term — simple visual analogy — was probably more useful.

There is not the slightest doubt, though, that the drawing of a building, and particularly a design drawing, *is* an iconic sign: Peirce says it is.

There is no doubt either that certain buildings are indices. That is true obviously, of any building which, by its actual form 'expresses' certain functions in ways which can be read by anyone, irrespective of culture, which do not require a learned response. A primitive shelter probably is an index in this sense, so, for that matter, is any sophisticated building which *indicates* by its planning, the route which one must take through its sequence of spaces.

One thinks, in this connection, of certain exhibition pavilions, such as the British one at Expo '58 in Brussels or — at an even more sophisticated level of the Maison la Roche of Le Corbusier which also was planned around a set route. This particular example, however, is a rather complex one in that the route itself has certain *symbolic* connotations (see Broadbent, 1969).

As for the building as symbol, one has no problem in defining that. Given that the essence of a symbol is the *learned* relationship between a signifier and a signified. Pugin's church obviously is a symbol in this sense, any building which displays the attributes he describes almost certainly *is* a church.

Peirce's terms, therefore, help us make distinctions between different buildings — or between different aspects of the same building — which are worth making. Discussions on them are certainly worth developing, but they will have to be the subject of a further paper.

I am indebted to Tomas Llorens for his detailed constructive comments on earlier drafts of this paper, and also for clarifying the issues I raised by means of a diagram which, greatly over-simplified, became my Figure 14.

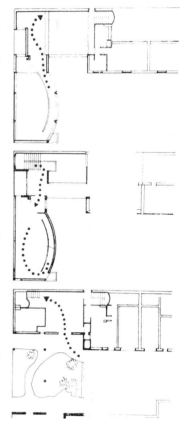

Figure 14
Le Corbusier's Maison la Roche is planned about a set route so that to proceed from the entrance to the Library we must move through a sequence of spaces as *indicated* by the plan. The building itself is an index of how we should move about it

References

Broadbent, G. (1969) *Meaning into Architecture* (ed. Jencks, C. and Baird, G.), London; Barrie & Rockliff, New York, Braziller.

Broadbent, G. (1973) *Design in Architecture*, Chichester, Wiley.

Bruner, J. S., Goodnow, J. J. and Austin, G. A. (1962) *A Study of Thinking*, New York, Wiley.

Eco, U. (1968) *La struttura assente. Introduzione all ricerca semiologica*, Milano, Bompiani.

Eco, U. (1972) Introduction to a Semiotics of Iconic Signs, in *Versus* 2/1.

Le Corbusier (1959) *The Chapel at Ronchamp*, London, Architctural Press.

Morris, C. (1946) *Signs, Language and Behaviour*, 1955 edition consulted, New York, Braziller.

Osgood, C. E. (1957) A Behaviouristic Analysis of Perception and Language as Cognitive Phenomena, in Contemporary Approaches to Cognitive Psychology. A symposium held at the University of Colorado, Cambridge, Mass., Harvard UP.

Peirce, C. S. (1897-1903) *Logic as Semiotic: The Theory of Signs*, in *The Philosophy of Peirce*, ed. Buckler, J Assembled from: Ms CP 2.227-9, c.1897; CP 2.231-2, c.1910; CP 2.274.302, c.1902, c.1895, c.1893; CP 2.243.52, c.1903, 245-65. Also from Baldwin: *Dictionary of Philosophy and Psychology*, 1902.

Peirce, C. S. (1940) *The Philosophy of Peirce*, ed. Buckler, J. (1956 edition consulted), London, Routledge.

Piaget, J. (1972) *Psychology and Epistemology*, Harmondsworth, Penguin.

Pugin, A. W. (1841) *The True Principles of Pointed or Christian Architecture*, London, Hughes.

Quatremere de Quincy, A. (1825) *Encyclopédie Méthodique d'Architecture* (Vol 3), Paris.

Venturi, R., Scott Brown. D. and Izenour, S. (1972) *Learning from Las Vegas*, Boston, MIT Press.

Volli, U. (1972) Some Possible Developments of the Concept of Iconism, in *Versus* 3/2, pp.14-30.

2.6 A Framework of Meaning in Architecture

Judith Blau

An earlier version of this paper was read at the American Sociological Association meetings, New York City, August 1976. Financial support for this study was provided by the Research Foundation of the City University of New York.

Analyses of architecture are generally based on the study of the aesthetic, or formal, properties of buildings. Yet the complex character of architecture, which includes technology, use, client characteristics, and environment, suggests that formal analyses should be supplemented to include these other facets as well. The concern here is with the 'structure of meaning' in architecture, that is, the multi-dimensional framework by which architects are related to their products in the fullest sense—as practice, as built structure, and as style.

Quite simply, we are asking what is the structure of shared meanings in architecture and what are the dimensions in terms of which that structure can best be described. The aim is to uncover a relatively simple paradigm by which we can account for a variety of particular patterns.* Attention will also be directed to the social processes by which some meanings become aggregated and others disassembled; some highly charged and others neutralized. And, since meanings have social consequences, we will try to grapple with the problem as to how meanings (particularly those that are aggregated and charged) make a difference in the architectural community.

The study is empirical in nature, on the assumption that meanings are so ingrained in architects' varied experiences, perceptions, and judgments that the opinions of many architects must be examined to determine the full range, inten-

*The term 'paradigm' is used here in the way that is defined by George Lichtenberg (Mauthner and Hatfield, 1969) and differs from Thomas Kuhn's more current conceptualization of it.

sity, and variability in these meanings. Questions were asked of every architect who works in a sample of 152 New York City offices rather than just the most illustrious (or 'promising', or 'articulate') among them. Thus, the views of both 'elite' and rank-and-file architects are reflected in the results.

Meaning in a specialized professional community is similar to other forms of meaning — common sense, religious, scientific — in that it is only comprehensible in terms of both cognitive and subjective elements.* The dialectical relation between cognitive and subjective — knowing and liking — demands analysis, but once they are distinguished from one another (empirically or theoretically) it must be recognized that as social properties they become inert. Thus, dissecting meaning into its two components must be followed by ultimately effecting a synthesis of the two, and it is this consideration that has guided the present analysis.

The distinctions between meaning and other theoretical concepts should be made explicit in order to clarify how the concept 'meaning' makes a unique contribution, especially insofar as it takes into account the linkages between individuals and work (or social praxis in general). Many investigations in the sociology of the professions have been concerned with the 'values' of professionals (see Hall, 1969 pp 81 — 91; Gauldner, 1957 pp 281 — 306; Parsons, 1939 pp 457 — 467). This term, however, typically centres attention on nonrational (expressive or cathetic) elements and minimizes the role of knowledge and ideas. Meaning (which encompasses individual elements — meaning codes — and the relationships among these elements — frameworks) is the appropriate term, as this concept places a dual stress on the importance of ideas as well as their subjective underpinnings. It is precisely because whatever develops out of and affects objective conditions of work must have both cognitive and subjective contents, that the prime interest here is specific meanings, not the broad and diffuse value orientations that many members of a particular category (for example, all professionals, or all architects) share. Values are briefly analyzed here, however, first to draw attention to the distinction between values and meanings, and second, to show, at least for the former — it is assumed to be true for meanings as well — how they are homologous with firm structure.

What are the similarities and differences between 'meaning', in the sense that it is used here, and the semiotic concept, 'signified'? In linguistics signified is the social significance, or idea, that accompanies sound (the 'signifier').

---

*My usage of the term meaning is consistent with the way in which it has been defined by American symbolic interactionists, most notably George Herbert Mead and Peter Berger. For an important contribution to this tradition, see Becker (1962).

In *Meaning in Architecture*, Charles Jencks (Jencks, 1969) and Geoffrey Broadbent (Broadbent, 1969), among others, discuss how these terms apply in architecture. Signified becomes the content (Jencks), or the abstract concept or meaning of architecture (Broadbent), and the signifier is the form (Jencks) or, more simply, the building (Broadbent), What is problematic in semiotics, the relationship between signifier and signified, is not of particular interest here, for I am more concerned with the complex patterns by which signifieds are structured and with the way in which they create and are created by social context. Coming to semiotics through the back door, so to speak, I hope to show that a behaviourist perspective sheds some light on the social origin and consequences of content and form in architecture, however content and form are themselves found to be related.

Since the concerns here are similar in some respects to the Lévi-Strauss version of structuralism, certain points should be briefly clarified. The structuralists would never assume, as is the case here, that the community of architects can be described in terms of its own generic framework of meaning, for while they are greatly interested in structures of meaning their search is for fundamental ones that are widely, if not universally, shared (Lévi-Strauss, 1969, pp. 220, 440, 464). However, certain aspects of Lévi-Strauss's work are fully a part of the study reported here: an emphasis on structure; relatively great attention to the cognitive component of meaning; an interest in identifying homologies that exist between the structures of social institutions on the one hand, and those of meanings and values on the other; and finally, the assumption that structured meanings are embedded in social action and give sense to it without individuals being fully conscious of these meanings nor of the logic that underlies that structure.

Value Orientations

This analysis of the framework of meaning in architecture is part of a larger study of 152 architecture firms and the architects who work in them. The firms were selected randomly from the listing of architects in the Manhattan telephone directory.* In the case of firms with at least four professional employees, a principal (or, in a few instances, an associate) was interviewed to obtain information about the firm and its characteristics; in the case of smaller firms, the principal was sent a questionnaire that included most of the same items.

*Of the principals who were contacted, 88 per cent agreed to provide information about their firms.

Table 1
Principals' criteria for a 'successful project'

Category	% mentioned	% emphasized
1. Financially successful; project on schedule; within budget; efficient	68.8	18.7
2. Client satisfaction	64.9	25.3
3. Aesthetically satisfying; architecturally exciting	49.4	16.0
4. Design adheres to objective (aesthetic criterion underlies answer)	36.8	10.7
5. Personally satisfied	31.6	6.7
6. Logical and functional (technical criterion underlies answer)	28.6	2.7
7. Serves people's needs	25.0	8.0
8. Have good relations with client; no major problem with owner or contractors	21.1	1.3
9. Contributes to architectural thinking; brings professional recognition	13.0	0.0
10. Project improves with use	6.6	1.3
11. Project continues to give pleasure	5.3	0.0
12. No compromises from architect's point of view	4.0	0.0
13. Project demonstrates how architecture can improve user's life; project educates client or user	3.9	0.0

Number of respondents = 77.

One of the questions that was asked in the interview (but not in the questionnaire sent to principals in small firms) was: 'How do you define a successful project?' (To clarify the question, if need be, they were asked, 'What do you aim for in your work?') Answers were coded in terms of the categories reported in Table 1, with the percentage of individuals whose answer or partial answer fell in each category reported in column 1, and the percentage of times that answer was emphasized, or mentioned alone, in column 2.

It is clear that economic criteria (item 1) and public relations (item 2) dominate these principals' concerns. This may be because the word 'success' appeared in the question and it triggered associations dealing with profit. However, this cannot explain that even though substantial numbers *mentioned* aesthetic criteria and users' needs (column 1, especially items 3, 4, 7, 10, 11) very few *emphasized* them, as shown in column 2.

There may be two reasons why financial matters and public relations are so important. First, as noted above, only in the largest firms was this question asked. Heads of very large offices seldom devote much time to design activities, and in their administrative roles they probably become preoccupied with the viability and financial health of their firms. Second, solvency—to say nothing of profits—is currently a problem for many architectural offices. These questions were asked in 1974, a year marked by severe recession in the building industry, especially in New York City.

It is useful here to draw attention again to the distinction between values, which are broad orientations, and meanings, which are highly specific codes that are inseparable from the content of knowledge of the specialized community. Due to the vagueness of the question, heads of firms responded in terms of their values and not in terms of specific codes of meaning. Nevertheless, we find that value orientations are realized in the structures and the activities of firms. It is beyond the scope of this paper to elaborate this point fully, but a few examples involving the three dominant value orientations—financial, client satisfaction, and aesthetic—can illustrate it.

Those firms in which principals stress *financial criteria*, whether they are large or small, are more productive than other firms; that is, they complete a relatively large number of projects each year.* This is clearly compatible with a dominant interest in pecuniary gain. Further, in these firms, staff architects tend to score very high on an alienation measure,§ which suggests that the bold pursuit of profits by top management undermines the morale and self image of professionals.

Firms whose principals consider *client satisfaction* very important tend to have more separate departments than other

*The partial correlation coefficient between the criterion of financial success and the number of projects completed per year, controlling for firm size, is 0.19 (significant at the 0.05 level).

§The partial correlation coefficient between the criterion of financial success and the alienation measure, controlling for firm size, is 0.40 (significant at the 0.01 level). (This measure is made up of four items including, for example, 'I find it pretty difficult to work with other architects'. Individual scores within each firm were averaged to obtain a value on this measure for every firm in the sample).

firms.*f* An interest in maintaining good relations with clients is consistent with a differentiated structure for it gives notice of the office's ability to offer a wide range of services and of the large number of top-ranking staff with whom the client can consult. These firms tend to deal almost exclusively, regardless of their size, with private individual clients.* While this is a logical choice for principals who are oriented to the personal needs and the satisfaction of clients, working with individual rather than with other types of clients pro- bably even further promotes such an orientation.

It appears somewhat paradoxical that special atten- tiveness to *aesthetic* criteria increases the number of hierar- chical levels,§ and thus, apparently, the degree to which responsibilities and decisions are delegated to staff below the senior and associate levels. However, the vast majority of responsibilities and decisions pertain to administrative and technical matters, and, as Brewer argues, in what are often called 'design oriented' (in contrast to 'production oriented') firms, these matters are relegated to low ranking professionals, whereas the relatively fewer, but more impor- tant, design responsibilities and decisions are centralized at the top (Brewer, 1972).

These results help to confirm, at least with respect to value orientations, an assumption made about values and codes of meaning, namely, that they establish, and in turn are maintained by, compatible social structures. Answers to two other questions tap facets of meaning codes and help to develop a paradigm or framework for understanding them. These data are superior in that information is available for a representative sample of all New York architects, not merely the heads of large offices.

Architectural Heroes

The two questions that deal with meaning codes appear to be somewhat oblique. It did not appear wise, however, to ask architects directly about the work they were doing and how it tied in with the work of others, for architects are notorious- ly unwilling to talk about their design strategies (Salaman,

---

*f*The partial correlation coefficient between the criterion of client satisfac- tion and number of divisions, controlling for firm size, is 0.21 (significant at the 0.05 level).

*The partial correlation coefficient between the criterion of client satisfac- tion and percentage of individual clients, controlling for firm size, is 0.25 (significant at the 0.01 level).

§The partial correlation coefficient between the criterion of aesthetics and the number of hierarchical levels, controlling for firm size, is 0.17 (significant at the 0.05 level).

1974, p. 98). For this reason, they were asked about their architectural heroes and how much they agreed or disagreed with statements that are fairly well known among architects. The question that deals with heroes is:

> Below is a list of individuals and groups who through their work or writings have been influential in contemporary architecture. For those that you know, indicate whether you generally tend to like or dislike their contributions. There will probably be some on the list that you do not know. Please indicate this by a check.

On the questionnaire the 50 names appeared in alphabetical order; in Table 2 they are ordered by the percentage of architects who liked their work. (The aim is not to report the results of a popularity contest — though the data are also interesting in this regard. For example, much of the criticism of Frank Lloyd Wright by architects during his lifetime appears to have become great posthumous popularity.)

The ratio is reported in column 3 of the number of times each architect was mentioned favorably by the respondents (column 1) to the number of times he or she was reported 'known' (column 2). From a comparison of columns 2 and 3 we can isolate a number of architects who are not generally known but who are well liked by a few followers (the value in column 2 is relatively low and that in column 3, high). This group includes Greene (no. 35), van Eyck (no. 39), Nowicki (no. 40), Esherick (no. 44), and, especially, Stirling (no. 30). Stirling is a young English architect who is probably best known for his History Faculty at Cambridge University, but who has also done various low-cost housing projects and worked with settlers in Latin American *barriadas* to help plan their communities. The high evaluation of his work by those who do know it may indicate the beginning of a growing school. On the other hand, for the older ones — Esherick, for example, is 62 — the pattern probably indicates the persistence of a dedicated small following.

Another group are architects neither widely known nor greatly appreciated by those who do know them (the values in columns 2 and 3 are relatively low). Speer (no. 50), the prominent Nazi architect, belongs not unexpectedly to this group, as do, though obviously for different reasons, two contemporary *avant-garde* movements — Archigram (no. 41) and Superstudio (no. 49). Other controversial architects who have relatively low visibility include Ehrenkrantz (no. 42), Kiesler (no. 43), and Wachsmann (no. 47). In different ways these architects are challenging assumptions that underlie prevailing design practices, arousing opposition in the process of gaining a few adherents.

Finally, an interesting group are those architects who are well known and controversial (the values in columns 2 and 3

Name	% 'Like' (1)	% 'Know' (2)	Ratio of 'Like' to 'Know' (3)
1. Le Corbusier	95	100	0.95
2. L. Kahn	95	99	0.95
3. F. L. Wright	93	99	0.94
4. E. Saarinen	92	99	0.93
5. A. Aalto	91	93	0.97
6. P. Nervi	91	97	0.93
7. Mies van der Rohe	83	96	0.87
8. W. Gropius	82	97	0.84
9. I. M. Pei	82	99	0.83
10. M. Breuer	78	98	0.79
11. R. Neutra	78	94	0.83
12. The Architects' Collaborative	78	90	0.86
13. K. Tange	78	86	0.91
14. C. & R. Eames	76	83	0.91
15. B. Fuller	72	92	0.79
16. P. Rudolph	72	99	9.73
17. J. Sert	67	82	0.81
18. O. Niemeyer	67	95	0.70
19. M. Safdie	66	87	0.76
20. The Cambridge 7	65	74	0.87
21. E. L. Barnes	65	86	0.76
22. P. Johnson	62	96	0.65
23. R. Guirgola	61	73	0.83
24. J. Johansen	60	83	0.73
25. R. Meier	60	80	0.75
26. C. Moore	56	72	0.78
27. Skidmore, Owings, & Merrill	55	96	0.57
28. H. Stubbins	51	76	0.67
29. P. Soleri	50	86	0.58
30. J. Stirling	49	54	0.92
31. J. Jacobs	46	68	0.68
32. V. Lundy	44	72	0.62
33. M. Yamasaki	44	98	0.45
34. R. Venturi	42	86	0.49
35. H. Greene	39	49	0.78
36. B. Goff	38	66	0.57
37. P. & P. Goodman	36	61	0.59
38. G. Kallman	33	43	0.75
39. A. van Eyck	32	36	0.88
40. M. Nowicki	28	36	0.78
41. Archigram	27	44	0.61
42. E. Ehrenkrantz	26	37	0.70
43. F. Kiesler	25	40	0.63
44. J. Esherick	23	29	0.77
45. W. Harrison	20	87	0.23
46. E. D. Stone	19	98	0.20
47. E. Wachsmann	18	27	0.66
48. M. Lapidus	17	88	0.20
49. Superstudio	7	15	0.49
50. A. Speer	4	47	0.09

Table 2
Attitudes about Architects
and their contributions

Number of respondents = 420.

are, respectively, high and low): Skidmore, Owings & Merrill (no. 27), Soleri (no. 29), Yamasaki (no. 33), Venturi (no. 34), Harrison (no. 45), and Stone (no. 46). The independence of Venturi (the champion of Las Vegas and popular taste), Soleri (whose houses appear as 'moonscapes' (Jencks, 1973 p. 195),) and Lapidus (whose hotels never feign seriousness) is well established. But it is indeed surprising that SOM, Yamasaki, Harrison, and Stone, major representatives of the International Style, which is still the major influence in contemporary building practice, are also very controversial. These results draw attention to an ironic situation. The aesthetic canons that have come to dominate American—and particularly Manhattan—architecture have scarcely any validity among architects themselves. That the International Style is still the dominant practice, yet is no longer accepted by most New York architects, is an important instance of what many view as the muddle in which architecture currently finds itself (Muschamp, 1974; Huxtable, 1975; Norberg-Schultz, 1968).

A statistical procedure, factor analysis, is used to identify dimensions that explain the meanings that underlie these patterns of knowledge and subjective evaluations (see Cattell, 1952; Harman, 1968; Rummel, 1970). Factor analysis isolates structures that correspond to the amount of ordered or patterned variation in the data. It is more than a procedure, according to Boudon, for a factor structure that is derived from empirical observations reveals the theoretical structure implicit in the empirical data (Boudon, 1971, pp. 52—89; 133).

Since factor analysis discloses the underlying dimensions in masses of complex data it is well suited for discovering meanings. The interpretation of each factor (and the label it is given) is determined by the factor loadings. They measure which variables are involved to what degree with a given factor (and can be thought of as the correlations between factors and variables). Whereas a factor loading indicates the relative importance of a given variable, that of a given factor is indicated by the amount of the total variance in all of the answers for which it can account. The loadings are reported in the tables, and the relative amounts of the variance for which factors can account are given in the text. The dimensions that result from a factor analysis are, if the data are sufficiently diverse, relatively stable. In other words, had other questions been asked of the same architects or had the same questions been asked of different architects, it is probable that similar or identical dimensions would have emerged.

Although 14 factors were generated,* four describe most

*A matrix of Kendall *tau* coefficients was the input for the factor analysis. A principal component, varimax rotation procedure was used.

Table 3
Loadings of 0.40 or higher of Architects on Four Factors

I.	*Subjectivism versus Bureaucratic*	
	Stirling	0.58
	Aalto	0.46
	Yamasaki	0.66
	Stone	0.66
	Harrison	0.63
	Speer	0.44
	Lapidus	0.44
II.	*Purist*	
	Neutra	0.56
	Niemeyer	0.55
	Nervi	0.42
III.	*Meta-art*	
	Wachsmann	0.49
	Archigram	0.45
	Superstudio	0.43
IV.	*Camp*	
	Meier	0.55
	Rudolph	0.44

of the variation in these data and, thus, explain by and large the underlying structure. The four factors are given in Table 3 in terms of the names of architects and groups that have a factor loading of 0.40 or higher. Before examining them in detail, it should be noted that the most popular architects (see Table 2; for example, Le Corbusier, Kahn, Wright, and Saarinen) do not appear in the first four factors, nor do they have high loadings on any of the 14 factors that make up the complete solution. The reason is that they do not have a distinctive group of followers; because they are so generally popular, opinions about them tend not to vary greatly and so do not explain the differences in opinions about other architects and their styles. In general, the higher the factor loading, the more distinctive the group of admirers.

It is antithetical meanings that are revealed by the first factor, the opposition of what I interpret as *subjectivism versus bureaucratic*. Because this factor accounts for more variance than any other (about three times as much), it can be inferred that it reveals most about the currents of thought in contemporary architecture. Furthermore, significance can be attached to its bipolarity, for it suggests underlying disagreement as to the assumptions that architects bring to their understanding of the field and to their own work. Specifically, from the results it is inferred that architects who

Figure 1
Alvar Aalto: Vioksenniska Church

like the subjective qualities in architecture evident in the work of Aalto and Stirling, tend to dislike bureaucratic tendencies revealed in the work of Stone, Yamasaki, Harrison, Lapidus, and Speer, and vice versa. Although the reverse pattern is rarer—the second set of architects are less popular than the first—the opposite evaluations highlight the bipolarity of this dimension.

What do members of the two sets have in common? Jencks's classification scheme, the 'evolutionary tree' (Jencks, 1973, pp. 28–94; 1971) and Joedicke's historical comparisons (Joedicke pp. 33–48) are helpful here, particularly for members of the set with the positive factor loadings—Stirling and Aalto. Jencks is nothing less than enthusiastic about the 'powerful rhetoric' of James Stirling (Jencks, 1973, p. 261):

> For the first time since the Palm House at Kew or the Crystal Palace, Britain had a designer who could handle glass with virility; for the first time since MacKintosh, an architect who could combine glass with a moulded masonry and send them rebounding around the facade; and for the first time since Hawksmoor an architect who could pile masonry on top of itself, one masterful conceit following another into the clouds.

Jencks describes Stirling as part of the 'metaphysical idealist' tradition because of his 'expressive functionalism' and 'alternatives to the existing social system' (Jencks, 1973, pp. 28, 31, 44–5). For him, the contrast between Stirling's and Aalto's work is formal, and not necessarily semantic for they share the belief that architecture must help realize a set of social ideals that are defined, however vaguely, in terms of liberalism and equality. However, unlike Stirling's complexity, Aalto's style is more organic; Jencks describes his interiors as 'undulating surfaces' and 'interrelated shapes' and, taken as a whole, his buildings as 'relaxed', 'solid', often looking like 'crouching animals'. In the classification scheme, Jencks places Aalto close to Stirling, in the 'heroic idealist' tradition, because of his 'plastic use of form and materials' and 'naturally expressive form' (Jencks, 1973, pp. 28, 167–184).

Joedicke, however, places them at different points in the same continuous tradition; Aalto is the forerunner and Stirling a highpoint of what he terms 'international brutalism' (Joedicke pp. 108–137, esp. p. 115). It is characterized by the breakdown of functional units, complexity, and individuality and, in more generic terms, by its subjectivity. And the links between Aalto and Stirling, as well as the label I have given them, become even more evident when Aalto and Stirling are compared with members of the second set.

With little sympathy, Jencks discusses Stone, Yamasaki, and Harrison as direct descendents of Speer—their work is 'self-conscious' and 'bureaucratic' (Jencks, 1973, pp. 28, 185, 200). Lapidus is not mentioned by Jencks but the fact that he is grouped by the factor analysis with Stone, Yamasaki, and Harrison indicates that the respondents perceive underlying similarities despite apparent differences in style. Although the objectives are different—garish chicness in hotel design and imposing monumentality for corporate offices—the ends they serve are similar for both express the corrupt values of a bureaucratic, consumer society.* Only in the social implications of their work is Joedicke more charitable than Jencks. He would describe the work of Stone, Yamasaki, Harrison, Speer, and, possibly, Lapidus, as formalistic, that is, stressing form over content, being monumental and artificial (Joedicke).

Thus, Factor I in Table 3 contrasts the subjective and expressive with the formal and contrived. There is little (built) evidence that American architecture is on the threshold of a humanistic transformation, but these results indicate that any future change will probably be consistent with the more humanistic tradition—at least by current standards—of Aalto and Stirling rather than with the monumental and impersonal tradition represented by the other group of architects.

---

*Aalto, himself, has contrasted two prevailing extremes with his own aims. Of one extreme, Aalto writes, 'parallelepipeds of glass square and synthetic metals—and the inhuman dandy-purism of the cities', and of the other, 'grown up children play with curves and tensions which they do not control. It smells of Hollywood' (*Zodiac*, 3, p. 78). Jencks labels these two extremes, 'sterile rationalism' and 'bombastic expressionism', and contrasts them both with the 'understated humanism' of Aalto (*Modern Movements in Architecture*, p. 179).

Figure 2
R. Meier: Smith House

Factor II, which is called the *purist* dimension, includes Neutra, best known for his West Coast houses made of steel and glass, and Niemeyer, one of the major figures of the Brasilia scheme. Both are placed by Jencks in the 'idealist international style' tradition (Jencks, 1973, p. 28). Nervi is also included in this factor. He is the most popular of the three (liked by 91 per cent of the respondents), and the relatively low factor loading of 0.42 indicates that he has a less distinctive following than either Neutra or Niemeyer. Nervi, an engineer, creates with concrete extraordinarily expressive structures, and is labeled by Jencks as an example of 'logical functionalism' (Jencks, 1973, p. 28), which is quite distinct from the 'ideal international style' attributed to the work of Neutra and Niemeyer.

But if style is not what Neutra and Niemeyer have in common with Nervi, why are they implicitly associated by the architects in the sample? While Aalto and Stirling's buildings have been praised for their intimate spaces and congeniality, Neutra, Niemeyer, and Nervi have exhibited a marked disregard, often contempt, for inhabitants and their needs. Niemeyer's Brasilia is practically uninhabitable by poor and rich alike. Neutra's work 'has always had an unreal, absolute look to it, as if it had just been extruded from some Platonic kitchen where dirt and age had been eternally expunged' (Jencks, 1973, p. 215). And Nervi's engineering masterpieces are beautiful sculptures—forbidding and uninhabitable. These are the qualities Nervi's buildings share with the architecture of Neutra and Niemeyer despite obvious differences in style.

Wachsmann, Archigram, and Superstudio are grouped

Figure 3
O. Niemeyer: Alvorado Palace, Brasilia

together in Factor III, which indicates that despite their obvious differences they are associated with one another in the minds of their colleagues. Political, technological, and societal objectives all figure in the explicit intentions of Wachsmann, Archigram, and Superstudio, albeit in different mixtures and with different emphases. A unitary theme they share, however, is that architecture must be redefined in non-artistic terms, that is, as an activity that transcends art.

This *meta-art* notion is evident in Wachsmann's writings and projects (for example, in his space frames and modular systems). Art, he argues, is the product of scientific and technical performance (Wachsmann, 1967, p. 31). Founded in 1961, as much a part of the pop art movement as an architecture style, Archigram declared itself to be 'beyond architecture'.* In one manifesto they express their idea for a technological environment that is totally responsive to the individual: 'What we want, clearly, is a miniaturized, mobile, cooking, refrigerating, sewage-disposing, VHF and three-channel-televiewing, trunk-dialing, dry-cleaning and martini-dispensing services robot with fitted ash-trays and book rest, that will follow us around the house riding on a cushion of air like an interplanetary hoover. (*The Architects' Journal*)

Members of Superstudio describe themselves as revolutionaries. Their most famous scheme is 'The Continuous Monument,' a single piece of architecture that extends around the world in which everyone has an identical room. That their critics ask whether it is fascism or democracy (Jencks, 1973, p. 56) is exactly the point—the relevant evaluative criteria for the projects of Superstudio (as well as for those of Wachsmann and Archigram) reside outside aesthetic realms.

The last factor includes two fairly well-known New York

*Title of the seventh issue (1966) of *Archigram*.

Figure 4
M. Webb: Cushicle

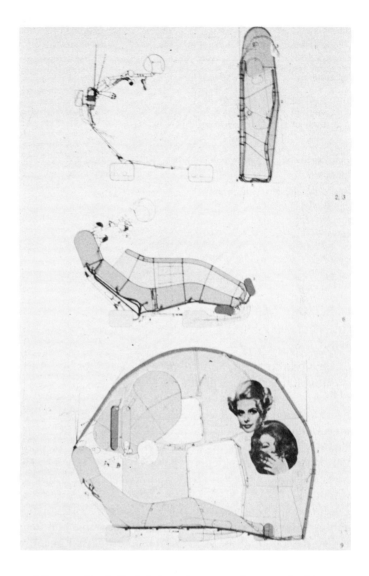

architects: Paul Rudolph, whose exuberant Architecture Building at Yale created so much controversy, and Richard Meier, a younger man who specializes in domestic architecture. The underlying theme here is an emphasis on texture, surface, and style. And this, Sontag writes, is one of the defining characteristics of *camp*, or what she calls 'the sensibility of failed seriousness' (Sontag, 1967, pp. 287 – 8):

> Camp refuses both the harmonies of traditional sensuousness, and the risks of fully identifying with extreme states of feeling. . . . It incarnates a victory of 'style' over 'content,' 'aesthetics' over 'morality,' of irony over tragedy. . . . The whole point of Camp is to dethrone the serious. Camp is playful, anti-serious. More precisely, Camp involves a new, more complex

Table 4
Classification of architects according to Sir Henry Wotton's dictum

Commoditie	*Firmness*	*Delight*
Wachsmann	Yamasaki	Lapidus
Archigram	Stone	
Superstudio	Harrison	
	Speer	
Commoditie and Firmness	*Commoditie and Delight*	*Firmness and Delight*
Meier	Rudolph	Neutra
		Niemeyer
		Nervi
	Commoditie, Firmness and Delight	
	Stirling	
	Aalto	

relation to 'the serious.' One can be serious about the frivolous, frivolous about the serious.

The four dimensions of this analysis—*subjectivism versus bureaucratic, purist, meta-art,* and *camp*—are briefly reconsidered in Table 4 in terms of Wotton's (1624) dictum, 'commoditie, firmness and delight' (Wotton, 1624, p1). An emphasis on 'firmness', or in contemporary terms, structure, is evident in the work of four architects described as bureaucratic—Yamasaki, Stone, Harrison, and Speer. Lapidus belongs with this group only because his buildings refer to the identical set of societal values and not because of communalities in design style. For as Wotton would say, Lapidus's hotels give 'delight'; they are just for fun (that is, for those who can afford it!). While the *purists*—Neutra, Niemeyer, and Nervi—have shown a high regard for structure ('firmness') and form ('delight'), they have consistently ignored the criterion of liveability, or 'commoditie'.

We can contrast the view that architecture should only be what people want, or at least ought to want—for their own good or for the good of society—which is expressed by Archigram, Superstudio, and Wachsmann, with the counterview, represented by Rudolph, that architecture must above all provide visual along with sensual pleasure, in other words, must satisfy the dictates of art as well as those of good living. But Rudolph's engineers have provided him with bad advice, or else he has not heeded their good advice; his buildings have suffered from mechanical and structural difficulties; those of 'firmness', Sir Henry Wotton would say.

While Meier's homes are not such hyperbolic performances, they are deemed liveable and structurally sound.

But all these traditions in architecture that only partially fulfil Wotton's criteria can be opposed with the synthesis of the three criteria that distinguishes the architecture of Aalto and Stirling. Apt, here also, is Jencks's concept of 'multivalence', or 'multivalued levels of meaning' (Jencks, 1973, pp. 13 – 14), for it is the fusion of elements that is evident in the work of these two architects, while univalence or bivalence characterizes that of the others. However, the empirical analysis shows that it is not merely, as Jencks implies, the fusion of elements at the levels of form and content, but also a fusion that is rooted in, and inseparable from, social context. That is to say, the community of architects itself has defined its univalent and (much rarer) multivalent structures of meaning in terms of its own social structure, and this reveals something about the nature of that community as well as about future developments in form and content.

In sum, the framework of meaning underlying architects' thinking about the field and its major contributors is best described as a differentiated structure comprised of four independent dimensions: *subjectivism versus bureaucratic, purist, meta-art*, and *camp*. This frame refers to architects' knowledge and subjective evaluations of the field as a whole, which is to say, the field that shapes and influences their own work while nevertheless being exterior to it. The rest of this paper deals with meanings in which architects are more personally involved, that is, the ideas and subjective evaluations that more directly relate to their own work.

Further Explorations into Meaning

In order to elicit the meanings with which individuals are more personally involved, 36 quotations by architects, planners, and critics were selected that were believed to represent the spectrum of ideas, opinions, and controversies that currently prevail in contemporary architecture (Table 5). For each quotation, respondents were asked to indicate whether they strongly agree, mostly agree, have no opinion one way or another, mostly disagree, or strongly disagree. The quotations are ordered in Table 5 by the combined percentage of strongly agree and agree (column 1). The percentage that checked 'no opinion' appears in column 2.

With the exception of item 5, 'texture is extremely important', formal or aesthetic criteria are ranked less high than those reflecting social or functional criteria. Generally statements representing *avant-garde* design philosophies (for example, 'It's good because it's awful' and 'Main Street is almost alright') are not yet very popular. Many architectural

Table 5
Amount of Agreement with Ideas Expressed in Quotations

Quotations	% Strongly agree or agree	% no opinion
1. Good buildings must relate to their environment	94.6	2.9
2. Spatial relationships can influence, and even determine, interpersonal social relationships	86.4	10.6
3. Architecture should not be designed for peers nor clients but for users	84.4	10.5
4. Much more attention should be given to the users' cultural values, spatial needs, and aesthetic preferences	83.7	9.4
5. Texture is extremely important	83.7	10.5
6. Top priority should be given to the serviceability of buildings: access to transportation, sunlight, public safety, acoustics, and so forth	81.4	9.7
7. The aim of architecture should be to restore the 'human scale'—to our buildings, to our cities	80.9	12.3
8. Form follows function	79.9	10.6
9. More than anything, the practitioner requires sound business capability, professional integrity, and the ability to communicate with others	77.8	12.7
10. Every age has its 'feelings' and its aspirations. These must be expressed in architecture	75.4	16.5
11. Buildings should be designed from the inside out, rather than from the outside in	67.7	19.8
12. Less is more	60.1	22.2
13. Architecture should be the result of a team effort and not the emanation from one isolated ego	59.1	15.2
14. The nature of space reflects what it wants to be	58.5	24.6
15. The really important thing in architecture is proportion	56.0	14.9
16. Buildings should have a sense of humor	48.0	30.8
17. Good design: flair, drama, excitement	47.4	19.5
18. Modern architecture should concern itself with the 'recycling' of existing structures, avoiding new structures whenever possible	46.4	15.1
19. We are not interested in architecture as a cultural object, nor as a status symbol. Anathema to us is the monument in architecture and 'prima donna' architect	43.6	24.3
20. A good design must be dynamic	42.3	15.7
21. The best architecture gives one the feeling that it grows out of the soil	41.9	23.3
22. Good design most often is a technical solution	40.1	11.1

Table 5
continued

23. Honesty is expressed in exposed surfaces	39.8	17.2
24. Good architecture should be a means of advertising	38.2	20.8
25. Monumentality is still a virtue	38.1	24.4
26. We need machines for living instead of cathedrals	36.7	21.2
27. Everyone should be able to build	29.3	24.2
28. Architecture is an affair of the élite	26.4	11.8
29. Less is a bore	23.4	31.0
30. An architect should refuse a commission from the Rhodesian government	23.4	28.0
31. The international style is just too flat chested	23.4	32.8
32. Main Street is almost alright	23.0	33.6
33. Sociologists don't know anything about how to build. It's only artists who know how	22.7	18.0
34. Who wants to know what the inside looks like from the outside	15.7	25.2
35. What we build will find its usefulness. Form does not follow function	14.6	12.6
36. It's good because it's awful	5.2	14.9

Number of respondents = 416.

critics would be surprised to learn how sensitive these architects are to the implications of projects for their surroundings, as indicated by the fact that item 1 ('Good buildings must relate to their environment') and item 7 ('The aim of architecture should be to restore the "human scale"—to our buildings, to our cities') were endorsed by more than three-quarters of the architects. Further, these results confirm Lipman's interpretation of data for British architects; namely, that architectural determinism (item 2) still appears to be a major premise in architectural thinking (Lipman, 1969, pp. 190 — 204), although the concept has been vigorously attacked in the professional literature for at least a decade (Gutman, 1966 p. 12; Rein, 1967, p. 150; 1963). A table of the relationships among all quotations and the names of architects, along with a brief interpretation, is given in the Appendix to this paper. It is useful for it provides an understanding of characteristics respondents attribute to architects—albeit unwittingly—and it elaborates on the frame developed in the paper.

The results of the factor analysis of these quotations* are reported in Table 6. The names given to the dimensions are: *humanist, liberal professional, technical, social responsibility,*

*A matrix of Spearman *rho* coefficients was the input for the factor analysis. A principal component, varimax rotation procedure was used.

Table 6
Loadings of 0.40 or higher of Quotations on Eight Factors

I. *Humanist*
  4. Much more attention should be given to the users'
      cultural values, spatial needs, and aesthetic preferences 0.57
  7. The aim of architecture should be to restore the
      'human scale' — to our buildings, to our cities 0.55
  2. Spatial relationships can influence, and even determine,
      interpersonal social relationships 0.50
  3. Architecture should not be designed for peers nor
      clients but for users 0.50
  10. Every age has its 'feelings' and its aspirations. These
      must be expressed in architecture 0.48
  14. The nature of space reflects what it wants to be 0.44
  1. Good buildings must relate to their environment 0.43

II. *Liberal professional*
  19. We are not interested in architecture as a cultural ob-
      ject, nor as a status symbol. Anathema to us is the
      monument in architecture and the 'prima donna' ar-
      chitect 0.54
  13. Architecture should be the result of a team effort and
      not the emanation from one isolated ego 0.46

III. *Technical*
  22. Good design most often is a technical solution 0.49
  23. Honesty is expressed in exposed services 0.47

IV. *Social responsibility*
  30. An architect should refuse a commission from the
      Rhodesian government 0.49
  16. Buildings should have a sense of humor 0.44
  18. Modern architecture should concern itself with the
      'recycling' of existing structures, avoiding new structures
      whenever possible. 0.41

V. *Anti-minimalism*
  29. Less is a bore 0.88
  12. Less is more 0.55

VI. *Anti-functionalism*
  35. What we build will find its usefulness. Form does not
      follow function 0.70
  8. Form follows function 0.58

VII. *Pragmatic*
  6. Top priority should be given to the serviceability of
      buildings: access to transportation, sunlight, public
      safety, acoustics, and so forth 0.64
  9. More than anything, the practitioner requires sound
      business capability, professional integrity, and the abili-
      ty to communicate with others 0.60

VIII. *Expressionism*
  17. Good design: flair, drama, excitement 0.61
  20. A good design must be dynamic 0.54

anti-minimalism, anti-functionalism, pragmatic, and *expressionism.* All factors account for roughly the same amount of statistical variation, except for the first, which accounts for nearly twice that of any of the others.

The first factor taps *humanist* concerns and unmistakably indicates the great importance architects attach to what users of buildings want and to the social relevance of design and architectural practice. If architects still are not giving priority to users' needs—and most critics feel they are not—the architects in this study indicate that this will be, or should be, the future trend. Whereas the frequency distributions in Table 5 show simply that many tend to agree, for example, that 'much more attention should be given to the users' . . . values . . . and preferences', and that 'architecture should not be designed for peers nor clients but for users', the factor analysis reveals that there are large numbers of architects who have the same attitudes about an entire set of issues, and that these issues are currently the most potent and significant ones.

It had been expected in advance of the analysis that the quotations indicating a concern with users would be part of a larger pattern and include the items that deal with the 'progressive' practice of architecture—specifically, an interest in team practice (item 13), and the anti-elitism expressed in item 19, which includes the statement, 'Anathema to us is the monument in architecture and the "prima donna" architect.' This is not the case. The progressive orientation to architectural practice that underlies these items is important, but it is quite distinct (statistically independent) from the humanistic perspective. Both items load high on the second factor, *liberal professional.*

The *technical* dimension (Factor III) brings together two distinct viewpoints: first, that design and technical problems are one and the same; and second, an emphasis on exposed services, as stressed by brutalism. Generally, this factor reflects a straightforward approach to materials and technology.

The fourth factor is especially interesting, for it is comprised of items whose similarity is not obvious. What they appear to have in common is the principle that architecture must serve ends that are not merely architectural, but are socially meaningful and relevant. The *social responsibility* of the architect is the underlying theme.

The *bureaucratic* pole of the first dimension of the factor analysis of architectural heroes is similar to the fifth and sixth factors of the analysis of quotations, *anti-minimalism* and *anit-functionalism,* respectively. These results —specifically, the negative loadings on all three of these factors—indicate that the dominant aesthetic is facing a large opposition within the architectural community. It appears, however, that individual architects are more likely to engender schools of opposition than are the ideas which they represent. This is argued on the grounds that opposition to the works of Yamasaki, Stone, and Harrison seems to be better organized, for it is represented by a more important factor (which accounts for more of the variance) than opposition to the ideas with which they are associated. It may be generally true that in a period of intellectual ferment—in science, academia, or art opinions become mobilized *against* individuals who stand for the older tradition, but not so much against the old as *for* a new set of ideals.

The *pragmatic* orientation (Factor VII) includes both the idea that buildings should be practical to live in and the idea that the architect must possess the sensible virtues of a successful, but enlightened, businessman. The more romantic image of the architect—neurotic, egoistic, creative—is excluded by this definition.

There is only one factor (if we exclude here the *technical* dimension) revealing advocacy for a particular design aesthetic that accounts for any significant proportion of the variation in the responses. This is *expressionism*, Factor VIII. Since other design-related statements (for example, 'texture is extremely important', and 'the really important thing in architecture is proportion') were not included in the factor solution, this indicates that the formal attributes revealed by Factor VIII, namely, 'flair, drama, excitement' and 'dynamic' qualities, are the only ones deemed currently salient. This may be an indication of future developments in architecture, particularly since this factor is somewhat parallel to the *subjectivism* pole of the first factor in the analysis of heroes.

But taken in their entirety, the results unambiguously show that the most important issues in architecture at the moment do not revolve around questions of design and form but rather the social uses—or what Herbert Gans has called the 'human' qualities of architecture (Gans, 1971).

Conclusions

What do these results suggest about future trends in both architectural practice and building design? The office dominated by one or a few senior design architects with the mostly routine work carried out by many specialized junior architects may soon be replaced—or, at least, many of these architects hope it will—by a decentralized structure made up of small teams of co-workers. Further, given the notable emphasis on users' needs, on the relationship between buildings and their surroundings, and on technical performance, architects imply the need (and the willingness?) for greater cooperation with other experts — planners, sociologists, and engineers.

For technological and economic reasons, many predicted after the 'energy crisis' of the early 1970s that glass-curtain, steel structures would become a relic of the past (Hitchcock, 1968 p. 418; Fitch, 1972, pp. 308 – 320). This study supports that prediction. If ideas count in architecture — and they apparently do, even in the United States in which architecture is governed so much by the market place — the research findings unambiguously indicate the demise of monumentality associated with the International Style, and the emergence of an architectural style that is more humane and more sensitive to the needs and the life-styles of the users of buildings.

Although the results of the factor analysis of quotations highlights the salience of social rather than aesthetic criteria, the only aesthetic style that is stressed, expressionism (as against functionalism and minimalism), is clearly compatible with the one revealed in the factor analysis of eminent architects. That is, while the work of the villains represents simplicity, linearity, and monumentality, that of the heroes reveals virtuoso and elaborate performances. The favored architects — Stirling and Aalto — in terms of which this contrast (and the root controversy it denotes) can best be understood, combine innovative engineering and an expressive design aesthetic with appeals to humanistic (although not strikingly democratic) values.

But more significant, I believe, is that the ideas and the feelings that architects have about their work are structured to a considerable extent in terms of social utility. It is in fact quite remarkable — given the character of the contemporary professional ethos — that this is the case. To be specific, the orientation of these architects is dramatically inconsistent with their training and with the prevailing professional view, as it is reflected in journals, the writings of all but a handful of established reviewers, professional schools of architecture, and — as we discovered in the analysis of value orientations — the attitudes principals have about their firms' projects. In my view, this dominant professional ethos will not change in a way that is consistent with the basic orientation of practising architects until there are fundamental changes in government policies and in the economies of the design — building industry. Whether practising architects can help to transform these policies and the industry's economy remains to be seen.

But, if America is nearing the threshold of a humanistic revolution, as Charles Reich (Reich, 1971) and Jean-François Revel (Revel, 1971) have argued, architecture may play a pivotal role in the expression of new social meanings. For architecture is, after all, meaning made manifest, and the evaluations and ideas advanced by these architects clearly portent a more humanistic and democratic architecture.

Appendix: Significant Relationships between Quotations and Names of Architects

If architects are asked to describe the work of eminent colleagues, one is always concerned that the 'textbook' answers are given, rather than personal and thoughtful ones. An alternative is to ask architects what qualities they think buildings should have and then to ask them which architects they like. And, by bringing these two sets of answers together, the results indicate those architects and those qualities that can mutually coexist, and those that cannot, 'in the minds' of the respondents. What this table shows, then, are some of the qualities that the respondents indirectly associate with the work of 50 architects.

Listed here are the significant positive and negative relationships* between the respondents' opinions about the 50 architects and the 36 quotations. A given positive relationship, reported in the left-hand column, indicates that respondents tend to agree with the statements and like the work of that architect (or, disagree with the statement and not like the work of that architect); a given negative relationship, reported in the right-hand column, indicates that respondents either tend to disagree with the statement and like the work of the architect, or tend to agree with the statement and dislike the work of the architect. In other words, the left-hand column of positive relationships shows the consistencies between architects and ideas, and the right hand-column of negative relationships, the inconsistencies.

There are many examples of corroboration of the interpretations made in the paper (for example, those who agree that 'monumentality is still a virtue' tend to like Neutra, Pei, and Stone). There are also some examples that contradict various interpretations (for example, those who are in favor of monumentality also like Meier). But, on balance, this table of relationships tends to support what is inferred from the results of the factor analyses, and also raises some interesting questions with regard to issues not discussed in the paper.

*Kendall's *tau* is the measure of association. Only those that are significantly related at the 0.05 level (two-tailed test) are reported. (This means, roughly, that, if chance were operating, the probability of obtaining a *tau* value of a given magnitude is equal to 5 out of 100.)

| Positive
Relationship | Negative
Relationship |

1. Good buildings must relate to their environment.

Positive	Negative
Fuller	Lapidus
Goodman/Goodman	Venturi
Giurgola	
Kahn	
TAC	
Tange	
Wright	

2. Spatial relationships can influence, and even determine, interpersonal social relationships.

Positive	Negative
Goodman/Goodman	Johnson
Giurgola	Stone
Jacobs	Yamasaki
Kahn	
Stirling	

3. Architecture should not be designed for peers nor clients but for users.

    Ehrenkrantz
    Kahn

4. Much more attention should be given to the users' cultural values, spatial needs, and aesthetic preferences.

Positive	Negative
Fuller	Tange
Lapidus	
Yamasaki	

5. Texture is extremely important.

Positive	Negative
Breuer	Venturi
Fuller	
Goodman	
Johnson	
Neutra	
Soleri	
TAC	

Positive Relationship	*Negative Relationship*

6. Top priority should be given to the serviceability of buildings: access to transportation, sunlight, public safety, acoustics, and so forth.

Positive	Negative
Breuer	Aalto
Goodman/Goodman	Eames/Eames
Harrison	Kisler
Johnson	Stirling
Niemeyer	Tange
Stone	
Stubbins	
Wachsmann	

7. The aim of architecture should be to restore the 'human scale'—to our buildings, to our cities.

Positive	Negative
Goodman/Goodman	Moore
Wachsmann	

8. Form follows function.

Positive	Negative
Breuer	Aalto
Goodman/Goodman	Giurgola
Gropius	Kallman
Harrison	Moore
Johnson	Stirling
Lundy	van Eyck
Mies van der Rohe	
Niemeyer	
Pei	
SOM	
Speer	
Stone	
Stubbins	
TAC	
Yamasaki	

9. More than anything, the practitioner requires sound business capability, professional integrity, and the ability to communicate with others.

Positive	Negative
Breuer	Aalto
Goodman/Goodman	Eames/Eames
Harrison	Esherick
Johnson	Giurgola
Lapidus	Kiesler
Mies van der Rohe	Moore
Niemeyer	Nowicki
SOM	Safdie
Speer	Stirling
Stone	Tange
Stubbins	
Yamasaki	

Positive	*Negative*
Relationship	*Relationship*

10. Every age has its 'feelings' and its aspirations. These must be expressed in architecture.

    Mies van der Rohe
    TAC

11. Buildings should be designed from the inside out, rather than from the outside in.

Breuer	Aalto
Goff	Stirling
Goodman/Goodman	van Eyck
Gropius	
Harrison	
Lundy	
Niemeyer	
SOM	
Stone	
TAC	
Wachsmann	

12. Less is more.

Breuer	Goff
Gropius	Greene
Johnson	
Kahn	
Meier	
Mies van der Rohe	
Pei	
Rudolph	
Saarinen	
Soleri	
SOM	
Speer	
TAC	

13. Architecture should be the result of a team effort and not the emanation from one isolated ego.

Archigram	Barnes
Ehrenkrantz	Esherick
Gropius	Meier
Wachsmann	
Yamasaki	

14. The nature of space reflects what it wants to be.

    Fuller
    Kahn
    Rudolph
    Safdie
    Soleri

Positive	*Negative*
Relationship	*Relationship*

15. The really important thing in architecture is proportion.

Breuer	Aalto
Harrison	Ehrenkrantz
Johnson	Esherick
Lapidus	Giurgola
Neutra	Kiesler
Niemeyer	Moore
Pei	Sert
Rudolph	Stirling
Soleri	Tange
SOM	
Speer	
Stone	
Yamasaki	

16. Buildings should have a sense of humour.

Aalto	Breuer
Archigram	Gropius
Ehrenkrantz	Harrison
Esherick	Johnson
Giurgola	Lundy
Stirling	Mies van der Rohe
van Eyck	Nervi
Venturi	Neutra
	Niemeyer
	Saarinen
	SOM
	Speer
	Stone
	Stubbins
	TAC
	Yamasaki

17. Good design: flair, drama, excitement.

Le Corbusier
Lundy
Niemeyer
Stone

| *Positive* | *Negative* |
| *Relationship* | *Relationship* |

18. Modern architecture should concern itself with the 'recycling' of existing structures, avoiding new structures whenever possible.

Archigram	Breuer
Eames/Eames	Gropius
Giurgola	Harrison
Kahn	Johnson
Stirling	Saarinen
	SOM
	Speer
	Stone
	TAC
	Yamasaki

19. We are not interested in architecture as a cultural object, nor as a status symbol. Anathema to us is the monument in architecture and the 'prima donna' architect.

Eames/Eames	Johnson
Nervi	Lundy
Sert	Rudolph
	Speer
	Stone
	Yamasaki

20. A good design must be dynamic.

Aalto
Fuller
Goodman/Goodman
Niemeyer
Pei
Rudolph
Stone
Yamasaki

21. The best architecture gives one the feeling that it grows out of the soil.

Goff	Meier
Johnson	Moore
Lapidus	Stirling
Niemeyer	
Soleri	
Stone	
Yamasaki	

| *Positive* | *Negative* |
| *Relationship* | *Relationship* |

22. Good design most often is a technical solution.

Breuer	Aalto
Gropius	Eames/Eames
Harrison	Giurgola
Johnson	Stirling
Niemeyer	
Saarinen	
Stone	
Yamasaki	

23. Honesty is expressed in exposed services.

| Lapidus | Aalto |
| Rudolph | Giurgola |

24. Good architecture should be a means of advertising.

Goff	Mies van der Rohe
Harrison	
Lundy	
Stone	
Venturi	

25. Monumentality is still a virtue.

Meier	Cambridge 7
Neutra	Safdie
Pei	
Stone	

26. We need machines for living instead of cathedrals.

| Meier | Nowicki |

27. Everyone should be able to build.

Archigram	SOM
Fuller	Stubbins
Stirling	

28. Architecture is an affair of the élite.

Stirling	Barnes
Venturi	Breuer
	Gropius
	Johnson
	Neutra
	Niemeyer
	Pei
	Stubbins
	TAC

	Positive Relationship	Negative Relationship

29. Less is a bore.

Positive Relationship	Negative Relationship
Giurgola	Breuer
Lapidus	Gropius
Stirling	Johansen
van Eyck	Johnson
Venturi	Mies van der Rohe
	Neutra
	Pei
	Rudolph
	Saarinen
	SOM
	Speer
	Stubbins
	TAC

30. An architect should refuse a commission from the Rhodesian government

Positive Relationship	Negative Relationship
Aalto	Johnson
Ehrenkrantz	Niemeyer
Esherick	SOM
Fuller	Speer
Giurgola	Stone
Moore	Stubbins
Stirling	Yamasaki

31. The international style is just too flat chested.

Positive Relationship	Negative Relationship
Lapidus	Aalto
Superstudio	Breuer
	Gropius
	Kahn
	Kallman
	Meier
	Mies van der Rohe
	Sert
	TAC

32. Main Street is almost alright.

Positive Relationship	Negative Relationship
Lapidus	Breuer
Stirling	Gropius
Venturi	Kallman
	Lundy
	Mies van der Rohe
	Nervi
	Neutra
	Niemeyer
	Nowicki
	Pei
	Sert
	SOM
	Stubbins
	TAC

*Positive
Relationship*

*Negative
Relationship*

33. Sociologists don't know anything about how to build.
    It's only artists who know how.

> Breuer
> Ehrenkrantz
> Fuller
> Gropius
> Lapidus
> Moore
> Safdie
> Superstudio

34. Who wants to know what the inside looks like from
    the outside?

> Barnes
> Breuer
> Pei
> Safdie
> Sert
> Soleri
> Stubbins
> TAC

35. What we build will find its usefulness. Form does not
    follow function.

Greene	Breuer
Stirling	Gropius
van Eyck	Johnson
Venturi	Mies van der Rohe
	Nervi
	Niemeyer
	Saarinen
	Soleri
	Speer
	Stubbins
	TAC
	Yamasaki

36. It's good because it's awful.

Lapidus	Barnes
Moore	Breuer
Stirling	Gropius
Superstudio	Johnson
Venturi	Mies van der Rohe
	Nowicki
	Pei
	Saarinen
	SOM
	Stubbins
	TAC

References

Boudon, R. (1971) *The Uses of Structuralism*, London, Heinemann.

Brewer, J. (1972) 'Organizations/Occupations Interfaces: The Case of Autonomy and Organizational Authority in Architecture', mimeo.

Broadbent, G. (1969) 'Meaning into Architecture', in George Baird and Charles Jencks (eds), *Meaning in Architecture*, London, Barrie & Rockliff, p. 56.

Cattell, R. B. (1952) *Factor Analysis*, New York, Harper Bros.

Fitch, J. M. (1972) *American Building 2: The Environmental Forces that Shape it*, Boston, Mass., Houghton Mifflin.

Gans, H. J. (1971) 'Some Observations and Proposals on the Role of Architecture in Today's America', mimeo.

Gouldner, A. W. (1957) Cosmopolitans and Locals. *Administrative Science Quarterly*.

Gutman, R. (1966) Site planning and social behaviour', *Journal of Social Issues*.

Hall, B. N. (1969) *Occupations and Social Structure*. Englewood Cliffs, N.J. Prentice-Hall.

Harman H.S. (1968) *Modern Factor Analysis*, University of Chicago Press.

Hitchcock H. R. (1968) *Architecture: Nineteenth and Twentieth Centuries*, Harmondsworth, Penguin Books.

Huxtable, A. L. (1975) The Architecture of the Ecole des Beaux Arts, *New York Review of Books*.

Jencks, C. (1969) 'Semiology and Architecture', in George Baird and Charles Jencks (eds), *Meaning in Architecture*, London, Barrie & Rockliffe.

Jencks, C. (1971) *Architecture 2000*, New York, Praeger

Jencks, C. (1973) *Modern Movements in Architecture*, Garden City, Anchor Press.

Joedicke, J. *Architecture Since 1945*, London, Pall Mall Press

Lévi-Strauss, C. (1969) *The Elementary Structures of Kinship*, ed., Boston, Mass., Beacon Press.

Lipman, A. (1969) 'The architectural belief system and social behaviour', *British Journal of Sociology*.

Muschamp, H. (1974) *File Under Architecture*, Cambridge, Mass., MIT Press

Norberg-Schultz, C. (1968) *Intentions in Architecture*, Oslo. The Norwegian Research Council for Science and Humanities.

Parsons, T. (1939) The Professions and Social Structure. *Social Forces*, Vol. 17.

Reich, C. (1971) *The Greening of America*. New York, Random House.

Rein, R. (1967) 'Social science and the elimination of poverty', *Journal of the American Institute of Planners*.

Revel, J. F. (1971) *Without Marx or Jesus*, Garden City, NY, Doubleday.

Rummell, R. J. (1970) *Applied Factor Analysis*, Evanston, Northwestern University Press.

Salaman, G. (1974) *Community and Occupation*, Cambridge University Press.

Schorr, A. (1963) *Slums and Social Insecurity* (Research Report No. 1, Division of Research and Statistics, Social Security Administration), Washington, DC, US Government Printing Office.

Sontag, S. (1967) 'Notes on Camp', in *Against Interpretation*, London, Eyre & Spottiswoode.

Wachsmann, K. (1967) 'Research: the mother of invention', *Arts and Architecture*.

Wotton, H. (1624) *Elements of Architecture*, reprinted, 1964 Charlottesville, Va., University of Virginia Press.

Section 3

3.0 Introduction to Section 3

Richard Bunt

'Sémiologie', Saussure's hopeful vision of a 'science that studies the life of signs in society', has given rise to many divergent interpretations since the publication of the *Cours de linguistique générale*. What is reasonably clear from this posthumous collection is that Saussure had in mind a vast enterprise in which the broad dimension of signification, which can be attributed to the various artificial operations of human culture, occupies a central place. Such operations generate both material and non-material artefacts, which may include both the material incidents of our culture — such as commodities, utensils, and buildings — and those non-material institutions — such as natural language and various systems of social convention — which serve to modify our attitudes to these material incidents as the bearers of 'meanings'. Indeed, the interaction between all of the various manifestations of human purposeful activity, which we collectively term 'culture', would seem to have an essential dimension of 'signification' bound up with it. For Saussure, the science of 'sémiologie' was seen as potentially encompassing the whole of this vast territory — no wonder that he refrained from indicating a detailed programme that such a discipline might follow.

More recently, a considerable amount of attention has been devoted to the possibility of developing a structural model of systems of signification in general, and of the relation of signification which is encapsulated by the linguistic sign in particular. The theory of the structure of the linguistic sign which has served most often as the basis for this widespread interest is, naturally, that developed by Saussure himself. However, within the Saussurean tradition there have emerged divergent approaches.* Broadly speaking, this divergence stems from two complementary facets of Saussure's thought—his emphasis on the study of language as a social institution, on the one hand, and his firm insistence on the need to study language as a structural system on the other. Perhaps the most eminent successor to Saussure was Louis Hjelmslev. He succeeded in formulating the structural properties of language in such a way that these properties could be sought in cultural phenomena which belong 'outside' natural language. It is thus inevitable that most of the theorists who are concerned with the semiological study of cultural institutions outside natural language should have been influenced by Hjelmslev to a greater or lesser extent.

Since Saussure and Hjelmslev, certain obstacles have arisen which have tended to obscure the basic theoretical positions which they adopted concerning the social nature of systems of signification and the structural properties of such systems. Attempts to apply theoretical positions within a general semiology have often taken the form of applying a relatively indistinct notion of linguistic structure to the study of cultural phenomena which are of a much less abstract nature than is natural language. The result of this is that the implied parallelism between such phenomena and natural language has either tended to be too literal—being conceived in terms of the cultural or material equivalents of specifically linguistic entities, such as 'monemes' and 'phonemes', etc[§]—or else too metaphorical—in which the notion of 'meaning' introduced has become so general, subjective, or epistemologically imprecise as to raise more questions than it answers. Unfortunately, it seems that attempts to apply Saussurean structural linguistics to a semiotic study of architecture have suffered from both of these defects.

A principal obstacle to the development of such a possible application of Saussurean linguistics concerns the whole

---

*On the one hand there are the followers of a strictly linguistic tradition such as André Martinet and Eric Buyssens, while on the other there are theorists who adopt a much wider ranging, all-embracing stance in seeking to make use of Saussurean insights in the most diverse fields of cultural study. Roland Barthes is probably the best-known author within this latter category; in books such as *Elements de Sémiologie* and *Systeme de la Mode*, in particular, he sought to indicate that the Saussurean and Hjelmslevian models of signification might usefully be employed in cultural situations which are not ostensibly 'linguistic' in nature.

§Approaches such as these tended to employ a literal analogy between material or spatial 'building blocks' and the constituent components of phonetic speech. In Italy, the early work of Gamberini and de Fusco provide examples of such approaches. This point is referred to also in Charles Jencks' article in Section 1 of this collection.

question of the usefulness of an analogy being set up between the characteristic features of a natural language and of any other signifying system. On the one hand, it has been argued that any descriptive model based on natural language must be capable of accounting for the specific properties of natural language insofar as they are pertinent to its signifying function: André Martinet, for example, suggests that the distinctive property of language in this respect is its 'double articulation' into 'monemes' (which have significance) and 'phonemes' (which do not).* Accordingly an applied semiology based on structural linguistics has often been bedevilled by what Paolo Ramat has lamented as attempts to assimilate into the province of linguistics other areas of study (fashion, cinema, cuisine, and, of course architecture) (Ramat, 1975 pp. 1 — 2). The object of this is to find 'embryonic second articulations in the most widely disparate fields'—efforts which have inevitably lost in theoretical rigour and accuracy what they have sought to gain in specificity—in their search for such basic entities as the 'cinematic sign' or the 'architectural sign' and their constituent, non-signifying, components. On the other hand, it has been argued that any attempt to construct a descriptive model based on natural language must of necessity be framed in such general terms as to be incapable of capturing the specific varieties of signification which are particular to the various phenomena to which such a model is applied. Surely, however, both of these pitfalls can be avoided if we follow Hjelmslev's suggestion that 'each discipline will be able to contribute in its own way to the general science of semiotics by investigating to what extent and in what manner its objects may be submitted to an analysis that is in agreement with the requirements of linguistic theory' (Hjelmslev, 1961, p. 108).

There is one final area of theoretical disagreement which remains to be considered. This concerns the distinction between a 'semiology of communication' and a 'semiology of signification'. The controversy hinges on the priority of one mode of semiotic emphasis over the other.§ Some theorists have suggested that there can be no proper study of the phenomenon of signification without that study being based on the process of communication. For example, Luis Prieto argues that the process of communication constitutes an essential example of human intentionality within a potential-

*André Martinet introduces this distinction in an elementary form in *Elements of General Linguistics*, trans, Elizabeth Palmer, Faber, London, 1960, pp. 24 — 25.

§The distinction is discussed in some detail by Georges Mounin in an essay in his *Introduction à la sémiologie*, Minuit, Paris, 1970, pp. 11 — 15. Also referred to in Charles Jencks's article in Section 1 of this collection.

ly signifying situation, and that accordingly the phenomenon of signification can only be demonstrated within the context of some intention to communicate. It seems that a model based on the priority of the process of communication can be applicable only to systems of signification involving an artificially delimited and arbitrarily conceived 'set of rules'—such as a finite range of signifiers and a one to one correspondence between signifier and signified.* Needless to say, the adoption of such a model places serious restrictions on the ways in which the phenomenon of signification can be conceived. On the other hand, Umberto Eco has argued that no communication can take place without there being present a context in which a relation of signification is first established. Eco holds that signification is a 'system'—a framework of relationships—while communication is a 'process' operating within such a framework (Eco, 1976, pp. 8 – 9). Also, Maria Luisa Scalvini admits that non-linguistic systems of signification, such as those bound up with architectonic objects, are 'not necessarily backed up by an intention to communicate'. (Scalvini, forthcoming) Furthermore, if we accept the priority of the phenomenon of signification we can recognize that a signifying code can be set up independently of any actual process of communication. We can accordingly speak of a system of codification in terms of which the members of a culture classify and organize phenomena with respect to their potentially signifying properties—which does not necessarily imply that any intention to employ these phenomena to communicate a 'message' necessarily exists. Thus, referring to Roland Barthes's examples of non-linguistic signifying systems, Georges Mounin notes: (Mounin, 1970, p. 14).

> this garment, this object, this gesture . . . which Barthes grasps with particularly fine psycho-social intuition, are very probably indexes . . . . And these indexes are very probably significations . . . To apply to them—because one has designated them as a signs or semiological system— a model of explanation involving 'communication' is to risk by-passing the question of the mechanism of their social functioning.

We can see from this introductory picture that, even within a general semiology, there exist fundamental theoretical conflicts. What the present section attempts to do is no more than to indicate the scope of certain of these theoretical positions as they have informed studies concerned with what we may call 'architectonic objects'.

---

*For example, such a restricted set of rules is adopted in such a code of signals or ciphers as constitutes the international Morse code, or semaphore.

In choosing to limit the selection of articles in this section to work recently carried out in Italy, we have had in mind the particular richness of a body of work already well established and also the usefulness of making some of this work available to English readers, either in translation at first hand, or at least in some form of summary.

References

Eco, U. (1976) *A Theory of Semiotics*, Bloomington, University of Indiana Press.

Hjelmslev L. (1961) *Prolegomena to a Theory of Language*, trans. Francis J. Whitfield, University of Wisconsin Press.

Mounin, G. (1970) *Introduction à la sémiologie*, Minuit, Paris.

Ramat, P. (1975) Semiotics and Linguistics, *Versus*, no. 10.

Scalvini, M. L. Structural Linguistics versus the Semiotics of Literature, (in this collection).

3.1 An Introduction to Italian Developments in Architectural Semiotics

Fernando Tudela

The semiotic approach to architecture, in Italy just as
elsewhere, has twin roots. It is the product of the convergence of two main clusters of interests. The first source is
to be found in architecture itself as a response to the increasing demand for a worthwhile theory of architecture, and this
demand usually appeared in connection with the crisis of the
theoretical assumptions of the Modern Movement. We
should refer briefly to the specific historical conditions in
which that demand for a theory appeared in Italy. The
Modern Movement started slightly late in that country, when
fascism was already in power and controlled not only
politics but culture as well. The first group of 'rationalist'
architects was founded in 1926: the Group 7 (L. Figini,
G. Frette, S. Larco, A. Libera, G. Pollini, C. E. Rava, G. Terragni). At the same time the Movimento Italiano per l'Architettura Razionale (MIAR) was created. It had a difficult existence and never managed to upset the dominant academic
structures. One of the sources of difficulty stemmed from
the ambiguous relationship that rationalist architects maintained with fascism. Rationalism, which never developed at
a triumphant pace in Italy, followed a more contradictory
line, much less dogmatic than in the rest of Europe. It never
lost a clearly distinguishable Italian flavour. Having always
kept the Modern Movement under control, Italian architects
felt with much less intensity the generalized crisis of its
tenets. They were however deeply worried about the so
called 'semantic loss' of modern architecture, and this was
one of the sources of the later development of theoretical
thinking on architecture. But there are others. Perhaps the
most relevant one resides in the need that all Italian archi-

tects have always felt to cope with the problem of inserting their work within an unusually rich historical context. The unbelievable density of buildings of historical interest made it necessary for them to have, as an everyday tool, some theory on the relationship between architecture and history. That need was especially acute during the post-war reconstruction activity. Since then, the rapport with the past constitutes the cardinal axis of Italian architectural culture.

There are other factors, again, to be pointed out, such as the long, unsolved economic crisis which caused a slow-down in building activity. Consequently, there has been little design work to be carried out, especially in the southern and central provinces; this scarcity has forced many architects to concentrate on research and theoretical work. A great many abandoned altogether any architectural activity: only a small proportion of graduates from schools of architecture now do architectural work. The access to educational jobs, even at the lowest levels, has become highly competitive. There has also been a remarkable expansion in the publishing industry. In the last ten years Italy has probably published more on architecture than any other European country.

As a result of all we have been pointing out, Italy has become, especially since the early nineteen-sixties, a main centre of theoretical interest in architecture. The theoretically-minded architects borrowed—mainly from the social sciences—the theories which appeared to be most appealing in the cultural context of the moment, and used them as a framework for their own activity.

The Anglo-Saxon cultural world was not easily available for that purpose, for linguistic reasons among others: until recently very few Italians set about learning English. The main tentative Anglo-Saxon responses to the crisis in the theory of architecture—that is, the study of 'Design Methods', and of Psychology as applied to environmental problems—remained basically alien to the Italian archi-tectural culture. We can hardly find any research of this type being carried out in Italy. French culture was, on the con-trary, extremely influential there. French Structuralism, in particular, received a great diffusion throughout the country. In the field of visual communication, industrial design, etc., authors such as Gillo Dorfles carried out dutifully the task of importing structuralism into Italy, and initiated a line of research which seemed to be extremely promising. Other scholars particularized and took that line further, often beyond the degree of development it had reached in France, where structuralism remained for a long time associated only with the fields of linguistics, philosophy, anthropology, and literary criticism. The publishing activity on structuralist semiotics was particularly intense in Italy during the nineteen-sixties, and it included not only a great many translations but original Italian works as well. Many architects started to dig for their theoretical framework in the midst of this cultural landslide. Books on linguistics made an unprecedented appearance on the bookshelves in architectural offices.

The other source for architectural semiotics is constituted by the work of those scholars who were not primarily interested in architecture (philosophers, researchers on aesthetics, mass communication, etc.) but who happened to use a comprehensive semiotic framework wherein architecture was included. These scholars derived from their consideration of the specific characteristics of architecture quite a set of puzzling problems about how that art could fit into the framework without too many contradictions. This provided an expansion in the interest in architectural signification and produced results that sometimes went deeper than the architects' own researches.

Architectural semiotics developed in Italy out of both these sources; and although it would be hazardous to speak of an 'Italian school' in that field of studies, some homogeneity can be found deriving from a basically common set of references.

3.2 The 'Language' of Architecture

Emilio Garroni

Translated by Deda Price and Richard Bunt.

Introductory Note by Emilio Garroni

This article constitutes—with certain modifications provided by the author—Chapter III of the first part of his book, *Progetto di Semiotica* (Laterza, Bari, 1972). In accordance with the approach adopted in this part of the book, which is both theoretical and intuitive, this article does not contain any rigorous justification of the legitimacy of considering architecture as a semiotic phenomenon, a problem which is confronted in another part of the above book in which Hjelmslev's semiotic theory is considered with reference to architecture among other phenomena. The *Progetto* represented, when it was originally completed, a stage of research which the author still maintains to be valid—even though this has subsequently been incorporated into other work, which accordingly does not contradict the major part of the considerations which follow.

Continuity and discreteness. A theory of the image and a theory of semiosis

It has been observed many times that one of the difficulties that could hinder a semiotic analysis of some (so-called) non-verbal languages — such as architecture, painting, cinema, and so on — could stem from their property of continuity as opposed to the property of discreteness which is peculiar to verbal language (see Granger, 1968). There are, indeed, difficulties in considering such 'languages' as true and proper languages, but we do not believe that these difficulties are to do with 'continuity'. In other words we do not believe that continuity in itself constitutes an insurmountable difficulty, such as would be encountered at a theoretical level if one were to demonstrate that the impossibility of analysing such 'languages' is a result of their character of continuity. On the contrary, *it seems to us that the question of continuity is based on a misunderstanding*, which is supported on occasion by certain unavoidable observations and undeniable technical difficulties which together have so far impeded the construction of an adequate theory and method. We want to make clear straight away that the question hinges upon the opposition between 'continuity' and 'discreteness' — above all with regard to what, according to Hjelmslev, we may call the 'plane of expression'.

Let us begin by observing that even verbal language, for instance in its concrete phonic manifestation, is evidently continuous and not discrete, even though one may conveniently analyse language into discrete phonemes and morphemes (although this is not so easy to accomplish from a diachronic point of view (see Alarcos Llorach, 1968_1). We can, moreover, see that music (to take an example of a 'non-verbal' language$_1$ has a strong character of continuity, since it seems that its continuity is not simply an accidental property linked to its concrete manifestation, but belongs to music even when considered in terms of its purely formal structure. And yet, even in this case, there exists a method of graphic codification which has not developed together with the evolution of music but has been elaborated and perfected relatively recently in successive stages. This method permits us to transcribe the continuity of music in terms of discrete notation, while also enabling us to consider all those pertinent aspects of continuity (which are an essential part of musical form) by employing a means of transcription analogous to co-called 'suprasegmental' linguistic features (for example, indications such as 'legato', 'staccato'). On this basis it would be possible to make a strict semiotic analysis of musical works in the same way as of literary works (Della Volpe, 1968). Even this simple example suggests that continuity in itself does not constitute an obstacle in strictly theoretical terms. *The above-mentioned misunderstanding, therefore, stems from a pseudo-semiotic approach, oriented towards material rather than formal considerations, so that what presents itself as being continuous appears, in the absence of an adequate tradition of transcription, to be decomposable into material parts, rather than being formally analysable. This would only involve cutting a continuum into material parts according to inadequate criteria.*

We do not mean to suggest by this that *if* there could exist, for all possible 'languages', methods of practical transcription, it would then be possible to resolve with ease every theoretical and methodological problem of analysis. We believe, rather, that in order to ensure a *semiotic 'survival' of culture*, in certain cases there is a practical necessity to institute a graphic equivalent as a presupposition of a more explicit and more accurate analysis. As far as verbal language is concerned for example, there seems to be no doubt that writing represents a method of transcribing oral language into a distinct semiotic medium—a method which implies both a theoretical and a practical preoccupation with capturing more or less precisely its potential discrete character. We must recognize in this coincidence of practical and theoretical requirements both an important factor of conventionalization, as far as discreteness is concerned, and a prerequisite for a possible subsequent theoretical analysis—a first step towards the formation of a metalinguistic awareness and an embryonic analytical attitude. A parallel practical requirement does not seem to exist within the scope of the figurative arts: painting, sculpture, or architecture do not need, in order to be transmitted or to survive, anything but their own material presence associated with empirical 'studio' practice. Painting and its transcription, so to speak, coincide. A marked 'metalinguistic' tension between an original medium and its transcription is not produced. *And yet there exists, if only in a weak form, a requirement for a method of transcription even within the figurative arts.* We cannot, for example, neglect the use of iconographic models, annotated sketches (as employed by the art historian Cavalcaselle), lists of procedures, verbal descriptions, etc., within the tradition of art criticism. One may even include in the case of architecture, its 'quasi-codification' (through numerical relations, geometrical schemes, verbal, typological, and stylistic categories, etc.) which has formed the subject of traditional treatises on architecture, and which has, perhaps optimistically, been considered as a sort of structuralism *ante litteram* (de Fusco, 1968). On the other hand, a certain metalinguistic distinction and tension can be often recorded also *at the same level* of the production of figurative and visual works. This is the case in those works which are, so to speak, more 'written', that is to say, provided with a strong conventional character of discreteness, in order to ensure *a semiotic, not a material, 'survival'.* We may consider, for example—in addition to the more obvious case of architecture—the case of the ancient, archaic, and 'primitive' painting and sculpture. However, while there are, indeed, important requirements in this sense, yet these have always lacked a powerful practical impetus, and there has never evolved either a sufficiently accurate method of transcription nor a coherent theory and method of analysis.

Furthermore we do not mean to suggest by this either that the existence of a practical requirement of transcription is a necessary (or even sufficient) condition for the development of a theory and of an analytical method, or that, in general, a practical method of transcription is always technically possible—*in the same way* that it is for verbal (or musical) language. *We will only note that this lack of practical constraint, combined with an instinct for cultural and specifically semiotic 'survival', has certainly contributed not only to painting, sculpture, and architecture remaining within the domain of the image taken as a whole (which has a communicative capacity only at an intuitional level), but also to the theoretical shift of emphasis as regards the undeniable continuity of the image, so that it becomes synonymous with unanalysability.* In this way there can arise a *theory of the image*, in which the image is conceived as that which is essentially unanalysable—presented immediately in terms of its individual 'being'—and about which we can only talk at a philosophical, and not at a theoretical/technical level. Such a theory is naturally counterposed to a *semiotic theory and analysis*, which aims to elaborate those models to which the image also refers—at least the image which is reproduced for the purposes of communication, whether artistic or not.

Naturally, the instances that give rise to such a theory of the image also have strong justifications, as we can see from the important contributions of C. Brandi. These stem from the unarguable need to capture in the work of art not only the 'message'—*in the restricted sense* of a message which is verbally translatable—but also all those further irreducible elements which for Brandi constitute the 'presence' of the work—its self-reference and self-consistency, its 'being' (Brandi, 1966). Certainly, such terminology is particular to a kind of problem rather different from ours; but on the other hand it is right to maintain an opposition to any *banal* reduction of the work of art to the status of a 'message' (in a restricted sense). Furthermore, this theory of the image (above all in its recent formulations) does not exclude the possibility that the work of art consists also of multiple communicative strata and that, accordingly, it could be considered *in this sense* as a semiosis by deferring to the appropriate code; however, *to the extent* that it is in a proper sense a work of art, a work of art cannot be considered as a semiosis. Nor, ultimately, does this theory exclude completely the possibility that, even *as* a pure work of art, it can *in some way* be analysed in terms of its very special structure (see in particular Brandi's *Struttura e architettura*, 1967). Even though such instances must be subject to certain important distinctions their importance must be recognized. A very simplistic semiotic approach would reduce any observable phenomenon and behaviour (including aesthetic contemplation) to a semiosis, and moreover to a semiosis in a restrictive sense. The most we could say in certain cases is that 'the aspect of a church informs us whether that church is catholic or protestant' (Brandi, 1967, p. 37). We cannot endorse, however, the opposition (which almost amounts to an alternative choice) between the semiotic approach and the philosophical/aesthetic approach — at least to the extent that this presupposes a parallel, objective opposition between the discreteness that characterizes the first approach and the continuity (or unanalysability) which characterizes the second.

But continuity and discreteness cannot be found, so to speak, in nature. If a continuum is that which we can consider, *in elliptic terminology*, as immediately and materially 'given' (equivalent to Hjelmslev's 'purport'), then the discrete can be introduced only through theoretical hypotheses. The opposition between 'sign' and 'image', between 'discrete' and 'continuous', is thereby revealed as the correct consequence of an incorrect assumption; i.e. that analysis consists in a material segmentation, finding in the thing itself objectively discrete parts to be considered as semiotic elements.

The Material Sign and the Formal Invariant

The problem of characterizing a non-verbal language as being discrete or continuous may well be more complex than it appears. In the case of the field of architecture, on which we propose to concentrate our attention, the property of continuity does not present an insurmountable obstacle, although (as in the case of music) it is doubtless a feature of central importance and not an 'accidental' property. *Only if we operate in terms of a material division — that is, by cutting the architectural continuum into material parts — would it be absurd to try to identify in this way the distinctive and pertinent elements of this continuum (which we will call 'invariants').* And yet some authors still look for the 'architectural sign', precisely in the sense criticized by Brandi and (in the field of cinema) by Christian Metz. In fact, it is probable that *there may be stronger reasons for adhering to the erroneous notion of the 'architectural sign' than those upon which the notion of the (ridiculous) cinematic sign is based.*

There is above all a cultural motivation behind the search for the architectural sign based on the very strong traditional requirement to refer both classical and neo-classical architecture to a 'code' (of a highly approximate nature, to say the least), thereby setting up a kind of metalinguistic reflection. It may happen, therefore, that the example of classical architecture (particularly of the architecture of Classical Greece) which appears *deceptively* to be appropriate in order to consider a code as a system of (material) signs, is extended so as to apply to the *whole* corpus of architecture. From this we derive the illusion of being confronted by works made from complex and macroscopic material components such as 'column', 'entablature', etc., which were initially discrete and could accordingly be codified as being supposedly invariant elements. In this connection, we must not underestimate also the misunderstanding which has resulted from a superficial reading of a famous extract from Saussure's *Course in General Linguistics*, doubtless within an atmosphere of semiological enthusiasm. Saussure takes precisely the example of a Greek temple in order to exemplify the idea of the twin types of relation — syntagmatic and associative (which we nowadays term 'paradigmatic'):

> From both [syntagmatic and associative] points of view a linguistic entity is *comparable* to a defined part of a building, e.g. a column. On the one hand, the column finds itself having a certain relation with the architrave which it supports; this arrangement of two entities which are actually present within the same space is *reminiscent* of a syntagmatic relation. On the other hand, if this column belongs to a Doric order, it suggests a mental comparison with the other orders (Ionic, Corinthian, etc.) which elements are not present in that space; thus the connection is associative. (Saussure, 1922, p. 171, editor's translation).

We have underlined those words in this passage that indicate the caution observed by Saussure in proposing this example — a caution which the editors of the '*Cours*' clearly perceived.

Saussure intended to demonstrate with this simple non-linguistic example that the elements of a context are determined to the extent that they are both distinguished syntagmatically from contiguous elements occurring within the same context, and are also distinguished from similar, paradigmatically correlated, elements which are not selected — not 'contextualized' — and therefore remain 'absent'. This example was perhaps susceptible to theoretical development, but in no way amounted to a theoretical indication of the possibility of constructing an architectural code.

It is clearly absurd to reduce the Greek temple or the classical tradition in general to a mere combination of large-scale material components, which are *at the same time* 'in-variants'. *The real invariants are not, and cannot be, the material components* (which may be in some cases similar to other material components), *rather they must be considered as formal elements. The reason is that a material component is susceptible of variation in terms of its dimensions, its proportions, and the distribution of its parts.* To assume that classical architecture can be analyzed typologically in such a way may seem plausible, so long as we confine ourselves to a very restricted field of application (such as the historical and typological context of the Doric temple), though this field is not strictly analysable in such a way. However, this assumption would jeopardize the possibility of comprehending analytically those diachronic phenomena that also require an adequate and flexible consideration, from a synchronic point of view, of the various models or systems involved in analyzing them. For example, the process which characterized the Italian Renaissance has been formerly considered as the resurrection of a 'dead' architectural language, whereas it was really a transformation, deformation, and actualization of a classical language in terms of a modern, differently structured, language.

If we were to consider instead other apposite architerctural examples (such as the shape of the internal space in a Byzantine church, the undulating concave/convex facade of a baroque building, or a tortuous wall by Gaudí), *the illusion of such a 'code' should not even arise.* In such cases, the continuity of the manipulation of fabric and of architectonic modulation is dominant—often, as in the case of Gaudí, deliberately not being susceptible to institutionalization in a material context and being strongly opposed to traditional codes of architecture, in particular to those codes which pertain to neo-classical architecture. Nor is this all; if Gaudí can appear as a limiting case of an architecture that has no precedent in history—something absolutely unique—baroque architecture has on the contrary very explicit and evident correspondences with that pseudo-discreteness which characterizes classicism. Baroque architecture is *also* characterized precisely by its adoption and deformation of a classical code, by means of the various types of correspondence between the code which is adopted and its deformation; for this reason there may be said to be a polar opposition between a 'classical' baroque and an 'anti-classical' baroque. (Incidentally, we may observe that the old question of giving an univocal definition of 'baroque' was simply based upon crudely material criteria: it was a question which fruitlessly afflicted the history and criticism of the baroque and compelled historians of the period to make continual exclusions, enlargements, and distinctions that were apparently subtle but were in point of fact vague and even contradictory. This problem, indeed, is reduced to insignificance from the point of view that we have sketched here.) It is precisely this fact which emphasizes that a model, which may be constructed in order to analyse architectural objects but which also in fact functions so as to produce them, is composed not of complex material components but of homogeneous formal elements which can be interrelated with the elements of other homogeneous models, heterogeneous among themselves. For example, the elements of figurative models can be interrelated with the elements of rythmical models in terms of *consonance* or *dissonance* with respect to a preceding interrelation, each type of interrelation establishing this or that constructive principle. In any case, we shall never find the invariant element in question *ready made*, but will have to determine it formally, at an appropriate level and type of specification. We shall have to identify such invariants, indeed, if it is to make any sense to say that a connection exists between, for example, baroque and classical codes.

Thus it is not the material idea of the 'sign', but the formal notion of the 'invariant' which is indispensable in order to explain the obvious similarities and differences (both synchronically and diachronically) between similar but individually well-defined architectonic objects — for example, to remain within the field of Roman baroque, between the façades of S. Vincenzo and S. Anastasio by Longhi Jnr. and of S. Maria in Campitelli by Carlo Rainaldi, or on the other hand between the façades of S. Carlino by Borromini and of S. Marcello by Carlo Fontana. The difference in the way in which these examples resemble each other clearly cannot be reduced to a superficial decorative taste, even though it should be made clear that, in principle, decoration is anything but irrelevant, having an important constructive role in the case of Iberian, Venetian, Neapolitan, and Apulian baroque. The similarities and differences of these examples are always realized by virtue of their formal structure, which is to say, by virtue of the presence or absence — as well as of a similar or different syntagmatic distribution — of classifiable invariant formal elements, which can be identified at appropriate levels of specification. A presence and an absence, that is to say, which both serve to indicate that what is present can be adequately perceived, in terms of its cultural determinateness and semiotic significance, not only in terms of sensory observation, but to the extent that it also establishes correlations of an associative or paradigmatic type with something which is absent. What is present is apprehended as something identified historically, insofar as it has been determined in terms of a series of differences with respect to a model or group of interrelated models. We must strive to exclude both the notion that the architectural work is something unanalysable as a whole, and the equally incorrect idea that it is structured and articulate (that is, 'analysable') in terms of material signs (which simply do not exist). *The problem is therefore to find appropriate methods of considering the 'continuous' architectonic object as consisting of discrete parts, or, better still, to construct models characterized by such discreteness which may be adequately applied to the continuous architectonic object, which thus becomes properly analysable.*

Methodological Views. The Typological Model

It should be made clear straight away that the methodological observations which follow do not claim to be adequate from every point of view. *They are intended to function only as examples of possible operative methods, with the aim of presenting concrete instances of a number of ideas which are primarily valid in the first place on a theoretical level. Basically, in the absence of a general theory and of explicit procedures of specification and application, it is our intention to identify some theoretical problems concerning certain so-called non-verbal languages and to suggest some preliminary answers, even if of a general nature, which may be formulated with regard to concrete semiotic phenomena.*

We should begin by stating that *investigating the properties of even a typological model can satisfactorily resolve the theoretical misunderstanding concerning the notion of continuity, providing that the entities established through such a model are formal, and not material, entities.* Even the usual elements such as a 'column', 'entablature', etc., may be legitimately considered within the scope of a current 'semiology', if by this it is intended to distinguish not the 'signs' whose realization and arrangement constitute the architectural object in its concrete entirety, but merely the formal elements of one of the possible models in terms of which an architectural object can be produced and analysed. On this basis, such elements permit a revision of the attempts to construct a semiology of architecture within the material plane. The difference is not merely terminological but the practical consequences are also important. A typological model, in fact, only permits one-sided and summary analysis of architecture; for example, the model from which the invariant element 'column' derives is applicable to a large number of architectural objects, each very different from the other, and the mere application of this model does not enable one to appreciate such diversity. By means of a model of this kind we bring together in the one class the Greek temple, the Christian basilica, the 'Tempietto' by Bramante, the Palladian building, etc. Nevertheless, we could define such a model more precisely both by specifying the formal typological elements and by imposing syntagmatic restrictions which allow the model to refer more adequately to certain sets of works. Finally, we could construct typological models not only with respect to the structural or plastic components of architecture (such as column, entablature, etc) but also with respect to its functional shape. This is what one generally does when one talks of architectural typology, embracing such types as the dwelling place, the school, the public building, the church, etc.

In this last instance we can even distinguish *two types of signification in relation to these two kinds of typological models* (probably interrelating with models of other kinds): a *'symbolic' type* of signification, common both to the 'column' (a typological element of the first kind) and also, for example, to the 'dome', 'rotunda', 'apse', and so on (typological elements of the second kind), and a *'referential' type* of signification, which is more closely linked to a typological model of the second kind. *In this way, we can distinguish between a metaphorical signification (an equivalence between an element and something else—a concept or a function—to which it refers), and a metonymical signification (a contiguity between a shape and the actual function with which it is connected).* Metaphor and metonymy are indeed—as Roman Jakobson has recently reaffirmed —complementary procedures, which may always be found together in the signifying role of concrete architectural objects, so that one has rather to appreciate the place of both within a complex hierarchy of procedures (Jakobson, 1967). For example, a metonymical signification, which stems from the strictly functional typology of an object (the contiguity of shape and function), must also be at the same time a metaphorical signification insofar as a certain connection of contiguity becomes inevitably institutionalized and so gains 'symbolic' significance (as, perhaps, in the case of the 'temple'). Sometimes an originally metonymical connection can give rise to a dominant metaphorical association (as in the transition from the basilica form to the Jesuit church). Conversely, we may also have to understand and accommodate the shifting of established metaphorical associations towards new metonymical functions, and so we may have to take into account a further stratification of metaphorical and metonymical signification (as in the case of the 'lay temple' during the Renaissance or the Neo-classical period).

At any rate, even bearing in mind all possible refinements and delimitations, *a typological model seems at the same time too general and too limited to allow adequate analyses* of architectural objects whatever they may be. On the one hand, it does not allow one to define an object or range of objects closely enough, since it cannot take into account all those further non-typological factors which contribute to establishing these objects in concrete terms. On the other hand, it cannot be sufficiently generalizable, since general and usefully applicative models can be constructed only in respect of a restricted range of objects. Furthermore, *it too easily permits the establishment of an equivalence between architectural significance and its verbal 'translation'*, according to one type of approach which is in danger of becoming simply a short cut, a way of facilitating a task which is in fact difficult (Barthes, 1967). In any case, it is more interesting and appropriate to tackle those aspects of architecture—and in general of many so-called non-verbal languages—which seem to be more 'specific' to it; that is to say, those aspects which differentiate architecture from language in a proper sense and at the same time identify it more accurately in terms of its actual structure, for example in terms of 'spatiality'.

Space as 'Essence' and Space as a Model

Naturally, we do not consider the 'essence' or specificity of architecture as if architecture were definable in a rigorous sense (any more than it would be for any particular 'art'), but it would seem that we still cannot deny that even the poorly conceived question of the 'essence' of architecture is a response to some legitimate requirement. This 'essence' has recently been determined, on the basis of an authoritative tradition, as consisting of that *space* which would constitute precisely that which is of a specific and pertinent nature within architecture. In reality, when we talk of 'space', we are employing an ambiguous notion which has a number of diverse meanings, depending on what point of view we adopt—whether geometrical, perceptual or practical (in the sense of a space being 'accessible') (Prak, 1968, pp. 11–13). Thus Bruno Zevi, when he introduced the idea of 'space', really referred to 'internal space'—a notion which is already somewhat more precise. However, this idea also introduces, as a result of its materiality, some unacceptable paradoxes. For example, it necessitates the exclusion from the field of architecture of such objects as the Greek temple, the pyramid, and the bridge, which would accordingly have to be considered more as sculpture on an urban scale than as architecture in a strict sense (Zevi, 1949).

This would not create so much of a problem if there did

not remain to be explained the strong parallelism which we feel exists between such urban sculpture and what we term 'architecture', rather than regarding such objects as being closer to what we prefer to call 'sculpture', and, *more importantly,* if there did not exist an infinite number of intermediate cases which prevent us from deciding clearly whether or not we have to do with an internal space. To what extent must a space be internal and practicable (that is, materially enclosed and accessible by man) in order for it to constitute the *essence* of architecture? Moreover, it does not seem either that the recent attempt of de Fusco to adopt and modify such a criterion within a semiological context is able to resolve the difficulties of Zevi's position while at the same time retaining the specificity of the criterion itself. In fact, the substitution for the concept of an internal and accessible space of the notion of a semiological space (which is not necessarily internal or accessible) either simply amounts to an unsatisfactory combination of formal and material considerations, which leaves intact the difficulties which stem from Zevi's attitude in this respect, or else it ceases to be a criterion according to which to define the language of architecture (de Fusco, 1969, pp. 6 ff.).

It is precisely this conclusion regarding non-specificity that particularly interests us, although we are afraid that it will be difficult for de Fusco (and those who have been approaching architecture from a semiological point of view) to accept it. And yet a 'semiological space' (space as 'meaning') cannot be other than a *'virtual space'*, and as such can be easily applied to perspective painting or to the 'schiacciato' technique of Donatello and his school. One could object that this technique is a mere representation of space, and that it is not 'space' in a strict sense, but even in architecture space is never reducible to a simple datum (internal or external, empty or full, accessible or not). Space is not 'something' articulated simply according to technical expediency; rather, it is really *a representational space—a space formed according to various schema and procedures.* In addition to this, there exist a number of intermediate cases which provide evidence of the close correlation which may be found between architectural space and pictorial or sculptural space: one has only to consider the most extreme illusionism of Bramante, which may be held to constitute an 'ideal' example of a link between Brunelleschi and Donatello (see, for example, Bruschi, 1969, p. 206).

For our part, we do not dispute such 'impure' examples, since they allow us to see what there is in common between different arts, but they do not support the notion of space as a 'specifically architectural' criterion. Intentionally or not, such a conclusion, which supports the non-specificity of a spatial model with regard to architecture, seems unavoidable in the work of de Fusco. Here, indeed, semiological space is considered as the essence of architecture; the meaning of such a space—and the meaning of architecture—corresponds not to its functionality, connected with an internal and accessible space, but to its symbolic value (as in the case of the Palladian 'Rotunda'—a microcosm which alludes metaphorically to the macrocosm). Such 'spatial meaning' will not be easily distinguished from the 'spatial meaning' of a column or of any other plastic element, even if it is solid, which has spatiality and possesses a symbolic value. From here it is only a short step to the spatiality of painting and sculpture, unless one again reintroduces *also* those very material characteristics (internality and accessibility) which a semiological perspective would require to be corrected in formal terms.

Thus the notion of spatial meaning appears to be interesting and productive precisely to the extent to which it renounces the materiality and specificity of spatial criteria as having the character of an 'essence', and leads us instead towards considerations of a more formal nature. Every concession to materiality, even if only partial, reintroduces serious analytical difficulties and in effect militates against a properly semiotic approach. However, if we are aware of these difficulties, this does not preclude the possibility of adopting the criterion of 'space' as being useful in order to discuss architecture (even if this criterion is not confined to architecture), that is, such a criterion is quite legitimate so long as it is determined according to the characteristics of appropriate spatial models—e.g. a model of a geometric kind.

The Hypothesis of a Geometric Model and its Syntagmatic Relations

In order to remain consistent with the examples already given, let us try to isolate the three-dimensional spatial configuration of baroque fabric, which may be determined by both internal and external structural elements, insofar as this serves to identify a 'structured space' in terms of points, segments, and surfaces. Alternatively we could simply consider a single two-dimensional aspect—for example, a section or, in particular, a plan. *We shall analyse such a space or surface according to a relation of combination of solid or planar geometric elements—that is, by means of the super-*

imposition or contiguity of such elements, the condition of linearity obviously not being required in assessing their interrelation. The analysis will be conducted in terms of contrastive relations between the elements, from a syntagmatic point of view, and in terms of oppositive relations from a paradigmatic point of view. By doing this, we will not have segmented the material object of analysis, rather we will have simply applied to it a formal geometric model. *Such a model is composed of discrete elements through which the spatial continuum is analysable (rather than 'decomposable') while, at the same time, each of these elements is characterized by its peculiar continuity.*

This particular hypothetical example might seem elementary and obvious, but it is not at all so from the more general point of view of theory and application. On the contrary, we cannot even tell with precision that it may be successfully and usefully applicable. To think of specifying our example in terms of concrete architectonic objects, while certainly not absurd, is nevertheless unadvisable, since it would be too easy to fall into broad oversimplifications, which would be theoretically unrewarding and even misleading. From a paradigmatic point of view, therefore, we have very little to add for the moment. However, it would seem possible to add something from a syntagmatic point of view (even though in a very incomplete way) which could throw some light on the actual constitution and useful application of geometric models or of models of a similar type. Such suggestions would *not* in general concern *all possible syntagmatic relations,* but—in order to simplify our propositions and make them more accessible—they would *only* concern *those relations of superimposition through which it is possible to assess whether or not one or more of the elements thus combined has a generating, or dominant, function in the context of hypotheses concerning, for example, syntagmatic arrangement.*

Within these definite limits, *we venture to suggest the possibility of considering such relations as falling into three distinct classes, between which there could be set up a correlation.* These are:

(a) *a class of 'syntactic' relations*—defined as a superimposition of certain elements to none of which is it possible to ascribe a dominant role (e.g. S. Carlino);

(b) *a class of 'hypotactic' relations*—defined as a superimposition of certain elements to one or more of which it is possible to ascribe a dominant role, other elements being subordinate or dependent (a possible example being the interior of S. Maria in Campitelli);

(c) *a class of 'paratactic' relations*—defined as the non-superimposition (or 'zero-superimposition') of elements.

Of course, there are other points of view from which it is possible to discuss the question of syntagmatic dominance, even among elements which are not superimposed. For example, there is the case of urban structures or complexes of constructions which are dimensionally articulated in both a syntactic, hypotactic, and paratactic way. In any case, in general it is not a matter of applying one or other type of syntagmatic relation, but of applying a number of interrelated types of relation in a complex syntagmatic hierarchy. This proviso would already seem to guarantee a certain productivity to our hypothesis, insofar as this method of application will not result in a schematic and mechanical classification.

Thus we would have, in the extreme case of a series of prefabricated units, a type of paratactic relation, whilst, in the Unité d'Habitation by Le Corbusier, we would have to integrate a paratactic modular relation with a subordinate hypotactic relation, which is applicable to the geometric element in the building insofar as it completely encompasses the individual primary elements and results from considering the sum of those elements. Precisely because it is based on addition, the hypotactic relation is hierarchically subordinate to the paratactic relation: it is not the enclosing space which generates, in the first instance, the enclosed spaces, but rather these enclosed spaces which, by virtue of their modular (paratactic) nature, determine the enclosing space. This is an observation which, whether or not it is true in the case of Le Corbusier, is certainly true in many examples of modern architecture including several projects by Nervi (such as the famous hangers or the Palace of Labour built for the Italia '61 exhibition in Turin) whose dimensions and overall proportions do not obey any rules other than those imposed by the number of spatial or structural elements selected. Furthermore, in some more complex instances of modular architecture (thinking principally of Le Corbusier's 'Modulor'), it is possible to further analyse the primary spatial elements in themselves according to a type of syntactic or hypotactic dimensional relation, which may even affect the determination of syntagmatic relations within the overall structure which results from the arrangement of these elements. For example, in the case of S. Spirito by Brunelleschi, a paratactic relation of great importance (between the spatial 'cells' of the aisles, the series of small apses which correspond to them, and so on) is subordinated to a primary hypotactic relation. Also, the basic syntactic structure of S. Carlino implies, as a subordinate hierarchical relation, a hypotactic structure (the connection between the space of the cupola, which ideally extends to the floor of the church, and the syntactic articulations of the lower space of the church). Furthermore, with respect of these spatial articulations, a paratactic structure is also implied which is not dominant, but which is nevertheless essential in order to grasp the complex syntagmatic interplay of the subspaces of this complex syntactic space—which are each equivalent one with another and yet which are disjunct in a paratactic sense. To clarify this last observation, we could perhaps also cite the syntactic space of S. Ivo (also by Borromini) which does not seem to imply a subordinate paratactic relation of equal relevance, being no longer a systematic *deformation* of a traditional concentric or longitudinal spatial schema, but which represents the institution of an original scheme which is thereby placed in a definite *opposition* to any traditional scheme.

The Hypothesis of a Graphic/Figurative Model and the 'Class of Variants'

The construction of a geometrical model such as we have described, however, still does not seem to be adequate to describe those complex architectural examples already cited, with regard to which we were only able to arrive at a very general level of analysis without sufficient explanatory power. In order to avoid this shortcoming we would have to specify such a model at a level over and above that of economy and manipulability. *In any case, it would be helpful to have appropriate geometric models able to render spaces analysable not in a direct way but—in conjunction with a type of analysis already suggested—in an intermediate way, through the analysis of the internal and external contours of a section. That is to say, we need a distinct geometrical model which can reveal the contours of the plastic envelope or of the spatial enclosure of the structure which has previously been analysed according to geometrical and more general models as consisting of two- and three-dimensional elements.* Such a further analysis, which is the more useful since the profile of these contours is not implicit in the spatial structure as such, apprehends, in fact, another aspect of the architectonic object which resides *not so much in its geometric spatiality as in its 'figurativity'.* This figurativity can have a subordinate, almost invisible, role as in the limiting case of a certain rational, and classical, architectural tradition, in which the profile of the contours is embodied, so to speak, in the underlying structure—where, in other words, spatiality and figurativity almost coincide. Alternatively, this figurativity can assume a dominant and almost exclusive role—this being the case in certain baroque facades which are completely independent, in visual terms also, of the spatial structure of the fabric.

We suggest that it is possible to construct (for example, in terms of a straightforward horizontal section, or 'plan') a graphic/figurative model composed of linear geometric elements, which can be expressed also by means of mathematically-based analytical methods. This has been suggested, although with differing intentions, by Garroni, (1967), and Eco, (1968). What seems more interesting here is that *an analysis of this type requires not the determination of elements through highly accurate representations of the actual curves which describe a figurative outline, but their determination by means of suitably approximate representations which then assume the status of invariants. It is also possible to establish that a pair of curves can represent the upper and lower confines of a range of curves, linked between themselves according to certain rules and which constitute in this respect an invariant element. Thus with regard to such an invariant, the curves which are actually given (or their graphic representations) act as variants.* Therefore, our aim is to construct a system of classes of variants determined in a manner appropriate to the type of analysis we intend to conduct. For example, we may be interested in studying the architectonic language of a given period, of a group of architects associated with a common objective, of a single artist, or even of a single work. On the other hand, we may wish to study common aspects of a group of works even if they are located at different points in time.

Apart from the possibility of considering even formal or geometric models as semiotic models, we should remember what has been said previously on the subject of possible typological models and on the possibility of analysis, by means of verbal equivalents, on the basis of homogeneity. It should be clear, then, that not only is it possible to interrelate appropriate geometric models and typological models—which are more evidently connected with what we intend to constitute the 'sense' of an architectonic work—but also that, through such interrelation, the geometric aspects cannot avoid having some effect on the sense established in terms of the typological models. This goes to emphasize that the formal and even geometric view of a work of art (such as was held by Wölfflin) is not in fact irreconcilable with the iconological model (such as was developed by Panofsky) which is simultaneously typological, symbolic, and employs verbal equivalents, and that an integration of these two viewpoints is possible if we recognize *the peculiarly heterogeneous character of artistic language.*

Theoretical Observations: the Criterion of Competence and the Procedure of Analysis Through Specification

As we have already noted, in order to construct such models it is unthinkable that we should proceed according to purely graphic or mathematical criteria. Furthermore, even if this were possible, there is no way that we can ensure that a model constructed in this way, which may be arbitrarily characterized by a high degree of simplicity and rigour, could then be actually applicable. The test of applicability obviously cannot be sacrificed in favour of an arbitrariness as splendid as it is useless (Hjelmslev, 1963); therefore the intervention of further constructive criteria is required for the construction of such models. Moreover, such criteria constitute a guarantee against the possibility that such an analysis may not prove to be semiotically pertinent, as, for example, a chemical or physical analysis of the material which actually realizes the form of a work would not be semiotically pertinent. *In other words, it is necessary to establish, apart from purely geometric or mathematical considerations, the criteria of pertinence of those elements which constitute the adopted model and in terms of which a group of concrete realizations can be effectively regarded as a group of variants with respect to one or more formal invariants.* At the lowest possible level—that of the mechanism of perception—such criteria will be governed by the laws or conditions of perception (a study forming part of a specialized branch of psychology); in other words, *by the competence (in the sense employed by Chomsky) of the perceiver.* At a higher level, *such competence will eventually become more complex by virtue of other implicit psychological structures, as well as considerations of 'taste', culture, and historical knowledge* which also seem to come into play at the level of perception as such. We mean that what can be grasped as being distinct in a pertinent way (i.e. as an 'invariant') at the level of perception, can also be apprehended, by changing psychical and cultural/historical parameters, as a variant of another, more general, invariant. Such a possibility will tend to attenuate and modify the strength of even the original perceptual invariant: in other words, perception always entails cultural aspects.

It is not a question of renouncing the pretensions to scientific respectability of a semiotic analysis, but rather of anchoring this analysis on a solid basis, that is, upon the phenomenon of communication itself, where signs are never simply something consistent in themselves but are in fact signs insofar as they can be analysed and interpreted at different levels with regard to various (historical, cultural, psychological) parameters. *This appeal to competence by no means necessitates that only a subjective result would be obtained*, even if we cannot claim that the notion of competence can be expressed in the form of universal structures or that different levels of competence can be strictly determined through defined operations of transformation. Assuming that it is in principle possible to construct very general models (not generalizable further and so applicable to a vast variety of objects), the different particular models will be obtainable not through operations of transformation according to universal rules, but through operations of specification—that is, through *constructive creative procedures*. Thus the models which are specified may prove adequate to the analyis of certain groups of objects of more restricted scope, while continuing to serve as analytic models and not simply as incoherent groupings of empirical data. In this sense, the restricted cogency of such models—the possibility, in fact, of violating the conditions they impose—together with the incidence of the factor of 'historicity' (which has sometimes led to a renunciation of the use of models in favour of a mythical 'individuality' and 'creativity' of the historical fact—as in the historicism of Croce) may nevertheless be expressed in analytical and 'scientific' terms.

Theoretical Observations: The Non-specificity of the Model

Concerning the problem of the identification of architectural codes, it has been said that *a geometric or mathematical model could not be considered insofar as it is not specific to architecture—that is, many other objects, even if they are not 'architectonic', can be described with reference to such a model—while other specific aspects of architectural language could not be explained and rendered analysable by such a model.* Eco has written on this subject: 'The fact that architecture is describable on the basis of a geometric code doesn't mean that architecture as such is based on a geometric code.' (Eco, 1968). Confronted with this type of objection, we must observe (having recognized the accuracy of Eco's conclusion that a 'langue' of architecture does not exist as such) that *a model or code (at whatever level of specification) is never, by definition, specific to any set of given material phenomena, nor can it ever analyse such a set exhaustively.* It seems to us that the question should be framed in another way. A model will always be legitimate so long as it can be referred (even if not exclusively) to a set of given objects, and it will be useful in operative terms with regard to these objects to the extent that it is possible to specify such a model adequately. This also applies in the case of architecture, or rather in the case of a certain range of objects that we call architectonic. With this reservation, such a model may still be termed 'specific' in a loose sense.

In particular terms, this means that a model specified to a certain degree with respect to a group of objects is only, properly speaking, useful as a model insofar as it finds itself in a twofold connection:

(a) *with parallel models specified differently, at the same level*, with respect to another set of objects (which are, for example, diachronically contiguous with the set of objects already considered);

(b) *with models specified more or less precisely*, i.e. with respect to subsets of the given set or, alternatively, with respect to sets which contain the given set as their subset.

Therefore there is a 'horizontal' relation between models which affect the (synchronic) analysis of an object in its internal diachronic dimension (for example, the object 'Renaissance classical architecture', as distinct from 'Gothic architecture'). There is also a 'vertical' relation between models which affect the synchronic analysis of such an object at varying levels of specification. For example, 'Renaissance classical architecture' may be variously specified in terms of 'the architecture of Brunelleschi' in a more detailed context or, alternatively, in terms of 'classicism' or even 'architecture' or simply as 'a means of forming visible objects'. Thus a model may be regarded as being 'specific' with respect to certain given objects simply to the extent to which it is applicable to those objects. In practical terms, then, a model is never an isolated model, but should rather be considered as a series of models, or as a model susceptible to being specified in different ways and at different levels. It is possible, therefore, that a very general model could be, in practice, specified in different ways, and could in this sense become 'specific' to objects which belong to sets having different 'specific' characteristics. Thus such a model could be considered to apply both to a group of architectonic objects, a group of pictorial objects, or even to a group of musical objects, and so on.

We can see this clearly enough at the level of current critical practice; for instance, when we introduce the notion of 'rhythm' and refer it to various different objects. In fact, such a notion either does not have any sense as a common yardstick (it being rather a matter of a multiplicity of notions which acquire a 'sense' only in the context of somewhat restricted applications), or—as seems more acceptable—it must be possible to demonstrate that underlying such a common notion there is a general model (and a general 'sense') which may be variously specified at different levels, and which is applicable to phenomena that require in addition some support or some residual distinct material. In fact, the notion of 'rhythm' has often been employed in a very general way, and in accordance with different usages—for example, with reference to both spatial and temporal phenomena—while other authors prefer to limit its use solely to the temporal dimension, so that with regard to the spatial dimension, such a notion would be nothing but an analogous extension—a simple 'metaphor' (Ejchenbaum, in *Formalisti,* 1971; Metz, 1971). A useful discussion of this problem is given by Seymour Chatman (1965) who seems in one way to accept the generalizing thesis, but against this tends to reduce the problem to one of semantics—as if, in other words, it would be simply a matter of coming to an agreement every time about the meaning of the word, adopting either a spatial or temporal sense; in any event, to take the meaning of the term 'rhythm' in a general sense would require the further distinction between 'two kinds of rhythms, temporal and spatial' (Chatman, 1965, pp. 18 ff.). This argument, however, seems clearly insufficient, even though it is apparently based on common sense. The very spatial reformulation of rhythm in a temporal sense which is adopted by Chatman (for example, in the sequences: * * * * ; ** ** ** ** ; ** * / ** * / ** * / ** * / etc.) seems to provide evidence that we must presuppose that there exists something in common between spatiality and temporality, that is to say that we must postulate a more general model, specifiable in different ways, which is applicable to both spatial and temporal phenomena. Kant was well aware of this in relation to very similar theoretical problems (Kant, 1959, Proposition 14) and this has also been clarified in a very convincing way from a mathematical point of view (Weyl, 1962).

In conclusion, from a strictly theoretical point of view, this notion of a highly specific code does not seem to be germane; even a highly specified model, which is therefore 'specific' in an approximate sense, is not necessarily applicable only to a given range of phenomena which we may call, for example, 'architectonic', even though we may not be able to actually determine to what other phenomena it could be applied. *The objection which we maintain here concerns the unacceptable hypothesis that there exists a bi-univocal correspondence between a code and certain material phenomena to which that code can be applied, according to which such phenomena are considered to be specific irrespective of the applicability to such phenomena of the code itself. It seems, moreover, that such a cor-*

respondence excludes the possibility of analysing the same
phenomena in a semiotically pertinent way with respect to
different models or codes. This hypothesis does not take account of the formal and arbitrary character of every procedure of constructing a model, even if this is conducted in
such a way that it is applicable and adequate to the set of
objects that we wish to study. Thus, either everything which
the constructed model turns out to be applicable to is defined as being 'architectonic' (thus compelling even common
language to observe the terminological arbitrariness of the
theory), or we simply accept the flexibility of an intuitive,
materially-based notion of architecture (foregoing to register
an objection to the non-specificity of that code, or model,
which is applicable to what we call 'architecture'). *This
means that the term 'architectonic code' must remain in a
strict sense incorrect,* since a 'code' or 'model' may be considered as such only insofar as it is something which is formal, whilst what is said to be specifically 'architectonic' is
simply a range of *given* material phenomena, surreptitiously
presented as a set of *possible* phenomena. It is on the basis
of the ambiguity of the notion of architecture ('architecture'
as a formal model, *and* 'architecture' as material
phenomena) that this misunderstanding is founded, and that
which is heterogeneous is mistaken for that which is
homogeneous. Once prepared, the applicability of definitions and models appropriate to what we call 'architecture'
is not necessarily restricted to the initial phenomena with
regard to which a model has been constructed. This certainly
does not exclude the possibility of speaking of an 'architectural code' (while being aware of the approximateness of
the term) when, for example, we have to do with an inter-
relationship of different models. However, this must not involve us in the mistake of considering as properly 'specific'
either these individual models or any combination of them.
As it happens, the use of such approximate terms does not
usually create important difficulties when we have to deal
with a fairly restricted area of application. The difficulties
arise when such an area of application becomes
larger—above all when we are faced with considerations
regarding the 'essence' of architecture.

   Finally, we must stress that while models based on
geometric criteria (or on any other criteria) can be
semiotically non-pertinent, this does not affect our insistence that semiotic models can also be based on an extra-
semiotic discipline (for instance, on geometry), while being
structured according to a principle which is genuinely
semiotic. We should like to repeat that if, for example, the
spatial organization of architecture has some bearing on its
communicative aims (as seems evident when we combine a
typological model and a spatial model and then examine a

typological architectural object — such as 'church' or 'public building' — in terms of its spatial and figurative features), then a model which permits such an analysis seems once again to partake of the nature of a class of semiotic models, at least at the level of connotation.

Variational Continuity in Architecture. Dynamic Invariants

We shall now attempt to clarify, if possible, *a further important aspect of the problem which stems from the character of continuity of some non-verbal languages;* in particular we shall consider our example of architectural language. In effect, until now we have simply presented the difficulties of considering the so-called continuous languages under the general heading of languages analysable in terms of models made up of discrete elements, the paradigm case of which being verbal language. These invariant elements have been determined according to classifying criteria, a simple example being the classification into 'concave'/'convex' curves — that is to say, into elements which are analogous, even if they belong to a specific, non-linguistic model, to traditional typological elements such as 'column', 'architrave', etc., or in one way even to phonemic elements such as $/x/,/y/$ etc. *However, it seems that we must also consider another type of continuity, or quasi-continuity, which is pertinent at the level of the model.*

Thus, while from a certain point of view we can determine invariant elements of the type 'concave'/'convex' (or, more specifically, a *certain* concave invariant or a *certain* convex invariant, etc.), it would be useful to adopt in addition another point of view so as to determine an invariant as consisting of, for example, the grouping together of certain concave curves, of certain convex curves, and even of certain ambiguous curves, or of straight or quasi-straight segments intermediate between concave and convex curves. (It should become evident that such terms as 'quasi-straight' or 'quasi-continuous' are only in part to be considered as geometrical terms, insofar as they refer to objects defined in terms of cultural and perceptual models; for the notion of 'ambiguous curve' see Arnheim, 1954). Such curves, in other words, could be considered not simply as variants of more than one invariant (e.g. the invariant 'concave' or 'convex' curve) but, more precisely, variants of a single invariant which is characterized by a greater extension. *This latter invariant is grasped as such through the competence (and not merely the perceptual competence) of the producer or of the consumer.* Naturally, the fact that such variants may also be subdivided into groups or classes of 'classificatory' variants (according to classificatory criteria), and that, depending on their falling within this or that group, these variants are eventually distributed according to certain syntagmatic rules, is not without relevance to an exhaustive interpretation of a given architectonic object. In other words, it is a matter of describing the same object in terms of two different models, which are susceptible to being interrelated. However, in the case of the more extended invariant to which we have referred above, the fact that the variants which comprise it can be regarded, from another point of view, as being opposed, means that we must introduce some important modifications to this notion of a 'variant'. Because the variants of such an invariant do not seem to be immediately substitutable one for another, it would seem that we can presuppose a certain variational continuity, or quasi-continuity, between them. Thus we can recognize both a continuity and, at the same time, an oppositional character, which are in some way constitutive of this more extended invariant. (Something of this kind occurs in the case of verbal language at a semantic level, where a class of similarity contains both synonyms and antonyms. See Jakobson, 1966, p. 27.)

Such further aspects of continuity seem to be in a sense more pertinent to the model as such and yet equally capable of being rendered in explicit and discrete terms. We will try to identify these aspects in the special variational connection in terms of which some or all of the variants, belonging to one or more classes of 'classificatory' variants, can be linked together. Thus continuity would cease to be a simple property of variants and invariants and would become a component of the definition of the invariant as such: continuity is considered as variation among variants. *We have thus to consider the possibility of constructing, besides models made up of 'classes of variants'—which we will call 'static invariants', and which are 'classificatory' or 'typological' in a broad sense—models made up also of 'classes of variations'—which we will call 'dynamic invariants' and which are 'formative' or 'structuring'.*

We will try to clarify initially the reasons which have led us to introduce the notion of the dynamic invariant by employing an analogy which seems quite appropriate. *We have in mind the distinction and connection which exists in verbal language between phonematic invariants and intonational invariants* (Jakobson, 1966, p. 18). We shall refer in particular to intonational invariants, considered from the point of view of 'quantity', there being still other types of intonational invariants possible, for example according to pitch, loudness, and size (in the case of written language). Now, when the linguist concerns himself with phonematic invariants, the quantitative intonational differences between variants are by definition simply ignored—but such differences can become pertinent, from another point of view, precisely for the purpose of identifying invariants of a different, 'quasi-dynamic' type. We say 'quasi-dynamic' because some confusion can arise concerning the variational character of the model, precisely as a result of the usual method of notation—justified no doubt by its convenience in relation to the usual analytical objectives. This may be exemplified by the correlation (or quasi-correlation) /x/, /x:/, where only the opposition or difference between 'short' and 'long' is notated explicitly and schematically—that is to say, there is simultaneously and ambiguously an opposition between the (properly correlational) absence or presence of a prolonging of intonation, and between the two extremes of *one and the same* variational entity. In other words, the usual method of analysis could lead us to think of a differentiation into discrete elements, analogous to the differentiation of phonemes; it also lacks the capacity to grasp, at the level of a model, the continuity of the variationality which characterizes the quantitative phenomena of intonation. It is appropriate, therefore, to consider a different and more explicit system of notation of the following type (although this is an imperfect instance which is employed in order to preserve and to extend the use of the usual symbols): /x*/ / [/x/,/x:/,/x::/,/x:::] where /x*/ stands simply for the absence of any prolonging of intonation, and /x/ stands for the lower extreme of the continuous or quasi-continuous variational entity contained by the square brackets[ ]. This type of notation, while very approximate, still suggests clearly enough the pertinent character of continuity or quasi-continuity which is established between the 'variants/variations' of one and the same invariant. Such an invariant may still be defined as a class of variants, but such variants, although they may still be considered as variants of a static invariant (whereby, for example we simply establish the opposition between the absence and the presence of an intonational prolongation), can enter into amongst themselves a further, variational, connection such that their differences as well as their identity contribute to the specific definition of the invariant to which they belong. We do not believe that, within the framework of linguistics proper, this simply amounts to a theoretical complication, without any semiotic consequences of application. Quantitative intonational difference, perhaps together with intonational differences of another type (extending even to include the 'influence of context'), comprise important differentiating conditions which affect the *formal* capacity of the invariant, of which these differences constitute 'variants/variations', to impart information. Let us consider the laconic reply, 'Yes!' This

may be realized according to different quantitative variations of intonation, which may constitute *substantial* (in the
sense used by Hjelmslev) expressions of, for example, 'self-
confidence' (/e/); 'respect' (/e:/); 'uncertainty' (/e::/); or 'impa-
tience' (/e:::/), etc.

It would now seem that, within certain approximate limits,
a comparison between the linguistic phenomena of intonation and the non-linguistic phenomena of variation is sufficiently exact to furnish a useful analogy. Let us consider, for
example, a verbal discourse or written text which possesses
an unambiguous and neutral aim of communicating. This requires a high degree of distinction between its elements — in
other words, these elements are unambiguously seen as
distinct realizations of static invariants. Such a discourse or
text can, however, allow for the presence in places of some
unpredictable intonational emphasis, although this has a
temporary role and does not force the listener or reader to
reinterpret the whole discourse or the entire text from an
emotional point of view. (If this were the case it would imply
that we should refer constantly to an intonational mode so
that a single distinctive element could be interpreted emo-
tionally as 'coldness', 'detachment', etc.) *In the same way, in
the case of architecture also, even if this is conceived according to a prevailing criterion of classification (for example,
classical architecture in a broad sense), we can observe such
aspects as 'accents', 'cadences', both calculated and unfore-
seen expressive 'liberties', all of which are closely comparable
to intonational variations.* As a limiting case, we may think of
the volutes of the link between the lower and upper parts of
some quattrocento façades (such as S. Maria Novella in
Florence, or S. Agostino in Rome): 'decorative' elements to
whose static invariance there must surely be associated a
noticeable dynamic invariance which confers an expressive
or intonational 'spark' to this single element, which we attempt to record as 'baroque taste'. *But above and beyond
such limiting cases, however easy to add to, there remains the
fact that any architectonic organism, or group of organisms,
even if strictly adhering to a static model, must present individual variations which it would be inadequate to interpret
'only' as variants, and which, accordingly, it is appropriate to
interpret also as 'variations', by referring them, that is, to a
variational model.* In this sense, the architectonic organism
can and must be interpreted also in terms of its particular intonation — an intonation which should be considered to be in
no way elusive or unanalysable.

So much for the general validity of this analogy. More
specifically it should be clear that with the notion of the
dynamic invariant and of dynamic models, we did not want
to simply present for consideration aspects which are in
some way superficial, purely contingent, and to this extent

easily deductible according to fundamental considerations which would be exclusively of a static type. Those aspects of architecture which we have called 'intonational' do not in any way possess that 'suprasegmental' character which linguists attribute to the intonational features of verbal language. In reality it is not strictly correct, even in this last case, to postulate a kind of *objective* basis as an 'essence' with regard to which those phenomena would be *objectively* 'suprasegmental'; instead it would be more correct to admit that it is appropriate *to select* a point of view which is more adequate in terms of the cognitive function of language. It is interesting to note that an architectural example, brought forward by a linguist, provides evidence of an incomplete awareness of the relative character of the distinction between communication in a cognitive sense and the other aspects of verbal language, even if the dominance of the cognitive function can be regarded as being obvious and quasi-objective from a practical point of view:

> Buildings aim to protect human beings against the elements. This is their primary and fundamental function. Doubtless it is not uncommon that a building could serve more to impress those who visit it than it would ensure efficient protection. But, even if, starting from its conception, we have never seen in it anything other than an expression of pomp; the building will never fail to testify, through its structure, its primary function of protection. (Martinet, 1965)

This conception of architecture is either simply tautological — in that architecture is indeed fundamentally protective *but only insofar as* we consider it from the point of view of protection — or it is frankly inadequate. This position is even factually unacceptable — one has only to think of the diachronic nexus between megalithic sacred enclosures and antique temples, and of the strong bearing of this on the suceeding architectural tradition. We can accordingly say that if in many ways the supposition of a 'primary' cognitive function in verbal language can be considered as being almost obvious, such a supposition does not come into effect, even at the level of common sense, in the case of architecture.

At this point, the possibility of applying the proposed distinction between static and dynamic invariants seems, in a number of different ways, to go well beyond the analogy with linguistic intonational phenomena. We shall merely content ourselves with some examples of possible applications. *In the first instance, it seems that it is precisely the notion of a dynamic model which is able to permit an appropriate analysis, both from a synchronic and diachronic*

*point of view, of architectonic objects. In this way, one can
realize analytically the unity of the vertical connection between models specified at different levels, and of the
horizontal connection between contiguous models, which
have been mentioned above.* Such a notion gives us the
possibility of constructing a fairly general model which may
be applied to a group of objects distributed over a large span
of time, and which at the same time contains in itself, in the
form of its variational character, the explicit possibility of
specification of differing types and at different levels. Such a
model clearly contains in itself in a systematic form the majority of those intonational aspects which at first sight seem
to be more superficial, with respect to the apparently dominant static aspects. Furthermore, it definitively eliminates
the conflict between the normative character of the architectural code and the individual architectonic realizations,
which deferred to the code only partially—a conflict which
was traditionally resolved as an ambiguous compromise by
virtue of the obscure idea of 'tolerance'. Such a conflict
arises from the fictitious opposition between the code on the
one hand and the concrete work on the other—that is, between two completely heterogeneous entities— but it can no
longer persist if we can encompass both the specifiability of
the code, so that it is never presented as a simple abstraction, and its variational property. This property allows us to
articulate the code in terms of its differences so that it has
the capacity to explain analytically even individually determined works, without in any way involving a mythical or
unanalysable 'individuality'.

Doubtless it is true that sometimes differences between
variants of the same invariant class can be considered as
secondary; this is in accordance with the view of those who
would emphasize, in a negative or positive way, that the proper function of the code can be specified only at a high level
of generality. It is also true that such differences cannot be
considered to be irrelevant in every respect, which observation at least allows us to understand the viewpoint of those
who unilaterally insist that the concrete work is 'the measure
of itself'. In the case of the Doric Greek temple, reference to
a model composed of static invariants certainly would have
priority (from a certain point of view) over a model composed of dynamic invarients; but, on the other hand, it is precisely this latter model which will be able to explain the determinate structure which is particular to certain subgroups of
Doric temples, or to a single temple as being differentiated
with respect to other subgroups or to other single temples. *In
other words, it is precisely dynamic models (even when they
have a secondary role) which enable us to understand more
completely not only the synchronic compactness of the
diachronic dimension itself, in which a certain group of archi-*

tectonic objects are located, but even those more delicate and elusive aspects (which are properly regarded as being 'original', 'creative', etc.) of architectonic phenomena which consist of 'concrete' or 'individual' works. Therefore we have defined the dynamic invariant also as a 'formative' or 'structuring' invariant, as distinct from the static invariant, which, in its 'classificatory' character, would seem to provide us only with a basis of general rule).

This analytical connection between the dynamic and the productive character of the model is even more evident in the following further example of application, somewhat different from the first example, but linked with it in many ways. *This second example involves those cases in which variational differences can be considered as being primary, when compared with the fact that recordable variations can be attributed from another point of view to one or more static invariants. In such cases the dynamic model would appear to demonstrate in an analytical manner the creative and productive choices of a certain group of architects or of a single architect or artist.* In contrast to the example of the Greek temple already cited, let us consider here the entrance steps and the Doric colonnade which dominates them in the Güell Park by Gaudí. In this case, in spite of the apparent static arrogance of the classical quasi-quotation, there seems to be a primary connection with a model composed of dynamic invariants (so long as we deliberately simplify the complex synchronic and diachronic questions of interpretation connected with this example). This connection exists insofar as such a model is better suited to the 'organic' character of the work in question, than would be one or more models made up of static invariants. These models would account, on the one hand, for the presence of a certain generic characterization) (e.g. pertaining to 'art nouveau' or to a certain 'Catalan modernism') and, on the other hand, for an even weaker 'neo-hellenic' or 'Doric' characterization, which is intentionally subordinate to a radically different type of organization through systematic and violent deformation. In this case an appropriate dynamic model could be constructed, such that it would reconstitute even the static models which may be opposed to it—such static models no longer being considered as static but considered as incidents of a more complex variational model.

We have intentionally made reference to 'organicity', which is a current notion within the context of architectural historiography and criticism, since we believe that the proposal of a general model of a dynamic type can contribute at least in part to a better definition of this phenomenon. If organicity is not to remain purely and simply a mystery—an indeterminate analogy derived from biology—it may be determined in one of the two following ways. In the first place it can be interpreted in terms of *static equivalences*—hence, for example, the geometric and rational organicity of certain concentrically planned buildings of late Roman imperial architecture or of the Renaissance; in the second place, it can be interpreted in terms of a *systematic employment of variational entities.* From the first point of view, 'organicity' may be considered as 'necessity'; from the second point of view, 'vitality'. Other definitions are also possible. For instance, organicity may be seen as a relation between architecture and nature, or between architecture and man (in the sense of scale, of congruence between architectural form, customs, culture, and so on), however, such definitions could cause us to regard architecture under other equally possible and useful headings, such as that of sociology, for example, rather than in terms of spatiality and figurativity. To return to Gaudí, the systematic use of variational elements is typical of the Casa Milá and especially of the chapel of S. Coloma at Cervelló, where we might almost say that we have to do with a single, highly complex, variational entity, in opposition to which there persists in a certain sense the static architectonic tradition, considered as an entirety simultaneously denied and retained (and hence 'aufgehoben'). It is this tradition, indeed, that permits Gaudí's chapel to be something which is determined and therefore to 'make sense'.

It is not a matter, in this case, of introducing unrepeatability and creative unanalysability under the guise of employing a model, but, on the contrary, of demonstrating how, even in extreme and apparently more difficult cases, we can speak in an analytical way of 'creativity' and 'originality', etc., only by virtue of having introduced adequate hypotheses. How many elements are there in the interplay within Gaudí's chapel? One? Twelve? Or two thousand? We cannot say, nor do we care. What it is important to establish is that, to the extent to which the 'organicity' of Gaudí's work is not adequately analysable in terms of static invariants, it must nevertheless be analysable in terms of dynamic invariants, even though such invariants are considered in interrelation with static invariants. The 'forms' created by Gaudí are not simply subjective or improvised inventions, such as the absence or feebleness of static invariants may lead us to suppose (Pevsner, 1968), but they respond to an undertaking which one can render in precise terms, as some authors have tried to show (Pane, 1964; Bohigas, 1969). Each of these forms comprises, in other words, variant/variations of one or more dynamic invariants. This is so not because Gaudí is, or is not, a 'genius', but because there does not exist a formation of objects that does not presuppose an implicit or explicit model, and because there is no formation of objects that cannot be analysed according to models. A form which is in any sense casual, contingent, unrepeatable, or unanalysable is something which simply does not exist, or which amounts to a contradiction in terms.

References

Alarcos Llorach, E. (1968) Les Representations graphiques du langage, in *Le Langage*, 'Encyclopédie de la Pléiade', Paris Gallimard.

Arnheim, R. (1954) *Art and Visual Perception: A Psychology of Creative Eye*, Berkeley—Los Angeles. The University of California Press.

Barthes, R. (1967) Semiologia e urbanistica, in *Op.cit., 10*.

Bohigas, (1969) *Architettura modernista, Gaudi e il movimen to catalano, Turin Einaudi*.

Brandi, C. (1966) Le due vie, Bari Laterza.

Brandi, C. (1967) *Struttura e architettura*, Turin Einaudi.

Brandi, C. (1968) Sulla nozione di codice nella critica d'arte, in *Rivista d'Estetica*, 13, 2.

Bruschi, A. (1969) *Bramante architetto*, Bari Laterza.

Chatman, S. *A Theory of Meter*, The Hague Mouton.

De Fusco, R. (1968) *Il codice dell'architettura, Antologia di trattatisti*, Naples Edizioni Scientifiche Italiana.

De Fusco, R. (1969) Significanti e significati della Rotonda palladiana, in *Op.cit.*, 16.

Della Volpe (1968) in *Linguaggio e ideologia nel film*, Cafieri.

Eco, U. (1968) *La struttura assente*, Milan Bompiani.

Formalisti (1971) Ejchenbaum, Brik, Sklovskij, etc, *I formalisti russi nel cinema* (Italian translation), Milan Garzanti.

Garroni, E. (1967) Popolarità e comunicazione nel cinema, in *Filmcritica*, 175, (appeared later in *Progetto di semiotica*, Bari Laterza 1972).

Granger, E. (1968) *Essai d'une philosophie du style*, Paris Colin

Hjelmslev, L. (1963) *Prolegomena to a Theory of Language*, Madison The University of Wisconsin Press.

Jakobson, R. (1966) *Saggi di linguistica generale* (Italian translation) Milan Feltrinelli.

Jakobson (1967) Conversazione sul cinema con R. Jakobson, in *Cinema e film*, 4.

Kant, I. (1959) *Kritik der Urteilskraft,* translated by K. Vorländer, Hamburg F. Meiner.

Martinet, A. (1965) Structure et langue, in *Revue Internationale de Philosophie,* 73 – 74.

Metz, C. (1971) *Langage et cinéma,* Paris Larousse.

Pane, R. (1964) *Gaudi,* Milan Ed. di Comunità.

Pevsner, N. (1968) *The Sources of Modern Architecture and Design,* London Thames & Hudson.

Prak, N. L. (1968) *The language of Architecture,* The Hague Mouton.

Saussure, de F. (1922) *Cours de linguistique générale,* Paris Payot.

Weyl, H. (1962) *La simmetria* (Italian translation) Milan, Feltrinelli.

Zevi, B. (1949) *Saper vedere l'architettura,* Turin Einaudi.

3.3 Structural Linguistics versus the Semiotics of Literature: Alternative Models for Architectural Criticism

Maria Luisa Scalvini

In recent years, the semiotic approach to architecture has moved from different starting-points, and among these two can be, in my opinion, identified as the most important ones. The first is that of general semiotic research, which eventually led to some specific applications in the architectural field; the second is that of some architects, aware of the present lack of theory, and aiming to find solid, scientific grounds for the theoretical construction—which is still to be built—of our discipline. Within Italian studies, Eco and Garroni are, in my view, the most important authors in the first group; Koenig and de Fusco in the second one, both having developed very interesting points of view, with reference respectively to Charles Morris and Ferdinand de Saussure.

I think I can also include myself in this second group, and I will try here to summarize, very briefly, my approach to a semiotic view of architectural criticism, aiming to put in doubt the so widely adopted linguistic model, and suggesting an alternative model of reference: that of literary criticism derived both from structuralism and from a semiotic approach to the literary text. My position is mainly based on Hjelmslev's theory, but with reference to other authors too (especially Prieto and Mukařovský), and it is developed in my last book (Scalvini, 1975).

Following Prieto (see Prieto, 1971a and 1971b), we can consider the whole sphere of semiotic systems as a realm—the so called 'sémiologie de la signification'—including the domain defined as 'sémiologie de la communication'; this, in turn, includes natural languages as a very special part of communication semiology. Some authors of the French School—as for instance Georges

Mounin (see Mounin, 1970—do not accept the idea of a semiotic realm including systems whose basic aim is not communication. In their view, semiotics' borders overlap exactly those of communication. But Prieto's theory allows us to consider the architectural system as a truly semiotic one, belonging to the 'sémiologie de la signification' (that is, to the semiotic realm), even if we must recognize that architecture's basic aim is not a communicative one, but rather that of providing a comfortable environment for human activities (see Broadbent, 1973).

So, if we reconsider the linguistic analogy within this conceptual frame, we can see that language and architecture seem, at first sight, to belong to very distant regions of the semiotic realm. Language is not only a part of the so-called domain of communication, but is also a part characterized by the presence of the double articulation as defined by Martinet. Architecture, on the other hand, belongs to the domain we have called 'sémiologie de la signification', where both the double articulation and the communicative aim are 'suspended', or put aside, so to speak.

However, in recent years as well as all through the history of architectural theories, the linguistic analogy (see Collins, 1965) has exercised such a strong influence that there must be a reason for its widespread adoption. In my view, the very reason behind the use of this analogy must be identified in the fact that both language and architecture are systems with overwhelming influence on human life and environment, the products of which can be plotted in a continuous range of levels, varying in aesthetic value from the poorest level of mere satisfaction of the basic aim within the system under consideration, up to the highest level where this of a more complex result. Now, with reference in particular to Mukařovský (see Mukařovský, 1973), we can distinguish between an extra-aesthetic sphere and an aesthetic sphere, the last one including art as an area whose borderline is very difficult and often impossible to determine. Indeed, difficulties also arise in trying to define the passage from extra-aesthetic to aesthetic domain. But it seems to be 'easier', or more correct, to distinguish between extra-aesthetic and aesthetic, than between aesthetic and art; so we will consider only the first of these two partitions.

Prieto says that, within the 'logic of instruments'—namely the semiology of those systems whose basic aim is not communication—every time the choice of a particular instrument is made, not merely aiming to satisfy a practical need (or, in his terms, to allow some 'operation'), but with the intention of communicating, by means of this choice, a specific conception of the operation itself, there we have 'art', as the particular choice (or behaviour) possesses what he calls a 'style' of its own.

So we can consider architecture as a system, belonging to the realm of the 'sémiologie de la signification', whose basic aim (within the extra-aesthetic sphere as defined by Mukařovský) is the non-communicative one previously mentioned, but whose instruments can be chosen (within the aesthetic sphere) to communicate specific conceptions of the operations they allow. Similarly, we consider language as a system whose basic aim is denotative communication, but whose units can be used to convey a richer significance, as, for instance, in literature, poetry being the most typical case.

The simplest way to synthesize these properties is, in my view, to consider both language and architecture as 'double-level' systems: I mean, as systems having a basic level (with basic aims corresponding to elementary 'products' of the system itself); these same systems, however, at the 'second' level, can be used in quite a different way, and with a much more complex aim, in which the basic aim is still 'enshrined', though having lost the main role which characterized it at the basic level.

Now, after the reference we have already made to Prieto's theory, a second one must be introduced: Hjelmslev's concept of 'connotative semiotics' (see Hjelmslev, 1961). As is well known, in Hjelmslev's theory the scheme of a typical semiotics originates from his concept of two main planes, that of expression and that of content. Both planes are split into 'form' and 'substance'; but two only of these four components (namely, the form of expression and the form of content) concur to constitute the semiotic system. In the case of language, for example, the scheme is as follows:

$$
\begin{array}{r}
\text{plane of content} \quad \dfrac{C_s}{C_f} \\[2mm]
\hline
\text{plane of expression} \quad \dfrac{E_f}{E_s}
\end{array}
\Bigg] \quad
\begin{array}{l}
\text{natural language (form of expression} \\
\longleftrightarrow \text{form of content)}
\end{array}
$$

In Eco's well-known transposition of this scheme in architectural terms (see Eco, 1971), we find functions corresponding to the plane of content, and spaces to the plane of expression; both, of course, only in terms of their 'forms': functions as the cultural units actually chosen among all possible functions; spaces as those spatial units which are actually shaped. My criticism of Eco's interpretation of Hjelmslev's scheme in architectural terms is based, firstly, on the fact that, in my opinion, in Eco's transposition function is put, so to speak, in the wrong place (I mean that function can be regarded in terms of 'aim', not of 'content', in the architectural field). The second point is that I think there cannot be space, in architecture, without 'something' we could call a physical enclosure actually shaping spaces we consider, featuring them in terms of texture, colour, and so on.

So, rewriting Hjelmslev's scheme for language in a shorter notation, and adding the basic aim as follows:

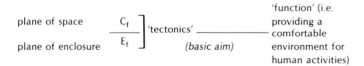

We can attempt to make a transposition for the basic level of architecture in this way:

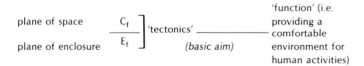

having decided to reserve the word 'architecture' for the second level, and to call 'tectonics' our system when considered at the basic level. We will try now to develop both schemes with reference to the second level.

A 'connotative semiotic' is, in Hjelmslev's theory, a non-scientific semiotic whose plane of expression is a semiotic in itself (whereas a 'metasemiotic' is a scientific semiotic whose plane of content is a semiotic in itself: for instance, linguistics, whose plane of content is natural language).

With reference to language, we will have for the second level the following scheme:

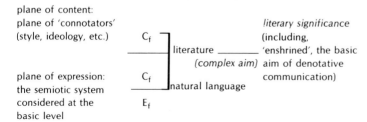

While with reference to the architectural system the scheme could be as follows:

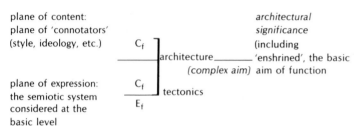

As it is easy to realize, all the theoretical developments synthesized above have actually needed a very complex series of 'passages', which I am obliged here to leave out for obvious reasons.

Now, the problem is that in carrying out semiological

analyses of real buildings, most authors have applied to 'products' belonging to the second level, theoretical tools derived from those of structural linguistics, which had been set up to analyse units belonging to the first level. In other words, a model analysis has been applied, derived from linguistics, to something we could easily compare to literary texts, regardless of the fact that this analysis is concerned with something very different from literature. So, the search for the 'minimal architectural units' corresponding to phonemes, or the attempt to recognize in architecture some degree of articulation in the same sense of Martinet's double articulation, can be explained as resulting from the choice of the wrong model of reference. But if we are interested in semiological analysis of architecture as represented by real, complex buildings (no matter whether designed by Palladio or by Denys Lasdun, whether historical or contemporary), our model must be the semiological criticism of literature, and not structural linguistics.

Some people may argue that we could also be interested in analysing individual 'elements' of architecture, as for instance Eco was in his brilliant essay on the column (see Eco, 1972). I cannot summarize here the arguments developed in my book about that topic, which are mainly derived from the awareness of the different values, extent, and implications involved in architecture — in comparison with language — through the well-known type token dichotomy defined by Peirce. I will only try here to give an example, and suggest that you evaluate the difference between the column as a part of the Greek temple, the column as an isolated monument, and so on, up to 'the column as skyscraper' proposed by Adolf Loos in the competition for the *Chicago Tribune*. Dimensional scale, material, colours, texture . . . all these factors seem to me to emphasize, in architecture, the 'gap' between type and token, in rather a different way from language. It seems, therefore, that semiotic analysis and criticism of architecture must be concerned with real 'texts', not with 'elements'.

I think we can now discuss some problems arising from the theoretical point of view previously exposed; problems which are mainly concerned with applications of these theoretical tools in the history and criticism of architecture.

The difficulties implied, in the historical field, by the reference to the concept of 'structure', are well known. Furthermore, many researchers have considered structuralism and semiotics as the starting-points for two quite different kinds of criticism, the first one aiming to analyse the individual text under discussion, considered as a self-sufficient entity; the second one aiming to consider each text as belonging to a highly interconnected set of works.

It seems to me that, on closer view, a semiotic approach

can help us in solving these difficulties, as it gives the text the greatest importance, making at the same time, however, reference to the notion of 'literary genre'. Thus we could conceive a history of architecture, starting from the semiotic criticism of an individual work or of a group of works (considered as 'architectural texts'), and founded on a series of hypotheses, some of which we could perhaps write down as follows:

—Identifying the total significance of the architectural text considered as a structure in itself (and not as a sum of parts). This implies the analysis of both the plane of expression (often the only one described by the traditional, 'philological' approach, and which in our interpretation is a semiotic in itself) and the plane of content (often the only one taken into account when starting from a preconceived, 'ideological' position);

—Using a methodology derived from both semiotics and structuralism, in the analysis of individual works (or groups of works) as well as in the analysis (aiming to determine more general and 'deep' structures) of the dialectic relationships between *work's structure* —— *author's style* —— *style of the particular age*, and so on.

—Searching for the structural constants of a particular architectural 'genre', or of specific groups of works, along both the synchronic and the diachronic axes.

In this view, semiological analysis is seen as a 'double' process, aiming to fulfil two co-existing objectives: the definition of the structure of the architectural text, considered as an individual, unique object; and the study of this same text considered as the 'ideal' centre of a series of possible associative chains, connecting it to other works in different directions, which imply typological, stylistic, symbolic, iconological, ideological relationships. It is useful to observe that in this 'double' process the two main directions of analysis (the object as unique, the object as the ideal centre of a 'galaxy' of interconnected objects) are not to be separated; on the contrary, they must always be related to one another.

So, we can say that a true semiological analysis must always relate its object(s) to other entities which, according to the different cases, could be the style of the author, other works of the same architect, contemporary works of different architects, and so on. In architecture, these entities can also be represented by what we usually call a 'typology': a concept which, in many respects, could be compared to that of 'literary genre'.

As is well known, among literary genres the folktale has been regarded by many authors—starting from Propp—as a typical problem of morphological structure. So, it is not surprising that the semiological analysis of literature I chose in my book as a model of reference for a possible, initial transposition in terms of architectural criticism was the 'structural analysis of the tale' set up by Roland Barthes (see Barthes, 1969).

The first problem arising in that transposition is the determination of the architectural 'corpus' of the analysis. Let us suppose for a moment that a 'certain' set of architectural texts could correspond, under given conditions, to the literary genre of the tale. Just as the folk tale, even in the variety of its morphology, is only *one* of the literary genres we could consider, in the same way the group of architectural texts our analogy will be concerned with will be *one* among many possibilities of choice. It is useless to try, here, to write down a 'list', so to speak, of all possible groups of architectural texts available for such an analysis. What is worthwhile is the attempt to define the characteristics such a group has to possess. I think that the 'tale analogy' could be quite correctly applied to any group of architectural texts, within which we could verify the presence of the same characteristic features having relevance for the particular analysis we want to develop. And this means that groups will not be identified 'once and for all'; on the contrary, they will be defined, every time, in relationship to the specific analysis to be undertaken. Furthermore, what we could consider as a group with regard to one programme of research could be part of a larger group (or could be split into different, smaller groups) in another; if anything, overlapping conditions must generally be taken into account.

We could decide, for instance, to consider the typology of the 'villa' as corresponding to the literary genre of the tale. Within each of these conceptual areas we could distinguish groups of works which in different degrees are, at the same time, autonomous and related to one another. It is somehow as if we had a set, within which we could identify a series of subsets, differently overlapping; each subset can be studied in relationship to one or more subsets, or even to the whole set.

Let us try now to follow, step by step, the structural analysis of the tale as proposed by Roland Barthes, seeking a possible transposition in architectural terms. Following Benveniste's theory of levels, Barthes reminds us that relationships in a text (for us, a literary text or architectural work) can be of two different kinds: 'distributional', if connecting units belong to the same level; 'integrative', if connecting units belong to different levels. A main problem in the structural analysis of the tale is the definition of the 'smallest narrative units'; these units, whose 'size' is originated by their own functional role within the story, are called 'functions'. 'Functions' can only be identified by starting from the individual text under analysis, as there are no *a priori* functions. It is easy to recognize that this approach is quite other from that which—inspired by structural linguistics—

aims to define the architectural equivalents for elements like signs, morphemes, phonemes, and so on. The process of literary structural analysis is indeed completely different from that of linguistic analysis, as in this last case minimal units are previously defined, whereas in the first we must every time derive our minimal narrative units ('functions') from the splitting of the individual text (and we must operate similarly when dealing with architectural works).

By means of this concept we are also helped in solving the old problem of an architectural system's 'continuity' (as opposed to the 'discrete' nature of natural language), because the 'splitting process' of semiological analysis, when applied to objects belonging to what we have defined as the 'second level', aims to define stylistically and not physically separated units (see also Garroni, 1972). Furthermore, we can say that, generally speaking, an architectural unit (or 'function', in Benveniste's terms) can correspond in one case to an individual entity, in another to an 'ensemble' of many elements.

We will try now to distinguish different types of 'functions', following the role they play in the text. According to Benveniste, these units must be divided into two main groups. The first one—that of true 'functions'—includes those units whose related term is a unit of the same level (implying 'distributional' relationships); while to the second group belong the so-called 'indizi', or units whose related term belongs to another level (so implying 'integrative' relationships). I have suggested, for what is the concern of the architectural field, considering as true 'functions' those spatial or enclosing units whose related term is, in turn, a spatial or enclosing unit belonging to the same architectural text (for instance, the dome and the crypt in Bramante's Tempietto of San Pietro in Montorio, which correspond to one another in the syntagmatic structure of the architectural text, as well as in the associative plane, conveying two related notions, namely those of Heaven and Hell).

As far as 'indizi' are concerned, I think we must take into consideration those architectural entities of the text whose related term is not another architectural unit, but a rather different entity, as for instance a 'parametric' term as defined by Ruwet. We could perhaps consider the pediment of the Turbine Factory by Peter Behrens as an 'indizio', whose related term is the whole idea of classicism, with all its overloaded connotations. Barthes suggests that the distinction between true 'functions' and 'indizi' overlaps another classical dichotomy, as functions imply metanymical relationships, while the nature of relationships implied by 'indizi' is a metaphorical one. Our architectural interpretation of 'indizi' does not seem to be in contradiction with this assumption, and we could also add that this same interpretation matches the remark—also made by Barthes—that only 'indizi' possess a true semantic value.

Let us now consider again the first group, that of true 'functions'. We can distinguish, within this group, between 'cardinal functions' ('nuclei'), corresponding to the great 'fragments' of the text, and 'catalysts', 'which only fill, Barthes says, the narrative interval (the 'empty space', so to speak) between the first ones'. Architectural catalysts, in my view, are typically the so-called connection spaces, and this interpretation, too, is confirmed by Barthes's further remarks, where he says that the role played by catalysts depends only on the 'nuclei' they relate, being consequently of a 'parasitic' kind; whereas 'cardinal functions', or 'nuclei', correspond to the great opportunities of choice in the text, to real (in his terms) 'dispatchers'.

One more point to consider is that of the dichotomy: consecutivity/consequentiality. Barthes observes that in the tale 'what happens *after* is read as *determined by*'. Of course, we cannot deny that in many architectural works the dimension of temporality (in a series of spatial perceptions, for instance) assumes a prior importance from the moment of the first conception of the design, of the first sketches. We have only to consider, as an example, the Guggenheim Museum by Frank Lloyd Wright, where the idea of a 'spatial path' is the generating concept of the whole architecture.

But in literary criticism, the dichotomy consecutivity/consequentiality has initiated two conflicting trends, the first one aiming to give priority to the chronological plane (Propp), the second one to the logical plane ((Lévi-Strauss, Todorov, Greimas). Alan Dundes, in his introduction to the second edition of Propp's *Morphology of the Tale*, remarks that in Propp's analysis 'the structure or formal organization of a folkloristic text is described following the chronological order of the linear sequence of elements in the text as reported from an informant', whereas in Lévi-Strauss's approach 'rather the elements are taken out of the "given" order and are regrouped in one or more analytical scheme'. It seems now that the winning approach is the last one, in which chronological aspects are put aside, in view of a 'relogification' (Barthes) of the narrative content. In my view, both trends have their own importance, and both give their contribution to the richness and 'ambiguity' of architectural significance. It is impossible to deny the importance of perceptual sequences in experiencing architecture (but in our field, excepting special situations, there is no 'given' order), but it is impossible, too, for a criticism of architecture based on the semiological approach and on structuralism to be satisfied with an analysis of the architectural text, in which only aspects related to the chronological plane are considered, neglecting the main problem of the 'logical structure' underlying this same text. Both planes—that of perceptual sequences and more generally of chronological aspects, and that of the 'logical structure'—are therefore to be considered, not separately but together: which implies, of course, additional difficulties in our task.

As a conclusion, I only want to say that applications of the theoretical tools here suggested are still to be carried out (and it is just this kind of research I am now trying to do). For the moment, we can only compare in terms of hypotheses —in view of a renewed criticism of architecture—the alternative models of analysis we could derive respectively from structural linguistics and from the criticism of literature based on structuralism and on the semiological approach to the text. Having worked using the first model, and being dissatisfied with the corresponding results, I have tried to determine the theoretical foundations of a possible alternative model, and my next work, I hope, will test the 'literary analogy' as an alternative step in place of the 'linguistic analogy'.

References

Barthes, R. (1969), 'Introduzione all' analisi strutturale dei racconti, in *L'analisi del racconto*, Bompiani, Milan. (Italian translation of a whole special issue of the French review *Communications*.)

Broadbent, G. (1973), *Design in Architecture*, Chichester, Wiley.

Collins, P. (1965) *Changing Ideals in Modern Architecture, 1750−1950*, London, Faber.

Eco, U. (1972). A Componential Analysis of the Architectural Sign/Column. *Semiotica*. 5.2.

Eco, U. (1971), *Le forme del contenuto*, Milan, Bompiani.

Garroni, E. (1972), *Progetto di semiotica*, Bari, Laterza.

Hjelmslev, L. (1961), *Prolegomena to a Theory of Language*, revised English edition, trans. Francis J. Whitefield, Madison, University of Wisconsin Press.

Mounin, G. (1970), *Introduction à la sémiologie*, Paris, Les Éditions de Minuit.

Mukarovský, J. (1973), *Il significato dell'estetica*, Turin, Einaudi.

Prieto, L. (1971a), *Lineamenti di semiologia—Messaggi e segnali*, Bari, Laterza.

Prieto, L. (1971b), 'Notes pour une sémiologie de la communication artistique', in *Werk*, no. 4, p. 249.

Scalvini, M. L. (1975), *L'architettura come semiotica connotativa*, Milan, Bompiani.

3.4 Linguistics into Aesthetics Won't Go

Richard Bunt

This commentary relies for its paraphrasing of the ideas of certain of the theorists mentioned (notably de Fusco) on material made available by Fernando Tudela[1], although the views expressed are the author's own.

This essay is concerned with some attempts to adopt a semiotic approach based on structural linguistics in the consideration of the distinctively material aspects of what we might call architectural 'expression'. This approach is characterized by what we may refer to here as an 'aesthetic' preoccupation, particularly on the part of some Italian theorists. This aesthetic preoccupation, seems to stem from an emphasis on the unique confrontation of the experiencing observer with the material presence of the concrete architectonic object. Moreover, this architectonic object is considered as a unique 'work'—in the sense of a 'work of art'—an object, therefore, of aesthetic contemplation. The semiotic orientation which seems to result from this preoccupation is accordingly presented as an opposition between the 'expressive' dimension of built architecture on the one hand, and the 'experiential' dimension of the individual encountering this architecture on the other. It is the broad contention of this essay that this opposition serves to confuse both the distinction between considerations of 'substance' and of 'form' (that is, between specific individual instances and the organization of such instances as examples of generic types) and the distinction between the material plane of 'expression' and the cultural plane of 'content', upon both of which distinctions a genuine linguistically oriented semiotic approach must be founded. In this essay, we will consider briefly the theoretical positions taken by certain key theorists in the field of architectural semiotics, and we will try to examine examples of the way in which the requirements of a semiotic analysis based on structural linguistics conflict with an analysis based on fundamentally aesthetic criteria.

The aesthetic orientation of certain Italian theorists concerned with a semiotic approach to architectural theory may be traced to the work of Cesare Brandi and Bruno Zevi. Both of these authors are concerned with what, for want of a better word, we may term the 'essence' of architecture. Brandi believes, for example, that in encountering the individual work of architecture, which he considers as a 'work of art', there is a need to capture not only the 'message' which the work may contain, but also its 'presence' (Italian *astanze*)—its being; in other words, its 'essence' (Brandi, 1967). While the ostensible message carried by the architectural work may be conveyed to the observer in terms of his basic comprehension of the work in a cognitive sense (which Brandi admits includes an implicit cultural component), Brandi seeks to locate the 'essence'—the complex aesthetic reality of the work—'outside' the cultural dimension through which one initially apprehends the individual work. To this extent, while he considers that the cognitive apprehension of the architectural work within a cultural context may be regarded as a semiosis—i.e. a transformation arising through the agency of a sign—Brandi obviously considers a semiotic approach to be inappropriate to describe the unique encounter with the architectural object—an experience which he regards as being of an aesthetic nature. Thus there is already implicit an opposition between a semiotic approach to the study of architectonic objects and what has been called a 'philosophical/aesthetic' approach.

Moreover, Brandi appears loath to admit that it is conceptually possible to break down the signifying or signified dimension of an individual architectonic object, of whatever scale, into dependent components. Referring to the notion that the capital of a column may be considered as a combination of subsidiary elements within a classical vocabulary, Brandi insists that such elements 'are not distinctive features of a capital, rather they are entities significative of themselves only—essentially un-analysable—their combination in the shape of a capital does not have the meaning 'capital', but actually *is* a capital' (Brandi, 1967, p. 37). This passage betrays a tendency to reject the possibility that an architectural object is analysable into signifying components at all, in the face of its overwhelming 'presence'.

From this aestheticaly oriented, not to say metaphysical, premise, Brandi insists on regarding the work of architecture as being characterized by an indivisible continuity, and as such, unanalysable, since he argues that the only way to conduct an analysis according to a structural linguistic model is to 'locate the discontinuum in the segments into which the continuum may be divided'. Apart from denying that such a discontinuum can be located in the individual architectural work, Brandi seems to confuse the identification of a 'significant form'* with the actual division of an object of study into individual material segments.

The other author to whom we may look as a source of the emphasis on the aesthetic dimension of architecture is Bruno Zevi (Zevi, 1957). For Zevi, the essential property of architecture is that of possessing 'internal space', by which Zevi means 'enclosed space' and not merely 'interior space'. Although Zevi's semiotic orientation is only implicit, it is none the less definite; this can be seen from the way in which he considers that this internal space can be delimited, arguing that facades and walls are only the container, of which *the content is the internal space* (Zevi's emphasis) (Zevi, 1957, p. 24). Although he says that the 'container' and the 'contained' are in many cases mutually interdependent, as, for example, in the case of French Gothic, this is by no means always true, as, for example, in the case of the discrepancy between the 'container' represented by a baroque façade and the 'contained' labyrinth of often illusory internal spaces.

These remarks reveal that Zevi may be thinking of a 'rightness of fit' between elements of external expressive form and internal content. Zevi is apparently most concerned with the role of solid architectural elements in determining enclosed spaces, but at the same time he stops short of admitting that this internal space can form the subject of a relation of signification. Indeed, he states that this space cannot be completely represented but only grasped experientially—that is, it is only through the process of actually experiencing a building that this internal spatiality becomes a concrete reality (Zevi, 1957, p. 27). In this way, Zevi envisages an experiential dimension of architecture which is similar to Brandi's notion of 'presence'. It is precisely at this point that the limitations of a semiotic approach to aesthetic phenomena become apparent; the very property of giving to an architectonic object or internal space a concrete experiential reality means that this 'essential' property of architecture cannot be represented by any indirect means of expression. As we shall try to show in this essay, the very emphasis, through which what may loosely be regarded as being 'significant' in an architectonic object is confined to the realm of individual subjective experience, lies at the root of the problem. Not only does this emphasis render the notion of 'meaning' which inevitably arises epistemologically imprecise, but it sabotages any hope of

*In the terminology of structural linguistics, the identification of a 'significant form' involves the conceptual division of an object of study into purely formal elements of 'expression' and elements of 'content' which are shown to be linked by a relation of signification.

setting up a uniform relation between material phenomena and non-material 'meanings' within any culturally determined context. For example, if we restrict ourselves to considering purely material phenomena in an experiential context, a uniform relation between a solid envelope and an enclosed space will not necessarily emerge since we inevitably have to consider 'types' of enclosure when formulating such a relation.

Renato de Fusco

It is with Renato de Fusco that we find a fully developed attempt to institute a semiotic study of achitecture as 'space', but one which is also subject to an aesthetic emphasis which is strongly reminiscent of Zevi. De Fusco, like Zevi, considers that the presence of an internal space is an 'essential' property of what we recognize as architecture. Indeed, he considers that internal space is directly equivalent to Saussure's 'signifié', with the difference that it is 'virtual' aspect, the implicit aspect, which de Fusco considers to be critical from a semiotic standpoint. This is to say, the fact that an internal space is indicated or 'signified', whether or not it is actually accessible, is the important consideration for de Fusco (De Fusco, 1973). The counterpart to this internal 'signified' space is an external space which acts as a 'signifier'. As a result of this complementary interconnection—this relation of signification—which, de Fusco believes, serves to link external with internal space, this external space can be regarded in material terms as the envelope enclosing the internal space, through which the presence of the internal space can be implied. We can see that this conceptual arrangement of complementary elements follows closely upon Zevi's complementary distinction between 'container' and 'contained'. In fact, the correlation between envelope and enclosed space, suggested by Zevi, remains at a somewhat elementary level in de Fusco's thinking. The specifically semiotic conception of the relation between the two elements is not developed in any detail, but is treated as being self-evident. That is to say, the question 'To what extent and by what mechanism can an internal space be inferred from its envelope?' is not asked. This is all the more surprising since, as Zevi had pointed out, the relation between the two is not always apparent.

There is a further parallel to linguistic elements as envisaged by Saussure, therefore, in that the external and internal spaces connected in the above way are indeed entities mutually defined by a complementary opposition. In the sense that one cannot exist without the other, they offer a parallel to Saussure's illustration of the 'two faces' of the linguistic sign as the 'recto' and the 'verso' of a sheet of paper (Saussure, 1966, p. 113). However, because the external envelope is conceived by de Fusco as the complement of the perceived internal space—and not, for example, as a topological or purely functional external skin—it can only be defined in terms of the internal space it encloses, and not in terms of the functional or topological properties which it may share with other envelopes. The external space conceived in this way, therefore, also has a 'virtual' aspect. We are accordingly confronted with a theory which asks us to envisage a pair of complementary entities—an external space and an internal space—between which there exists a relation of signification in that one implies the other. Thus we have the possibility of considering the relation between an 'actual' internal space and an implied 'virtual' external space, or conversely between an actual external space and an implied virtual internal space. Surely we must conclude that in each case it is the 'virtual' space (internal or external) which constitutes the 'signified' entity (Garroni, 1972, p. 93), since there is nothing apart from the complementarity of their interrelation to suggest a specifically semiotic 'content' for which the counterpart would serve as an 'expression'. This stems from the emphasis de Fusco places on the material aspect of this relation, with no attempt being made to suggest a way of conceiving a typology of use, or even of geometry, in terms of which a distinctive semiotic 'form' could be set up in order to organize the purely material spatial 'substance' in some clearly identifiable way. ('Form' and 'substance' are here used in a specifically semiotic sense wherein 'form' comprises a generic 'type' of entity and 'substance' constitutes a particular instance of that type of entity.)

A word about the 'inside/outside' dichotomy. Quite obviously, the means by which an enclosing or enclosed space is implied is distinct from the means through which it is actually generated. Thus an external (enclosing) space is generated by solid volumes being placed within it, while an internal (enclosed) space is generated by solid objects being placed around it. In other words, space can be regarded as being a property of objects perceived in some relation to each other—often simultaneously generating both enclosed and enclosing spaces. It is in this sense that the notion of an enclosed or enclosing space being generated in perceptual terms is more useful than the notion of a mutual implication of 'inside' and 'outside' conceived in purely spatial terms.

The fact that a 'signified' space is conceived by de Fusco as including a 'virtual' aspect also in itself admits of the category of representational or even illusionistic space as a legitimate aspect of the mode of signification which the architectonic object comprises (Garroni, 1972, p. 93). It is this aspect of de Fusco's 'signified' space which specifically contradicts the emphasis on actually experienced space which had hitherto been considered as an essential property of the architectural work, regarded as an object of aesthetic contemplation. We are therefore prevented from concluding that de Fusco's notion of 'virtual' space attempts to achieve a genuine compromise between the idea that the essential aspect of architecture is the experience of space (and hence an aesthetic property) and the incorporation of such an aspect in a relation of signification. In addition to these reservations, there are a number of issues concerning which this attempted compromise also fails to provide convincing answers, to which we shall now turn.

A further difficulty arises from the fact that the signifier/signified relation, which, de Fusco argues, constitutes the 'architectural sign' is considered to obtain only at the level of enclosed or enclosing spaces. When de Fusco subdivides these elements he not only does so in purely material terms, but confines his attention to the 'solid' components of the enclosing envelope; moreover, these material components are considered independently of any spatial properties that they might have. De Fusco thus confines himself to what he would call the plane of the 'signifiers'.

One might be justified in assuming that de Fusco tries to divide the architectonic object in this way in order to find a parallel to Martinet's 'second articulation'—the division of signifyng 'monemes' into non-signifying 'phonemes' in natural language—an articulation which Martinet also only conceived in the plane of expression (Martinet, 1964, pp. 22 – 4). However, the fact that de Fusco apparently regards these solid components as having some signifying properties in their own right, suggests that this division is a mere material segmentation, and not a genuine 'second articulation' into non-signifying components (Tudela, 1975). In factr, to pursue a linguistic analogy, de Fusco believes that the signifiers and signifieds, which may be identified in terms of enclosed and enclosing spaces can be considered as the counterpart of linguistic 'phrases' or 'sentences', rather than 'words'. If this were so, however, then where would we look for the counterparts of individual monemes (words, or roots of words)? De Fusco might argue that these counterparts are to be found in the solid material components of the external envelope, but in that case we would require evidence of an equivalent subdivision of the plane of content, which de Fusco considers solely in terms of space, and which he seems reluctant to subdivide. Accordingly, in denying the spatial properties of the solid material components, and faced with the difficulty of subdividing the 'continuum' of internal space—a notion which he has inherited from Brandi—de Fusco is compelled to fall back on a somewhat evasive and unsatisfactory conclusion. On the one hand, he maintains that an equivalent to the linguistic 'second articulation' can be found in 'the lines of architectural drawings' (!) while, on the other hand, he calls the material components of the external envelope 'subsigns'—a compromise term which implies elements which yet have signifying properties but which remain outside his schema of purely spatial signifying elements. It seems that the inescapable conclusion must be that a semiotic analysis, which is confined in its original terms of reference to purely spatial criteria for setting up signifying elements, is exhausted when one is confronted with components which are not admitted to have spatial properties. The fact that such a limitation would severely restrict the usefulness of such an analysis is, of course, in itself a damaging criticism—not only of the adoption of purely spatial criteria, but of the general view that such criteria constitute the 'essence' of architecture.

It would seem that de Fusco introduced the notion of 'subsigns' in order to provide a level at which to entertain the notion of a 'code' based purely on the material characteristics of the component parts of an enclosing envelope. However, de Fusco also considers that it is in terms of the articulation at the level of spatial signifying and signified elements that the 'message' of the work of architecture can be recognized. Clearly one cannot construct a message from subsigns unless the 'code'—the rules according to which a signifying element is attached to a signified element—is made explicit at the level at which the subsigns are identified. As it is, in de Fusco's theory, the lowest level at which this signifying/signified relation is explicit is that at which the relation between external envelope and internal space is considered, therefore surely the rules of the code in question must be sought at this level and not at the level of subsigns. It seems that the reason de Fusco sought the rules of a code at the level of subsigns was that he envisaged a sort of 'typology of constituent elements of form' although by 'form' de Fusco undoubtedly meant material form and not semiotic form.

There is one further confusing consequence of de Fusco's insistence on the material and spatial nature of the signifying and signified elements comprising an architectonic object. De Fusco apparently associates a decrease in the arbitrariness of the connection between signified and signifying elements with an increase in the 'materiality' in which the enclosing envelope and the enclosed space are conceived in concrete rather than 'pure' spatial terms. Indeed, de Fusco opposes the material properties of these elements to their purely 'formal' (de Fusco's term) spatial properties. This notion of 'form' de Fusco considers to be eroded by any increase in the way in which the signifying and signified elements are conceived in strictly material (as opposed to spatial) terms. Because he also regards utilitarian function as being directly associated with this material emphasis, de Fusco concludes that such an erosion of a 'pure' spatial conception is the result of an increased emphasis on what he considers to be the crass utilitarian aspects of built elements. We may suppose that such an 'impure' conception of space would occur where a space is considered in terms of the material and functional properties of its enclosing elements, or of the functional relationship set up between these elements in enclosing a space, rather than in 'pure' geometric or formal terms. Thus he states: 'In an architecture of totally motivated signs, deprived of any degree of arbitrariness, "function", in some respects equivalent to the "substance" of the linguistics, annihilates "form" ' (De Fusco, 1973, p. 131). This surprising equation appears to lie at the root of much of the confusion in de Fusco's semiotic schema, as well as illustrating his insistence on the archaic 'function versus form' dichotomy. In the first place, 'motivation' is associated with the emphasis on 'materiality' instead of being regarded as a product of the relation between the signifier and the signified. In the second place, to assume that the functioning of a built element is not only self-evident in the physical properties of that element, but is actually coincident with it, is to miss the culturally conditioned relation between the dimension of 'use' and that of 'material'—in which, for example, the notion of a typology of both functional (or purposive) and material attributes plays a part. Finally, to equate spatial 'form' with linguistic 'form', without recourse to a model abstracted from the material properties or the purposeful attributes of spatial enclosure (such as we might construct in order to consider the 'geometry' or the 'use' of that space), and in which the Saussurean notion of 'form' might be legitimately employed, is to fail to appreciate the essentially 'abstract' nature of linguistic or semiotic form. For example, a space might be considered in terms of a 'type' of shape (geometry) or in terms of a 'type' of use (purpose).

Maria Luisa Scalvini

The second theorist whose work we shall consider is Maria Luisa Scalvini (1975). For Scalvini, the problems of applying a semiotic model based on structural linguistics to what she considers to be the 'specificity' and complexity of architecture are recognized at the outset. At the same time, she consciously fragments the phenomenon of the architectonic object in order to emphasize the 'essential' properties of architecture. Scalvini distinguishes between 'building' ('edilizia') and 'architecture' ('architettura')—a distinction also made by Cesare Brandi under the headings 'tectonics' and 'architecture' (Brandi, 1967). The basis for this distinction, Scalvini finds in the notion of 'aesthetic' versus 'extra-aesthetic' which had its initial semiotic formulation in the work of Jan Mukařovský (Mukarovský, 1966). Scalvini's use of the term 'tectonics' refers to what Mukařovský called the 'extra'aesthetic' dimension. For Scalvini, tectonics embodies the purely functional aspects of architecture at what she calls a 'basic' level, which she distinguishes from the 'second' level of 'architecture' proper which embraces the aesthetic aspects of architecture. Furthermore, Scalvini regards the extra-aesthetic dimension of tectonics as being equivalent to ordinary language, while the aesthetic dimension of architecture is regarded as being equivalent to literature.

The difficulties which arise as a result of her adopting such an unequivocal position are not necessarily inherent in the parallel between works of architecture and works of literature. Rather, they stem from the way in which she envisages the formulation of a semiotic relation at the basic level of tectonics, since it is upon the semiotic relation which she postulates at this level that she attempts to construct a semiotic framework appropriate to the 'second' level of architecture. In the event, the two specifically linguistic models (based on the work of Luis Prieto and Louis Hjelmslev) which she attempts to apply in order to account for the distinction she makes between the extra-aesthetic and the aesthetic level, do not prove adequate to cope with the complex nature of the second level of architecture to her own satisfaction. Accordingly, she eventually seeks to apply semiotic models based not on structural linguistics but on the study of literary and narrative texts.

Luis Prieto distinguishes between two kinds of semiotic systems—those whose basic aim is to communicate and those whose basic aim is not to communicate (Preto, 1975(a), p. 179—189). In fact, Prieto is concerned to distinguish, even in the structure of systems whose ostensible aim is not to communicate, some *de facto* phenomenon of communication, in whatever way this might be recognized. For Prieto, the phenomenon of communication ultimately resides in the intention, of an 'emitter', of what is then treated as a 'message, to 'communicate' in however indirect a way. Among semiotic systems whose basic aim is not to communicate, Prieto identified what he termed a 'logic of instruments'. This concerns operations of an ostensibly utilitarian type, such as the making, use, and deployment of useful artefacts (tools), the semiotic aspect of which Prieto subsumed under the term 'instruments' (Prieto, 1975(a), p. 186).

For Prieto, communication resides in the 'selection' of an instrument which has the effect of communicating a particular concept of an operation which that instrument can be used to carry out. It is clear, however, that this selection depends on two factors. Firstly, the recognition by the user of the instrument of the class of operations which can be carried out by that instrument (which Prieto terms its 'utility') (Prieto, 1975(a), p. 183), and secondly, the recognition of a particular way of conceiving the objective of the operation in question — its purpose in other words. Both of these factors involve the recognition of a particular culturally conditioned context. Underlying both these factors is the dimension of signification since it is only within the context of a relation of signification that the utility of an instrument and the way in which its deployment is conceived may be articulated. This relation of signification would be implied between the utilitarian properties of an artefact and the purpose for which it is to be used within a particular cultural context.

The main lines of Prieto's theory in this respect have been adopted by Scalvini as being applicable to the phenomenon of what she calls 'aesthetic communication'. Prieto himself adapted his theoretical terminology in an essay devoted to the subject of 'artistic communication' (Prieto, 1975(b), pp. 115 − 124). Scalvini considers that it is the presence of an intention to communicate the way in which an operation is conceived which imparts an aesthetic quality to the selection of the instrument employed to carry out this operation. Conversely, we may assume that if there is no evidence of such an intention present, then the selection of the instrument takes on a basic, non-aesthetic character. Following from this, Scalvini considers that the lack of any intention to communicate characterizes the tectonic dimension of architecture. However, Scalvini has elsewhere made it clear that she considers this tectonic aspect to embody the 'merely functional' properties of architectural elements (Tudela, 1976, note (2)). How, then, would she regard the purposeful use or deployment of a utilitarian artefact? Would she insist that this deployment be considered as a realized act of communication? If so, then the already tenuous link between 'communication' and 'aesthetic' intentionality can only with difficulty be employed to distinguish between the 'functional' and the 'more-than-just-functional'.

Scalvini's argument, while it tries to identify the role of communication within a loosely defined 'aesthetic' dimension and thus define this dimension more precisely, can also be interpreted as leading to the somewhat absurd conclusion that every communicative act is also an aesthetic act. In fact, Scalvini states that the selection of architectural built elements at the basic utilitarian level is not a matter of intentional communication but of interpretation, and also that such a selection is not carried out with the intention of indicating some particular conception of the functioning of these elements. Surely, however, the conception of the functioning of such elements is in fact shared by their makers and users and also influences their selection, deployment, and use. The sum total of such activity, in other words, constitutes a cultural context in which a dimension of intentionality is inevitably manifested.

Scalvini pursues her argument concerning the way in which the functioning of architectonic elements considered at the 'tectonic' level may possibly be indicated, without relying on the notion of a distinct intention to communicate, by referring to Adam Schaff's idea of a 'transparency of communication' (Schaff, 1962). This is conceived as the dominant property of a linguistic unit, whereby the 'sense' of the linguistic entity dominates its material embodiment so that this sense is conveyed 'directly' to the receiver without him necessarily being aware of the role of the material configuration of the linguistic unit in conveying that sense. Scalvini suggests that the functional dimension of what she calls tectonics may likewise be transmitted directly through its material embodiment in basic architectonic elements, so that one would be able to speak of a 'transparency of function' in such a case. This is an intriguing idea which locates the 'functioning' of architectural elements squarely in what Hjelmslev calls the plane of content. The trouble is that 'function' in itself cannot be said to belong to the realm of 'sense'. If it is to be incorporated into the semiotic dimension of 'content', the notion of function must be considered in the context of the way in which particular operational or functional properties are conceived and manipulated by man; in other words we must also involve the notion of 'purpose'. Accordingly, it would be the expression of such a conception—the expression of a definite purpose—which would convey a 'sense' to the user of basic architectonic elements. Here again, then, we would be involved in the dimension of intentionality—the articulation of the way in which a particular functional operation is conceived.

In order to tackle the more complex domain which Scalvini calls the 'second' level of architecture, she turns from the notion of aesthetic communication, in terms of which she initially distinguished this 'second' level from a basic level of material functioning, to a broader-based model furnished by Hjelmslev's notion of a 'connotative semiotic' (Hjelmslev, 1961, pp. 114–121). This postulates a complex semiotic hierarchy in which a basic semiotic relation between a plane of expression and a plane of content is itself incorporated into the plane of expression of an overall system whose plane of content is inferred through a relation of 'connotation' as opposed to 'denotation' (Scalvini, 1979).

Scalvini's interpretation of this arrangement is that the

basic semiotic relation of denotation is appropriate to the tectonic level of architecture, while the overall semiotic relation is appropriate to the whole domain of architecture, of which the plane of content constitutes the aesthetic dimension of architecture. Following from de Fusco, Scalvini considers that in order to identify a basic relation of signification at the level of tectonics, we must treat the external envelope in its material aspect as a 'signifier' which contains a 'signified' internal space. It will be immediately apparent that the functional aspect of the tectonic level is not made explicit in this interpretation of Hjelmslev's basic semiotic relation of denotation, in that it is not specifically included in the setting out of the semiotic relation between signifying and signified elements, which are considered in purely material terms. It seems, in fact, throughout Scalvini's argument, that a marked disjunction between a 'functional' basis and an 'aesthetic' superstructure is evident.

The reluctance to base a semiotic description of an architectonic object on an interpretation of its functional properties reveals a limitation of a strictly aesthetically oriented approach to the study of the products of human culture. The whole point of being able to recognize an 'artefact' is to be able to identify in it some evidence of an artificial intention on the part of its maker, which intention must have some correspondence in our apprehension of the cultural role played by that artefact. If we cannot identify what that cultural function is, then we are prevented from understanding that artefact *as an artefact*. Any 'aesthetic' apprehension which remains will thus be indistinguishable from the appreciation we would bestow upon a product of the operation of nature. Thus it cannot be through aesthetic criteria considered in this way that we are able to apprehend artefacts as products of artificial human activity; in such an aesthetic context, the material properties of such an object are given 'formal' significance by the operations of perception and cognition alone—we do not have through such criteria direct access to the minds of the makers and users of the artefacts in question.

It seems that if we adopt a specifically functional conception of what Scalvini calls the tectonic level of architecture, we may find that the aesthetic, rhetorical dimension of architecture may not be derived from the tectonic dimension in the same way that a relation of connotation may be derived from a relation of denotation, but rather that the two levels at which we consider the architectural object are simply independent of each other. On the other hand, we can see that if the basic semiotic relation is envisaged in terms of exterior and internal spaces, even if this is confined to the material properties of basic architectural elements,

Scalvini can more easily arrive at an aesthetic consideration of architecture which is simply derived from the material and spatial properties of the built envelope, ignoring the function and purpose of architectonic elements almost entirely. We might, therefore, conclude that Scalvini involves herself in considering the functional aspect of architectonic elements when interpreting Prieto's model primarily because she had based her distinction between tectonics and architecture on implicitly functional criteria.

Scalvini concludes that the most promising parallels between language and architecture are found at the level of literature, which she ultimately equates with the aesthetic dimension of architecture. For this reason she has tended to seek models in the semiotic study of literary and mythological texts. This approach is based on a number of sources, including Roman Jakobson's notion of the self-referential function of poetics (Jakobson, 1963)—in which the literary work is held to refer to itself alone—as well as on more specific parallels developed by Barthes and Todorov, directed at formulating a general semiotic framework for the analysis of literary texts—parallels whose scope is beyond that of this essay. We may remark in conclusion, though, that distinctive aesthetic characteristics of individual works of architecture have been said to be governed by a 'rhetorical' or a 'stylistic' code. Since such terminology is itself derived from the study of literature, a further study of architectural objects is not likely to illuminate the notions of 'rhetoric' or 'style' used as critical tools in that context. In this sense, the borrowing of literary tools is bound to be one-sided, with the result that architecture would tend to be studied as a 'text'—as a form of 'literature', as it were—with the danger that its specific 'essential' properties, which earlier aestheticians such as Brandi were so keen to emphasize, might be neglected. One thing that is apparent, however, is that such literary parallels can be conducted without recourse to an argument over the adoption of 'functional' or 'extra-functional' criteria in order to identify the 'significant form' of a building. The 'signified' elements of built architecture are not to be found in a consideration of the material elements which comprise a building, but in a cultural 'reading' of that building—architectural 'meaning' would indeed seem to be contextual. A common mistake is to assume that this contextual meaning is connected with what past generations of theorists have called the 'aesthetic' dimension—by which was meant some subjective, non-quantifiable aspect abstracted from the very material elements—solids and voids—which, as we have tried to show, prove so resistant to a semiotic analysis based on structural linguistics.

Emilio Garroni

In conducting a semiotic analysis of an object of study, one is seeking to articulate a distinctive relation between the elements of 'sense' incorporated into that object through the operation of human culture and the elements which can serve to express that sense. This articulation consists of a differentiation of elements within the constitution of an object of study which possess a distinct 'formal' identity as a result of their connection with a given sense. This articulation is accordingly quite separate from the process of merely breaking down an object into its material parts. The aim of a formal semiotic analysis is therefore 'not to divide the object of study into separate pieces but to detect its innner relationships'. This distinction between formal analysis and material segmentation has been emphasized by Emilio Garroni, and is one of his chief contributions towards resolving the confusion which has attended certain attempts to divide the continuous medium of architecture into 'architectural signs', usually on a purely material basis. Garroni argues that the process of revealing distinct elements within any set of phenomena is an artificial activity, involving just such a formal analysis (Garroni, 1972, pp. 82 − 3).

Garroni believes that in order to conduct a formal analysis one must make reference to an artificially conceived 'model'. His conception of a model, using terminology derived from Hjelmslev's *Prolegomena*, is of a finite range of invariant elements of form (Garroni, 1972, pp. 83 − 8). This may be briefly elaborated by saying that for Garroni the notion of an 'invariant element' may be compared to entities such as spoken words in verbal language. What constitutes a spoken word is a range of individual sounds which have in common the fact that they can all be employed to express a single 'meaning'. Thus a word has what may be called a formal, rather than a material (or substantial), nature, since it does not coincide solely with a given utterance of a sound or group of sounds, but encompasses a whole range of sounds—varieties of pronunciation, intonation, etc.—which differ phonologically. Such individual varieties of sound-expression were called 'variants' by Hjelmslev—a usage which Garroni follows.

An invariant element of form, then, consists of a range of variant entities which all have a common formal identity. A model may accordingly be constructed in order to identify certain elements of form in the constitution of the phenomena to be studied in the same way as 'words' may be identified in the study of an example of a verbal language. In the case of architecture, Garroni considers and rejects a number of possible models which may be potentially useful for describing the distinctive properties of an architectonic object in such a way as to reveal a genuinely semiotic constitution within the phenomena of architectural objects in general. Thus Garroni considers models based on the typology of the 'use' of a building, models based on purely 'spatial' elements (such as Zevi and de Fusco employ—for example, the notion of a 'virtual semiological space'), and models based on strictly 'geometrical' elements (cubes/cylinders/cones, etc., or their two-dimensional representations). Garroni finally considers the essential requirements of what he terms a 'graphic/figurative' model constructed from elements which encompass ranges of outlines, profiles, and contours, which may be abstracted in a two-dimensional plane from architectural objects, in the form of elevations, sections, or 'plans'.

However, according to Garroni, any one of these models taken separately will not necessarily be able to describe what Garroni calls the 'specificity' (the essence, as it were) of the architectural phenomena which a given architectonic object represents. Garroni argues that to do this we must employ not a single abstract model, but an interrelated series of such models which, between them, are capable of covering a whole range of attributes which embody the distinctive properties of any architectural phenomenon—that is, properties which are specific to the realm of architecture. It seems that such an exhaustive description can be achieved in two ways. First, we may use a range of models which are so constructed that they are capable of describing a given object at a greater or lesser level of abstraction. Thus, from the examples which Garroni gives (Garroni, 1972, pp. 107−8), a given architectonic object may be considered as: (a) a unique work in its own right; (b) as a particular example of an architectural period—for example, the Italian Renaissance; (c) as an example of the work of a particular architect, for example, Bramante. Second, an individual model may be employed in conjunction with a model constructed from formal elements of a distinct type. For example, models based on geometrical elements may be employed in conjunction with models based on figurative elements (profiles, contours, etc.) to describe the expressive surface of a building. Alternatively, models based on geometric elements may be employed in conjunction with models based on purely spatial elements or categories, or even with models based on elements consisting of types of use, in order to describe the interior of a building.

The chief difficulty is that Garroni seeks to employ a number of models, all of which are based on a particular invariant element of form, each of which is by definition independent of purely material criteria and could therefore in theory apply to a number of differently constituted material phenomena. Nevertheless, Garroni requires that such models should, between them, be capable of describing individual material objects and artefacts in a way that is distinctive to their employment in an architectural context. Furthermore, it seems that the types of models which Garroni eventually chooses for this purpose are abstracted from the purely material properties of architectonic objects, even though these properties are held to be bound up with the expression of some aesthetic 'content', which Garroni implies may be interpreted in a strictly semiotic context. In other words, it seems that underlying Garroni's approach there is an aesthetic orientation which implies that architecture is an expressive activity, in which the individual work of architecture is the principal level at which an aesthetic content may be recognized.

The problem of conducting a properly semiotic analysis based upon this premise seems to us to be twofold. Firstly, faced with the overwhelmingly unique nature of the architectural work considered as a whole — a 'thing-in-itself' — there is the problem of describing the expressive components of a given work in terms of elements of form which are not only non-specific to the work in question, but which may be common to any expressive plastic medium of which architecture is just a part. Secondly, it seems that the actual elements which comprise the models which Garroni selects are illustrated increasingly in terms of what Hjelmslev called the 'plane of expression'. In consequence, it is not always clear precisely in what the distinctive semiotic dimension of 'content' consists in the case of architectonic works. The majority of Garroni's examples are selected from an architecture containing a well-defined classical vocabulary. The continuous variations which can be identified in such a range of architectonic phenomena are accordingly seen to take place predominantly in the expressive surface of such an architecture. Furthermore, these variations are inevitably referrable to a preceding or subsequent 'norm' of expression — in other words, these variations are subject to a sort of 'code' of expression. It is in terms of 'outline', 'profile', and 'contour' that Garroni seeks to identify formal elements in terms of which such variations may be described. However, as a result of their very abstraction from the material plane, such elements cannot be identified through their connection with any specifically 'architectural' content, or indeed with any content which derives explicitly from the products of human activity. It would appear, therefore, that we would have to imagine a content born of what we can only describe as an aesthetic contemplation of pure shapes.*

*We must add that it appears that Garroni is aware of these difficulties and that in formulating 'dynamic' models to describe the expressive dimension of architecture in terms of the various parameters of 'intonation', he may be implying the presence of what for want of a better word we may call an 'emotional' content. (See his essay in this collection)

Conclusion

Accordingly, we must conclude that the entire enterprise of a semiotic study of architecture based upon such premises must be confined within an aesthetic convention which either remains self-referential within the plane of expression, or else refers us to a 'content' which is so abstracted from any evidence of specifically cultural activity that it would be difficult to speak of a 'meaning' being present, other than in the mind of the perceiver. Of course, this hinges on what we mean by 'content' in a strict semiotic context. The view which we have taken throughout this essay is that the identification of a semiotic 'content' is bound up with the recognition of a dimension of human purpose or intentionality, and that this is what we have in mind when we speak of the 'meaning' of an artefact or of an element of a building. This dimension of purpose is, of course, culturally conditioned — it is not just a question of a simple operational function, but of the way in which such a function is conceived in a particular cultural context. Thus, although the attributes of 'geometry' or 'figuration' which we can read into the expressive surface of an architectural object are in a sense culturally conditioned, these attributes cannot in themselves tell us anything about the distinctively artificial nature of a given three-dimensional object — that is, about the intentions and purposes which went into the making and the using of that object. This means that the identification of attributes of geometry, etc., in their pure form, must be amplified by setting up some correspondence between these shapes and some identifiable purpose on the part of the designers, makers, and users of a given architectonic object, before a legitimate relation between 'expression' and 'content' can be articulated. The mechanism for articulating such a relation is well established within structural linguistics, but, as we have argued, a precondition for the establishment of such a relation would be the adoption of criteria other than purely aesthetic.

References

Brandi, C. (1967). *Struttura e architettura*, Turin, Einaudi.

de Fusco, R. (1973). *Segni, storia e progetto dell'architettura*, Turin, Einaudi.

Garroni, E. (1972). *Progetto di semiotica*, Bari, Laterza.

Hjelmslev, L. (1969). *Prolegomena to a Theory of Language*, Madison, University of Wisconsin Press.

Jakobson, R. (1963). *Essais du linguistique général*, Paris, Minuit.

Martinet, A. (1964). *Elements of General Linguistics*, London, Faber.

Mukařovský, J. (1966). *Aesthetic Function, Norm and Value as Social Fact,* Ann Arbor, University of Michigan.

Prieto, L. J. (1975). Signe et instrument, and Notes pour une semiologie de la communication artistique, both in *Etudes de Linguistique et de Semiologie générales,* Geneva. Droz.

de Saussure, F. (1966). *Course in General Linguistics,* trans. Wade Baskin, ed. C. Baily and A. Sechehaye, New York, McGraw-Hill.

Scalvini, M. L. (1975). *L'architettura come semiotica connotativa,* Milan, Bompiani.

Scalvini, M. L. (1979). Structural Linguistics versus the Semiotics of Literature (included in this collection).

Schaff, A. (1962). *Introduction to Semantics,* London, Pergamon.

Tudela, F. (1975). *Hacia una semiotica de la arquitectura,* Publicacciones de la Universidad de Sevilla.

Tudela, F. (1976). Maria Luisa Scalvini, mimeo.

Zevi, B. (1957). *Architecture as Space,* trans. Milton Gendel, New York, Joseph Berry.

Index